THE NATIONAL RIFLE ASSOCIATION ITS TRAMWAYS AND THE LONDON & SOUTH WESTERN RAILWAY

TARGETS AND TRAMWAYS

Christopher Bunch

PEN & SWORD
TRANSPORT

AN IMPRINT OF PEN & SWORD BOOKS LTD.
YORKSHIRE – PHILADELPHIA

First published in Great Britain in 2019 by
Pen & Sword Transport
An imprint of
Pen & Sword Books Ltd
Yorkshire - Philadelphia

Copyright © Christopher Bunch, 2019

ISBN 978 1 47389 174 6

Typeset by Aura Technology and Software Services, India
Printed and bound by Replika Press Pvt. Ltd.

Pen & Sword Books Ltd incorporates the Imprints of Pen & Sword
Archaeology, Atlas, Aviation, Battleground, Discovery, Family History,
History, Maritime, Military, Naval, Politics, Railways, Select, Transport,
True Crime, Fiction, Frontline Books, Leo Cooper, Praetorian Press,
Seaforth Publishing, Wharncliffe and White Owl.

For a complete list of Pen & Sword titles please contact

PEN & SWORD BOOKS LIMITED
47 Church Street, Barnsley, South Yorkshire, S70 2AS, England
E-mail: enquiries@pen-and-sword.co.uk
Website: www.pen-and-sword.co.uk

or

PEN AND SWORD BOOKS
1950 Lawrence Rd, Havertown, PA 19083, USA
E-mail: Uspen-and-sword@casematepublishers.com
Website: www.penandswordbooks.com

CONTENTS

FOREWORD

Christopher Bunch has been working on Targets and Tramways for many years and I have witnessed his dedication and studiousness on many occasions while visiting the NRA Museum.

The book is a unique reference to the close and often intertwined history of the NRA and the Railways, from the days of Wimbledon common to the Association's new home at Bisley.

The book narrates how transport to Camp, at first from Putney and Wimbledon Stations on the London and South Western Railway and the Omnibus from the city and in later years with the spur line from Brookwood has been integral to shooting and its community and has literally shaped Bisley Camp.

Targets and Tramways is a historical reference like no other, able to draw parallelism between two powerful allies, the NRA, founded in 1859 for the protection of the realm and the London and South Western Railway, whose Court of Directors, once informed of the desired move from Wimbledon , directed its General Manager, Charles Scotter, to do anything in his power to persuade the NRA to remain on LSWR Territory!

Whilst focussing on the relationship between the NRA and the Railways Companies, Targets and Tramways narrates the history of the Association and its activities revealing a rich tapestry of anecdotes and little known historical facts that have shaped its world and given birth to the sport of target shooting in its current format. From the choice of the Enfield for distances closer than 600 yards and the Whitworth for greater distances, to the change in major competitions from the use of the .303 Military Rifle to specialist rifles using NATO ammunition in 1968 to today where different rifles are used not just for different distances, but also different forms of shooting.

The book is an eye opening read for all those who hold the NRA and Bisley close to their heart as it recounts of a time when railway companies would offer 1/6d return fare for Volunteers in uniform between London and Brookwood.

Chris has written a book that no target shooter can be without whether they have an interest in the railways or simply a great love of shooting and the varied and rich history of the NRA.

Andrew Mercer
Group Chief Executive & Secretary General

NATIONAL RIFLE ASSOCIATION

ACKNOWLEDGEMENTS

I should like to express my grateful thanks to the following:

Ted Molyneux, Honorary Curator of the Museum of the NRA, a former leading marksman and captain of many national and international NRA teams, for his help at all times.

Roger Mundy, Hon. Deputy Curator of the Museum of the NRA who links together the worlds of shooting and railway enthusiasm, for his great assistance and finding many items of interest in the archives.

The Chief Executive of the NRA, Andrew Mercer, and Katia Malcaus Cooper for their support and encouragement as well as other past and present members of the NRA staff.

Peter Harding for letting me have access to his photographic collection and in particular his collection of Southern Railway documents from the Cullum Collection which were invaluable for filling a large gap in the 1930s and later.

Colin Chivers and Nick Pomfret of the South Western Circle for giving me access to items from their own collections and research.

Tim Price for his local knowledge of the Bisley area, especially regarding the nearby Princess Christian Homes, local schools and institutions as well as the loan of photographs.

I would also like to remember with special thanks the late Eric McGibbon who was so helpful to me when he was assisting at the Museum towards the end of his life.

Photographs and documents reproduced in this book are from the NRA Museum Archive unless otherwise acknowledged.

PREFACE

In 1859 Britain perceived itself to be threatened by a French invasion which encouraged the urgent formation of a Rifle Volunteer Movement for home defence. The National Rifle Association of Great Britain was founded towards the end of 1859, and constituted at the beginning of 1860, for the purpose of providing this Movement with an effective forum in which teams and individuals could improve their rifle shooting skills by competing for prizes. In order to allow this to happen it was necessary to establish a suitable location which was easily accessible to the Volunteers through the fast-developing railway network. The selection of Wimbledon Common through the good offices of the Lord of the Manor, Earl Spencer who was a co-founder of the Association, was fortuitous. However, it only permitted the rifle competitions to take place during the short period of the annual Meeting; just over a week in the first instance but rapidly evolving into the traditional July fortnight. This proved an attractive enough proposition for the still growing London and South Western Railway Company, the L&SWR, to exploit its near monopoly of the Volunteer traffic by offering attractive fares between its terminus in London, Waterloo, and its two nearby stations to the chosen venue of Wimbledon and Putney

After a hesitant start, a cordial business relationship soon began to develop between the railway company and the NRA. Each July, Wimbledon Common became a major centre of spectacle and the growth of the Volunteer Movement allied with the increasing popularity of the Prize Tournament there resulted in an extraordinary democratic mixed gathering every year of all the classes of contemporary Victorian society in Britain. At the same time riflemen from the far reaches of the Empire made every effort to attend the Meetings.

The relationship with the L&SWR was well on the way to full maturity by the time the NRA moved to Bisley where the Association ceased to be restricted by the increasing Wimbledon constraints. The establishment of a permanent new site near the L&SWR's mainline station at Brookwood and connected to it by a short branch line enabled the railway company, after playing a key role in its selection, to continue that relationship now based on a much more substantial business footing as the site could now be opened throughout the year. The relationship lasted throughout the period of the Southern Railway, which absorbed the L&SWR in 1923, and continued into the 1960s under the nationalised British Railways regime, only ceasing when road transport had largely displaced rail.

The year 2012 marked the sixtieth anniversary of the closure of the Bisley Camp Tramway, that obscure and very short railway branch line originally planned by the L&SWR in collaboration with the Association and laid in 1890 to connect the main line at Brookwood with the Bisley ranges. I had come across this line, or tramway as it was known, as a boy just before it closed in 1952 when my father, who had been a distinguished rifle shot at Bisley throughout the 1930s, used to take the family there on a regular basis to attend the prize-giving at the end of the Annual Meeting in July. Later I read much of the literature that had been published about it which tended to reflect the popular view that it was opened solely for the Annual Meeting and then resumed its slumbers until the following July; there seemed little more to add. However, a few years ago I came across vague references to an even more obscure steam worked tramway which had apparently once transported competitors in the various competitions to some of the more distant Bisley ranges. This tramway had apparently disappeared, seemingly without trace, around about the time of the First World War.

Summarily dismissing the former 'tramway' as being already fully documented, it was the latter 'range' tramway that now particularly intrigued me and it lead me to contact the NRA Museum at Bisley to see if any further information might be available. My introduction to Ted Molyneux, the Hon. Curator of the Museum, and his willingness to allow me to delve into the extensive archives opened a world that I had not even started to contemplate.

The collection contained a large collection of original documents some dating back over one hundred and fifty years to the Association's beginning. These had been recovered when the Museum, as it exists today, was formed in the mid-1990s although they had remained largely unread. There were gaps, largely due to 'clear-outs' in the past, but enough information remained to develop a detailed history of the Association's various Camp Tramways and the special relationship built up with the L&SWR and its successors. In addition, there were photograph albums and individual pictures that, although primarily devoted to the shooting activities, included scenes of camp life at both Wimbledon and Bisley. There was also a fine collection of contemporary prints and newspaper cuttings that included a large number from various periodicals of the Wimbledon period. Detailed reports of each Meeting were contained in the NRA's own Annual Report and also a largely complete set of the Volunteer's own weekly newspaper, the *Volunteer Service Gazette* (later the *Territorial Service Gazette*), which, although an independent periodical, was closely associated with the NRA. The Council Minute books also became available and these of course recorded all the Council's own deliberations and the various policy decisions reached since the very earliest meetings of 1859.

Nearly all the NRA Letter Books, containing copies of the letters written almost exclusively by successive Secretaries of the Association between 1859 and 1921, had survived. These were all carefully indexed under the addressee's name. After this date, however, such letters had been parcelled up, albeit in date order but no longer indexed, making it rather a more onerous task to study! In addition, there was a complete set of Account Books covering the opening of Bisley right through to the Second World War. These contained receipted invoices, each of which had been carefully pasted by diligent clerks into the pages of enormous leather-bound ledgers giving details of every transaction, generally in great detail. A prime example was the volume covering the move to Bisley and its immediate aftermath which naturally proved of immense value.

From 1890, with the NRA removed to Bisley, the Association's Secretary had acquired far wider responsibilities than simply looking after the target shooting and the temporary camp arrangements for the annual meeting at Wimbledon. He was now in charge of a vast area of ranges which included a listed village of unique buildings supporting the various shooting activities which now continued throughout the greater part of the year. In particular, before the advent of mass motoring in the late nineteen twenties, this included ensuring that both shooters and visitors could easily reach the site by train encompassing a shooting season that lasted, at Bisley, from April to October as well as the particularly busy annual Meeting in July. It was this aspect particularly and the local railway company's policy of 'retaining the business' that lead to the establishment of the extremely close working relationship between the National Rifle Association and the L&SWR over a period that covered about three quarters of the latter's existence.

Victorian and Edwardian letter writers displayed a fortunate habit of paraphrasing the letters they received into their replies and, as most of the received letters dating from the nineteenth century were missing from the collection, this gave an invaluable source of information. In addition, there was a vast archive of photographs of the shooting and other activities dating back to the earliest days. From about 1908 onwards many incoming letters had in fact survived and it has been found possible so far to locate more than one hundred and fifty letter-headed L&SWR communications, the great majority of which were sent under the signature of senior officials of that company. Letter-headed invoices from the railway company were also found in great abundance commencing in 1890 and these were extremely helpful in filling the gap. Contemporary national newspapers and journals also contained articles and pictures of the NRA's activities with the Annual Meetings being reported on and analysed in detail generally on a day by day basis.

Another important aspect was the connection with the Association of well-known contemporary personalities. Many of these can be found listed in the Appendix.

The intention of the book has been to put the history of the NRA, already covered in great detail in other publications, into context with the extraordinary relationship that developed between the Association and the L&SWR and its successors, as well as other major railway companies, over very many years.

The possibility of developing all this interrelated information into a coherent narrative using verbatim quotes from actual letters and other documents had become increasingly apparent. Certainly over much of the period under study, especially that before the 1914-18 Great War when the art of letter writing seemed to have reached some kind of literary zenith, it became possible to gain an insider's view of the Association's day to day business mainly through the incumbent Secretary's eyes.

THE VOLUNTEERS AND THE FOUNDING OF THE NATIONAL RIFLE ASSOCIATION

For thirty-nine years after the end of the Napoleonic Wars Britain was not involved in any major conflict. This was to end with the outbreak of the Crimean War in 1853 and, by its conclusion in 1856, an increasing national consciousness of international events and affairs, especially in Europe, had been brought about. At this time, large conscript armies had been established on the continent with France fast assuming the mantle of the dominant military power. This was further demonstrated by the intervention of the French Emperor, Napoleon III, in what became known as the Second Italian War of Independence. At the Battles of Magenta and Solferino in 1859 an alliance of France and the Kingdom of Piedmont-Sardinia had comprehensively defeated the forces of the Austrian Empire. At the same time Napoleon had made certain speeches effectively impugning Britain with having sinister designs on French sovereignty, fully reflected in and supported by the French Press. This caused increasing public concern about the ability of Britain to withstand a foreign invader with voices strongly advocating a revival of the old Infantry Volunteer movement for defence of the realm that had been stood down in 1813 towards the conclusion of the Napoleonic Wars but before the climactic Battle of Waterloo in 1815.

Initially this was not supported by the Government but a strong intervention by the Duke of Cambridge, the Commander-in-Chief of the British Army, in which he stated that 'the spirit of the Regular Army would be destroyed, the public demanded the right to train men for the country's defence' seemed to have had a positive effect on their attitude although, much earlier than this, in 1852, a pamphlet written by General Sir James Napier entitled *Defence of England by Corps of Volunteers and Militia,* in which he strongly urged the formation of Volunteer corps for the country's defence, seems to have already acted as an important catalyst.

Things were now moving rapidly and in April 1859, a meeting, which was to become known as 'The Long Acre Indignation Meeting.' was held in London at St. Martin's Hall, which made a strong protest against the insufficiency of the National Defence.

This public expression of concern, and the national attitude to affairs on the other side of the Channel, evoked a poetic contribution to *The Times* by the Poet Laureate, Lord Tennyson, under the title 'Form, Riflemen, Form,' which seemed to capture the spirit of the moment. The poem was published on 9 May, 1859:

> *There is a sound of Thunder afar,*
> *Storm in the south that darkens the day.*
> *Storm of battle and thunder of war!*
> *Well, if it do not roll away,*
> *Storm, storm, Riflemen, form!*
> *Ready, be ready, against the storm,*
> *Riflemen, riflemen, riflemen, form!*
> *Let your reforms for a moment go!*
> *Look to your butts and take good aims!*
> *Better a rotten borough or so*
> *Than a rotten flesh and a city in flames!*
> *Storm, Riflemen storm, Riflemen storm!*
> *Ready, be ready against the storm!*
> *Riflemen, Riflemen, Riflemen, form.*

The Government, now being fully aware of the national feeling, resurrected an old statute, 'the Yeomanry and Volunteer Consolidation Act' of 1804 that was drawn up under the emergency of the Napoleonic Wars. It was not repealed with the subsequent disbandment of the infantry Volunteers (but not the Yeomanry, who were volunteer cavalry). The Establishment of the new Rifle Volunteer Force was sanctioned by a War Office Circular dated 12 May 1859, signed by General Peel, Secretary of State for War, under the provisions of the original Act (44, Geo. III, Cap. 54 of 5 June, 1804).

On the same day, the War Office sent out a circular stating that Her Majesty's Government, having had 'under consideration the propriety of permitting the formation of Volunteer Rifle Corps', as well as Volunteer Artillery Corps in the maritime towns in which forts and batteries were situated, called upon the Lords-Lieutenant to implement the Act and, in greater detail, in the circular. The main points stipulated were:

Volunteer Corps should be formed under officers holding a commission of the Lord-Lieutenant of the County.

All members would take an oath of allegiance.

The force should be liable to be called out under arms in the case of invasion, appearance of an enemy force off the coast, or in the event of rebellion arising out of those causes.

Whilst so under arms, the members of the force would be subject to military law and entitled to pay 'in like manner as the Regular Army' That officers disabled on service under these conditions should be entitled to half pay, whilst N.C.Os. and men would be entitled to the benefits of Chelsea Hospital.

Members should not quit the Corps when actually on service, although they could do so at other times by giving fourteen days' notice, and that they would be considered effective on completion of eight days' training in each quarter or a total of twenty-four days drill or exercise each year.

A second circular, of the same date, laid out in great detail the Volunteer Constitution. Section 7 of this circular seems to have influenced more than anything else the ideas that shortly manifested themselves in the formation of the National Rifle Association:

'The instruction, therefore, that is most requisite is practice in the use and handling of the rifle; and with a view to this, sites for firing at a target should be established, if possible, in every locality where companies or bodies of Volunteer riflemen are formed, and every encouragement given to the men to avail themselves of them, leaving it to themselves to select their own hours of practice, or for such further instructions, as sharpshooters, as it may avail themselves of cover.'

There was huge enthusiasm by the public on the formation of the Volunteer Force and units sprang into existence with such rapidity that by 1861 numbers exceeded a hundred and seventy thousand men of all classes of society with an estimated rate of recruiting during this period of seven thousand a month.

Three months after the formation of the Volunteer Movement a group of men, who attended the first musketry course for Volunteers held at the School of Musketry at Hythe, came up with the idea of organising a national competition for marksmen and formed themselves into a Committee 'for a National Volunteer Rifle Meeting'. At the same time, a similar idea had been entertained by members of the London Rifle Brigade and when this became known Earl Spencer (one of the two leading supporters of the idea, the other was Lord Elcho) convened a meeting on 29 October at his London residence, Spencer House, with the idea of bringing the two embryo organisations together. At this meeting, a resolution was passed proposing the formation of a National Association for the encouragement of Volunteer Rifle Corps and the promotion of Rifle Shooting throughout Great Britain. A constitution was decided on and it was resolved that a paid Secretary and Treasurer be appointed and that prize meetings for riflemen be held periodically in different parts of the country.

A further meeting was held at Willis's Rooms at the Thatched House Tavern, in St. James's Street, on 16 November of all those friendly to the proposed Association, the outcome of which was the formation of the National Rifle Association.

During the meeting, chaired by Lord Elcho, Earl Spencer moved the first resolution providing for the formation of the Association. He had then gone on to state that:

'he was most anxious that one great society should be formed, in order that there may be no rivalry. This Society would not be connected with one corps or one locality; to secure success it must be National. There was every prospect of their receiving the highest sanction for this Association.'

Spencer then described a conversation he had had with the Prince Consort on the subject of the Association in which the latter indicated he would support it in every way. Spencer also had the impression that the Queen and the Prince Consort would like to offer prizes for competition amongst the members.

Another significant motion, by Captain Wilbraham Taylor, was also moved at the meeting and carried:

'That the first Meeting of this Association be held in the neighbourhood of London on the first Monday of July, 1860, or as near that date as can conveniently be appointed.'

The Working Committee met for the first time on 19 November at Spencer House under the Chairmanship of Lord Elcho and it was at this meeting that Edmond St John Mildmay was put forward as the leading candidate for the important post of Secretary to the Association at a salary of £300.

"He served in the Austrian Army from 1834 to 1844. Was Equerry in waiting to the late Duke of Cambridge from 1844 to 1850 – then became equerry to the present Duke. For some time temporarily attached to the Legation in Vienna. Served as British Commissioner to the Austrian Army in Italy. Is a very good Linguist. Lord Elcho undertook to see him on the subject.'

At the second meeting of the Working Party on 24 November it was announced that Capt. Mildmay had accepted the Office. He was to remain in office throughout the thirty years that the Association held its Meetings on Wimbledon Common.

The aims of the Association were publicized through the columns of *The Times*, and on 9 December, an explanatory letter from Lord Elcho was published:

'Sir,-As many of the letters which the Committee of the National Rifle Association daily receive show considerable misapprehension as to its nature and objects, the Committee hope that, for the sake of the public convenience, and in the interest of the Rifle movement, which you have done so much to promote, you will find a place in your columns for a short explanatory statement on the subject.

'The Association is formed for the purpose of encouraging the volunteer movement, and fostering a taste for Rifle shooting; but it does not propose to do so, as many would appear to think, by in any way aiding or assisting in the formation of Rifle Corps; it does not intend to draw up any rules for their guidance; neither does it presume to offer advice, or undertake to give information on matters connected with the organization, management, discipline, arms, accoutrements, dress, &c., of Volunteer Corps; and there is no idea of making the Association a kind of court of appeal in cases where any differences of opinion may exist. It is, no doubt, desirable that there should be some recognized central authority to whom reference might be made, and from whom information might be obtained on all such matters. But it appears to the Committee that they do not come within the province of the Association,

Lord Elcho in 1860. He became the first Chairman of the NRA and is regarded as the Association's founding father.

Capt. St John Mildmay, the first Secretary of the NRA who spanned the entire Wimbledon era. Always easily identifiable by his luxuriant and spreading whiskers, he is depicted in his tent on Wimbledon Common during the 1863 Meeting. The photograph is by Herbert Watkins, a well-known mid-Victorian photographer who was appointed Official Photographic Artist to the NRA in 1862.

and that the only proper authority on such questions is the department of the War Office, which has been especially devoted to the volunteer service.

'Having said this much in explanation of what the National Rifle Association does not propose to do, let me now shortly state what its nature and objects really are.

'The National Association is formed 'for the encouragement of Volunteer Rifle Corps, and the promotion of Rifle-shooting throughout Great Britain,' by raising funds for the establishment of a great annual national meeting for Rifle-shooting, similar to the 'Tir Federal,' which takes place every two years in Switzerland, at which prizes will be competed for. The principal prizes will be opened only to enrolled effective volunteers, and it is thus that encouragement will be given to the volunteer movement; but, at the same time, with a view to promote Rifle-shooting as a national pastime and custom, it is proposed likewise to establish prizes which will be open to all comers, whether volunteers or not.

'It is further intended that the Association should embrace Scotland as well as England in its operations; and that, following the example of the Royal Agricultural Society, it should hold its annual meetings in different towns in the United Kingdom. The first meeting will be in the neighbourhood of London, and it is proposed that it should take place the second week in July.

'Such, shortly, are the nature and objects of the Association. It has been formed in the belief that something of this kind will be necessary to give permanence to the volunteer force, and to render it, as it ought to be, part and parcel of our institutions, for, when once a large volunteer force has been organized, and the present excitement on the question of national defence has subsided, there is danger of our becoming lukewarm on the subject, and again relapsing into the state of fancied security from which we have recently and happily been roused. Nothing, therefore, it appears to the promoters of the Association, is more likely to keep up these Corps, and to nationalize in this country a taste for Rifle-shooting, than the creation of a spirit of rivalry and emulation, such as a great and annual gathering for prize shooting could not fail to call forth. We see the good effect of such meetings in Switzerland, for the best Rifle shots flock from all parts to the 'Tir Federal,' where a truly patriotic feeling prevails, and a national brotherhood in arms is established. The taste for Rifle-shooting is thus thoroughly nationalized; it penetrates into the remotest valleys, and the natural fastnesses of that small country, thus garrisoned by a people trained to arms, become the home and stronghold of a nation in the enjoyment of the utmost political freedom, though surrounded by despotic Governments. In our own country, archery was formerly the chief national pastime, and therein lay the nation's strength and security. What the bow was in former times, the rifle should now be. Competition is the life and soul of our national sports. How long would cricket flourish without 'Lords,' or horse racing without 'The Derby'? We want, then, to encourage volunteers and Rifle-shooting in Great Britain by establishing an annual 'Rifle Derby'; but this cannot be done without money; the number of prizes and their value will necessarily depend on the number of those who join the Association, and on the amount of their donations.

'At the 'Tir Federal' at Zurich, in 1859, the total value of the prizes shot for amounted to £10,000. Let it not be said that the people of Great Britain are less liberal and patriotic than the Swiss.'

I remain, your obedient servant.
ELCHO
(On behalf of the Committee).

23, St. James's Place,
December 9th, 1859.

At the Working Party meeting of 24 November, it was agreed that the translation of the Swiss Rules be printed and circulated among the Committee and Council. This enabled the Working Committee, after being engaged for many weeks in organising the Association, to present a draft set of rules to the Council at a meeting held on 25 February 1860. This Committee, being recognised as having completed its work, was then disbanded and its responsibilities were handed over to an expanded Council. This immediately resolved, firstly, that Mr. Sydney Herbert be asked to request the Prince Consort to become Patron for the National Rifle Association.' and secondly to request the Duke of Cambridge to subscribe to the Association. At the following meeting, held on 8 March it was confirmed that the Prince Consort had agreed.

The Council were also heavily involved in drawing up the draft Bye Laws for the regulation of the Prize Shooting in 1860. Previously, on 1 December, the Working Committee had agreed that Ladies should be invited to subscribe towards the formation of a fund for establishing a Ladies Prize to be shot for by Volunteers.

The Queen had already signified her wish to found a prize of £250 to be competed for annually by Volunteers. This now translated into the Queen's Prize, (or King's Prize as it became known when Edward VII came to the throne in 1901. It is collectively known as the Sovereign's Prize and is still the Grand Prize of the tournament). To this, the Council added their Gold Medal. The Prince Consort also offered a prize of £100 to be competed for by all comers from all nations, and, significantly, the Duke of Cambridge presented a prize of £50 for breech loading rifles in seeking to improve firearms; all contemporary British military rifles were muzzle loaders.

Another item of significance was the design to be applied to the Association's Gold and Silver medals.

'The Council are indebted to the celebrated Artist, Mr. Watts [George Frederick Watts 1817-1904 who later also designed the Elcho Shield and the original Running Man target for the Association] for the design for the Medal which was beautifully modelled and executed by Mr. Adams [George Gammon Adams 1821-1898] the sculptor. Mr. Adams obtained the prize for the Exhibition Medal of 1851, which he subsequently executed, and is deservedly celebrated in this department of art. The medal as illustrative of

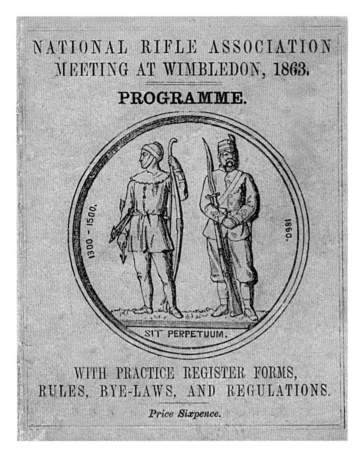

The Symbol of the NRA as it appeared on the cover of the 1863 Programme Book (or 'Bible' as it became known); the first to be issued in bound book form.

the objectives of the Association, represents an archer of the time of the Plantagenets and a rifleman standing side by side, the motto at the bottom of the medal being *Sit Perpetuum* [May It Last Forever].'

This design, of course, also became the symbol and seal of the National Rifle Association.

The newly founded NRA also required a permanent Office and this became established in London at 11, Pall Mall East.

The Rifle Trials at Hythe

The type of rifle that would be used at the first Meeting also needed to be defined. The standard military rifle of the time was the Enfield, a muzzle loader of .577 inch calibre, which was also used by the great majority of the Volunteers. The Government's willingness to lend such rifles for the duration of the Meeting made its adoption an almost foregone conclusion. However, the Enfield was only deemed accurate up to 600 yards and, longer ranges having been proposed for competitions such as the Queen's Prize, it was necessary to find a rifle that produced high accuracy at distances up to 1000 yards and more:

'This, it was decided, should be the long Enfield up to 600 yards; because, although the Lancaster rifle, the Sea Service rifle, and the short as well as the long Enfield rifles are in use amongst the Volunteer corps, the latter is the weapon with which nine-tenths of the force are armed. The Council are indebted to the authorities at the War Office for enabling them to give effect to this principle, as they kindly placed at their disposal 1000 long Enfield rifles, 1853 pattern, made in the Government Factories. These rifles were lent a month previous to the meeting to such Volunteers as by the rules of the Association were entitled to compete for the Volunteer Prizes, and were after the close of the meeting returned into store, where they will be kept until required next year for re-distribution.

Prizes of considerable value were at the same time offered for competition with any description of rifle of a Government pattern in use amongst Volunteers. The range for the competition with the long Enfield was limited to 600 yards, because it was considered that beyond that distance sufficient reliance could not be placed upon its accuracy; and it was thought advisable that Her Majesty's prize, and the gold medal of the Association, should be competed for at ranges of 800, 900, and 1000 yards, in order to show the world the power of English rifles, and the skill of English marksmen. At these long ranges the extreme accuracy of the long Enfield was known to fail; and the superiority of small bore rifles had been incontestably proved. It only remained therefore to decide upon the description of rifle which was to be used in 1860 by the Volunteers, who might be entitled to compete for Her Majesty's prize at these long ranges.

Before any decision upon this question had been come to by the Council, it was publicly stated that they had decided in favour of a rifle made by Mr. Whitworth, of Manchester; and Mr. Goodman, on the part of the Birmingham Arms Trade, wrote to the Times newspaper, remonstrating against this decision.'

This had apparently come about when the type of rifle to be used in respect of long range shooting was discussed at the Sub-Committee meeting held on 22 March 1860 chaired by Elcho.

'General Hay made some suggestions as to how the shooting ought to be carried on, and Lord Elcho read a paper from Mr. Ross on the subject. Mr. Ross suggests that the Volunteers in shooting at the long range should be allowed to use any kind of Rifles – General Hay objected to this and suggested that the only Rifle to compete with on strict equality ought to be Whitworth's which had been proved to be, for the present at least, the best.'

The Council, being anxious to show that they had acted in a spirit of fairness and impartiality, resolved to arrange a trial of Whitworth's rifle against those of the gun makers of Great Britain and this was duly held at the Government's Hythe Ranges on Romney Marsh:

'Council of the Association were represented at Hythe by Lord Spencer, Lord Elcho, Lord Vernon, General Hay, Mr. T. Fairbairn, and the Secretary, Capt. St. John-Mildmay. The programme of the trials was drawn up on Tuesday, and in spite of the high winds which prevailed, some score shots were fired from the rival rifles, each firing alternately at the same target at a range of 800 yards. The experiments were begun at too late an hour of the day to admit of their being long continued. The results, as far as they went on the first day, were greatly in favour of the Whitworth. On the following day, in spite of the wind, which was blowing a complete gale, the trials, under the judicious arrangement of General Hay and his well-organised staff, were proceeded with. The United Gunmakers insisted that all the shooting should be from the machine-rest, as that was the most satisfactory mode of testing the guns, without depending on the marksman's skill. They had not, however, provided a rest of their own, but made use of one constructed by Mr. Whitworth for the Hythe School of Musketry. Mr. Whitworth brought with him a similar rest, and both were placed side by side in the first instance at 800 yards from the target. The superiority of the Whitworth rifle was manifest from the first, and the United Gunmakers, after trying two of their best rifles, found it hopeless to continue the contest, and withdrew their rifles from further competition. The mean deviation of 40 shots of the Whitworth rifles was 21-36; of 40 shots of the gunmakers' rifles 70-80 inches, at 800 yards. It should be stated that the wind continued to blow down the range with the greatest violence throughout the trials, and in fact, about half of the 40 shots of the United Gunmakers failed to hit the target, which was 18 feet square. All the Whitworth shots hit, as the Whitworth projectile, owing doubtless to its greater velocity and lower trajectory, was much less affected by the wind. With the view of rendering the comparison more complete, the best of the rifles of the United Gunmakers, 39 inches long, was fired against a Whitworth 33 inches long, at a range of 1100 yards, and the result, as was in fact anticipated, more fully confirmed the superiority of the Whitworth rifle. It can hardly be said, considering the results which have been obtained from these trials, that the Council of the National Rifle Association committed an error of judgement when they proposed that the Whitworth rifle should be used at the National Rifle Meeting in July by those who intended to compete at the longest ranges.'

The Selection of the Site

Requisites laid down for the site were 'great space, safety, accessibility and vicinity of the Metropolis' to which was added 'picturesqueness and charm of situation'. Various sites were investigated including Woolwich, Epsom, Aldershot and Chobham, but none was entirely satisfactory.

At the very first meeting of the full Council, held on 25 February, item 8 on the agenda was 'Ground for July Meeting.'

'Resolved that no time be lost in making enquiries about a piece of ground in the neighbourhood of London where the meeting in July should take place.'

Shortly afterwards Mildmay, the NRA Secretary, suggested Wimbledon Common as the place which best fitted these criteria and in this he was fully supported by Lord Spencer, Lord of the Manor, who offered it to the Council. The site was inspected by Col. J. Clark Kennedy, appointed by the Horse Guards (Headquarters of the Army), who was a member of the Council, and he was able to draw up a report which was universally accepted.

Woolwich, 11th May, 1860.

SIR, - I have the honour to report, for the information of His Royal Highness the General Commanding in Chief, that in obedience to the instructions contained in your letter of yesterday's date, I proceeded to Wimbledon Common, for the purpose of inspecting and reporting upon the ground proposed by the National Rifle Association, as the place where their Annual Meeting for the Prize Rifle Shooting Competition for the current year, should be held.

Lord Elcho being present upon the part of the National Rifle Association, and Colonel Oliphant and Mr. Francis accompanying us (the former a Military Officer who has resided 21 years near the Common, and the latter gentleman, the representative of Earl Spencer, as lord of the manor), the ground was carefully inspected with reference to its adaptability for competitive Rifle Shooting on a large scale, and especially with reference to the safety of the various ranges proposed, and marked upon the plan prepared for and shown upon the ground by the Association.

The ground generally is well adapted for the purpose. It is proposed to place ten pairs of targets across the Common, facing the east, at a distance increasing from 750 to 1000 yards from the road, forming the western boundary of Wimbledon Park - these ranges to be used for distances up to 600 yards.

An eleventh pair of targets to the southward of this line was proposed, but upon examination, not proving perfectly satisfactory, this range was condemned, and struck out of the plan.

Four long ranges for 1000 yards are also laid out in the same line of fire as the ten double 600 yard ranges, but are not to be used simultaneously with them.

The general line of fire is from east to west, and the various lines converge somewhat towards their centre; behind the targets, the prolongations of the lines of fire extend over the Common for about 1400 yards of open ground.

The firing points are so situated, that there is little or no probability of accidents arising from the firing frightening horses on the public road.

The most stringent regulations should be framed and carried out for the prevention of trespassing across the lines of fire in rear of the targets, by guarding and watching both flanks up to the rivulet, forming the western boundary of the Common. Not less than three danger signal posts should be erected-one on the north, and at least two on the south side of the Common.

Provided that the usual and proper precautions are observed, I do not consider that a safer or more eligible site for the Meeting of the Association could be found than Wimbledon Common.

I have the honour to be, SIR,

Your most obedient Servant,
(Signed)
J. CLARK KENNEDY, Colonel.
The Quarter-Master-General of the Forces &c.,
Horse Guards

PART 1
WIMBLEDON
1860-1889

CHAPTER 1

THE NATIONAL RIFLE ASSOCIATION AT WIMBLEDON 1860-1889

Opening

2 July 1860 had been fixed as the date for opening the first Meeting on Wimbledon Common with the Queen signifying her intention of inaugurating it in person by firing the first shot. Estimates for erecting the butts (£622) and the laying out of the enclosure (£250) were based on the hard, dry conditions existing on the Common at the time with the Government promising the loan of tents, mantlets (iron shelters for markers) and other necessary accoutrements. However, the rain then started to fall and did not finally let up until the day of the opening of the Meeting thus turning much of the Common into marsh with parts under water:

'Nothing could look more hopeless, and the Council were obliged to issue orders from day to day for works to be done and preparations to be made which were never contemplated, and for which it was necessarily impossible to obtain estimates or enter into contracts. The Common had to be drained and ditches opened, roads had to be made, many hundred yards of planking for roadway had to be laid down; and large sums had to be expended in providing

The front cover of the first Meeting Programme in 1860. It was not until 1863 that the small but comprehensive pocket book, which became the famous 'bible', was first issued.

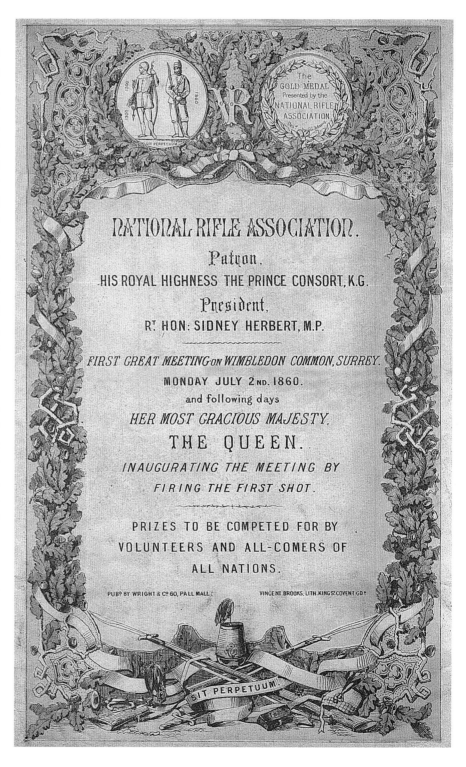

NATIONAL RIFLE ASSOCIATION.

Patron,
HIS ROYAL HIGHNESS THE PRINCE CONSORT, K.G.

President,
RT. HON: SIDNEY HERBERT, M.P.

FIRST GREAT MEETING on WIMBLEDON COMMON, SURREY.

MONDAY JULY 2ND. 1860.
and following days

HER MOST GRACIOUS MAJESTY.

THE QUEEN.

INAUGURATING THE MEETING BY
FIRING THE FIRST SHOT.

PRIZES TO BE COMPETED FOR BY
VOLUNTEERS AND ALL-COMERS OF
ALL NATIONS.

PUBd. BY WRIGHT & Co. 60, PALL MALL.   VINCENT BROOKS. LITH. KINGS ST. COVENT GDs.

SIT PERPETUUM

additional tents and accommodation for the protection of those who might be expected to be present at the inauguration; thus the estimated outlay has been more than doubled, as will be seen on reference to the printed statement of Accounts. Whilst referring to the preparation of the ground, the Council cannot omit recording their grateful sense of the services rendered by Colonel Bewes, by whom the butts were admirably laid out, and who for many weeks was constantly on the ground; and they would likewise acknowledge the efficient manner in which the butts were erected and the drainage and other works performed by Mr. Scott, who was engaged almost night and day in superintending the various operations up to the very hour of Her Majesty's arrival. But notwithstanding the zeal and energy displayed by them, as well as by many other members of the Council and other gentlemen, the inclemency of the weather, and the difficulty of procuring labour, caused so many delays that at the last the Council were obliged to apply for fatigue parties of the Guards, and for some Sailors from Woolwich Dockyard. This aid was readily granted, and it was mainly owing to their exertions and the heartiness with which they worked, that everything was in readiness for Her Majesty's reception at the opening of the Meeting.'

In recognition of the assistance given by the Swiss Tir Fédéral in setting up the Association one hundred and fifty riflemen from Switzerland paraded at the opening ceremony.

'The Queen arrived about three o'clock and was received by the Premier, Lord Palmerston; the Secretary of State for War, Mr. Sidney Herbert; Lord Elcho, the great officers of State, and commanding officers of a large number of units of the Volunteer Force.

A guard of honour was mounted by the competitors, and with them were associated a hundred and fifty Swiss riflemen, the best shots of their respective societies or clubs, who had come over to take part in the first English national shoot. The Swiss wore no uniform beyond the badge or ribbon of their society, and they marched on the ground preceded by the flag of the Swiss Confederation. The Common was thronged with Volunteers in the varied uniforms of the numerous recently raised Corps. 'In such a young force,' it was recorded in a contemporary account, 'it is not to be wondered at that the civilian was more apparent than the soldier,' and the prints of the period show 'the curled whisker, the shaven upper lip, the long and aristocratically dressed locks of hair, and the shirt collar of the civilian, worn in conjunction with the military uniform. The uniforms also were more picturesque than soldierly, there being a general tendency to wear skirts to the tunic, nearly as long as those of a French vivandiere.'

After addresses had been presented to Her Majesty and the Prince Consort, the Royal party proceeded to the Pavilion, where Mr. Whitworth had, by means of a mechanical rest, fixed the rifle with which the Queen was to fire the first shot, the distance being 400 yards. A silken cord attached to the trigger was handed to Her Majesty by Mr. Whitworth, and the rifle having been fired by a sharp pull, it was found that so accurately had the rifle been adjusted that the bullet had struck the target within a quarter of an inch of the centre. A duplicate of the gold medal of the Association was then presented to the Queen by Lord Elcho, the chairman of the Council, while a salvo of artillery announced the opening of the meeting.'

The first Queen's Prize was won by Private Edward Ross of the 7th North Yorkshire Volunteer Rifle Corps using a .451 Whitworth Rifle, with Lord Fielding of the 4th Flintshire Rifle Volunteers as 'runner-up.' The prize-giving was held, on the Monday following the meeting, at the Crystal Palace (a practice which continued until 1864), and a crowd of twenty thousand assembled there to watch the distribution of the prizes by the Under-Secretary of State for War, Earl de Grey and Ripon, Sydney Herbert not being available. *Chambers Magazine* for 4 August carried a vivid eye witness description of the Meeting including the conclusion of the Queen's Prize Competition in which Edward Ross finally triumphed over Lord Fielding.

'.............. Passing through the entrance, where we paid one shilling, we found ourselves on the common - a wide heath, with patches of furze, and a fringe of

Roger Fenton's Photograph of 'Her Majesty firing the First Shot' at Wimbledon on the 2nd July 1860. The target is mounted on the left Butt of Number 1 Pair seen in the distance. (*Roger Fenton - Royal Collection Trust / © Her Majesty Queen Elizabeth II 2016*)

'The Queens Target'. The 'first shot' mark of the bullet fired by the Queen from the Whitworth Rifle. (*Roger Fenton - Royal Collection Trust / © Her Majesty Queen Elizabeth II 2016*)

tents. The eye took in the arrangements at a glance. Within the fringe of tents, which contained mainly refreshments, were a row of others in pairs, about a hundred yards apart, opposite and corresponding to pairs of butts 500 yards off. These were mounds of earth, some 15 feet high, and 30 feet wide. Beyond them was a still more distant line, nearly a mile off. In front of each stood the targets - plates of iron about half an inch thick, and six feet square, white-washed, with a black centre two feet in diameter. The furthest were so distant that the centre was just visible as a little black dot not much bigger than that of an 'i.'

The tents from which the firing was going on were surrounded by crowds of people, who were kept from interfering with the shooters by a rope passed round a ring of stakes driven into the ground. The firing-tents to the right were occupied by the candidates for the Queen's Prize of £250; those on the left were hard at work at 'Aunt Sally.' We visited these first. 'Aunt Sally' is adapted from the popular venture of that name at fairs and races. You pay a shilling for your shot, and the receipts are divided at the close of the day among those who hit the centre. I walked up to the tent opposite the third pair of butts; a crowd of gallant volunteers were waiting for

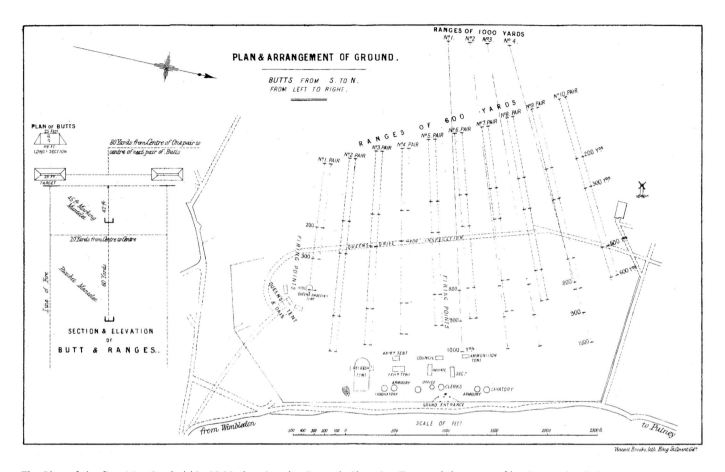

The Plan of the first Meeting held in 1860 showing the Queen's Shooting Tent and the route of her Inspection Drive.

their turn to shoot. The tent from which they fired in rotation was about eight feet wide, open before and behind. At the entrance, a man sat with pen, ink, and paper, ready to receive the moneys, and put down the names of those who hit the centre. Some twenty men were standing in single file, treading close on each other's heels, and shuffling forward as the turn of the leading man came to fire; after which he moved off to the right, round the tent, reloaded, and took his place again in the line - like the processions in the smaller theatres. You might fire in any position. This liberty was freely used. Some stood; some knelt in the approved Hythe posture; others sat down, and gathered up their knees as if they were going to take their place in a circle of 'Hunt the Slipper;' others lay flat down upon their stomachs. The mistakes made were occasionally odd enough - 'Hollo! sir, you have forgotten to cock your rifle.' 'You have not put up your sight.' 'That is the wrong butt you are aiming at.' One fat fellow sat down with a jolt and fired right up into the air!

Close beside each target was a bullet-proof iron shed, shaped like the body of a Hansom cab off its wheels: in this the marker sat, and signalled the result of each shot. A dark-blue flag shewed that the centre was hit; a white one, that the white part of the target had been struck; a red, waved close to the ground that the ball had fallen short. Armed with a race-glass, lent to me by one of the bystanders, I sat down on the grass at the entrance of the tent, and watched the shooting. The target, I have said was 500 yards off, and the centre two feet in diameter. No one was allowed to fire from a rest. This, then, was no child's play, though many of those present joined in it with great merriment. The party who were firing belonged to a genuine London corps; many of them, till within the last few months, never had a rifle in their hands. The shooting however, was remarkably good. One smart young fellow was telling me how he knew nothing whatever about shooting until lately. When his turn came, he laid himself flat down on the ground, and quietly drove his bullet right into the centre - that is, he would have hit a man more than a quarter of a mile off. I stood by the tent for some time; again and again the distant flag was waved, shewing that the target had been struck; and this was the skill of men who hitherto had spent their lives behind the counter or at the desk. Think of that, ye sneering martinets and swaggering French colonels!

Here were thorough-bred Cockneys, poking fun at one another, but all the while making practice that would rival or even beat the famous Chasseurs de Vincennes, without seeming to think they were doing anything out of the way. A soldier alone, who stood by me, expressed any surprise.

Presently the order came to cease firing; and the markers, waving large red flags to indicate danger, came out of their holes, and went to dinner. Most of the spectators turned into a huge refreshment marquee, furnished by Strange, the caterer at the Crystal Palace. All tastes were suited; you could dine at any figure at well-ordered tables, or be happy on the grass with a slice of bread and cheese and a pot of porter. During the armistice, I walked up to the butts. For many yards in front of them the ground was covered with flakes of lead, the bullets that struck the iron having been, not flattened - that is too gentle a word - but actually splashed about. The targets were spotted all over with hits. Those untrained, inexperienced Londoners would have utterly cut up a body of horse or foot half a mile off!

When the firing began again, I went to see the conclusion of the contest for the Queen's Prize - the highest honour of the week. The competitors had already been shooting at the 800 and 900 yard ranges; and when I walked up, a party of the Scots Fusilier Guards; in undress, were fixing up the tent to fire from at the final distance of 1000 yard. The target was also in this case white, with a centre two feet in diameter. It looked hopelessly distant. Imagine yourself standing at the Oxford Street circus, and expected to hit a tea-tray in Tottenham Court Road. There was quite a purple haze, that made the butt look like a distant hill, the target shewing like a white cottage at its foot with one small window.

Thousands of spectators had now assembled to watch the progress, or rather final struggle, of the match. The signal-flags were so distant, that many would not trust their naked eyes, but used a telescope.

In a very short time, the strife became exceedingly interesting. Mr. Ross and another gentleman were ahead of the rest, and equal. It was Mr. Ross's turn. He knelt down, aimed deliberately, and pulled the trigger. Alas! his rifle was only at half-cock. This threw him out for a minute. Several voices sympathetically enough, said: 'Ah, now he will miss.' A shade of nervousness crossed his mind. His close competitor, strung up to the tightest strain of excitement, lay down flat upon the grass, and hid his face. Ross, having now cocked his rifle, missed as was predicted. The other gentleman picked himself up from the ground, and came forward. See! he kneels down, steadies himself upon his heel, and puts his rifle to his shoulder. No - not yet - something dazzles him. He takes it down for a moment, and passes his hand over his eyes. Another aim - crack! Yes - up goes the white flag; the target is hit - he is one ahead. Now, Mr. Ross, this is the crisis of your fame: miss, and you lose the prize; hit the centre, and you win - that will count two, and leave you victor by one point. It is a trying moment. The little dot on the white target seems to move further off; you can barely see it; but to hit it, with that small candle-end of lead you have just pushed into your rifle, shade of Robin Hood, behold! Now for nerves of steel, and a pulseless heart. All hold their breath. The marker's hand stops midway with fresh-dipped pen; the very policemen on duty shade their eyes with their palms to catch sight of the possible signal. The gallant young volunteer kneels coolly down in the door of the tent, and raises his rifle. Crack! a puff of smoke; no other sound breaks the silence. No! - yes, yes, it is the dark flag; he has struck the centre, that little hopeless dot, no bigger than a parasol, nearly a mile off; and the suppressed breath of the multitude bursts forth into a well-earned cheer. After this, he shot off one or two ties, and established his victory.

And now fresh bodies of volunteers came pouring into the common, dusty, and, to judge of the rate at which they rushed into the refreshment-booth, when they had piled arms, thirsty as sand.'

At the first Council meeting after the Wimbledon tournament some significant decisions were made and subsequently recorded in the minutes. Roger Fenton, already well-known for his photographs of the Crimean campaign and who had also attended the first Volunteer

Edward and Horatio Ross. Edward Ross was the first 'Sovereign's Prize winner (then The Queen's Prize) at Wimbledon. Horatio Ross, his father, was a member of the NRA Council and a noted sportsman. (*Roger Fenton - Royal Collection Trust / © Her Majesty Queen Elizabeth II 2016*)

Course at the Hythe School of Musketry, had been commissioned by the NRA to photograph the Meeting and had passed the copyright to the Council. They in turn agreed a vote of thanks, made him a life member and also asked him to be the official photographer to the Association. They also resolved to present a set of his pictures to the Prince Consort. It was also agreed that General Hay should negotiate with Whitworth to secure the rifle with which Queen Victoria had fired the opening shot of the Meeting.

Consolidation 1860-1869

Throughout the 1860s the Meeting evolved from the comparatively unsophisticated single week to the very professionally organised fortnight still familiar today. During the same period rifle, cartridge and bullet designs were fundamentally improved, especially with the introduction of the military breech loader, and developments in bullet ballistics provided increasing accuracy particularly over the longer ranges. At the same time, lightweight canvas targets had begun to replace the heavy and cumbersome wrought iron ones'.

It had been originally proposed that each Meeting would be held in a different part of the country but the experience with that Meeting, with all the complications and expense of preparing the ground, indicated that it should remain at Wimbledon. On 12 February 1861 that Resolution was adopted by the Council.

'That while retaining the power of holding the Annual Prize Meeting of the Association in such part of Great Britain as may appear desirable, it is the opinion of this meeting that the objects of the Association would be best promoted by holding the Prize Meeting of 1861 at Wimbledon.'

The first Meeting was of only one week duration and this had caused one of the competitions to be cancelled for lack of time. During the first Meeting, in order to make best use of the limited number of targets used for shooting the Queen's Prize as well as allowing for the time taken to reload contemporary muzzle loading rifles, competitors were placed in squads of up to five, each man advancing to the firing point in turn while the others reloaded. The 'squadding' method proved so efficient that it was later extended into other competitions where the number of competitors exceeded the number of targets. Later the same year it was agreed that the Meeting should be thrown open to Volunteers from the Empire thus encouraging a strong showing of overseas competitors. In 1861 the first Colonial competitor, a single Volunteer from Australia, took part. Also that year, the first Camps were introduced, pioneered by the Victoria Rifles, who thereafter were always first on the ground and the last to leave at the end of the Meeting. Tragically, on 14 December, the Patron of the NRA, the Prince Consort, died and the Association approached the Prince of Wales to fill the position. He very willingly acquiesced, and remained enthusiastic and supportive until his death in 1910 as King Edward VII.

In the same year a trial introduction was also made, on one of the long ranges, of the Swiss system of canvas targets, the existing targets being wrought iron which returned a satisfying 'clang' when hit. Naturally the canvas target made no sound under the same circumstances and this was much deprecated by some (to miss the iron target was referred to as 'dropping a clanger' – a phrase which has entered the language). Nonetheless the canvas target system, much cheaper and more

The Rifle Contest Wimbledon in 1864. A panoramic view of the ranges. The Running Deer Range can be seen just above the No 6 Shooting Point sign. Lord Elcho is on the left, riding the white horse, while, on the right, a successful Volunteer is carried in triumph by his friends. The ladies are dressed in the voluminous crinolines of the time.

practical than the iron, was eventually adopted and its direct descendants are still in use.

In the early years many of the well-known Cups and Prizes were introduced. In 1861 these included, for the first time, 'The Ashburton', shot for by cadets from the leading Public Schools, and the Spencer Cup. The Elcho Shield and St. George's Vase were introduced in 1862.

1862 was a significant year which saw the introduction of the Running Deer target, that year lent to the Association by a leading gunmaker. The following year the Association introduced their own Deer, to the design of Sir Edwin Landseer, the famous animal painter, and the alternative Running Man, designed by George Frederick Watts. Boys from the Shoe Black Brigade, a charity of the time, took over certain duties at the Camp.

Entertainment for the Volunteers was not forgotten during the Meetings. A notable example in 1863 was entertainment by Madame Goldsmidt, better known as Jenny Lind the 'Swedish Nightingale'. The most famous and distinguished singer of her day she was then living close to the Common and was always willing to contribute to the Meeting.

'The evening concluded with a charming musical soiree, held in the club tent of the Association, which was not only crammed to overflowing, but the spectators stood ten deep outside; and it was no wonder, for Madame Lind Goldsmidt, with her accustomed kindness, had consented to sing some of her very best pieces. This she did in a manner that was sweetness itself. Her 'I must be ever singing,' was a most wonderful effort of the highest musical

power; 'The love warble of the linnets throat' was combined with every other excellence. It can only be heard to be appreciated. She was accompanied on the piano by her husband, Mr. Otto Goldsmidt. Mr. Blagrove also gave one of his admirable performances on the violin, and in one in which he accompanied Madame Goldsmidt it was difficult to detect the voice from the accompaniment, so entirely were both blended. It is a great feather in the Volunteers cap that a corps of them should possess so fine a performer on this most difficult of instruments – for Mr. Blagrove is a sergeant in the Artists' Corps. Captain Drake also contributed to the amusement of the evening by reading a scene from 'Pickwick,' which elicited all his comic powers, and they are great; he did full justice to his author, and kept the audience in a roar for half an hour. Three hearty Volunteer cheers were given to Madame Goldsmidt; and the party separated after singing 'God save the Queen,' which Madame Goldsmidt was so kind as to lead.'
(*Volunteer Service Gazette*)

Captain Drake was the Royal Engineer Officer in charge of the Camp.

The following year the famous singer had every intention of appearing again but an accident that took the life of one of the markers brought all the entertainment to an abrupt end. Strictly against regulations the scorer for a particular target had fired a shot into the Butts to warn the marker who had been slow to respond to a signal. The bullet passed through the canvas target and hit the marker, Private Henry Cooper of the Coldstream Guards who was collecting spent bullets, piercing his lungs. He died a few days later.

Competitors had begun to meet socially in the evening round a large Camp fire and the Council decided this could be turned into an occasion for discussing rifle politics. Lord Elcho was the main organiser and presided at the first of these 'meetings' in 1862. Anybody had freedom to speak and the meetings became something of a rifle parliament. One of the first points aired were objections to the Hythe kneeling position underlining the NRA's willingness to break away from the rigid military doctrines of the day. The midnight meeting was held again in 1863 in a festive atmosphere. It was however discontinued in 1865 as the ground was required to accommodate additional Camps.

In order to increase the element of chance the system of 'carton' shooting was introduced in 1863. This employed a circular card fixed exactly to the centre of the bull's eye. Each card was unique to an individual firer and was removed as soon as it was hit. At the end of the Meeting the most central shots could be exactly measured with a special measuring instrument of Swiss manufacture and the prizes were awarded on this basis. This competition proved extremely popular over a number of years

Even the most distinguished members could fall foul of the strict rules. One of these was the disqualification from the competition of any firer who had shot on the wrong target. In 1863, Elcho, while firing for the Scottish Eight in his own competition, the Elcho Shield, fell victim but the English Team requested that his sentence should not be implemented for this competition! This was complied with and became to be generally applied in other team competitions specifically where the circumstances were not due to unfair or dishonourable conduct.

In the same year an American, Mr Mont Storm, introduced his breech loader in a competition held over 200 yards. The Council were so impressed with the 'rapid, accurate, and destructive fire thus obtainable from breech-loaders' that they brought it to the attention of the Commander-in-Chief and the Secretary of State for War.

In 1864, the Marquis of Tweeddale offered two prizes, one for muzzle and one for breech loading rifles. This encouraged the NRA to offer their own prize for breech loaders the following year but the development of a suitable rifle for the British Army was now under investigation by the War Office and in 1866 a committee of seven army officers came up with a recommendation, initially as a temporary measure, for the conversion of a limited number of Enfield rifles to breech loaders based on the invention of another American, Joseph Snider. The success of this adaption resulted in 'the Snider' becoming the British Army's standard issue rifle, but it was not until 1871 that it was finally made available to the Volunteers when the Army were converting to the Martini-Henry rifle.

The NRA, however, had continued to lead in the development of suitable breech loaders for military use by offering a prize for the best weapon in this class. By 1867 the Secretary of State for War was offering

Capt Drake RE (centre), the Engineer Officer in charge of Wimbledon Camp, and Lord Elcho (right), Chairman of the NRA. Lord Elcho later became the Earl of Wemyss and March.

substantial rewards for the overall best rifle, the best breech action and the best ammunition. A committee was appointed to consider this development and three out its five members joined the Association's Council. It was this body which was responsible for eventually recommending the Martini-Henry rifle as the standard infantry weapon.

By 1865 the Association was able to state publicly that:

'Rifle Shooting has become so nationalized in Great Britain, and has likewise taken such root in her Dependencies, that the time appears to have arrived when the Rules and Byelaws of the National Rifle Association might be adopted with advantage by other associations. The Rules of Marylebone govern cricket, Newmarket governs provincial races, a standard set of byelaws is now being framed for football; and in like manner Wimbledon should rule all Rifle Meetings in connection with the parent Association'.

At the Winter General Meeting of the Association it was announced that Volunteers in Hong Kong and Shanghai had clubbed to together to subscribe towards a large silver cup to be called the China Cup. It was initially shot for by teams of 'Efficient Volunteers' each representing their County. This enormous and magnificent Cup was created in Canton by a firm of silversmiths named Lee Ching.

The nature of the Ranges at Wimbledon was such that a walk of about three quarters of a mile from the centre of the Camp to the farthest firing points was required – not a pleasant prospect for competitors loaded with rifles, ammunition, telescopes etc. on a hot and dusty July day. In 1864 this was alleviated by the introduction of a horse-drawn Camp Tramway which rapidly became extremely popular.

In the same year a wooden prefabricated pavilion was introduced by Jennison, the Camp refreshment contractor. This was the forerunner of a set of such buildings which gradually replaced the larger tents and marquees.

As time went on, individual Rifle Corps began to produce their own magazines during the Meeting, whose literary style was generally in a light vein. Of these the best known were the 'Owl' and the 'Earwig', both introduced in 1864. The 'Earwig' was named after the insect which inflicted itself on the Campers; the Common was alive with them! The Journal, edited and produced by a member of the Victoria Rifles, was patterned after the contemporary *Punch*. It also sponsored a competition, 'The Earwig' Prize, which was offered at each annual Meeting until the demise of the Journal in 1872. The other journal, the 'Owl' also sponsored a competition which, although short lived, became unique in the history of the Association.

'Owl Shooting Extraordinary. O yes! O yes! Take notice all. A prize of £50 has been given by the Venerable the Owls, of the Owl Newspaper, to be competed for on such terms as the Council may fix. Out of consideration for the generous but benighted donors, the Council have determined that the competition shall take place in the dark, at the 200 yards pool targets. Lights, called Owls'-eyes, will be substituted for the plates now used as bull's-eyes at these pools. Conditions.- Each competitor shall pay 1s. per shot, as at pool; and if the Competitors do not appear in great numbers, 'the moping owl will to the moon complain.' The prize, which will be in the form of a beautiful Silver Owl, shall be adjudged to the Competitor who shall, by the end of the Meeting, have made the greatest number of owls' eyes, or broken the glasses by which it will be shaded. Every precaution has been taken to guard against accidents. The shooting will commence at dusk.'

The shooting took place on only two consecutive nights but it was discontinued as being unsafe. The Owl itself however remains in a place of honour at the Bisley Council Offices of the Association, as does the giant image of the Earwig.

In 1863 'Squadding', originally introduced for the Queen's Prize competition, was extended to other competitions. It was recognised that more attention should be given to breech loaders as the Government intended to introduce such rifles, as well as self-igniting cartridges. A trial was arranged between the long-established Prussian needle gun, the first with a form of bolt action, and the standard British military rifle, the muzzle loading Enfield. The Enfield proved to be the more accurate but the needle gun was quicker to load, although the breech mechanism was seen as rather too delicate for military use.

At the 1864 Meeting the Prince of Wales made one of his many visits to Wimbledon where he shot on the Running Deer Range, beating some distinguished members of the Council in the process.

In May 1865, a Competition for the best rifle, of a maximum weight of 15lbs and using telescopic sights at a range of 2000 yards, was held at Gravesend. Only Sir Henry Halford and Metford, (William Ellis Metford – a British engineer who went on to make fundamental developments in breech loading rifle barrels and ammunition) took part both sharing a rifle designed and made by the latter. Although the results were inconclusive – for example the target was only 12 feet high and the elevation difficult to sustain – conclusions drawn were that a good, serviceable weapon could be developed for use at these ranges. Such a weapon could have wreaked havoc against a contemporary enemy army. The Confederates, in fact, had already used Whitworth Rifles for long range sharp shooting very effectively in the recent American Civil War, but sad to relate the British Army of the day and much later did not take the hint.

During the year the Council received complaints of stray bullets reaching the Duke of Cambridge's estate at Coombe Wood which was largely situated behind the Butts. It was probably not realised by the Council but this was an ominous foretaste of a problem that would come to a head in the 1880s resulting in the Association receiving notice to quit. This time a diplomatic letter to the Duke's Agent seems to have quietened things down.

In 1867, 1,100 Volunteers under the command of Lt. Col. Loyd Lindsay VC (afterwards Lord Wantage) had travelled to Brussels on invitation from the Belgian Volunteers. The following year the latter were invited to Wimbledon and, such was their enthusiasm, substantially aided by free travel offered by the London, Chatham and Dover Railway, that 2,000 of their Riflemen arrived. Colonel Gregoire, the Belgian Commandant, presented the NRA with a handsome commemorative trophy at a parade on what turned out to be an extremely wet day on the Common.

By 1868 the workload for maintaining the Wimbledon site was such that, even though the Meeting only occupied a fortnight each year, the Association decided to appoint a permanent Foreman of Works. Captain Drake of the Royal Engineers, responsible for the engineering aspects of the Camp site, was asked if he knew a suitable retired Royal Engineer for the post:

'Appointment of Foreman of Works – Resolved that the Secretary communicate with Captn. Drake with a view to obtain information relative to employing a pensioner from the Royal Engineers as Superintendent of the National Rifle Association Stores at Wimbledon, and to be at the same time Foreman of Works as well as Assistant Clerk.'

(Council Book 1)

Drake managed to locate an extremely capable man, C.S Stockman, who had served twenty-one years in the Royal Engineers, and he was appointed in late 1868. About this time the Council decided to buy a farm on the Common which became the Association's Stores and Engineering base. In the 1870s, Stockman constructed two large prefabricated buildings there – the Pavilion and the Council Offices respectively. The soundness of his construction was demonstrated by the transfer of both buildings to Bisley where the Council Building still remains in full use.

The Government had issued an order in 1866 that all new muzzle-loading Enfields were to be converted to Snider breech-loaders. This caused problems for the NRA as they normally borrowed muzzle loading Enfields from Government stores for the shooting of the Queen's Prize in the first stage of the then two stage competition. Such rifles were no longer available and the Government declined to lend breech loading Sniders on the grounds that there were not enough to spare. The Association was forced to fall back on privately owned Enfields for the competition.

Earl Spencer had been elected Chairman in 1867 after the resignation of Elco, however his term of office had come to a premature end in 1869 when he was appointed Lord Lieutenant of Ireland. As an emergency measure Elcho agreed to take over the reins once again but only on a temporary basis. In 1870 the position was taken by the Earl of Ducie.

By 1869 the Camp had reached a degree of maturity and wooden prefabricated buildings had started to be erected in place of tents.

'THE WIMBLEDON PRIZE MEETING.
A RAMBLE ROUND THE CAMP.
(FROM OUR OWN CORRESPONDENT).

As we approach the camp this year the first thing that strikes us as being something new is the tower which has been erected over the Putney entrance. It and the Bell tent and the Windmill are now the three most prominent objects on the common. On heading the entrance we find that there has been an entirely new arrangement of this part of the Camp. On the right of the turnstiles the office of the National Rifle Association, which was formerly in the centre of the Council tents, has been substantially built. To the left, as you enter, is the telegraph office, and further to the left again the handsome new restaurant which has been built by Messrs. Spiers and Pond, who have taken the contract for the refreshment department, in place of Messrs. Jennison, the caterers for the Volunteers for several years past. The new building, which is pretty in design and gaily painted, is much more spacious than the structure with which Volunteers are familiar. It comprises handsome first and second class dining-rooms, and an extensive buffet. There, too, will be found the lavatories, a ladies' cloak-room, a lost property-office, and, what will be a welcome acquisition to quartermasters, a store, at which any article of food likely to be in demand in the camp will be on sale. We have not heard that arrangements have been made for supplying ice in small quantities; but we hope Spiers and Pond will not be behind Jennison in this respect. Still keeping round to the left, we notice the large Umbrella tent which Messrs. Piggott and Son, the contractors to

Earl and Countess Spencer at Wimbledon circa 1867 with the N.R.A. Staff. Spencer, standing behind his wife, was Chairman of the N.R.A. from 1867 to 1868. Others in the picture include Capt. Drake, the R.E. Officer in charge of the Camp (front left), Capt. St. John Mildmay, the NRA Secretary (standing right) and Capt. Salmond (standing third from right), Drake's deputy at the time.

the National Rifle Association, have again erected, and the tramway which this year will have a station at each of the starting places, and also one at about half-way along the line near the 1,000 yards firing-points. Closer in to the palings are the County Tents and the quarters of the officers on duty in the Camp. Farther on in the same direction will be found the firing-points for the targets at which the First Stage of the Queen's will be shot for, and at the extreme end of the encampment southwards are tile tents and canteen for the soldiers who are employed in registering scores, marking, &c. Turning back, we come to the Exhibition Tent, which is, as usual, filled with a most attractive display of useful and ornamental articles suitable for prizes. Passing the great clock and Pastorelli's meteorological stand, we come at the Council tents, which are ranged in an oval form, and numbered from 1 to 14. Herein is the

bulk of the business of the Meeting transacted; and in a sanctum sanctorum, in the very centre of all, the 'Executive' of the Council sits permanently, to adjudicate upon the numerous questions and complaints which are sure to arise during the meeting.

We now approach the Windmill, and pass on our left Earl Spencer's cottage and Captain Drake's charming little tent and garden. At the angle facing the Putney entrance is the tent of the Volunteer Service Gazette, a penny daily edition of which journal is, as has been the custom in former years, published there every morning at six o'clock during the Meeting, and giving, amongst other useful information, the authorized squadding tables and all official notices. This is No. 1 tent of the Bazaar, the most frequented spot in the Camp. Here are tents at which everything required to make a man comfortable under canvas can be obtained, and all the necessary odds and ends of rifle-shooting, from a bottle of sight-black to a complete match rifle, can be had for money. Outfitters, photographers, pith hatmakers, lamp-sellers, and five or six gunmakers, are located here. In the rear towards the Putney entrance, is the Guards' camp, and straight before us the NRA camp. To the left is the hospital, and the Camp Commandant's and Camp Adjutant's quarters; and to the left front, the firing-points for pool, for the running deer, and for breech-loading rifles. Keeping away to the right, we come to the Members' camp, and have now gone over all the ground, except that allotted to the Regimental camps, of which there are this year, as last, seventeen in all. The best way to pay them all a visit is to retrace our steps to the Putney entrance, and starting from there, turn to the right, along what has been named

Strathnairn-road. Passing on our right the post-office, the police-station, and the police encampment, we come to the camp of St. George's, which is on our right. Next comes the 19th Middlesex, and following on, in succession, the 37th Middlesex, the South Middlesex, and 1st London Engineers. A road to the right leads to the 19th Surrey, who have opposite to them the London Irish, and to the left, abutting on the main road, the 7th Surrey. These three last-named corps are new campers, and have got a roughish bit of ground to encamp on, but not worse than many of the others had when they first came to Wimbledon. Beyond the 7th Surrey, towards the 'Iron House,' and occupying the ground on which the 3rd Middlesex Artillery encamped last year, is the camp of a detachment of one of the mounted troops of the Royal Engineers, with stabling for thirty horses, Turning

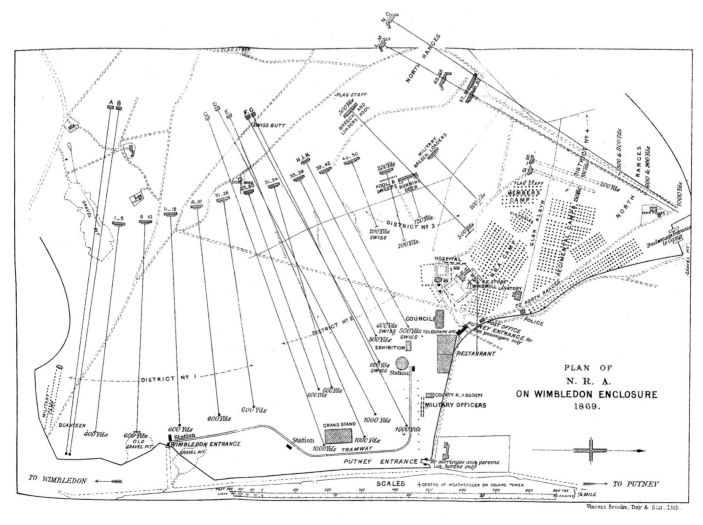

The plan of the Camp in 1869. This now includes the two by now well established 'tramways' – the Range Tramway and the Running Deer and Man.

back, we next come to the camp of the Tower Hamlets Brigade, and in their rear, on the slope overlooking the North Ranges, is the spacious encampment of the Civil Service Rifles. Joining the Tower Hamlets, and facing Strathnairn-road, is the 40th Middlesex, and next to them, occupying the apex of the triangle, we find the 26th Middlesex. Still keeping along the main road, we next come to the Queen's, and, following the line of their tents, we turn to the right, and come on to the slopes of Glen Albyn, overlooking which charming spot are situated the camps of the 1st, Surrey; the London Scottish, and the. London Rifle Brigade. On the opposite side of the Glen; over against the London Scottish, is the famous camp of the Victoria, Rifles; who were the first campers at Wimbledon. They are always the first on the ground, and last to leave it. This completes our stroll round the Camp. We shall have noticed that some of the campers are inclined to be as showy and luxurious as possible, while others apparently wish to make their life in camp as near as they can what it would be in actual service; and this is, no doubt, what the whole encampment should aim at. It should have an eye to instruction in military life as well as to enjoyment, and it is so far satisfactory to see that the arrangements of most of the campers are framed to meet that requirement. Colonel Colville, who is again Camp-Commandant, has issued his standing orders, which are in most respects similar to those of last year. The most noticeable points are that the 'Assembly' is never to be sounded except in case of fire. The rule against entertainments after eight o'clock, except with express permission, is repeated. 'Reveilles' will Sound at 6 a.m.; orders at 10.45 a.m.; tattoo at 10.30; and last post at 11 p.m. At ten minutes past eleven, 'Lie down' will be sounded, and after that time; for a quarter-of-an-hour certain of the officers will be allowed lights, and then all will have to be settled down quietly for the night.

With the view of obviating as much as possible the inconvenience of the crowded Camp on Sundays, it has been arranged that passes shall be required, as on week-days, or special Sunday passes, which will be obtainable from commanding officers, and that admission for those not having such passes shall be by refreshment-tickets, issued at 6d each by Messrs. Spiers and Pond.'

(Volunteer Service Gazette)

At the conclusion of the 1869 Meeting a claim for £100 compensation was made by one of the tenants of the Duke of Cambridge's Coombe Wood Estate who had to stop farming work while shooting was in progress. This was a sign of problems to come.

Maturity – 1870-1879.

The Snider Rifle was finally issued to the Volunteers in 1871 after sustained pressure by the Association, and the muzzle loader was withdrawn from the normal competitions. However, the newest service rifle, the Martini-Henry, was just then coming into service with the army and it would be some time before this weapon generally came into the hands of the Volunteers. As the Snider was not accurate at ranges greater than 600 yards, the Council asked the Government to lend them sixty-five Martini-Henrys to be used for shooting the second stage of the Queen's Prize. This was agreed.

Two of the most important competitions in the NRA calendar still shot for today, The Imperial Challenge Cup and the Grand Aggregate, were established in 1871 and 1873 respectively. The former, now known as the Kolapore after its presenter, the Rajah of Kolapore, was in fact a pair of identical silver vases. The Grand Aggregate consisted of the highest aggregate score from a number of major competitions with a shoot off in case of a tie.

1871 saw the appearance of the first international team, from Canada, to take part in the annual Meeting. It was commented on that their smart appearance contrasted strongly with that of the average British Volunteer! Ensign Humphry won the Gold Medal of the Queen's Prize. He was to become a distinguished and long serving Member of the Council and acted as Secretary during the move from Wimbledon to Bisley. The Council banned evening entertainments without their permission. This was in part a response to the Putney Vestry's long-standing complaint about Sunday 'roudiness.' The standing order read 'No entertainments after 8 p.m. will be allowed, except by permission of the Council, NRA this permission will never extend to fireworks, balls and dancing parties'! Shooting positions were also fast evolving. By virtue of allowing 'any position' over 200 yards (previously over 600 yards) the virtual abolition of the Hythe kneeling position, at least in NRA competitions, was achieved.

In 1869 Spiers and Pond, the Catering Contractors, had entered on a seven-year contract with the NRA, on

29 December 1870, after a dispute, they pulled out and the Association had to look elsewhere. Four days before the opening of the Meeting the new Contractor defaulted but fortunately, Drake who had much experience in large scale catering, offered to take over at very short notice. The catering was successfully secured (although it was reported that liqueurs came to be served in claret glasses!) but overall a substantial loss was made, not surprisingly in the circumstances. Fortunately, the Council already had available their own prefabricated Refreshment Building, constructed in early 1871, which had come about in the following way.

In 1870 the Report had noted that -

'All carpenters work, including office and entrance buildings, and nearly all the painting, is now done in the NRA workshops on the ground and under the superintendence of the foreman of works, Mr. Stockman, to whom also is entrusted the whole of the engineering work necessary for the erection of butts, mantelets, &c.'

The Council had decided to construct a prefabricated Refreshment Building because of previous difficulties with contractors and the design had been developed under the guidance of a specially formed Building Committee and constructed on the Common by Mr. Stockman, the NRA's Clerk of the Works.

St John Mildmay, in one of his directives to Stockman, had made the following comments when it was under construction.

'March 16 1871
…... Mr. Young suggests that we should not paint the Building as the work is so good that it ought not to be concealed by paint - Would it not therefore be as well to finish a 25ft bay, gable and all and then Plain and Varnish it? The inside of the Panels above should be Stained leaving the raised parts the original colour of the wood. We could then put up the vanes belonging to the Bay so as to see the effect. What do you think of it? …...'

This building, or 'The Pavilion' as it became known, elaborately decorated in front but primitive behind this façade, was completed in time for the 1871 Annual Meeting. It was moved to Bisley, serving the same purpose, and lasted until 1923 when it had to be pulled down as by then it had become 'unhygienic and rat-infested'! It was replaced with the current red-brick building.

In 1873 Drake was promoted to Major and felt compelled to resign as his new duties precluded him from fulfilling his usual office at the annual Meeting. His place was taken by his equally competent deputy, Captain Salmond R.E.

The Pavilion depicted just after it was constructed in 1871. Offering restaurant and mess facilities it was the first prefabricated building owned by the N.R.A. on the Common. It was especially designed for the Association by Mr. Young, a member of Council, and constructed and erected for the 1871 July Meeting by C.S. Stockman, the Association's Foreman of Works. (*The Graphic*)

Wimbledon Common Conservation

In November 1864, Lord Spencer had outlined plans for enclosing the Common to a meeting of local residents but they put up a strong opposition as they regarded themselves as having full access rights to the Common. So strong was the opposition that in 1866 a suit of Chancery was brought against the Earl but later withdrawn. These actions had raised some alarm in the NRA but it had quickly become clear that Spencer had no intention of interfering with the annual Meeting.

The situation was eventually resolved when in 1871 the Wimbledon and Putney Commons Act was passed which effectively wrested control of the Common from Spencer, although he received a very beneficial settlement. This Act, effective from early 1872, vested the Commons in a body of Conservators for the benefit of the public. It at least regularised the presence of the Association on the Common but did not extend permanent or unhampered rights.

By the time of the Council meeting on 10 February 1871 it was necessary for the NRA to work with the new Conservators who were to be awarded full control of the Common from 1872 and it was therefore resolved to set up a special Committee in the first instance to discuss items of mutual interest.

> Captain Page read a letter (103) from Mr. Forster, Solicitor to Lord Spencer, relative to some alterations contemplated by the Council in the arrangements of the Butts at Wimbledon and requesting that plans showing the proposed alterations, be drawn up, so that a committee of the gentlemen who will after this year have the general control of Wimbledon Common may have an opportunity of making suggestions.
>
> Resolved that a Committee be appointed to meet the Committee above referred to, and that the Committee consist of three members of Council, viz;
>> Lord Elcho
>> Lord Bury
>> Captn Page'

The Association were able to protect their rights on the Common to a certain extent through the terms of the Act and were also permitted to appoint two representatives to the Board of Conservators. Some points remained vexatious to the Association as the Conservators insisted on maintaining an overall control which included permission to cut back vegetation obscuring the ranges and alterations to the butts and firing points. Often enough receipt of their decisions proved subject to delay but the Council found they were able to weather these more onerous conditions satisfactorily.

The Council Offices

An important event in 1876 was the authorisation of the design and construction of another building, this time to house the Council Offices. The marquees previously used for this purpose were no longer adequate for the steadily increasing workload of the Council staff and flooding problems had occurred. The new prefabricated building was designed by Salmond and constructed at the NRA Workshops by Stockman and his team. This building was transferred to Bisley and still remains in use although with considerable modifications to the roof.

> 'Wimbledon Office Building
>
> Captain Salmond, R.E., having stated that the plan of building which he had submitted would be found more applicable to the requirements of the various departments than that submitted by Mr. Young, and that besides ensuring better ventilation, it also allowed of more expansion if at anytime this was found necessary –
>
> The Committee recommended that Captain Salmond's plan be adopted in lieu of that submitted by Mr. Young. And approved of at the former meeting of the Committee – the details as to arrangements and distribution of rooms to be left to Captain Salmond, Colonel Peel and the Secretary.'

In early 1871 it was resolved that the Government would be requested to loan sixty-five Martini-Henry rifles to be used for shooting the second stage of the Queen's Prize and this was agreed to by the War Office. The Enfield rifles still in use were replaced with Sniders for the first stage thus permitting the entire match to be shot for with breech loaders. The issue of Martini-Henrys for shooting all stages of the competition did not occur until 1878 when the rifle was made generally available to the Volunteers. The following year the membership made it clear that they wished to use the Martini-Henry in place of the Snider in its entirety. This was the rifle that gained a degree of immortality in the defence of Rorkes Drift in 1879 during the Zulu War.

One of the major prizes of the Meeting, the Grand Aggregate, satisfied a desire for 'consistent success in the chief service rifle competitions'. At that time, the competition was made up of the aggregate scores of the First Stage Queen's Prize, the first stage of the St George's Vase, the Alexandra, the Alfred and the Windmill. The Volunteer with the best united score in these competitions became the winner.

In 1874 the system of target frames and sliding canvas targets based on the Swiss system, first proposed some ten years before but rejected by senior members of Council, was introduced. It superseded all iron targets except those used for the Running Deer, volley firing and mounted competitions. Present targets on the major Bisley ranges are direct developments. In addition, the present system of aiming marks consisting of concentric rings was introduced.

At the 1878 Meeting telephones were tried out for the first time between firing points at 800, 900 and 1000 yards, and the Butts and worked well. The telephone had only been invented two years before by Alexander Graham Bell in the USA and had been demonstrated to the NRA taking part in the international match shot at the US rifle range at Creedmoor in 1877. This was its first use

in Britain and it quickly replaced the old telegraphic system of communication (in turn a development of the original flag semaphore signals) and in the following years was expanded to other key areas of the Camp.

The Wimbledon meeting by this time had become internationally well-known and the *Gazette* for 21 September 1878 contained a letter from an American that had originally been published in a New York periodical under the title 'Annual Shoot of the Britons'.

'That portion of Wimbledon Common used by the National Rifle Association for its Annual Meeting, is little more than one mile and a quarter in length, and little more than three-quarters of a mile in width. During forty-nine weeks of the year it is an unfenced and uncultivated common, with no signs of the battles fought upon it save the long series of embankments, in front of which targets are erected for the meeting. Not a gun is allowed to be fired upon it, nor may an unruly boy "fire" a stone or other missile thereon, without being pounced upon by the "bobbies," if seen.

'About July 1st, a grand transformation may be seen. By a contract with Parliament during three

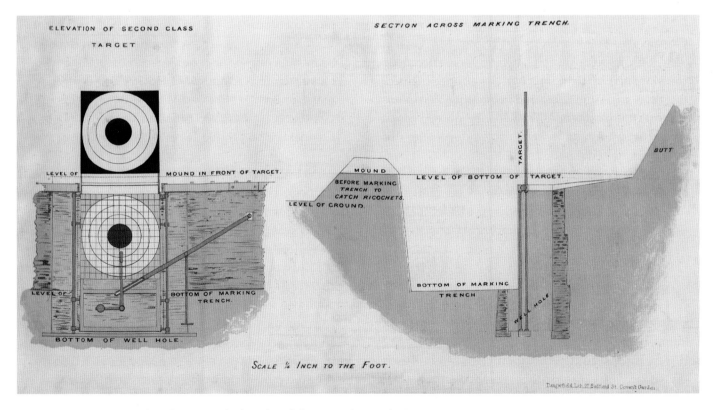

The Canvas Targets introduced in 1874 which replaced the original wrought iron ones.

weeks in the year, the NRA have control of the Common for their purposes, between the hours of 8 a.m. and 8 p.m. A few cottagers who reside within possible range of bullets, move out during this period, and are compensated by the NRA for their trouble, and whatever damage their property may receive. As if by magic a small city springs into existence. A substantial fence is thrown around the grounds, a railway put in operation, post office and telegraph-office stare one in the face, with police station on opposite corner, an immense refreshment pavilion, dealers in all sorts of wares, the offices of the Association, some twenty in number, are erected, and by Saturday night over three thousand inhabitants sleep in the magic city. About one hundred targets of the various classes are erected, and in the conduct of the meeting about eight hundred men are employed, including working parties, markers, score-keepers, orderlies, officers in charge of firing points, ticket sellers and officers of the Association. With the exception of the last named, all officers and men are supplied by the War and Navy Departments.

'On Monday morning following the week of preparation, three thousand competitors, more or less, commence to the shooting, as though it had been the business of their lives. Everything moves with the precision of a perfect machine, no confusion, no wrangling, no complaints, and but very few challenges of shots or appeals from decisions of officers are heard. The rules governing are well known, and every competitor, whether Director of the Association, peer of the realm, private soldier, or citizen, must comply with them.

'"How does Wimbledon compare with Creedmoor?" have asked a score of riflemen. The mechanical aids to the shooter are far inferior. There is no wind vane nor clock, the flags are small and placed apparently with reference to ornament rather than use, and the light, except on cloudy days, is simply beastly. The shooting is mostly done to the south-west, so that after 11 A.M. the sun shines directly into the sights and faces of the marksmen; the target is in the shade, while a plentiful supply of London smoke adds to the difficulty. The long range rifle sights used by a majority at Creedmoor are next to useless here, as through them a bull's-eye is as plainly descried on the outer wings of the target as in its proper place. The

habitués of Wimbledon use Goodwin bars, split bars, or very large calipers, and have peep-hole in vernier from four to six hundredths in diameter. Another difficulty, especially at the longer distances, is liability of shooting at wrong targets, the letters or figures indicating them being too small to be distinguished, and the only recourse being to count the targets from left to right on line. As the line of fire to the 500 and 600 yards carton targets intersect diagonally, and the firing points being of about the same line, it is not an uncommon matter for one intending to shoot at one distance to find himself aiming at a target belonging to the other. At Creedmoor all shooting is in one direction, but at Wimbledon there are nearly as many directions as distances. Whether from this cause entirely, or possibly because distances are varied, I found that elevations obtained at Pool and carton targets were not reliable enough to give me always a bull's-eye for an opening shot in a match – , between six hundred carton and six hundred regular targets I found a difference of three points.

'But if difficulties at Wimbledon are greater than at Creedmoor, comparison of the rewards to the successful marksman is decidedly in favour of Wimbledon. Second-hand ammunition boxes, sewing-machines, and other prizes of that ilk, take a second place; no price is set upon them, separate matches are shot for them, and the maker of the best score takes his choice of the lot, second best next choice, &c. Money prizes, however, are the principal features of the prize list. The total amount this year footed up about $45,000, and probably the value of the extra prizes, challenge plate, cups given by the Association (none of the latter are less than $250 in value) will foot at least $15,000 more. Turning for comparison to the prize list for 1877 of the NRA of America, I find the sum of about $350 in money and, excluding those that are perpetual, about $2,000 worth (at their valuation) of trophies. It is worthy of note that, although the NRA of Great Britain receives a considerable sum of money from the Queen and others for prizes, yet their receipts for entries far exceed the whole amount of the prize-list, the number of entries to regular matches being about 30,000, and upward of 40,000 shots being fired at carton targets. The Pool targets I failed to get. The highest entry fee is for the Albert (any rifle), £3.15s.; the lowest, in some of the military matches, being but a shilling. All Pool and carton shots cost one shilling each, and blowing-off shots cost from two to fourpence each. The highest prize a soldier can win is the Queen's, £250 in money, and a gold and silver medal. The highest prize for any rifle is £100, and the lowest £2. Ties are decided as with us, except in case of absolute ties for a number of prizes (as full scores), if for money prizes; by dividing and shooting off (three shots), if for prizes in kind or a single money prize. A notable and praiseworthy feature of their prize list is that, with very few exceptions, it is open to all comers whether for Snider rifle, military, breechloader, or any rifle.

'"Can we beat them on their home ground?" is best answered by a comparison of scores. Last spring at Creedmoor 34 in possible 35 (any rifle) at 900 yards, won first prize. At Wimbledon four 35's were made in one match, and three in another. At Creedmoor, 33 at 1,000 yards took first prize. At Wimbledon 35 was made in one match and 34 in the other. In fact, at all distances with any rifle, in but three instances did anything less than full scores take a prize in a seven-shot match.

'A comparison of scores made with military rifles will prove more interesting and instructive, for, while we have defeated all teams that have measured strength with us at Creedmoor in "any" rifle matches, we have yet to measure our strength with foreign riflemen with a practical military weapon.

'An American at Wimbledon
'from a letter to the New York *Spirit of the Times*.'

In May 1877, the NRA received an invitation from the USA to compete in the American Centennial Trophy and the Championship of the World competitions to be held at the Creedmoor Ranges in Long Island. Sir Henry Halford was appointed to lead the British Team which, however, was defeated by the Americans over a two-day

THE VOLUNTEERS AT WIMBLEDON—POOL SHOOTING AT 500 YARDS

An 1875 view. The Running Deer Range can be glimpsed at the left hand end of the line of trees. (*The Graphic*)

shoot. A full report put this down to a combination of the latter's organisation and their excellent breech loading rifles – the British were using muzzle loaders (for which this match sounded the death knell). Another aspect that was commented upon was the physical position adopted by the shooters, the Americans generally adopting the back position. Of particular note was that the telephone, only recently invented, was used to communicate between the firing points and the butts. Opportunity was taken in 1882, at the same location to avenge this defeat.

The Final Decade at Wimbledon – the 1880s

In the final decade that the annual Meeting was held on Wimbledon Common a series of problems arose that seemed to threaten not only the Meeting but the very existence of the NRA.

Early in 1881, a Bill was raised in Parliament for a new railway, the Guildford, Kingston & London, aided and abetted by the Metropolitan District Railway, the route of which at the London end would have sliced right through the Common in a cutting, thus threatening to put an end to all shooting on the site. Furious opposition from the NRA and others caused a substantial modification to be made to the route so that it would tunnel under Putney Common instead. However, the residual threat remained until 1886 when lack of money caused the Bill to run out of time.

Late in the same year the Putney Vestry put in a substantial complaint about the unruly nature of the crowds who attended the Meeting, especially on Sundays. This was the culmination of a longer campaign by the Vestry to force the closure of the Meeting altogether. The Volunteer Service Gazette of 3 December printed the minutes of the Vestry Meeting in full and also made its own pithy comments.

'The Putney Vestry and the NRA Meeting

A meeting of the Putney Vestry was held on Thursday last week, and the Mid-Surrey Gazette gives the following resolution, which, after a long discussion, was carried as : -

(1.)   That a letter be written on behalf of the Vestry to the National Rifle Association, stating that for many years past the meetings of the Association

have been a source of constantly increasing nuisance and annoyance to the residents in Putney. That the Vestry is most anxious not in any way to interfere with the legitimate development of the Volunteer movement. That such meetings have become, to a large extent, a kind of picnic, where Volunteers who care very little about drill, but who may be called professional marksmen, meet to contend for large money prizes subscribed by various Associations and persons, and do very little to promote the efficiency of the Volunteer Force, and that therefore the reason of the Association's existence has to some extent, passed away. That the injury to the trees, furze, and turf on the Common, when used for the legitimate purposes of the camp, is very great, but is much increased by the illegitimate uses it is put to. That the principal nuisance of which the inhabitants of Putney complain is, that on the three Sundays of the camp the traffic on the roads leading from the Metropolitan District Railway Station at Putney Bridge and the London and South-Western Station, in Putney High-street, deprive the inhabitants of Putney of the orderly Sunday to which they have been accustomed, that from about 10 a.m. until after midnight on those Sundays, a continuous stream of persons is passing first up and afterwards down the hill, and that the noise and dust created by the traffic is a source not only of annoyance, but of considerable injury to all persons living within a reasonable distance of each side of the road. That the noise and confusion during every day of the week are a sufficient annoyance, but that these are intensified after nightfall, and that from about 9 o'clock p.m. to 1 o'clock a.m. the shouting, screaming, laughing and so-called singing, by crowds of roughs and disorderly persons – the songs being frequently of a ribald and disgusting character – entirely destroy the quiet of the neighbourhood, and are calculated to produce very serious results in the case of aged and infirm persons and invalids. That the remedies for what is complained of may possibly be found in stopping the sale of drink in the camp in any form after a certain hour, say 8 p.m., preventing the general public from entering the enclosure without payment, or by ticket on week days and by entirely closing the camp on Sundays to all except authorised persons. That by the 40th section of the Wimbledon and Putney Commons Act, 1871 the Association is entitled exclusively to occupy and use part of Wimbledon Common as a rifle shooting ground and place of encampment for the purpose of the annual meeting of the Association, and is not entitled to use it for any other purpose, or in any manner not authorised by the Act. [Here quotations from the 42nd and 43rd sections are inserted as to avoiding inconvenience to residents and injury to the Common.] That by the 45th section of the same Act, the Association may during the shooting period keep off and remove from the enclosure any person other than such as are authorised in pursuance of the Act to enter thereon, and may, during such period, take re-payment for admission, and allow the erection of tents or booths for the sale of refreshments, or otherwise, for the use of persons admitted within the enclosure. That the Association has therefore ample power to protect the Common and the Inhabitants from the injury and nuisance complained of, the Vestry will take steps to apply to the Wimbledon and Putney Common Conservators to exercise the power given to them by the 66th section of the Act above referred to. [This section gives the Conservators power to give notice to put an end absolutely to the permission for the Association to occupy and use any part of the Common, at the expiration of six months from the expiration of the notice.*] That in the opinion of the Vestry the legitimate purposes of the Association would be more fully carried out if its meetings were to be removed to Aldershot or some other military camp, in the same manner that the National Artillery Association holds its annual meeting at Shoeburyness.

(2.) That copies of the above resolution be sent to the Vestries of Wandsworth and Wimbledon, with a request that they will take the same into consideration and support the action of this Vestry, with a view to the abatement to the nuisance complained of, also to the Conservators of the Common, to the Secretary of State for War, and to the Commander-in-Chief.

(3.) That a copy of the above resolutions be also sent to the Justices of Surrey, in Quarter Sessions, praying that on any occasion licence to be hereafter granted for the purpose of supplying refreshments during the Wimbledon Camp Meeting, it be a condition that all refreshment rooms shall be closed at 8 o'clock at night.

*[There is a very important proviso in the 66th Section for the protection of the Association which is not here adverted to. – Ed. V.S.G.]'

The Editor of the Volunteer Service Gazette wrote a strong editorial in reply which was printed in the same Journal.

'Some of the inhabitants of Putney are again endeavouring to get rid of the Meeting of the National Rifle Association, and have induced the Putney Vestry to pass a resolution, which we print on another page, and of which copies are to be, or have been, sent to the Vestries of Wandsworth and Wimbledon, to the Conservators of the Common, to the Secretary for War, and to the Field Marshall Commanding-in-Chief, and to the Justices of Surrey. We have examined this document elsewhere; but we may also call attention here to the fact that the framers of it are quite at sea in their notion of the work really done by the competitors at the NRA Meeting. It is gravely asserted that Volunteers, who may be called professional marksmen, meet 'there to contend for large money prizes subscribed by various Association and persons,' and do very little to promote the efficiency of the Volunteer Force! The framers of the resolution are also under the mistaken impression that the Rifle Meeting could be usefully and conveniently carried out in the same manner as the Artillery Meeting is carried on at Shoeburyness.

'The chief grievance of the residents of Putney and the neighbourhood is, of course, the presence of the noisy crowds of visitors to the Camp on the Sundays, especially on the middle Sunday. This is a very serious grievance, and is one which we can certify is at least as much felt by those in Camp, as by the inhabitants of the neighbourhood. And, assuredly, the Council of the National Rifle Association would be only too obliged to the Putney Vestry, or anyone else, who would show them how the nuisance can be practically dealt with. Unfortunately the method suggested by the Vestry has been, to some extent, tried, and been found eminently unsuccessful.'

(Volunteer Service Gazette)

The Vestry had already objected about the provision of restaurant facilities on a Sunday. This was totally undermined when it was pointed out that it was necessary to feed Volunteers, and all the other attendees, on every day including Sundays!

The NRA experienced a heavy blow when Stockman who had experienced increasing health problems during 1881, died in February 1882. The Council met on 22 March 1882 to select a replacement from a list of the candidates who also attended the interview. It was decided to appoint the Secretary's choice, Mr John Hoey, late Regimental Sergeant Major of the 1st Royal Scots and now Sergeant Major of the 3rd Surrey Rifles.

'......and after a lengthened deliberation the Committee decided upon recommending Mr Hoey for the appointment. He was well known to the late Mr Stockman with whom he had been in the habit of working for some years past and especially latterly when Mr Stockman was for some time under Medical Treatment. He gave the Committee every assurance that he had full knowledge of the work required at Wimbledon, and that he was well acquainted with all the workmen employed by Mr Stockman.'

The Committee recommended that he should be appointed on a salary of £100 per annum together with the free use of a house and garden. The choice of Hoey turned out to be most fortunate and he went on to oversee the layout of the Ranges at Bisley together with the successful transfer of the Association there in 1890.

The Final Years at Wimbledon

In 1885, the Queen's Prize was finally divided into the three stages which is still current today. In the same year the use of the Snider Rifle was finally dropped from the Meeting regulations having been virtually superseded by the Martini-Henry the previous year. But things had already moved on. A Committee had been appointed by the War Office in 1885 with the intention of producing a rifle to supersede the Martini-Henry.

The eventual outcome of this was the development of the Lee-Metford rifle having bolt action and a magazine. Lee was an American who had designed a suitable bolt action and Metford had developed the rifling of the barrel. It was this rifle which eventually evolved into the classic British infantry weapon of the first half of the twentieth century, the .303 inch calibre Short Magazine Lee-Enfield, or SMLE as it became known, used in both World Wars.

The development of the Lee-Metford magazine rifle was also a factor in the move of the NRA to Bisley. By 1887, building development in the region of Wimbledon Common had reached the stage where the power of modern rifles was making the Ranges unsafe. Stray bullets had fallen into the area of Coombe Wood since the 1860s. Although Cambridge was the President he now felt forced to issue an ultimatum regarding the future of shooting on the Common. He, however, was willing to permit shooting to remain on the Common until a new site had been selected.

In January 1885, Major (later Lt. Colonel) Charles Ford, an NRA member, moved a resolution at the next Winter Meeting that Revolver Shooting should be introduced at the next Rifle Meeting. He had first raised it with the Council in 1878 and it was believed to have gained the support of Elcho. By 1889, the last year at Wimbledon, there were three revolver Ranges in operation, but it was not until the move to Bisley that Revolver shooting became really popular.

The third of the prefabricated buildings also constructed on Wimbledon Common, was introduced in 1885. This became known as the 'Staff Pavilion', having replaced a large tent previously used for that purpose, and was destined to be transferred to Bisley where it became the 'Council Club'. It was designed by Major Waller and constructed by the NRA's chief carpenter, Terry, under the supervision of Hoey.

The final Meeting at Wimbledon in 1889 brought out, unsurprisingly, a 'sense of melancholy' in many of those associated with the shooting there and at the end of the Meeting, Mildmay resigned as Secretary, a post he had held since the very first Meeting in 1860. The reason was his advancing years but the Council had already decided that they did not wish to burden him with the additional responsibilities of the move to a new site and this was probably a factor in his decision. Mildmay was made a Vice-President of the Association.

A whimsical look at Wimbledon scenes in 1886 including the original 'shed' design for the Revolver Range.

Incidents and Anecdotes
The Peake Case of 1868

The Queen's Prize Competition of 1868 gained notoriety as it resulted in the only disqualification of the apparent winner in the history of the NRA. This incident, which attracted a large display of partisanship, was extensively reported in *The Times* and *Telegraph*. Corporal Peake, who had won acclaim for his excellent shooting in the two stages of the competition, had already been awarded the winner's badge by the NRA Secretary and had been feted by the crowd. Acting on a protest, the Council made extensive investigations into Peake's alleged tampering with the wadding (a wad of grease, held between two copper discs attached to the base of the bullet, designed to inhibit the fouling to which the Whitworth rifle barrel was prone) used with the Whitworth hexagonal ammunition.

'Queens Prize (Second Stage)

The Council having enquired into an allegation made that Cpl Peake, of the 6th Lancashire Rifle Volunteers, a Competitor for the Queen's Prize, has in shooting for the second stage yesterday used a wad other than that prescribed by the regulations for the same have decided that Cpl Peake has not complied with the regulations, and he is therefore disqualified as a competitor for the prize; and that the Queen's Prize be awarded to the Competitor making the next highest score.

By order E. St. J. Mildmay
July 22nd 1868'

Later that year, Peake, fully supported by his commanding officer and others, wrote to *The Times* still protesting his innocence. However, in the letter he described how, on several occasions, he had separated the wadding from the cartridge to which it was normally attached, laying himself open to the original accusation that he had effectively interfered with the ammunition which was strictly against regulations. He had of course been deprived of the £250 prize money – enough to buy a house at the time.

The following year the unfortunate Peake attended Wimbledon again where, early in the Meeting, he won the Prince of Wales Prize. However, while demonstrating the action of a breech loader using a supposed 'dummy' cartridge in the Camp lines, the rifle was discharged and delivered a bullet which passed through a number of tents. Fortunately there were no fatalities or injuries but under the strict rules of the Meeting, Peake was barred from further competition and also lost his entrance money although he was able to retain his competition prize as it had been won before this incident.

The Crowing of the Cock

Under the strict rules of the Wimbledon Camp the rather odd 'lie down' was sounded at 11pm with all those in Camp commanded to bed down and fall silent (Officers were allowed another fifteen minutes grace). However there had been the odd incident after this late hour of the night in which certain of the more boisterous and probably intoxicated Volunteers had seen fit to mimic the sounds of animals, including the braying of donkeys and the crowing of cocks, to the disturbance of all others. The night guardians of the Camp were always ready to clamp down hard on such defaulters.

On one particular occasion during the 1868 Meeting all had fallen silent after the 11 o'clock deadline only to be disturbed in the early hours of the morning by the sound of a crowing cock:

'In a community of marksmen it is held to be of the first importance that the shooting men in Camp shall be punctually fed, and that their rest at night should be undisturbed. Accordingly, as soon as 'lights out' has been sounded, there is much vigilance in suppressing irregular noises. The officer of the night hearing an admirable imitation of the crowing of a cock from one marquee, proceeded thither and requested that silence might be preserved, - a promise that was faithfully given, and for the time adhered to, so that during some hours all was peace. Between 2 and 3 a.m., however the sound was repeated, and the wakeful officer, wishing to catch the offender in the act, stole over to the tent in question, but did not show himself until chanticleer had once again proclaimed the morn. Then, throwing open the canvas triumphantly, he proceeded to lecture the inmates on the enormity of their offence, when he discovered that of Volunteer occupants the tent was empty, but that he was face to face with a genuine rooster. The sequel may be more easily imagined than described.'

(The Times)

Apparently the unfortunate creature ended up in a cooking pot for its sins.

Uniforms

The original volunteer constitution had allowed much latitude in the design of uniforms permitting Volunteer Corps to choose their own, subject to the Lord-Lieutenant's approval. Throughout the Wimbledon period there had been many attempts in applying strict uniform dress rules to the Volunteers who attended the Camp. These had varying degrees of success as the uniforms worn tended to vary in both design and colour, normally the brighter the better according to the whims of the various county Lord Lieutenants and Corps commanders with the men themselves sometimes wearing a mixture of uniform and civilian dress which tended to send senior officers into apoplectic fits.

With the appointment of Edward Cardwell as Secretary of State for War in 1868 major reforms of the regular army were started. From 1872, the Regulation of the Forces Act 1871 removed jurisdiction of the Volunteers from the county Lord Lieutenants and placed them directly under the Secretary of State for War. They became increasingly integrated into the Regular Army culminating in the Childers Reforms of 1881 whence they became Volunteer Battalions of the regular line regiments. This tended to force a much stricter discipline in the wearing of military uniform even when shooting.

In one particular incident, recorded in the Volunteer Service Gazette, a Private was actually disqualified from a competition for wearing brown shoes instead of the regulation black boots. A print from the *Graphic* journal depicting 'The Last Days at Wimbledon Camp' includes a depiction of a Volunteer being warned by a scorer to 'Button your tunic before firing'.

The British Army did not standardise on the use of camouflage for uniforms until the South African War (1899 to 1901) when it adopted khaki throughout including the volunteer battalions. It is noteworthy that Lord Elcho's own Corps were clothed in a uniform of drab green derived from that worn by the Rangers and Deer Stalkers on his estate in Scotland.

The Whitworth at War - The Death of General Sedgwick at Spotsylvania, May 9th 1864.

During the American Civil War, a number of Whitworth Rifles had been acquired by the Confederacy and the latter had exploited their long range accuracy, with the help of telescopic sights, by putting them into the hands of their sharpshooters for the main purpose of wreaking havoc in the Artillery lines of the Union forces as well as for general harassment. In May 1864, during the Battle of Spotsylvania, the Union Major-General John Sedgwick, was inspecting his Corp's front line estimated to be anything between 500 and 1000 yards from the nearest Confederates. He had been warned that sharpshooters were active and that a number of Union soldiers had become casualties. He had chided his men, dismissing the danger with words recorded as '- come on boys they couldn't hit an elephant at this distance', and was immediately shot through the head by a bullet from a Whitworth rifle.

CHAPTER 2

THE NRA AND THE RAILWAY COMPANIES

Lord Elcho, the first Chairman of the NRA, had foreseen that the Prize Meeting at Wimbledon would rely for its success on the attendance of sufficient numbers of Volunteers from all parts of Britain, yet whose means of reaching the Camp were largely dictated by a railway network whose fares were expensive and which had yet to reach full maturity. Railway travel was beyond the resources of the great majority of Volunteers, drawn, as they were, from all levels of Victorian society and particularly from the labouring and artisan classes, although some were supported by their respective Corps. Negotiation of fare reductions with all the principal railway companies therefore became an urgent requirement, especially with the L&SWR which held the rail transport monopoly in the area surrounding Wimbledon Common. The Company responded by offering return fares from Waterloo for the price of a single ticket, but only to those Volunteers in Corps, while individual Volunteers were offered the 'military rate.' These concessions only seemed to have lasted for the duration of the first Meeting.

Wimbledon Common was served primarily by two L&SWR stations, Wimbledon on the main line from Waterloo to Southampton to the south and Putney on the Windsor branch to the north. Wimbledon Station, within a few years, also came to offer connections to the networks of two other major southern railway companies, the London, Brighton and South Coast (LBSCR) and the London, Chatham and Dover (LCDR) with the latter also offering easy access to the Continent. However, the initial travel arrangements from the L&SWR's Waterloo Station to Wimbledon during the Meeting suggested that there was considerable scope for improvement!

'The great week of the Volunteers terminated on Saturday, and ended with a brilliancy only inferior to that of its opening day, which was graced by the presence of the Queen. In all public gatherings that extend over several days some of them are marked out for particular distinction; Epsom has its 'Derby,' and Ascot its 'Cup.' Saturday was the 'Queen's Prize' day at Wimbledon, and drew from London a greater number of spectators than had been seen on the ground since the inauguration. On the Putney road there was a continuous stream outwards of carriages and equestrians; at the Waterloo station there was again a crush, confusion, and a succession of very bad quarter hours to be passed by the public before they could disburse their cash for tickets. The impediments the railway authorities put in the way of those who come to them money in hand are sometimes singularly perverse; but with a week's practice the difficulties were brought to perfection on Saturday at the Waterloo station. Every 'one and return' is fixed at a sum that in nine cases out of ten requires change to be given from two shillings or half-a-crown; and one clerk at one small window was the receiver and payer for the whole rush. With the least foresight and arrangement these scenes of mobbing and scrambling, disagreeable to the strong, and really dangerous to the weak, might be avoided. But, as usual, the public endured, paid, and at last got to Wimbledon.'

(The Times)

An account was also carried in Chambers Magazine for 4 August 1860.

'Special trains had been running from Waterloo to Wimbledon throughout the 'rifle-week,' as fast as passengers accumulated at the station. On Saturday, when the Queen's Prize was contended for, when what has been called the examination for double-first in rifle-shooting came on, crowds filled the carriages as fast as they could be got ready. We went down in the morning. Volunteers in all shades of uniform, with rifles, and pouches well stored with ammunition, were waiting on the platform, and took the train by assault as soon as it was formed. I sat opposite a gentleman

SOUTH-WESTERN RAILWAY.—Rifle Volunteers—Competition on Wimbledon-common, on Monday, 2d of July and following days.—The COMPETITION with RIFLES for PRIZES given by the Queen, the Prince Consort, the Duke of Cambridge, the National Rifle Association, &c., will take place upon Wimbledon-common, on Tuesday, July 2, and following days.

The Queen will open the Competition on Monday, at 3 p.m.

Rifle Volunteers desiring to attend the competition in companies or corps, and in uniform, from any station on the South-Western lines, at a distance from Wimbledon, will be conveyed to Wimbledon (or Putney) and back for a single journey third-class fare in second-class carriages. Officers (and others) in first-class carriages, at double that fare.

Rifle Volunteers travelling to Wimbledon (or Putney), not in companies or corps, but in uniform, will be charged the military fares, viz., 1d. per mile in second-class carriages, and 2d. per mile in first-class, or the ordinary fares in their option.

On Monday and during the competition all the up-trains on the main line will stop at Wimbledon after 11 a.m. up to 3 p.m., and all the up-trains on the Richmond and Windsor Lines will stop at Putney after 11 a.m. and up to 3 p.m. to set down passengers for these stations.

All the down trains on the main line will call at Wimbledon after 4 p.m.; and all the down trains on the Richmond and Windsor line will call at Putney after 4 p.m., to take up passengers.

There will be frequent trains between London and Wimbledon and Putney on Monday and during the week.

RIFLE VOLUNTEERS' COMPETITION, on Wimbledon-common, on Monday, July 2, and following days.— The Competition with Rifles for Prizes given by the Queen, the Prince Consort, the Duke of Cambridge, the National Rifle Association, &c., will take place upon Wimbledon-common, on Monday, July 2, and following days.

The Queen will open the competition on Monday, at 3 p.m.

Frequent TRAINS will run upon Monday, and daily during the week, from Waterloo and Vauxhall bridge Stations, to Wimbledon and Putney. Returning from each of those stations.

NATIONAL RIFLE ASSOCIATION.——Prize Meeting at Wimbledon-common, on 2d July.—The London General Omnibus Company (Limited) will RUN OMNIBUSES from their offices, 109, Bishopsgate-street; 106, Edgware-road; 256, King's-road, Chelsea; and from the Peacock, Islington; commencing from 10 a.m., and returning from Wimbledon after the firing ceases. Fare 2s. each way.

Places may be booked at the above-named offices. Omnibuses for private parties of not exceeding 18 passengers, £2 10s., inclusive of all expenses, may be engaged on application to the undersigned.

By order,   A. G. CHURCH, Sec.

No. 31, Moorgate-street, June 25, 1860.

Advertisements for the London & South Western Railway Company, along with the competing London General Omnibus Company, offering certain reduced fares to Volunteers travelling to the inaugural Meeting. The Peacock Inn had been an important stop for 4-in-hand Coaches before the advent of railways. It is celebrated in literature. (*The Times*)

in braid, with a long Enfield, and very positive opinions about the match. The carriage was full. We talked butts and projectiles all the way down. Wimbledon Station was reached in about a quarter of an hour, and we found an irregular stand of cabs waiting to take us to the common. 'Here you are, sir; Hansom! half-a-crown; two shillings.' 'Bus! plenty of room inside; shilling each.' We went by the bus. It bristled with arms, and was double loaded outside; the volunteers

sitting with their legs dangling down like those of mutes on a return-hearse. There was quite a study of pendent boots from the window at which I sat. In about a mile and a half, we were set down outside a fence like a hoarding round a half-built house.'

(*Chambers Magazine*)

The Camp was about midway between Wimbledon and Putney and some two miles uphill from both. In the early days Volunteers generally had a choice of either walking, loaded with their rifles and packs, hiring a 'fly' (a one-horse Hansom cab) whose drivers, in the early days at least, had a habit of charging exorbitant fares or, with luck, an omnibus from Wimbledon but not then available from Putney. A letter to the Volunteer Service Gazette summarised the situation at Putney station and offered the suggestion that local omnibuses, at very much reduced fares, be substituted!

'WIMBLEDON
TO THE EDITOR OF THE VOLUNTEER SERVICE GAZETTE

Sir,—as the time now approaches when we shall be once more encamped at Wimbledon, I trust you will allow the following remarks to appear in your columns. It is well know that at least one-half of the Volunteers who spend the fortnight at Camp are obliged, for business and other purposes, to go to London daily. According to the system hitherto adopted (I believe for want of a better), we are compelled either to charter a fly from Camp to Putney Station at sixpence a head (if one passenger, two shillings) for the single journey, or walk the whole distance. The monopoly exercised by the drivers of flys has hitherto been a great tax on us Volunteers, and I am told that the owners of the vehicles make an uncommonly good thing out of it. The distance from the camp to the station is, say, one-half of that from Paddington to London-bridge, for which the London General Omnibus Company charge threepence. I am sure that the Company would find it well worth their while to send down to Putney during the encampment half-a-dozen omnibuses (some of them with three horses). Many campites, from motives of economy, and not wishing to pay sixpence for so short a ride, would, I am convinced, gladly avail themselves of the chance of avoiding a hot and dusty walk, and at the same time of an attempt to do away with extortion. The fare by omnibus should be three-pence. Will the managers of camp affairs give this matter their consideration?—Yours truly,

L.R.B.'
(Volunteer Service Gazette)

For the duration of the first Meeting, Mildmay kept in close touch with Archibald Scott, the L&SWR Traffic Manager (equivalent to General Manager to which the title was changed in 1870) regarding the fares charged and travel arrangements.

'9th August 1860

'Archibald Scott Esq.
Sir,
I beg to enclose a cheque for £2.1.0 for conveyance of Mr. Godfrey & 40 men of the Coldstream Guards to Wimbledon and back - I have to request that you will send me a receipt for the same.'

'Sep 8 1860

'A. Scott Esq.
Sir,
You would much oblige me by informing me what charges would be for the following number of Volunteers in uniform - from Waterloo Station to Wimbledon and back - '22 Men, 6 days travelling expenses'

These 22 men belonged to the Band which went down to Wimbledon during the Great Association Meeting.'

However, in the following two years of the Meeting, the Directors of the L&SWR, secure in their monopoly of the Wimbledon traffic, made no further attempt to offer reduced fares to Volunteers. This apparent shift by the L&SWR was strongly contested by the NRA although other Railway Companies, keen for a share of the potential traffic, came forward with offers of assistance.

'August 2nd 1861

Sir
I have the honor to request that you would convey the thanks of the Council of the National Rifle Association to the Directors of the Midland Counties Railway for the assistance rendered during the time of the Meeting at Wimbledon in permitting some of their Clerks to place their services at the disposal of the Association - I am directed to inform the Directors through you that nothing could be more satisfactory than the measure in which the Clerks acquitted themselves of their duties.'

The habit of employing clerks from certain railway companies on a temporary basis for the duration of the Meeting continued. Many years later, a Council minute dated 18 May 1878, indicates that this was still common practice. The request concerned an application for an increase in pay by a Clerk from the London, Brighton and South Coast Railway.

'Letter from Mr. Geo Russell, Clerk LB&S Coast Railway accepts offer to come again to Wimbledon as temporary Clerk, but asks for an increase in pay.

Mr Russell states that 'he will be pleased as before to accept the Offer of temporary Clerk at Wimbledon but thinks it right to mention that this will be the fifth year of his engagement and he hopes his rate of pay may be increased from 12/- to 15/- per day'.

The Secretary to inform Mr. Russell that the Council regret that they cannot take into consideration his request as to increase in pay.'

The following minute then proceeded to recommend substantial pay increases for two Association Clerks!

On 11 April 1861, Elcho, in a letter addressed to the 'Railway Association', moved to establish a comprehensive fare reduction policy agreement with the major railway companies, placing particular emphasis on their 'expensive fares.'

'As Chairman of the National Rifle Association I have to request the favor of your bringing before the Board of the Railway Association* the subject of the Coming

Prize Meeting which will take place on Wimbledon Common on the 24th June.

'By one of the rules of the N.R. Association the number of Volunteers sent up to compete may be in the following ratio '4 from a Corps consisting of any number of enrolled Volunteers above 500; below 500 and above 300, 3; below 300 and above 100, 1; What the actual no of Competitors will be we are at present unable to State, but we do not Calculate more than 600 or 700, as many will, we fear, be deterred from coming by the expense of Travelling. It is therefore on this point that I would now Call your attention in the hope that the Railway Authorities may be induced to Concede to the Volunteers who are sent up as Competitors by their respective Corps the privilege of travelling at reduced fares. Nothing would I am Confident Contribute more than this to the Success of our Prize Meeting, and I venture to hope that the great public importance of this Annual national rifle gathering may lead the Board to view this subject with favor.'

At a meeting of the Council held on 5 of May, Elcho was able to announce that the majority of the railway companies to whom he had written had consented to make the required reduction.

The notable exception was the L&SWR, although Mildmay was able to maintain his own arrangements with Archibald Scott; for example, in a letter dated June 26 1861 regarding the display of posters at L&SWR Railway Stations announcing the forthcoming Meeting.

'In furtherance of the arrangements entered into by the South Western Railway Company for the conveyance of Volunteers to and from Wimbledon during the next Contest I have given instructions for (quantity) of our latest large posters to be delivered at your office and would suggest that they be exhibited at the stations mentioned overleaf or otherwise as you may think best.'

In 1862, the directors of the South Western Company appear to have rescinded their general fare reduction policy for Volunteers, although other major railway companies had made such reductions. This became an important item of discussion at the Association's General Meeting for that year and appeared in the Report.

'The Council have to express their thanks to the railway companies for their liberal conduct in bringing up Volunteers to Wimbledon at reduced fares; though they regret to state equal facilities were not afforded by the South-Western Railway. A remonstrance, however, having been addressed to the directors of this company by the officers commanding metropolitan corps, it is hoped that next year they may be induced to deal more liberally with the Volunteers.'

Time Table of Trains between Putney and London and Wimbledon and London

PUTNEY, WEEK DAYS.

Leave Waterloo (Branch Line).	Leave Putney.		
7 20	*5 0	†7 18	6 37
†7 35	*8 6	*8 19	6 46
8 30	†6 15	†8 19	7 30
8 40	6 35	†9 2	†7 49
†9 0	7 10	9 26	8 48
*9 35	7 30	†9 57	†9 8
9 50	†7 55	†10 24	9 44
*10 25	†9 0	†11 26	10 26
†10 25	†9 50	11 36	10 49
10 50	10 15	†12 41	
†11 10	11 0	1 33	
†11 20	*12 0	2 26	
†12 15		†2 36	
1 15		3 59	
†2 15		4 36	
2 25		5 39	
†3 15		†6 9	
†4 15			

PUTNEY, SUNDAYS.

Leave Waterloo (Branch Line).		Leave Putney.	
8 10	10 30	†8 28	7 49
†8 30	10 0	†8 59	†7 59
†9 20		†9 59	†8 18
*10 10		10 19	8 29
†10 30		†10 59	8 48
†1 15		†12 13	†8 59
1 45		†1 49	9 32
†2 30		2 28	9 43
2 45		3 43	10 4
†3 25		†3 59	10 18
†4 10		†4 43	10 50
†4 25		5 43	
†5 30		†6 4	
†6 15		6 18	
7 15		†6 43	
†7 25		†6 54	
8 35		7 29	
		7 43	

WIMBLEDON, WEEK DAYS.

Leave Waterloo (Main Line).		Leave Wimbledon.	
6 15	6 35	‡8 12	‡8 54
7 10	7 10	8 23	9 23
7 15	8 5	‡8 51	10 15
7 35	9 30	9 20	10 50
9 0	10 15	9 40	
9 15	12 0	‡9 46	
9 40		‡10 23	
10 20		‡11 51	
11 15		1 6	
11 45		‡1 21	
12 35		2 39	
1 20		‡2 59	
2 0		‡3 31	
3 15		‡4 20	
4 20		5 54	
4 30		‡6 1	
5 35		7 43	
5 45		‡7 53	

WIMBLEDON. SUNDAYS.

Leave Waterloo (Main Line).		Leave Wimbledon.	
8 25	9 0	‡8 59	9 23
9 15	10 10	‡9 55	9 52
9 30		‡11 7	
9 45		‡12 7	
10 20		1 4	
10 55		‡1 59	
1 20		3 20	
1 35		‡3 37	
2 0		4 38	
2 20		5 38	
2 40		6 22	
3 20		‡6 38	
4 20		‡6 51	
5 0		7 38	
5 30		‡8 22	
6 20		8 59	
7 20		‡9 8	

* *These Trains do not stop at Vauxhall.* † *These Trains meet the Kensington Trains.* ‡ *Kensington Trains change at Clapham.*

The 1863 L&SWR Timetable between Waterloo and both Putney and Wimbledon. Note the reference to 'Windsor (Branch Line)' which was the original designation for the 'Windsor Line' Platforms located on the north side of the station.

By 1863 the directors, influenced by the protest as well as future competition, changed their attitude by offering reduced fares in connection with the Annual Meeting. In 1864, they even contributed a Cash Shooting Prize. This appeared in the NRA general Report for the year and was entered in the competition list in time for the 1865 Meeting.

'The Directors of the London and South-western Railway Company have given a prize of £50 to be competed for at Wimbledon, the conditions to be set by the Council.'

The NRA Report for that year contained a list of competitions requiring special notice, the L&SWR Prize being listed as Number 15.

'The London and South-Western Railway Company's Prize, value £50.

This Prize was presented through the liberality of the Directors of that Company, and at their request was given as one Prize. The Council added £25, which were divided and awarded as second and third Prizes.'

The competition was arranged for 'Volley Firing', between 'ten 'Efficient Volunteers' from each Consolidated or Administrative Battalion'. A Volunteer became 'efficient' when he had completed eight days' training in each quarter or a total of twenty-four days drill or exercise each year.

The L&SWR proved to be slow payers and, in 1866, the NRA having written to Scott asking if his Directors intended to contribute the same prize that year and receiving an affirmative reply, immediately sent another letter noting that the previous year's prize money was still awaited!

'May 14 1866

I have the honor to acknowledge the receipt of your letter of the 10th inst informing me that the Directors of the London and South Western Company would again this year kindly offer their valuable prize for Competition at Wimbledon. I am directed to request that you will be so good as to convey the thanks of the Committee to the Directors of the London and South Western Railway Company for their liberal contribution to the Prize list, and that you will at the same time state that the conditions for the Competition of their Prize will be the same as last year when the Prize was one of the most eagerly contested.

In reply to your question relative to the cheque for last year's Prize, we cannot find that it has been received.'

However, in October the NRA Secretary had to write to the L&SWR again to state that the cheque for the 1866 competition had not been received and would they mind sending it by the following month in order to balance the books. This short-lived competition did not appear in the list for the following year and it was not until the mid-1890s, with the NRA firmly established at Bisley, that the L&SWR offered to fund another competition. The reason for its withdrawal may have been due to a serious rift between the railway company and the Volunteers that developed at this time and, with which the NRA was unwittingly associated. This was brought to a head by certain 'incidents' in 1868...

The 1865 Report also made enthusiastic reference to another item of note, the planned construction of a branch from the South Western that would have passed near the Camp enclosure.

'A regular line of Railway is, it is said, to be brought before Parliament next session, which, without injury to the surface of the common, will connect it with the South-Western, and as there will be a station at the Wimbledon side of the enclosure, and another near the Iron House, great accommodation will, when this line is open, be afforded to visitors to the National Rifle Association Meeting.'

The 'regular line of Railway' was one of a number of similar schemes put forward at the time that would have potentially served the NRA Camp but all failed to make any headway.

In 1866 a return visit to Wimbledon by the Belgians caused Mildmay to write to the London Chatham and Dover Railway (LCDR) regarding reduced fares.

'May 29th 1866

Sir,

'The Council of the National Rifle Association having received intimation through the Belgian Legation that it is the intention of several Belgian Riflemen to come to Wimbledon to return the visit paid last year by our Riflemen to Brussels. I am directed to request that you would be so good as to ascertain from your Directors whether they would entertain the idea of bringing over the Belgian visitors at a reduced fare both by train and Steamer.

The Secretary
London, Chatham and Dover Railway'

The LC&DR went much further with an unprecedented agreement to bring the team over with no charge and, such was the enthusiasm, that the full text of the reply was released to the Volunteer Service Gazette, which duly published it in the 16 June 1866 edition.

'The Belgians at Wimbledon

Through the kindness of the Directors of the London, Chatham and Dover Railway, the Belgians coming to Wimbledon will be conveyed free of charge over their line. This great boon, conferred by the liberality of the Directors, will be thoroughly appreciated by the Volunteers of England. The following letter has been received by Captain Mildmay on the subject :-'

'General Manager's Office,
Victoria Station, Pimlico, S.W., June 12, 1866

'Sir, - In reply to your favour of the 29th ult., which has been laid before the Board of Directors of this Company, I am requested to state for the information of the Council of the National Rifle Association, that my Board has consented to bring over the Belgian Riflemen for the Wimbledon Meeting gratis, under certain restrictions, which will be communicated by us to M. Fassiaux, the Director-General of the Belgian States Railway.

'If the Volunteers come from Belgium viâ Ostend we will convey them free from Dover to London; if viâ Calais we will convey them free from Calais to London. - I have the honour to be, Sir, your obedient servant,

'A.S Forbes, General Manager

Captain E. St. John Mildmay, NRA,
12 Pall Mall.'

(Volunteer Service Gazette)

The Engineer and Railway Volunteer Staff Corps

In 1867 a letter of some significance was sent to the Volunteer Service Gazette, possibly from Lord Elcho. This suggested that the Engineer and Railway Staff Corps, a body set up two years before to assist the movement of large bodies of troops in times of crisis, should be considerably expanded. This letter may have acted as a catalyst for, by the end of the century, many senior officers of the major railway companies had become members. It was of especial significance to the L&SWR as the railway company eventually came to serve not only the NRA Bisley Camp site but many military installations and Camps as well as providing highly efficient troop transport arrangements during both the Boer and First World Wars.

'The Engineer and Railway Volunteer Staff Corps

The first inspection of this corps was held by General Sir John Burgoyne R.E., G.C.B. Inspector General of Fortifications at the head-quarters, 24, Great George Street, Westminster, on Monday the 6th of November, at 4 p.m. The Engineer and Railway Volunteer Staff Corps was enrolled in January 1865 'for the purpose of directing the application of skilled labour, and of railway transport, to the purposes of national defence, and for preparing in time of peace a system on which such duties should be conducted.' As a staff corps it consists only of officers who are defined by the rules as civil engineers and contractors, and officers of railway companies.' At present the only commissions filled up are 21 of the Lieutenant Colonels, who constitute a council for considering the various questions submitted by the Secretary of State for War. This Council is selected from 'civil engineers of standing and experience, who have directed the chief railway and other important works of this country, and general managers of leading lines of railway.' The chairman of the Council, as well as honorary colonel of the corps, is Colonel M'Murdo, C.B., and the lieutenant-commandant is Mr. G.P. Bidder, past president of the Institution of Civil Engineers.'

(The Times)

Colonel M'Murdo was also a prominent member of the NRA's Council and George Parker Bidder was a distinguished engineer who had worked with and been a friend of the great railway engineers George and Robert Stephenson. Bidder's son, also named George Parker was, for many years, an ordinary member of the Association and shot at Wimbledon.

'CORRESPONDENCE.
THE ENGINEER AND RAILWAY STAFF CORPS.
TO THE EDITOR OF THE VOLUNTEER SERVICE GAZETTE.

'Sir,-.At the dinner of the Institution of Civil Engineers some short time ago, Lieut.-Colonel Hawkshaw alluded to the corps of which he is a member-viz., the Engineer and Railway Staff Corps - as one which, though comparatively little known, is a very important one; and I cannot help thinking that it is a great pity that this corps is not enlarged to a very considerable extent, and that commissions in it, for captains, lieutenants, &c., should be given to the railway engineers and district superintendents all over the country, as far, of course, as those gentlemen could be induced to accept them; and that they should hold meetings at stated times, in their respective districts, and arrange plans for collecting large bodies of troops at different points in the shortest possible time, the general outline of the plan being furnished to them, from time to time, by the present lieutenant-colonels of the corps in London, who are no doubt the leading men of their respective professions, but who cannot have that local knowledge which is so necessary for the proper execution of any scheme.

'At the different county reviews, also, the members of the corps might be employed to great advantage, and thus gain experience, and I think that they would supply a want long felt-viz., some one to make the necessary railway arrangements for the conveyance of the Volunteers, who should know something of their requirements, and also of the best means of providing for them.

'The engineer members of the corps might also direct their attention to the best means and routes for making temporary railways to convey troops in times of emergency to points which are likely to be attacked, sea-coast defence lines, and means of communication between railways belonging to different companies which at present have no connexion, but over which it might be desirable to run through trains, and many other matters.

I think that if the corps was extended in the manner which I propose, it would become one of the most important branches of the Volunteer service; nay more, it would supply a want which the regular army would feel in the event of an invasion of this country, and which the Royal Engineers could not supply so well as the gentlemen whom I hope to see enrolled as members of the Engineer and Railway Staff Corps.

'Hoping you will be able to find space in your valuable columns for these remarks, and enclosing my card, I am, yours truly, L. E.'

(Volunteer Service Gazette July 13th 1867)

It is tempting to conclude that the signatory 'L.E.' was in fact Lord Elcho. The letter is very characteristic of his talent for advanced military thinking, outside the accepted mores of the time, in conjunction with his unwavering support for the Volunteer cause.

The Windsor Scandal

In the late 1860s, the relationship between the L&SWR and the Volunteer Movement deteriorated badly, a situation for which the management of the railway company seems to have been largely responsible. There appears to have been a general breakdown in the L&SWR organisational structure specifically in connection with the provision of train services for special events. Due to the large numbers involved this significantly affected the Volunteer Movement which relied almost totally on rail transport for Reviews and Meetings. The impact on the NRA was relatively minor.

Two incidents in 1868, particularly, became notorious as they served to highlight problems within the railway company and also disturbing indications of disciplinary problems within the Volunteer Movement. The occasion was the transport arrangements surrounding the Royal Review held at Windsor in June 1868 and attended by Queen Victoria.

The L&SWR's arrangements for the transport of Volunteers to the Camp proved chaotic and even more so, at the start of the return journey, when the organisation of the railway service virtually collapsed. This lead directly to a breakdown in discipline within certain Volunteer Corps, occasioning the Volunteer Service Gazette to write vitriolic comments about both the L&SWR and, initially, the Volunteers, but later reserving its main criticisms for the railway company.

The main points of the initial report by the *Volunteer Service Gazette* are taken from an editorial in its 27 June edition:

'The Conductors of this Journal have always endeavoured to place before the force and the public a perfectly accurate statement of all facts bearing on the Volunteer movement, whether such facts told for or against their own views. We have never attempted to explain away or make light of any foolish or insubordinate act or word, and in the course of the last eight years have had occasion to report and comment on several such. That this part of our duty has been hitherto so light, is a proof of the healthiness of the growth of the national force in its early years. Last week we should have maintained confidently enough that in its maturity this healthiness was even more settled, that our constitution was improving and strengthening with age. To-day we are obliged to admit, and are humiliated while admitting, that the occurrences of last Saturday night, on the return of the troops to the Datchet railway-station, after the Royal Review, were of a character to bring discredit and disgrace upon the force, and to prove either that the reins of discipline have been culpably relaxed in many cases, or that they have never been drawn tightly enough. We do not propose here to enter into details, which will be found at length in another part of our columns. We are perfectly aware that a large share of the blame rests on the South-Western Railway Company, whose arrangements at the Datchet station were utterly inadequate. If we were on the look-out for other shoulders on to which to shift the burden, we might spend a large amount of plausible indignation on the Company, the police, the owners of punts at Datchet, and other public and private bodies and persons. With these, however, we have nothing here to do; and after all excuses that can possibly be made,

the broad fact remains, that the Volunteers disobeyed general orders, which had been published and circulated, and the purport of which was perfectly well known to the whole force assembled. They were ordered to march to the stations in military formation, and they did not and would not do so. They saw General Lindsay and his staff at the pontoon bridge and the railway-station; they heard their positive and reiterated orders, and defied or evaded them. It only remains for us to examine the cause of this lamentable state of things, and to consider the remedy, leaving the many excuses which are available to be pleaded by others. ....'

Having castigated the L&SWR as being largely to blame for being the root cause of a breakdown in discipline of some of the Volunteer Corps due to inadequate arrangements at Datchet Station, the rest of the editorial devoted itself to roundly criticising the behaviour of elements of the Volunteers on leaving the Review.

In the next edition of the *Gazette*, that of 4 July, a more balanced account appeared. It was headed 'The Windsor Scandal.'

'There is still hesitation at head-quarters as to what action, if any, is to be taken with respect to the confusion and insubordination at the pontoon bridge and Datchet Station, on which we were constrained to comment so severely in our last number. This, at least, is the only conclusion to which we can come after the reply of Sir John Pakington to Lord Elcho's1 renewed inquiry. General Lindsay had gone on a tour of inspection to the North, and it is probable that in his report when made, and in the official comment upon it, serious notice, whatever that may amount to, will be taken of the transactions in question. This is all we can gather from the public utterances of the Secretary for War, and we need hardly say that such a conclusion is as lame a one as could possibly have been reached, and one which will not be accepted willingly by the Volunteer Force. Now that we have had time to compare the different statements and to weigh the evidence, the facts come out clearly enough. A considerable number of corps behaved badly, and showed a grievous want of discipline. On the other hand, there were corps - and, having regard to the very trying circumstances of the case, no inconsiderable number - who were orderly, obedient, never broke their ranks, and, in short, conducted themselves as men under arms should do, and in such a manner as to deserve the approbation of the Inspector-General and his staff; and the thanks of the. country. This being so, it is not to be borne without protest that the wholechapet force present at Windsor should lie under the stigma which undoubtedly rests upon them at present in the public mind, and which we venture respectfully but very confidently to assert will not be removed except after an official inquiry shall have been held, and a discriminating report put forth as to all the causes of the miscarriage, and the conduct of the several regiment, concerned.

'We say all the causes, because it is clear now that the chief blame rests with the South-Western Railway, and there is no reason whatever why the Volunteers should be debited with discredit which properly belongs to that company. It is not easy to understand their conduct, except upon the supposition that they deliberately intended to make the Review a failure if possible. They charged high fares, and made the most inconvenient arrangements, to begin with. Thus at least one Middlesex corps, from the North of London, was obliged to give up the Review altogether, because in order to attend they would have had to muster at eleven o'clock in the morning to reach the rendezvous at Windsor by means of the South Western Railway at 4.30pm! But perverse as the arrangements were, they were not adhered to, even in the early part of the day. The trains were not started at the named hours, though the Volunteers were, so far as we have heard, punctual at their musters, and in several instance, notably in that of the London Scottish, the journey of twenty miles occupied upwards of two hours. This morning performance was a fitting prelude to that of the evening, when the confusion of trains and the indifference of the company's servants reached their climax. We do not mean to say that the men were uncivil, but that they appeared simply to have lost their heads, and given up the business as hopeless, in the truly British reliance that somehow or other without their intervention things would right themselves, and the station be cleared some time or another in the course of the Sunday. We should not have been inclined to censure them so severely, but for the contrast of the Great Western Company. At the Windsor and Slough Stations there was no confusion, time was well kept on the whole, and neither the Volunteers, nor the public had any fair cause of complaint. If the one company could so manage, there can be no excuse for the other. All we can do is to let the facts be known as widely as possible. Of course remonstrances are useless, and the time spent on endeavouring to bring the company to acknowledge and amend their shortcomings will be thrown away. But a few such occurrences as the Windsor Review will prepare the public for a careful and favourable consideration in the not distant future of proposals for the transfer of the railways to Government. With this consolation we must be content for the present.

'To return to the Volunteers. What we think the force has a right to demand is that there shall be a searching inquiry into the causes of the disorder. Such an inquiry must spare no one if it is to be of the slightest use. The Inspector-General put forth certain carefully considered and very explicit general orders, and what we require to know is, how far these were obeyed by the Volunteers of all grades. Did the brigades leave the park in formation, and, if not, which brigades were broken up, and who allowed them to be broken up? What brigadiers brought their commands to the railways? And so on with corps and companies. We want to have as accurate a list as can be now obtained of the corps which were brought to the station in proper formation and obedient to order. and, lastly, of the regiments and companies, if possible, to which the stragglers belonged who were thronging the station, defying the staff, and firing off their rifles in the air. We shall then have the whole case before the force and the country, and shall know how far the occurrences of Saturday, June 20, indicate real unsoundness.

'We trust, then, that Lord Elcho will continue to press the Government strongly on these points, and that he will be backed up by every Volunteer officer in the House who has the credit of the force at heart. Neither he nor they need trouble their selves about the consequences. Let them be what they may, they can only benefit the force. For our own parts, we should be glad to see not only inquiry, which will distinguish between those officers and corps who did their duty and those who grossly neglected it, but the application of some searching remedial measures, which will reach those who have disgraced us, and be likely to hinder the possibility of the recurrence of such scenes as followed the Royal Review at Windsor.'

(Volunteer Service Gazette)

Poor relations between the Volunteer Movement and the L&SWR notwithstanding, the NRA's arrangements remained relatively unaffected, other than through an apparent retaliation by the L&SWR in withdrawing their Prize sponsorship, for throughout this period the Association was still able to negotiate the introduction of special stops at Wimbledon and Putney for the convenience of Volunteers attending the Annual Meeting although this may have been due more to the relationship built up between Mildmay and Scott.

'July 10th 1868

'Sir,

The Council will esteem it as a favour if you will be so good as make the same arrangements during the Prize Meeting, as regards the stopping at Putney of trains which do not usually stop at the Station, as were made by you in 1867.

Archibald Scott Esq.
Waterloo Bridge Station'

However further trouble was to follow. Following the Association's Annual Meeting, a Review was planned to be held on Wimbledon Common requiring Volunteers to assemble on the Common and Putney Heath. Those trains carrying Volunteers to Putney were, at very short notice, diverted to Wimbledon, causing a total collapse of the Review. This now dragged in the War Office who, having drawn up the original scheduling, was now accused of being party to this last minute change of plan instigated by the L&SWR for its own convenience. The Gazette was now positively incandescent about the Railway Company!

Putney Station in the 1860s The ornate building with its massive chimneys was swept away when the number of tracks was quadrupled in 1887. It was designed, with three other brick-built Tudor Gothic-style stations on the Richmond branch, by the architect William Tite in 1846. The others were Barnes, Mortlake and Richmond of which Barnes is the only survivor. (*Philip Brown collection*)

'THE RAILWAYS AND THE VOLUNTEERS

'There is a point beyond which a Government cannot safely go in allowing itself to be ignored, or defied, by any section of its subjects; and we would humbly ask the military authorities whether they are not of opinion that that point has been reached by the South-Western Railway Company, in the case of the arrangements connected with reviews? Surely one has a right to expect that when official orders have been printed and published by the War-office, giving minute instructions and directions as to places and times of muster, and other details, the plan indicated therein will be carried out. If there is no power of insuring this in the British Isles, we have been living in a fools' paradise; for we venture to say, that you shall take the first hundred men you meet in Fleet Street, and every one of them will answer that of course such power exists, and that no private firm, or corporation, or individual can for a moment resist the national will expressed by the Government in official orders, provided that there is no interference with the rights of person or property. Now, in the case of the Review of last Saturday there was no such interference. The only persons whose leave was necessary (if any one's leave is legally required) in order that the Review might be held on the Common, were Lord Spencer and the copy-holders, and this had been obtained. This being so, surely, if the Government had really cared about the matter, or been the least in earnest about encouraging Volunteers to attend on Saturday last, they might have insisted on the programme they had themselves laid down being carried out, and the Railway Company would have been advised by its lawyers that it would be safer to knock under, and do the bidding of the Government. It is the doubt - and we own not an unreasonable doubt, under all the circumstances - whether the military authorities cared a straw about the matter, whether, they might not be, on the whole, rather pleased than otherwise at any breakdown which should occur in connexion with Volunteer doings, that makes many of the best of our metropolitan corps so bitter when they see the way in which the South-Western Railway Company were allowed to ride rough-shod, certainly over us, and apparently over the War-office, on Saturday last. There is not a man in the force who believes that if Lord de Grey had been Secretary at War, the Company would have been allowed to alter all the arrangements of his department at the eleventh hour, when it was physically impossible that proper notice could be given of the alterations to the persons most interested, the rank and file of the different corps scattered all over London and the suburbs. Let us again remind our readers that General Orders were out last week, and had been circulated in the ordinary way, specifying that certain brigades were to be formed on Putney-heath, and certain other brigades on Wimbledon-common, and every corps had made its arrangements accordingly. On Friday only a sudden notification is made at the headquarters of corps that the South-Western will not take a single Volunteer to Putney, but insists on landing the whole at the Wimbledon Station. The War-office acquiesces, apparently without even a remonstrance, and the Review accordingly collapses. Not that we believe that in any case there would have been anything like a good muster. After the Windsor Review, and pending the inquiry which is in progress (or is at any rate supposed to be in progress) as to what took place there, no one at all acquainted with the public opinion of the force could expect that. But it is within our knowledge that the utter breakdown as to numbers was caused in many cases by this bewildering and inexplicable change of purpose.

'We have heard that the South-Western Railway Company never wishes to carry another Volunteer if they can help it. We can well believe from their conduct that this is so, and could sincerely reciprocate the wish that no Volunteer might ever again travel by that most inconvenient and ill-managed line. But, unluckily, Wimbledon is entirely commanded by the South-Western, and therefore if that company is to be allowed now to carry matters with a high hand, our yearly gathering for the Prize Meeting is at their mercy. After the brilliant success of their late audaciously impudent interference with the War-office, we may well expect further aggressive movements; and the least we may look for next year will be double fares, and some hampering and meddlesome restrictions as to the conditions upon which they will convey the marksmen of England to their yearly competition. Now, if the Government are prepared to stand this sort of thing from a Railway Company, is the country?

We cannot believe that the nation wishes to suppress the Volunteer movement, or snub the Volunteers. We hope, therefore, that between this time and next session the Metropolitan Commanding Officers will take steps to bring this matter seriously before Parliament. If the country is ever to be put in a satisfactory state for defence, it is perfectly clear that the railways must be utilized, and that the more thoroughly in hand they are the more efficient will our fighting power be. We have been contributing to this efficiency for the last nine years, and if we are to go on educating our great lines, it must only be on reasonable conditions. What our leaders should arrange, therefore, to demand with very decided insistence on the part of the force they represent, is, that the railways shall be bound to carry out the national will, and not their own caprice, whenever it is a question of any military ceremony or movements. If the Government has not the necessary power in this matter, it is high time that it had. We cannot doubt that the new Parliament will readily pass any Act which may be necessary (if any be, which we cannot yet believe) to give the Government the power of taking control of the stations, line, and rolling stock of railway companies whenever it considers it expedient to do so for military purposes, and we hope that the matter will be pressed on their attention. It would work a marvellous reform on all Railway Boards and staffs, if under such an act the War-office were to occupy Waterloo Station by a clear-headed and short-tempered General and his staff for the first week, say, of the next Wimbledon Meeting.'

(*Volunteer Service Gazette*)

In spite of the *Gazette's* rhetoric, to the L&SWR the commercial rewards offered by the transportation of large numbers of Volunteers to their various Reviews as well as the Wimbledon Meeting were, no doubt, regarded as rather more important than angry words in a newspaper. By 1869 the L&SWR had put its affairs in better order and the *Gazette*, all ill-will forgotten, produced a business-like editorial regarding the fare arrangements for the Annual Meeting of that year.

'We observe the South Western Railway Company have arranged to issue fortnightly tickets this year from to-day to the 17th, inclusive, at 13s. (first class)

and 9s. (second). In a pecuniary point of view, there is no advantage in this arrangement, but it will save the trouble of crushing up to the ticket-office everyday. The prices for day tickets are the same as last year, but special arrangements will have to be made for the day of the Grand Review, July 17. Like most of the other railways, the South Western will issue tickets at a single fare, available till July 20th, from all places over thirty miles from London, For further particulars, we refer our readers to our advertisement columns.'

(*Volunteer Service Gazette*)

Irritation with the Railway Company, however, persisted in other quarters and the Volunteer Service Review, a contemporary rival to the *Gazette*, continued to publish cutting paragraphs in its editorials. For example, as late as 1883, the following appeared:

'Aldershot Notes

It is a very odd thing that the London and South-Western managed to dispatch three thousand and odd men to Aldershot some three weeks ago without sending all the different detachments to their wrong destination or committing some other blunder; and for that once the station authorities exhibited a generous civility of manner which is quite foreign to them. This spurt, however, could not be kept up for long. When, on the 18th ultimo, the last Provisional Battalion went down, the little official we have had occasion to comment on before lost his equanimity and presence of mind, and made himself objectionable. Moreover, although the strength of the battalion had been communicated to the London and South-Western Railway authorities, they had not sufficient gumption to provide the requisite number of carriages, so had to hitch on others, and thus cause an easily avoided delay and confusion.'

(*Volunteer Service Review*)

The Tooting, Merton and Wimbledon Railway

On 1 October 1868, the Tooting, Merton and Wimbledon Railway opened. This line, which was jointly owned by the L&SWR and the London Brighton & South Coast Railway (LB&SCR), connected the former's network to that of its partner, the LC&DR, and the latter's network to Wimbledon via a loop starting at Tooting Junction. This added an important new route for reaching the Camp.

LONDON, CHATHAM, AND DOVER RAILWAY.—NEW ROUTE TO WIMBLEDON VIÂ HERNE HILL.

Every effort will be made to ensure punctuality, but the connexion of these Trains cannot be guaranteed.

FROM LONDON.		WEEK DAYS.										SUNDAYS.			
		a.m.	a.m.	a.m.	p.m.	p.m.	p.m.	p.m.	p.m.	p.m.	p.m.	a.m.	p.m.	p.m.	p.m.
L.C.&D. Line.	LUDGATE HILL ...... dep.	8 52	10 2	11 35	1 5	2 50	4 3	5 22	6 42	8 0	9 0	9 50	1 35	4 35	7 37
	Blackfriars Bridge ...... ,,	...	10 4	11 37	1 7	2 52	...	...	...	...	9 2	9 52	1 37	4 37	7 39
	Borough Road ...... ,,	...	10 7	11 40	...	2 55	...	...	...	...	9 5	...	1 40	...	7 42
	Elephant and Castle ...... ,,	8 56	10 9	11 42	1 11	2 57	...	5 26	6 47	8 5	9 7	9 56	1 42	4 41	7 44
	Walworth Road ...... ,,	...	10 12	11 45	1 14	3 0	4 10	...	6 50	8 8	9 10	9 59	1 45	4 44	7 47
	Camberwell Road ...... ,,	...	10 15	11 48	1 17	3 3	4 13	5 31	6 53	8 11	9 13	10 2	1 48	4 47	7 50
	Trains leave Victoria for Herne Hill at ......(A)	...	9 15	11 30	...	2 5	3 30	5 18	6 25	7 15	8 40	9 0	1 0	4 0	7 30
Tooting Line.	Herne Hill (and for Dulwich) ,,	9 3	10 20	11 53	1 22	3 8	4 18	5 35	6 58	8 16	9 18	10 7	1 53	4 52	7 55
	Tulse Hill & Lower Norwood ,,	9 8	10 25	11 58	1 27	3 13	4 22	5 39	7 3	8 21	9 23	10 12	1 58	4 57	8 0
	Streatham ...... ,,	9 13	10 30	12 3	1 32	3 18	4 27	5 43	7 8	8 26	9 28	10 17	2 3	5 2	8 5
	Tooting ...... ,,	9 18	10 35	12 8	1 37	3 23	4 32	5 48	7 13	8 31	9 33	10 22	2 8	5 7	8 10
	Haydons Lane ...... ,,	9 23	10 39	12 12	1 41	3 27	4 36	5 52	7 17	8 35	9 37	10 26	2 12	5 11	8 14
	Wimbledon ...... arr.	9 26	10 42	12 15	1 44	3 30	4 39	5 55	7 20	8 38	9 40	10 29	2 16	5 15	8 18

TO LONDON.		WEEK DAYS.										SUNDAYS.			
		a.m.	a.m.	a.m.	a.m.	p.m.	p.m.	p.m.	p.m.	p.m.	p.m.	a.m.	p.m.	p.m.	p.m.
Tooting Line.	WIMBLEDON ...... dep.	8 0	9 6	10 34	11 38	1 50	2 56	4 16	5 45	6 57	8 0	9 6	12 48	3 37	6 18
	Haydons Lane ...... ,,	8 3	9 9	10 38	11 41	1 54	2 59	4 19	5 48	7 1	8 3	9 9	12 52	3 40	6 21
	Tooting ...... ,,	8 7	9 13	10 42	11 46	1 58	3 3	4 24	5 53	7 5	8 8	9 13	12 57	3 45	6 26
	Streatham ...... ,,	8 12	9 17	10 47	11 51	2 3	3 8	4 29	5 58	7 10	8 13	9 18	1 2	3 50	6 31
	Tulse Hill & Lower Norwood ,,	8 18	9 22	10 52	11 56	2 8	3 13	4 34	6 3	7 16	8 18	9 23	1 7	3 55	6 36
	Herne Hill (and for Dulwich) ,,	8 24	9 27	10 57	12 1	2 13	3 17	4 38	6 9	7 21	8 23	9 28	1 12	4 0	6 41
L.C.&D. Line.	Camberwell Road ...... ,,	8 28	9 31	11 2	12 6	2 18	3 22	4 44	6 14	7 26	8 28	9 33	1 17	4 5	6 46
	Walworth Road ...... ,,	...	...	11 5	12 9	2 21	3 25	4 47	6 17	7 29	8 31	9 36	1 20	4 8	6 49
	Elephant and Castle ...... ,,	8 33	...	11 8	12 12	...	3 28	4 50	6 20	7 32	8 34	9 39	1 23	4 11	6 52
	Borough Road ...... ,,	...	...	...	12 14	...	3 30	...	6 22	7 34	8 36	...	...	4 13	...
	Blackfriars Bridge ...... ,,	8 37	9 37	11 12	12 17	2 26	3 33	4 54	6 25	7 37	8 39	9 43	1 27	4 16	6 56
	LUDGATE HILL ...... arr.	8 39	9 39	11 14	12 19	2 28	3 35	4 56	6 27	7 39	8 41	9 45	1 29	4 18	6 58
L.C.&D. Victoria Line.	Herne Hill ...... ,,	...	9 27	10 57	12 1	2 13	3 17	4 39	6 9	7 21	8 23	9 28	1 12	4 0	6 41
	Herne Hill ......(B) dep.	...	9 43	11 33	12 59	2 44	3 57	4 59	6 14	7 28	9 14	9 35	1 52	4 27	7 58
	Brixton ...... arr.	...	...	11 36	1 2	2 47	4 0	5 2	6 17	7 31	9 17	9 38	1 55	4 30	8 1
	Clapham (Town) ...... ,,	...	...	11 39	...	...	4 3	5 5	6 20	7 34	9 20	9 41	1 58	4 33	8 4
	VICTORIA ...... ,,	...	9 55	11 50	1 15	3 0	4 13	5 15	6 30	7 45	9 30	9 53	2 8	4 43	8 15

A. Or Passengers from Victoria, Clapham, & Brixton may travel by the Local Trains from Victoria to Ludgate Hill changing at Camberwell Road.
B. Or Passengers for Victoria, Brixton, & Clapham may change into the Local Trains running between Ludgate & Victoria at Camberwell Road Stn.
All Trains are 1st, 2nd, and 3rd Class between Ludgate Hill and Kingston and intermediate Stations.

The LC&DR's Timetable for the 'New Route to Wimbledon' covering the period of the NRA's July 1869 Meeting. It is noteworthy that of the six stations listed on the LC&DR Line only Elephant and Castle and a new Blackfriars Bridge remain open today. Ludgate Hill, for example, closed to passengers as long ago as 1929 but was not finally dismantled until 1990.

The Tooting, Merton and Wimbledon Station at Wimbledon in the 1870's with a London Brighton & South Coast train standing at the platform.

At this time the original L&SWR Station was on the other side of the road bridge out of sight to the left of this picture but platforms had been extended to allow interchange with the TM & W Station. In 1881 the TM & W Station was reconstructed to accommodate a re-sited L&SWR Station and the opportunity was taken by the L&SWR to adapt what remained of the up platform from their former station for handling the Wimbledon Volunteer traffic. (*Lens of Sutton*)

Time Table of Trains between Putney and London, and Wimbledon and London.

LONDON, BRIGHTON, AND SOUTH COAST RAILWAY.

VICTORIA TO WIMBLEDON.
WEEK DAYS.—6 24 A.M.—7 0—7 16—8 45—10 30—2 38 P.M.—3 10—4 29—5 40—6 15—7 59—9 50.

LONDON BRIDGE TO WIMBLEDON.
WEEK DAYS.—6 20 A.M.—7 18—7 55—8 40—8 55—10 25—12 15 P.M.—2 25—3 5—5 18—6 40—8 15—8 28—10 15—11 45.

WIMBLEDON TO LONDON BRIDGE.
WEEK DAYS.—7 30 A.M.—8 5—8 25—9 9—9 37—9 40—11 6—11 53—1 50 P.M.—3 1—4 50—5 53—6 0—7 17—8 3—8 56—9 53.

WIMBLEDON TO VICTORIA.
WEEK DAYS.—7 51 A.M.—9 19—9 40—11 1—11 53—1 50 P.M.—3 18—4 50—4 59—6 10—8 3—9 53.

LONDON, CHATHAM, AND DOVER RAILWAY.

LUDGATE HILL TO WIMBLEDON.
WEEK DAYS.—8 25 A.M.—9 45—11 15—1 3 P.M.—2 52—4 8—5 9—6 45—8 0—9 10.
SUNDAYS.—9 50 A.M.—1 35—4 35—7 37.

WIMBLEDON TO LUDGATE HILL.
WEEK DAYS.—8 0 A.M.—9 6—10 29—12 0—1 50 P.M.—2 56—3 45—6 0—7 0—8 0.
SUNDAYS.—9 6 A.M.—12 50—3 37 P.M.—6 18.

The 1872 Timetables, combining those of the LC&DR, LB&SCR and L&SWR, covering the Tooting, Merton & Wimbledon route. (*Volunteer Service Gazette*)

A Volunteer ticket over the South Eastern line from Woolwich to Waterloo East and then changing on to a LSWR train from Waterloo to Wimbledon. (*Keith Romig Collection*)

The Times of 8 August 1868 had already carried a short paragraph about the approaching completion of the new line:

'The Tooting, Wimbledon and Merton Railway had been inspected by the officer of the Board of Trade, and would be ready for traffic on the completion of the Brighton Company's line to Knight's-hill. The small piece of line constructing between Knight's-hill and Herne-hill would be completed by the same period, and within the contract time, when the whole of the line acquired under the agreement with the Chatham Company, including the Tooting line, would be brought into work between Wimbledon and Ludgate stations.'

(*The Times*)

Both the LC&DR, which had agreed running rights over the joint Tooting line, and the LB&SCR issued comprehensive timetables for the 1869 Meeting but it was not until 2 July 1870 that the LB&SCR published its own detailed advertisement for the 'new' route. Ludgate Hill gave Volunteers a direct connection initially to King's Cross and later to St Pancras stations on the Great Northern and Midland Railways respectively, thus providing in due course additional easy access to the Annual Meeting for those from the Midlands, the North and Scotland. It was not until its 9 July 1870 issue that the Volunteer Service Gazette finally commented on the new route. However, this only mentioned the LB&SCR routes from Victoria and London Bridge.

'The new route to Wimbledon from Victoria and London Bridge is a most welcome addition to the means of access to the camp, especially as the journey can be performed in about half an hour, and the trains run at frequent intervals. The fortnightly tickets too will be issued.'

(Volunteer Service Gazette)

The Carlisle Accident of 10 July 1870

In the early hours of 10 July 1870, the extraordinary dedication of Volunteers in reaching the Annual Meeting was demonstrated by two Lieutenants who had started their journey in Scotland. Just south of Carlisle, while travelling on a mail train over the London & North Western Railway, their train was involved in a serious collision with a goods train of the North Eastern Railway that not only injured them both but killed five other passengers. Instead of returning home, they continued their journey to Wimbledon, amazingly enough, in the remains of the same mail train involved in the accident!

'We regret that the Hospital, which is again under the able superintendence of Surgeon-Major Wyatt, had two occupants before the meeting began. It seems that Lieutenant Thomas Whitelaw, 102nd Lanark (Motherwell) Rifles, and Lieutenant R. Renton of the 42nd Lanark (Uddingstone) Rifles, both of the 1st Admin. Batt. Lanark (Hamilton) - were on their way from Glasgow in the mail train, and at 1.45 a.m. had just passed Carlisle when they were run into by a goods train. The carriage in which they sat was smashed, they were both thrown out on the line, and the only other occupant, an old gentleman, was driven by the force of the concussion through the roof of the carriage and killed. The two lieutenants, with some other Volunteers, who, fortunately, entirely escaped, came on by the mail train, and posted on to Wimbledon where, by the advice of Assist.-Surg. Mayo, they were put to bed in the Camp Hospital. Lieutenant Whitelaw has his left hand badly hurt and his head bruised, and will not be able to take part in the rifle contest. Nor will his companion, who, though he has escaped without broken bones, is much bruised about the head and body.'

(Volunteer Service Gazette)

The Treatment of the two Lanark Volunteer Lieutenants involved in the Carlisle accident was duly noted in the Wimbledon Camp Hospital Medical Record Book. Lt. Renton was an experienced shot at Wimbledon and had come second in the St Georges Competition of 1868.

The accident was investigated by the Board of Trade Inspector, Lt. Col. C.S. Hutchinson, who coincidently, in the rank of Major-General, inspected the new NRA Tramway at Bisley twenty years later.

'Board of Trade
(Railway Department)
30th July 1870

'Sir,

'In compliance with your instructions contained in your minute of the 11th instant, I have the honour to report, for the information of the Board of Trade, the result of my enquiry into the circumstances attending the collision which occurred at St Nicholas' crossing, near the south end of Carlisle station, early on the morning of the 10th instant, between a mail train from Scotland to the south belonging to the London and North-western and Caledonian companies and a North-eastern goods train crossing from West to East.

'This collision has, I regret to state occasioned the death of five persons; in addition to which, one passenger has sustained a compound fracture of the leg, 29 others, as well as one of the guards of the mail train, have been bruised, shaken or otherwise injured.

'At St Nicholas' crossing which is situated 520 yards south of the south end of the joint Citadel station at Carlisle, the main lines of the Lancaster and Carlisle railway are crossed on the level by a goods line of the North-eastern railway Company called the Canal line which connects their Newcastle and Carlisle line (by means of a junction called the 'Gates' junction, 120 yards east of the crossing) with a goods yard of the Maryport railway and with the North British railway at the Canal station Carlisle...........

'[The driver of the mail train] on going back found that his train had been run into by a North-eastern goods train proceeding from the Canal station to a goods yard on the Newcastle line about half a mile east of the crossing. The collision had separated the mail train at the fifth carriage from the front, the rear buffer beam having been torn out of this carriage; this was just off the road, but remained coupled to the front of the train, in which nothing had been damaged or had left the line. The sixth carriage from the front had its near side smashed in (probably from striking the masonry buffer stop) and was lying mixed up with the wreck of the one behind it, on the buffer bank; the seventh carriage was completely broken up with the exception of its floor and roofs. It is supposed that the goods engine must have struck between the sixth and seventh carriages and thrown and crushed them both against the masonry buffer stop...........

'The five passengers who were killed were travelling in the sixth and seventh carriages...............

'After a detention of about 2 hours and 20 minutes the mail train was able to proceed on its journey'.................

Easter Monday Reviews

From 1861 it had become the custom for the Volunteers from the London Metropolitan area and the south east to hold an annual Review at Easter. The transport of a large number of Volunteer Corps to and from the chosen site of the Review demanded a high degree of planning and coordination especially by the railway companies involved. The NRA, with its close ties to the Volunteer Movement, sat on the Metropolitan Commanding Officers' Council where the Association's representatives fulfilled important roles.

In March 1864, the Easter Review was held near Guildford in Surrey. It required a total of fourteen L&SWR trains and two South Eastern Trains to carry the Volunteer Corps involved from Waterloo and London Bridge respectively. Other trains belonging to both companies brought Volunteers south from Reading and north from Portsmouth. All those taking part, along with their equipment and horses, were delivered efficiently and without incident. At the start of the return journey, bad weather and the type of rolling stock used combined with delays to some of the departing trains at Guildford, led to a major complaint directed to the Secretary of State for War by the commanding officers. The correspondence regarding this incident was published in the *Volunteer Service Gazette* for 4 June and included a stout defence of the railway company by Scott. This gave a comprehensive insight into the train movements required for the exercise with interesting allusions to the use of rolling stock with roofs but otherwise open at the sides; a type of passenger carriage assumed to have been scrapped some years before or otherwise modified with glazed windows!

'The following is the correspondence on the above subject laid before the recent meeting of the Metropolitan Commanding Officers.

'War Office, May 13th, 1864

'My Lord, - I am directed by the Earl de Grey and Ripon to acknowledge the receipt of a communication, dated the 1st ultimo, from the special Committee appointed by the Commanding Officers of Volunteer Corps in the Metropolitan Districts to report upon the circumstances connected with the conveyance of the Volunteer force to and from the Shalford and Guildford stations on the 28th March last. Upon the receipt of this communication the Secretary of State called upon Lieut.-Colonel Hume, Assistant Inspector of Volunteers, and Major Brownlow, Adjutant of the 3rd Administrative Battalion of Surrey Rifle Volunteers, for any remarks they may have to make in relation to the facts therein reported. Copies of the replies of these two officers are enclosed. I am also to transmit for your information a copy of a letter dated the 29th ultimo, and its enclosure, which have been received from the Secretary of the London and South-Western Railway Company, in answer to a communication from this office, requesting him to furnish the Secretary of State with any explanations which he might wish to offer in regard to the complaints made against the railway. – I have the honour to be, my lord, your lordship's obedient servant,

HARTINGTON

Lord Elcho, M.P., National Rifle Association, 11, Pall Mall East.'

'The London and South-Western Railway, Traffic Manager's Office, April 26, 1864.
'To the Directors of the London and South-Western Railway Company.

'Gentlemen,- As instructed, I beg to report upon the communication which has been received from the Marquis of Hartington, Under-Secretary for War, with reference to the conveyance of Volunteers to and from Guildford on Easter Monday.

'First. It appears, from the letter addressed to the War-Office by a Committee of the Commanding officers of Volunteer Corps in the Metropolitan Districts which accompanied the communication above referred to, that the complaints on the subject of railway

accommodation refer to 'rather to the conveyance home of the forces than to their despatch from London.'

'I think it right, however, to show that, as regards the conveyance of the Volunteers from London, there is really no room for complaint, for, while the understanding was that the trains should leave Waterloo Station at intervals of ten minutes, the actual departures averaged one train every nine minutes, as the following table will show : -

Departures from Waterloo	Arrivals at Guildford	Time on Journey
A.M.	A.M.	H. M
6.25	7.41	1 16
6.40	7.48	1 8
6.50	8.8	1 18
6.55	8.14	1 10
7.12	8.33	1 21
7.20	8.40	1 20
7.25	8.46	1 21
7.35	9.5	1 30
7.45	9.25	1 40
7.55	9.38	1 43
8.5	9.45	1 40

'In all eleven trains stated within one hour and forty minutes; average, one train every nine minutes.

'In addition to the above, other trains with metropolitan district Volunteers arrived at Guildford as follows :-

From Staines, &c., at	8.32 A.M.
From Kingston at	9.0 '
From Kensington at	9.40 '

'In all, there arrived at Guildford fourteen trains with metropolitan corps in two hours and four minutes, averaging one arrival every nine minutes.

'Second. With respect to the arrangements for the return of Volunteers from the Guildford Station, the complaints made are these: Mismanagement at that station, and the failure of the railway authorities to perform what were understood to be their engagements. These complaints appear to be based upon the following statements :

1. That, contrary to express stipulations to forward the Volunteers before the ordinary passenger traffic,

consecutive trains were repeatedly sent off, filled with ordinary passengers, while the Volunteers were kept waiting.

2. For example, during an interval of three-quarters of an hour between the departure of the Queen's (Westminster) and the South Middlesex, three or four ordinary trains were filled and started.

3. that some Volunteers broke over the railings, and filled up trains, to the exclusion of other Volunteers.

9. That some of the carriages used for conveyance of Volunteers were open, and the seats wet.

'In answer to these complaints I will give, as briefly as possible, the facts as they occurred, and I can speak to those facts from personal knowledge. : -

1. There was no stipulation, promise, or understanding that the Volunteers should be conveyed from Guildford before the ordinary passenger traffic, and such an arrangement would have been, and must, under similar circumstances, always be, quite impracticable.

What was arranged and carried out was this: the interval between the departure of the Queen's (Westminster) and that of the South Middlesex was thirty-five minutes (not forty-minutes). To explain this interval it is necessary to state that the empty trains for Volunteers stood on one of the main lines of rails set apart for that purpose, about a mile below the Guildford Station, and occupied then about two miles of railway. Each empty train had its engine attached to it, ready to proceed at once to Guildford when telegraphed for. In proceeding from that point to Guildford, those trains had to pass the junction where the South-Eastern line towards Shalford joins the South-Western line, and to pass through a long tunnel, and, for safety, it was necessary to provide that no one train should pass through the tunnel until the preceding train had been telegraphed as having arrived at the Guildford Station.

'It happened, therefore, that after the train with the Queen's (Westminster) left Guildford, and before the next empty train had got past the South Eastern junction, that two heavy trains conveying Volunteers from Shalford to the Reading line, got before the empty train, and so prevented it from getting to Guildford Station, and a similar occurrence accounts for an interval of thirty minutes, which the following table shows to have occurred.

P.M.

No. 1	5.40 This train was standing ready.
No. 2	6.0 No Volunteers at the station for this train till 5.55.
No. 3	6.25
No. 4	7.0
No. 5	7.20
No. 6	7.50
No. 7	8.5
No. 8	8.15
No. 9	8.30

'In all, nine trains within two hours fifty minutes, or an average of one train every nineteen minutes.

'Between the hours above-mentioned, the following South-Western trains left Guildford Station towards Woking and London – viz:

P.M.

6.11	Special with passengers.
6.21	Ditto	ditto
6.50	Ditto	ditto
7.15	Ditto	Hants Volunteers
8.4	Ditto	passengers
8.20	Ditto	ditto

'Thus making fifteen trains in two hours and fifty minutes, or a departure every (eleven and one third) minutes.

'In addition to these trains there were the South-Eastern trains passing through the Guildford Station, proceeding from Shalford to Reading, with Berks Volunteers and the public, in all, I believe, five trains, so that a train must have left Guildford on an average every eight minutes.

'The Queen's (Westminster) left at 6.25 P.M. and between that hour and the next Volunteer departure, 7.0. one South-Western train with the public left, but two heavily-laden South–Eastern trains passed through, and it was those two trains that caused the delay to the Volunteers, and lead to the erroneous impression that the public were being preferred to the Volunteers.

3. No precautions were taken by the railway authorities to preserve order among the Volunteers, that duty devolving upon the commanding officers, consequently no responsibility can attach to the railway company as respects

those Volunteers who are said to have occupied trains to the exclusion of others.

4. With regard to some of the carriages being open and the seats wet. It is true that three of the trains employed consisted of carriages with roofs, but open at the sides; one of these trains consisted of South-Western, another of Eastern Counties, and the third of Brighton carriages. The fact is that similar carriages, and I believe the identical carriages, were used on the occasion of last year's Review at Brighton.

'Upon such a night as that of last Easter Monday, when the rain and wind were so heavy, such carriages must necessarily be excessively uncomfortable, while on a fine day they are preferred by excursionists. As, however, eighteen trains in all were employed in the conveyance of Volunteers from London and the country the use of the carriages complained of was unavoidable, and but for the bad weather would have, as on former occasions, caused no inconvenience.

'It appears unnecessary to refer to the reports of Major Brownlow and Colonel Hume, as their statements have already been answered in my previous remarks.

On the whole subject, I respectfully submit, that while the passage through Guildford of the South-Eastern trains caused a greater delay than was anticipated, the departure from that station of trains proceeding northward at the rate of one every eight minutes disproves the complaint of mismanagement, inattention, or absence of proper regulations, but were unavoidable under the circumstances.

'I personally superintended the arrangements so far as the Volunteer trains were concerned, and affirm that not a moment was unnecessarily lost, and that, second to considerations of safety, everything that man could do was done to despatch the trains quickly.

'My expectation was that the departures of Volunteer trains would have averaged one every fifteen minutes, the actual average was one every nineteen minutes, or inclusive of the Hants Volunteer train, one every seventeen minutes; and must not expect that the return journey could be accomplished with such ease and despatch as the journey from London; and if the weather had not been so excessively bad, my belief is that the departure of all Volunteer trains by 8.30 P.M. would have been considered satisfactory.

'I may also state, that while the work already referred to was proceeding at the Guildford Station, three very heavy trains were being loaded with Volunteers at Godalming Station, for Portsmouth, Brighton, &c., and the commanding officers of the country corps expressed themselves as well pleased with the accommodation provided for them, and the despatch given. – I am, &c.,

(Signed)
ARCHIBALD Scott'
(*Volunteer Service Gazette*)

The Easter Review of 1882 involved both the L&SWR and the LBSCR and was held at Portsmouth. A detailed plan was issued which laid out the railway arrangements to be followed respecting the various Corps of Volunteers who were to take part in the review.

One item of particular note, issued in the very comprehensive general travel arrangement plan, was the route to be used by the 3rd Kent (Royal Arsenal) AV who were scheduled to cross the rarely used Waterloo junction, the connection between the South Eastern line into Charing Cross Station and the L&SWR's Waterloo Station. All went well and there were no complaints.

The District Railway Extension to Putney Bridge

Both the Underground lines, The Metropolitan and Metropolitan District Railways, had noted the growing importance of the Meeting and each made efforts to attract passengers as soon as they had extended their lines to within reasonable distance of the Camp. As early as 1873 the Metropolitan, in partnership with the Great Western Railway, offered a service between Moorgate and Hammersmith, the section between Paddington and Hammersmith having opened on 1 August 1872. This later became the Hammersmith and City Line of the London Underground network.

However, it was not until 1880 that the Metropolitan District saw itself in a similar position. The opening of its extension to Putney Bridge on 1 March that year now posed a threat, albeit minor at this time, to the L&SWR's transport monopoly of the Meeting. The company was now in a position to advertise a direct railway service from Mansion House in the City to Putney Bridge, which was within reasonably easy reach of Wimbledon Common by public transport.

In July 1883, the Volunteer Service Gazette finally noted the Metropolitan District Railway's extension to Putney Bridge.

'It may be useful for some competitors to know that the Metropolitan District Railway affords a new, and to those living near its lines, a very convenient route to the Camp. From the Putney Bridge Station, at Fulham, very well appointed omnibuses run about every quarter of an hour to the bottom of Putney Hill close to the London and South Western Putney Station, where there are always plenty of conveyances to the Camp itself. It would, we should think, pay the District Railway, , to run special omnibuses from the Putney Bridge Station straight up to the Camp.'

(Volunteer Service Gazette)

With the completion of the Circle Line in 1884 by an extension joining Mansion House to Liverpool Street via Aldgate, the District Railway was able to offer access to more routes including east and south east London.

The Guildford, Kingston and London Railway

In May 1880, the integrity of the Common itself was threatened by the projected 'Guildford, Kingston, and London Railway.' This scheme had been largely promoted by the Earls of Onslow and Lovelace and was actively supported by the Metropolitan District Railway, With the completion of their line to the temporary terminus at Putney Bridge they were anxious to extend across the Thames to link up with the proposed new line at Surbiton, thus gaining access to the country beyond and competing directly with the L&SWR in that Company's heartland. The scheme involved construction of a new line which would involve a deep cutting straight through the Common.

The Association naturally became extremely alarmed, realising that the scheme would affect Wimbledon Common so much so that their Annual Meeting would no longer be tenable. They therefore resolved to oppose the Bill in any way they could. Ironically their own President, the Duke of Cambridge, was in favour largely because of the perceived commercial advantage to his adjoining land holding at

METROPOLITAN AND GREAT WESTERN RAILWAYS.

Trains run between the City (MOORGATE STREET) and Hammersmith, and all intermediate Stations, at intervals of about 10 and 15 minutes, at cheap fares. Omnibuses will run between the Camp at Wimbledon and Hammersmith Station from 8.20 a.m. till 10 p.m., at short intervals. Omnibus fares, 9d. each way.

BY ORDER.

22

METROPOLITAN RAILWAY
AND
WIMBLEDON CAMP.

MR. NEWMAN engages with the Public to run Omnibuses as below, and, in addition, other Omnibuses will run as required each day :—

From HAMMERSMITH.		From WIMBLEDON CAMP.	
8. 0 A.M	3.30 P.M.	9.30 A.M.	4.50 P.M.
9. 0 ,,	4. 0 ,,	10.40 ,,	5.40 ,,
10.20 ,,	4.40 ,,	11.30 ,,	6.10 ,,
11.40 ,,	5.40 ,,	12.50 P.M.	6 40 ,,
12.20 P.M.	6.40 ,,	1.30 ,,	7.50 ,,
1.25 ,,	7 40 ,,	2.30 ,,	8.50 ,,
2.40 ,,	8.40 ,,	3.40 ,,	10. 0 ,,

On SUNDAYS, the 5th, 12th, and 19th JULY, Omnibuses will run to and fro as frequently as the traffic requires.

Omnibus Fares, 1s. each way.

A Metropolitan and Great Western Railway joint Advertisement introducing a route, via part of the 'Middle Circle', between the City of London and The Camp in 1873. The equivalent advertisement in 1874 now also included a timetable for the Hammersmith – Putney Omnibus Service. Fares had now risen by a third! (*Volunteer Service Gazette*)

Coombe, through which the new railway would run for several miles. He, however, fully realised the delicacy of his position and took great care not to be seen to promote his private interests.

At a meeting of the Council dated 10 December, it was agreed that a special Committee of NRA Members of Council, the majority of whom were also Members of Parliament, should be formed – 'The Committee to consider action to be taken in Parliament on Bill about to be brought forward for construction of Railway thro' Wimbledon Common.'

'That the attention of the Solicitor of the Association be called to the Bill about to be brought before Parliament for the construction of a new Railway through Wimbledon Common and that he be requested to consider the position of the Association with regard to the said Railway and advise the Council accordingly and that the following be appointed a Committee to communicate and advise with the Solicitor of the Association upon this subject and with power to take such action in Parliament as may appear advisable.

1. Earl Stanhope
2. Viscount Bury
3. Lord Elcho
4. Lord Kinnaird
5. L Col Loyd-Lindsay
6. Mr Martin Smith'

The first meeting of the newly formed Railway Bill Committee took place on 23 December.

'The Committee having considered the plan of the Bill about to be brought before Parliament for the construction of the "Guildford, Kingston and London Railway" and that the said line would render the Rifle shooting at the Wimbledon Meeting impossible,

Resolved that:

'Mr Markby be requested to prepare a draft petition against the proposed line to be submitted to the meeting of Council on the 12th of January next.'

At that meeting, a second plan for a railway in the same line of country had also to be considered! This was entitled the 'Wimbledon Common Railway' and Alfred Markby, the Association's solicitor, was similarly requested to prepare a draft petition with the same object in view. The 12 January Meeting of the Council formally approved these minutes and on 4 February Markby tabled the two draft petitions:

'The Petitions against the two Bills in Parliament entitled The Guildford Kingston and London Railway and the Wimbledon Common Railway Bill are approved and that the Chairman and four Members of the Council to sign the Petitions and that the Bills be opposed on behalf of the Association.'

The Petitions, having been agreed, were signed by four members of the Council who were also MPs – Lord Elcho, Sir Henry Fletcher, Earl Waldegrave and Sir Henry Wilmot.

In early January, the L&SWR had held a special general meeting of their shareholders to express the Board's opposition to the proposed scheme. The meeting was reported in *The Times* of 8 January 1881.

'The Chairman (The Hon. Ralph H. Dutton) said the second object of the meeting related to the construction of new railways in Surrey. There had been several schemes in past years affecting this part of their district, but from one cause or another they had failed. In the present year, however, much larger schemes and in the judgement of the directors highly detrimental to the company's district, had been designed. He referred in particular, to the undertaking projected by the Metropolitan District Railway Company, to extend from that Company's system at Fulham and to pass by Putney, Wimbledon, Kingston, Surbiton and Stoke, near Cobham, to Guildford with branches to Bookham, and also to join the Epsom and Leatherhead Railway at Ashstead. This was a line which would very seriously affect the company's interests and they had determined to bring forward a scheme which they believed would not only answer as well, but a great deal better for the interests of the district affected. The line projected by the District Railway Company would, he said, interfere very seriously with Wimbledon-common and the Rifle Range; and as far as Surbiton was concerned, he should think that, while it would answer no practical purpose, it would meet with very serious opposition.'

On the 12 February, the *Volunteer Service Gazette* published two letters on the subject, one from a Wimbledon Common Ratepayer and the other, in answer to it, from the Clerk of the Wimbledon Common Conservators.

'WIMBLEDON COMMON AND THE PROPOSED RAILWAYS.

'The following letters on the subject of certain proposed encroachments on Wimbledon Common have appeared in the Daily News this week :

'Sir,

'The correspondence which has taken place in your columns respecting the prospective incursion of the Great Eastern Railway Company into Epping Forest has rather diverted the attention of the public from what is proposed with respect to Wimbledon Common. This beautiful common, extending to a thousand acres, and comprising almost every variety of wild loveliness from smooth turf to thick copse and underwood, was, at great expense, preserved to the public by an Act of Parliament passed in 1871, by which the interest of Lord Spencer, as lord of the manor, was transferred to a body of Conservators, of whom three are appointed by Government departments, and five are elected by residents within three quarters of a mile of the Common. By these residents a considerable rate is paid for the maintenance of the common and the payment of an annuity to Earl Spencer by way of an equivalent for his previous rights. By the same Act the enjoyment of the Common by the National Rifle Association for the purposes of their Annual Meeting, and by four Volunteer rifle corps for practice all the year round, was secured; while the Common was made over without stint to the general public for the purposes of recreation. So strongly did Parliament insist upon the value of the Common to the public that the Conservators are strictly enjoined to resist every encroachment or appropriation of any part, and are forbidden to consent to any species of alienation. Since the Conservators have been in office – now more than nine years – they have laid out considerable sums of money in the drainage and improvement of the common, which is without doubt the principle attraction of the neighbourhood; while on Sundays and holidays and notably during the meeting of the National Rifle Association, it is frequented by large numbers from London, from which it is of the easiest access by road and rail.

'One would have thought that this, of all Commons, was the least likely to be attacked even by the most inconsiderate railway projector. It would be well if such a gentleman would understand that by taking common land of any kind they perpetrate a peculiar kind of injustice; for in the case of private lands they can give compensation, and it must be a very singular case in which terms of some kind cannot be arranged which will leave the landowner no worse off, if not better off than before; but in the case of common land the public at large suffer by the destruction of an open space previously accessible to them, while no penny of compensation accrues to their benefit. But it will probably be some time before railway promoters appreciate this truth; the habit of looking on common land as unprotected and cheap to buy has taken to deep a root. Still it might almost have been expected that a Common so peculiarly situated as Wimbledon – a Common expressly dedicated to the public, preserved and kept up at great expense, and the scene once a year of a gathering from all parts of England of an altogether unique character – might have claimed some consideration at their hands. But no; the promoters of the Guildford, Kingston and London Railway Bill – a Bill designed to introduce the Metropolitan District Railway into the area hitherto served by the South Western Railway – have not only selected Wimbledon Common out of several alternate routes between Putney and Kingston, but have deliberately deflected from their straight course to traverse about a mile of the Common in an opening cutting, destroying some of the prettiest copse-wood, and severing a large area which would henceforth be almost useless. Whether it would be possible for the National Rifle Association to continue its meetings after the construction of the railway, it will be for that body to consider. It is certain the railway will directly traverse the line of fire, and probably the public will not be altogether easy under such circumstances, though engineers may assure them that every precaution has been taken. But, however this may be, the Common will be effectually despoiled. Several of the prettiest walks and rides of the neighbourhood will be destroyed, and the common will lose that wild character which is at present one of its chief charms.

'The Wimbledon Common Railway Bill is a less formidable aggressor. It is not difficult to guess that it is promoted on the chance of being taken up by one of the big Companies in the railway fight that must ensue if ever the Guildford scheme gets into Committee; and if the latter were to drop we should probably hear little more of its small competitor. Moreover, not only does this line encroach upon the Common to almost as great an extent as the District scheme, but the promoters have also the temerity to propose the appropriation of twelve acres of Richmond-park, and they asked to be allowed to cross on the level the high road between Hammersmith and Richmond, a proceeding which would lead to an accident at least once a month, on the most moderate computation. However, so long as it exists, this Bill also threatens the Common with irremediable injury. It is to be hoped that both bills will be met with the most determined opposition, not only from the Conservators, on whom the duty of protecting the Common devolves, but also from all who are interested in the preservation of Commons, and, we may with reasonable expectation add, from the Government of the day, in whose ranks are some of the foremost champions of the public rights and interests in the open spaces of the country. – I am, Sir &c

A Wimbledon common Ratepayer'

'Sir, - In a letter in your columns today on the subject of Wimbledon Common and the Guildford, Kingston and London Railway Bill, allusion is made to the duty cast upon the Conservators of that Common to resist all encroachments on it. In order to avoid any possible misconception, I am directed by the Conservators to state that they have throughout offered, and will continue to offer, a determined opposition to the Bill in question, under the powers sought, by which the greatest injury would undoubtedly be inflicted on the Common, and they trust that that their opposition will receive the support of all those who are interested in the preservation of Commons in the neighbourhood of the metropolis. The Wimbledon Common Railway Bill to which reference is also made in the letter you have inserted has, since the date of that letter, been abandoned. – I am, Sir, your obedient servant,

Robert Hunter
6, Lincoln Inn Fields
Clerk to the Conservators
London, Feb. 1.'
Volunteer Service Gazette

Although the 'Wimbledon Common Railway Bill' had now disappeared, wind of these developments had reached other areas of the press and a new journal called the Volunteer Service Review, a rival to the Volunteer Service Gazette, gave them some prominence.

'It appears that a railway company propose to invade the sanctity of Wimbledon Common. When we find a railway company brimming over, so to speak, with affection for the Volunteer force, and promising to confer great benefits on riflemen only if they will just allow the Company to take a slice off the Common, it is not to be wondered at that not merely the Volunteers, but the public at large, look rather askance at their proposals. We are not prepared to say yet how far the railway being covered in may do away with the objections to the scheme, but there is an obvious danger involved on which too much emphasis cannot be laid. If a railway is brought on to, or near the Common, it involves a station. A railway station involves housing, shops &c., surrounding it. Therefore if any inhabited dwellings begin to press in on the Common from all sides some fine morning the NRA may find itself subject to an injunction from the Court of Chancery. It is sincerely to be hoped that Members of Parliament who are connected with the Volunteer Force will scrutinise the proposals of this Bill very closely, and that they will see that under no circumstances shall either the line, the station, or any dwellings which may be incidental thereto, or the erection of which may flow from the construction of this station, shall in any way be in any risk of receiving a stray bullet from the Common.'

(Volunteer Service Review)

However, such was the opposition to the Bill, especially the apparent violation of Wimbledon Common, that the proponents agreed to alter the route so that it would now pass under Putney Heath via a deep tunnel thus neutralising the main objections of the NRA and others. These changes were incorporated into the Bill just before its second reading which took place on March 31st.

'House of Commons, Thursday, March 31st

'The main objection to the Bill was that it interfered with Wimbledon-common. No doubt to the railway as first proposed great objection could be taken, for it was to cross the common, partly by a cutting and partly by an open line. But the promoters had made an important diversion, which ought to satisfy the opponents of the Bill. They applied to a neighbouring landlord to assist them to avoid Wimbleon Common, and he did assist them. The result was that the line as now proposed would only skirt Wimbledon Common without touching it at all, and would go by a deep tunnel under Putney-heath, so as not to affect the drainage or injure the trees or shrubs. It was said that the line would interfere with the rights of the National Rifle Association. But when he stated that the landowner who had given the assistance to which he had referred was his Royal Highness the Duke of Cambridge, the House might infer that no great damage would be done either to the Rifle Association or to Wimbleon Common. He begged to move the second reading of the Bill.'

Lord Elcho, in his role as an MP, also took his opportunity to enter the discussion, although now he proposed to confine his opposition to the Bill as an individual:

'He said that as the company had diminished the objections taken to their original proposals by the National Rifle Association, the Association had withdrawn from opposition, reserving the right to appear before the committee; but personally he should still oppose the Bill, which he hoped the house would reject by way of giving a lesson to promoters not to bring in Bills destroying commons and overriding rights such as those which had been conferred on the Association by Parliament. As the Bill stood until Monday last it would have stopped all rifle shooting, and it would have severed the common by an open cutting, which would have taken away a large portion of the ground, for intersection would be severance in spite of the communication by bridges. But now it appeared that the company could carry the railway across the common by tunnelling.'

(The Times)

The second reading of the Bill was passed by a large majority of Ayes (275) against Noes (49).

The Council met again on 6 April where they were now able to accept the two new Clauses which had been inserted in the Bill to alter the route of the line and place it in the tunnel under Putney Heath. At the meeting of 27 April, Markby tabled a letter from the Conservators of the Common who had requested a voluntary contribution of £3-3s-9d from the Association towards the expenses of opposing the Bill. This was declined by the Council although they still requested the Secretary to forward a copy of the Petition against the Bill to the War Office.

'8th April 1881

'The Under Secretary of State for War
'War Office. Pall Mall.

'I have the honor to forward by direction of the Council of the National Rifle Association copies of the Petition against the 'Guildford, Kingston etc.' Railway Bill in Parliament, signed for the Association by four Members of the Council, and of which the Council request that will be so good as to lay before the Secretary of State for War, who they have been informed has been asked by the Conservators of Wimbledon Common to oppose the Bill.'

The Bill continued to divert the attention of the Council until their November meeting which Markby again attended. At this Meeting, he advised the Council to drop further discussions about the proposed railway presumably as the revised Bill had now been passed.

By this time the District Railway had formed a partnership with its old enemy, the L&SWR, and a new company – 'The Kingston and London Railway' – had been created to build the Fulham to Surbiton section.

'THE KINGSTON AND LONDON RAILWAY

'By this Bill it is proposed to transfer the undertaking of the Kingston and London Railway Company to the London and South-Western and Metropolitan District Railway Companies. By the Act of 1881 the Kingston Company was incorporated with a share capital of £675,000, and a borrowing power of £225,000, to make a line from the South-Western Railway, near Surbiton Station, to the Fulham Extension of the Metropolitan

The view north west from the Windmill across Kingston Vale circa 1889. The location of a possible station at Stag Lane on the Kingston and London Railway would have been near the end of the small valley left of centre. The range, whose butts are visible to the left middle distance, was leased to a Volunteer Corps and were not used during the Annual Meeting. The NRA Staff Camp is in the foreground with the Victoria Rifles behind.

District Railway at or near the Putney Bridge and Fulham Station. The Wimbledon and Putney Conservators by the Act of last Session sanctioned two shafts to the tunnel on Putney Heath, and Parliament is asked by this Bill to allow of additional tunnels (not exceeding four). There are certain deviations at Wimbledon and Putney. The capital to be raised by the South-Western and District Companies is £730,000 and a borrowing power of £943,000 is also given. Dyson and Co. and Mr. Rees are the Parliamentary agents.'

(The Times)

With the passing of the Bill there now was nothing to stop the new railway being built and this caused *The Times,* in a report covering the conclusion of the rather lack-lustre 1882 Meeting, to introduce a pessimistic commentary regarding the Association's immediate future on Wimbledon Common coupled with a vague allusion to commencement of construction of the new railway.

'Year by year the discipline becomes stricter, and the conditions of a military camp are more nearly approached. For instance Regulation VIII. of the Camp Standing Orders reads: No entertainments after 8p.m. will be allowed except by permission of the Council of the National Rifle Association. This permission will never extend to fireworks, balls and dancing parties'. Whether this will have been the last meeting of the Association at Wimbledon or not, it is as yet impossible to say. The construction of the railway now in progress would not necessitate a removal, as it would be easy with screens behind the butts to obviate any danger to those passing on the line, but if the Coombe-wood and other estates on that side of the common should be sold to house builders when the railway is made, a change of site for the encampment and shooting might be found necessary. Should some place in the Aldershot district be chosen, the camp, less easy of access from London, would soon lose even such of its popular features as still remain to it, and the Association would to a considerable extent lose the addition to the funds derivable from gate-money, and this in favourable years has been £1,800 or more.'

(The Times)

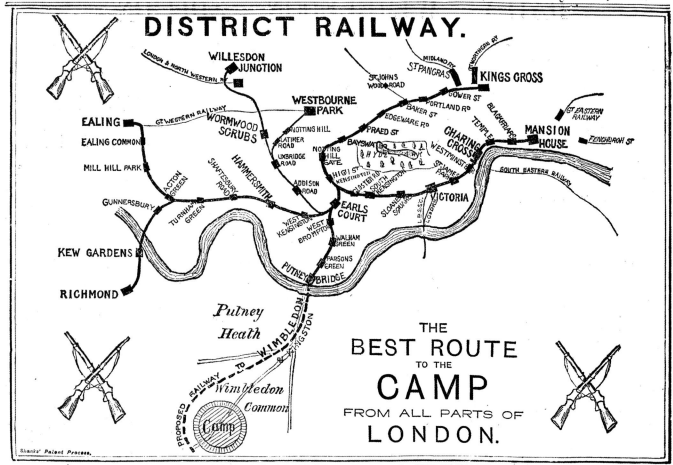

2   VOLUNTEER SERVICE GAZETTE.   [July 11, 1881.

FREQUENT TRAINS AT REGULAR INTERVALS THROUGHOUT THE DAY.
CONVEYANCES AT CHEAP FARES WILL RUN AS OFTEN AS REQUIRED BETWEEN WIMBLEDON CAMP AND PUTNEY BRIDGE (FULHAM STATION).
VOLUNTEERS IN UNIFORM, or BEARING ARMS, will be conveyed at the SINGLE FARE for the DOUBLE JOURNEY.

The District Line advertises 'The Best Route to the Camp' in the 11 July Volunteer Service Gazette with the distinctive outline of the military weapon of the day – the Martini-Henry Rifle.

By July the planned route of the Guildford Kingston & London Railway, after protests, had been altered to skirt around Wimbledon Common instead of passing through it in a deep cutting. However, at this very early stage, it now mysteriously appears to terminate at Wimbledon instead of crossing the South Western mainline at Surbiton. Was this to allay the general fears about its route especially those of the NRA?

Vehement concerns were still being expressed as late as 1883 about the disastrous effect that the new line would have on shooting on the Common. Again, this found expression in a *Volunteer Service Review* editorial published in August of that year which echoed in much more detail *The Times'* gloomy prognostications. It did however serve to clarify other reasons behind some of the numerous objections and in the process highlighted the very circumstances that forced the Association to abandon Wimbledon only a few years later!

'WIMBLEDON COMMON

'The time has arrived when the Government, through one of its departments, should take official notice of the position in which the National Rifle Association and a number of Volunteer corps stand with regard to Wimbledon Common. It is known to the majority of our readers that a large amount of money has been sunk by the National Rifle Association in the erection of butts on the Common, which are used at the great annual meeting; and it is also known that a considerable sum of money has been invested by various

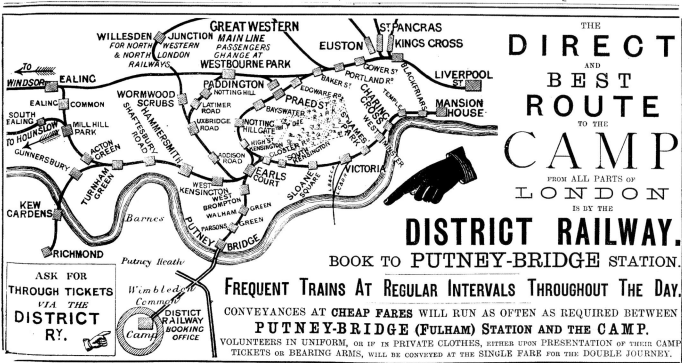

DAILY WIMBLEDON EDITION

OF THE

Volunteer Service Gazette

AND STRANGER'S DAILY GUIDE TO THE CAMP AND SHOOTNG.

DAILY SERIES, No. 1, VOL. XXIV.]   MONDAY, JULY 9, 1883.   [PRICE ONE PENNY.

THE

DIRECT

AND

BEST

ROUTE

TO THE

CAMP

FROM ALL PARTS OF

LONDON

IS BY THE

DISTRICT RAILWAY.

BOOK TO PUTNEY-BRIDGE STATION.

FREQUENT TRAINS AT REGULAR INTERVALS THROUGHOUT THE DAY.

CONVEYANCES AT **CHEAP FARES** WILL RUN AS OFTEN AS REQUIRED BETWEEN **PUTNEY-BRIDGE (FULHAM) STATION AND THE CAMP.** VOLUNTEERS IN UNIFORM, OR IF IN PRIVATE CLOTHES, EITHER UPON PRESENTATION OF THEIR CAMP TICKETS OR BEARING ARMS, WILL BE CONVEYED AT THE SINGLE FARE FOR THE DOUBLE JOURNEY.

ASK FOR THROUGH TICKETS VIA THE DISTRICT RY.

The District Railway's 1883 advertisement in the Daily Wimbledon Edition of the Volunteer Service Gazette. The so called 'Circle Line', incorporating the final connection between Mansion House and Liverpool Street, was not completed until 1884.

Volunteer Corps in the construction of butts at which their class-firing is carried on throughout the whole year. It is also known, to a still smaller section of our readers, that it is in contemplation to construct a railway through Putney under Wimbledon Common. It would emerge in Kingston Vale, where a station will be constructed, somewhere about Stag-lane or Beverley Brook. The construction of this line is deferred for the present for the want of necessary capital; but it is absolutely certain, that if the capital is raised and the line is made every rifle butt at Wimbledon will be permanently closed. The whole of the land on the other side of the Beverley Brook, and between the Common and the Kingston road, will at once become extremely valuable for building purposes, villas innumerable will be built, and the first bullet that drops into the conservatory of one of these dwellings will settle rifle shooting at Wimbledon Common for ever and for aye. Now, we do not believe in rushing to the Government for assistance in everything, but we are distinctly of opinion, that without the direct aid of the War Office and the House of Commons, a great national injury will be perpetrated, and one which, when accomplished, it will be impossible to rectify. Rifle ranges have been closed all over the country, and the increased range of the Martini-Henry renders it certain, that with the issue

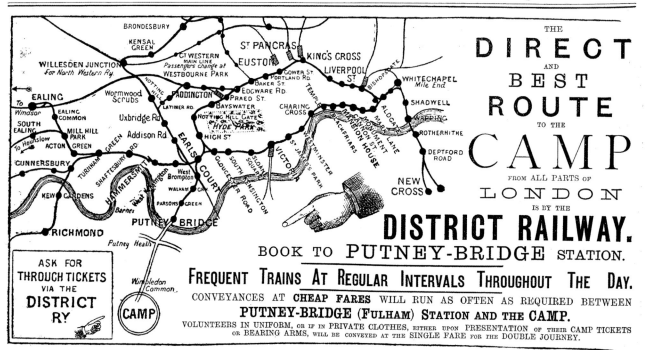

The District Line Map issued for the 1885 Meeting shows the completed Circle Line with other additions, but no sign of the projected London and Kingston Railway which would have skirted Wimbledon Common to the north and west by means of a tunnel under Putney Heath.

of this weapon to the Auxiliary Forces more and more ranges will be shut up annually. From measurements taken it is rendered absolutely certain, that even now if the land in the Vale is used for building purposes, rifle shooting on the Common will be rendered impossible. Under these circumstances, we submit to the proper authorities whether it would not be a wise and a just thing to frame a Bill which would have for its object the incorporation with Wimbledon Common of as much arable land in the district as may be necessary to ensure a safe range for rifle bullets, and to take such precautions as will ensure the use of this land to the public for ever, subject only to the continuance of the existing rifle practice. We must warn the authorities, that the time will come when it will be impossible to carry such a measure through successfully, but there is a time now, and with the sanction of the House of Commons it can be done. We are sure that all parties will combine on such a question as this, and the sooner the authorities set about it the better.'

(Volunteer Service Review)

Although the L&SWR was now effectively in complete control, the District's inability to raise their share of the funds required contrived to put the scheme on hold and by 1886 the Bill, having run out of time, had to be abandoned. By now the L&SWR had developed other plans; a revised route connecting Putney Bridge with Wimbledon and skirting the east of the Common through Southfields, thus entirely lifting the threat to the Association's Annual

DISTRICT RAILWAY.

CHOOSE THE "MANSION HOUSE" DIRECT ROUTE

TO WIMBLEDON CAMP.

BOOK TO PUTNEY BRIDGE OR TO THE NEW "SOUTHFIELDS" STATION.

Conveyances at CHEAP FARES and at frequent Intervals between PUTNEY BRIDGE STATION and the CAMP.

THROUGH BOOKINGS to and from PUTNEY BRIDGE STATION and HANWELL, SOUTHALL, WEST DRAYTON (for Uxbridge, Colnbrook and Staines), SLOUGH & WINDSOR, via EALING, and also to and from STATIONS on the METROPOLITAN, NORTH WESTERN, NORTH LONDON, TILBURY & SOUTHEND, and GREAT EASTERN RAILWAYS.

MANSION HOUSE is the Central City Station.

SOUTHFIELDS Station, on the new WIMBLEDON LINE, is about 20 Minutes' walk of the Camp.

ALWAYS ASK FOR TICKETS via "DISTRICT RAILWAY."

One Shilling.

EVERYONE GOING TO

WIMBLEDON

SHOULD BUY EITHER A COPY OF THE "DISTRICT RAILWAY"

MAP OF LONDON

TO SEE

THE DIRECT ROUTE TO

PUTNEY OR SOUTHFIELDS

FOR

WIMBLEDON CAMP.

PRICE SIXPENCE

Mounted on Linen	1/6
Do. in Leatherette Case	2/6
On Rollers and Varnished	5/-

OR A COPY OF

The "DISTRICT RAILWAY" GUIDE to LONDON:
Price SIXPENCE.

Both Maps and Guide are obtainable at District Railway Booking Offices, and at Station-Bookstalls.

The District Railway's final advertisement regarding the Wimbledon Meeting. The District Railway's 1889 Advertisement announcing the opening of the revised route which largely followed the valley to the east of the Common with a short tunnel at Putney. By this time the NRA had already announced that their move to Bisley Camp would take place in time for the 1890 Meeting. (*Volunteer Service Gazette*)

Meeting. Although this deviation was eventually constructed and owned by the L&SWR they decided to drop their original plans to gain access to other parts of the District's network and it was operated, ironically, almost exclusively by the District from its opening in 1889, although certain South Western trains used the southern section to connect with the Windsor lines at Putney.

The whole saga was finally resolved when the District Railway opened its extension from Putney Bridge to Wimbledon on 3 June, exercising running-powers over L&SWR track. This offered but a single season of direct but illusory competition to the L&SWR's virtual monopoly of the Annual Meeting before the NRA moved to Bisley.

CHAPTER 3

THE WIMBLEDON TRAMWAYS

THE RANGE TRAMWAY

The Horse Tramway

In February 1864, the NRA Council and the Secretary, Captain St John Mildmay, accompanied by certain Association members, attended the annual rifle trial that was held at Woolwich Arsenal. During the trial the party, which also included a member, Lieutenant Goodliffe, travelled over a tramway that connected the 1000 yard firing point with the Butts. This left a strong impression on both Goodliffe and Mildmay and, at the Winter Meeting of the NRA that followed shortly afterwards, Lt Goodliffe's suggestion was noted.

'Mr. Goodliffe concluded by suggesting that a tramway on the Range, such as that at Woolwich, would be a great convenience to shooters, who were often heavily laden, and would speedily repay the cost of construction.'

Mildmay had already advocated the provision of a tramway to the Council and these proposals encouraged a decision to lay one down in time for the 1864 Wimbledon Meeting. Progress on the development of the Tramway was recorded by Mildmay in his notebook dated 23 April.

'J. Hill writes to say that the Tramway is of so simple a nature that it requires no engineering and that the person who does the fencing could put it up. I have sent copy of plan etc. to Gooch, and Thompson and I think that the latter guided by Drake will do it well. I have written about the trucks to the W.O. If we can have them made at the Carriage Dept. it will be a great thing - Those we used at Woolwich are awfully heavy being built to carry ton loads of iron etc.'

William F. Gooch was the Works Superintendent at the Great Western Railway's Swindon Works and the younger brother of the celebrated Daniel Gooch, then the Locomotive Superintendent of the GWR. Gooch had

The Woolwich Tramway. February 1864 and a heavy rainstorm over the bleak Woolwich Ranges greets representatives of the N.R.A. Council and Members as they travel from the 1000 yard Firing Point to the Butts in one of the trucks designed to carry the heavy iron targets. Edmond St John Mildmay, the N.R.A. Secretary, is seated second from left. (*Illustrated London News*)

constructed the Running Deer track at Wimbledon in 1862 and the 'Deer' and 'Man' targets with their trucks in 1863 and it is probable that he had been requested to provide the wheels, axles and other iron work for the four tramcars ordered.

The plan was announced during the NRA Spring Meeting:

'For the use of Competitors, a tramway was to be laid down, at an expense of between £200 and £300, for communication between the different ranges. This would be found a special convenience this year, as the ground used was to be increased by the addition of the butts belonging to the London Scottish Corps on the extreme right. The idea of such a tramway had been suggested by that in use at Woolwich. Through the kindness of Colonel Kennedy, the carriages would be horsed by the Military Train.'

The early design of the tramway was probably 'too simple'; the remark likening its ease of construction to that of a fence seems to confirm this and may have been the underlying cause of a number of derailments during its early years. In fact, it took until nearly the end of the decade and a serious accident before the Council were persuaded that the track needed to be improved but ignored the safety of the tramcars themselves!

Oddly there was no mention of the new Tramway in the Council Minutes other than a single reference, at the meeting held on 24 May 1864, where it was recorded that Sir Joseph Paxton MP, a member of Council and celebrated as the designer of the Crystal Palace constructed for the 1851 Great Exhibition, was also now involved. Thompson, the Camp contractor, laid a portable track of a nominal 3 feet 6 inch gauge (the actual measurement was 3 feet 5⅜ inches) linking the firing points of the various ranges for the convenience of both competitors and visitors. The Carriage Department of the War Office at Woolwich provided four small horse-drawn wooden cars for passengers, equipped with back to back seating and running on a light un-sprung 4-wheel underframe, the iron wheels and axle-boxes of which were constructed, most probably, at the Swindon Works of the GWR under Gooch's supervision. The origin of the track is not mentioned but may also have been provided by the GWR.

The Times of 12 July provided a full description of the new tramway and its cars:

'One inevitable result of the widening of the ground suggests itself to every mind. The great difficulty of locomotion has to be met and solved. Λ competitor who has been told off to fire at a range near the Wimbledon end of the common, and after doing his duty in that quarter finds that he is interested in another competition going on at the new north ranges, would find it no joke to march a good mile and a half under a broiling sun, such as that of yesterday, carrying one, or it may be two rifles, and a proportional supply of ammunition.

'The Council foreseeing this difficulty, and determined to march with the times, procured, at an outlay of some £400, a tramway readily movable to any part of the common, but at present laid down from the site of the old Grand Stand to the 'Guards Camp' at the southern extremity of the enclosure. The tramway is of the same elementary but serviceable kind which existed many years ago in a few rural and mining districts, where it formed the precursor of the existing system of railways. The carriages, four in number, and intended to start at intervals of ten minutes, are roomy, well adapted to the object in view, and can be mounted or quitted with the greatest ease. Their shape may be described as an exaggeration of the Irish long-car, the steps descending so low at either side as to hide the wheels completely from view. Those who have never seen the vehicle in question can form a good idea of the Wimbledon omnibus by imagining that the point or upper half of a capital A were struck off and the lower portion mounted upon wheels. At least six can be accommodated on either of these sloping sides, and as many more in 'the well' in the centre. The motive power will be supplied by horses and men belonging to the Military Train which can be spared for the moment from ordinary duties, and, in the opinion of the authorities, will be usefully employed in furthering the operations of this valuable Association.'

The general Report of the NRA, issued after the Annual Meeting in July, reported enthusiastically on the

PLAN OF THE GROUND AT WIMBLEDON.

(Copied from the Official Programme of the National Rifle Association.)

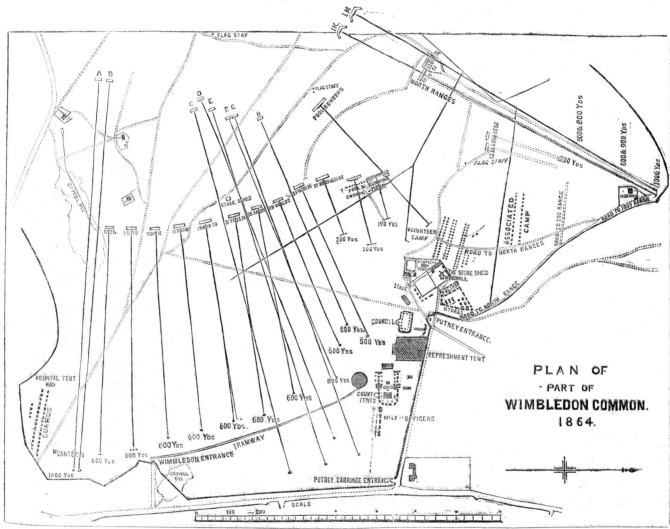

Plan of the N.R.A. 1864 Meeting showing the route of the Wimbledon Tramway as first constructed. (*Volunteer Service Gazette*)

tramway but blandly glossed over certain 'incidents' which detracted from the success suggested!

'The construction of butts, the making of roads, the drainage, clearing and levelling of the ground, and, generally speaking, everything connected with the targets and shooting as well as the Tramway, the great novelty of the Meeting, were well and efficiently executed by Mr Thomson of Wimbledon. The Council, feeling that some acknowledgement was due to him on the part of the Association for the admirable and punctual way in which everything undertaken by him is invariably done, have presented him with a silver punch bowl.

'The Tramway was a great success, notwithstanding one or two trifling incidents that unfortunately occurred to the passengers, the result of too great speed, as is frequently the case in railway travelling.

'The Association Wimbledon line was opened by His Royal Highness the Prince of Wales, when he visited the ground and inspected the preparations for the Meeting, previous to its commencement.

'The carriages were, by kind permission of F.M. His Royal Highness the Duke of Cambridge, horsed by the Military Train, Colonel Kennedy, Commandant, making the necessary arrangements.

'The scrip of the Association Great Wimbledon Trunk Line is not, it is true, quoted in the market, as it may be considered to a great extent a private concern, but it would be well if railways of greater pretension showed as good a dividend on capital expenditure. The total cost of construction, plant, &c. was £404; and although the line was only six whole days in actual working the total receipts amounted to £44 14s 11d.

'Next year it may be found necessary to have a branch line made to the London Scottish Shooting House on the extreme right of the ground.'

Following the Meeting, on 9 August, Mildmay sent a letter of thanks to Col. Kennedy.

'I am directed to request that you will accept the thanks of the Council of this Association for having kindly placed at their disposal during the Wimbledon Meeting a detachment of the Royal Military Train under your command.

'I have great pleasure in certifying for the satisfactory manner in which Sergeant McNeil and the men under his charge acquitted themselves of their duties – as well as to their general good conduct and their readiness to make themselves useful.'

The track of the Tramway was re-laid every year for the Annual Meeting and was taken up and removed to the NRA's Store, together with the rolling stock, at its conclusion. Although this must have been one of the earliest examples of a portable railway track, no specific details of its construction have so far come to light other than that it incorporated rails believed to weigh 24lb per yard, and was constructed in short panel sections which could be stacked for storage.

The *Volunteer Service Gazette*, in its 1864 daily report on the Meeting entitled 'The Prize Meeting of the NRA', paid particular attention to the new tramway.

'Monday July 11th
'… the new tramway was being laid down for the conveyance of shooters to and from the firing posts in the far south. This tramway and the new refreshment house are among the most conspicuous improvements in the laying out of the ground.'

'Wednesday July 13th
'The aspect of the ground was gay enough at mid-day, under a bright sun, many ladies visiting the ground, and the excellent band of the London Scottish playing a succession of lively airs. The tramway from the Wimbledon entrance was used today for the first time, and found to be a great convenience. The sum of two pence is charged for the ride, which is performed upon a plain vehicle, resembling in shape the Bianconi Cars of Ireland.'

However, the *Gazette* was not so sanguine as the NRA about the 'incidents' that occurred to passengers:

'Thursday July 14th
'In one particular, however, matters did not run quite so smoothly to-day; for about one o'clock, one of the cars came off the line of the tramway, and the wheel passed over the left foot of a gentleman who had been sitting in front. The sufferer was conveyed at once to the hospital tent, where an examination was made of the injury, which we are glad to hear, is not of a serious nature. But the fact that this is the second accident which has occurred on the line, some persons having been thrown out by a collision which took place on Wednesday evening, through inefficiency of applying the break, will, we trust, draw the attention of the Council to the subject, and so ensure the perfect safety of passengers in future.'

In spite of this, the NRA Report for the following year, 1865, mentioned the Camp Tramway in rather glowing terms and particularly remarked on the 'absence' of accidents!

'The Railway was in good working order, and happily no accident occurred, either to the public or to the 'Company's Servants,' i.e., the Military Train employed in working it. Judging by the way in which the cars were always crowded, the Wimbledon Grand Trunk is a decided success, and should the Association continue to thrive as it has hitherto done, there is little doubt that the Council will extend the line to the Iron House; the ground, however, is unfavourable, and the cost of making the line would be great; it will therefore not be undertaken in the coming year.'

This view was not entirely supported by the NRA Secretary who, in 1868, stated that no year had been accident free. The design of the passenger cars and the 'loose coupling' method of horse haulage as well as the zeal of the military horseman and the uncertainty of the primitive 'break' and track seemed to presage further accidents and a letter of 7 September 1867 addressed to Thompson refers to such an occurrence which, because of its seriousness, was well documented and finally jolted the Council into action to improve the safety.

'7th September 1867

'Dear Mr. Thompson

'I see from a letter received from the War Office that there is at the Hospital Marquee, a valise, etc., belonging to the Marquee as well as a few Small Stores belonging to Government which have not yet been returned to the Tower. These stores were probably left at the site for the use of the woman whose leg was broken in the tramway accident. Be so good as to see if they are in the Marquee and if so send them at once to the Tower

Yours truly
Edmond Mildmay'

The 'Sanitary' section of the 1867 Report described the injury as a 'severe case of compound fracture of the leg' and went on to say that 'the lady in question had been treated in the Camp in a well-boarded Marquee, and is progressing more favourably in this pure atmosphere than could possibly have been expected had she been subject to the effects of a journey to any hospital after the occurrence of the accident.'

The cause of the accident was a derailment which 'jolted off all the passengers who sat on one side of the vehicle'. The *Volunteer Service Gazette* for 13 July identified the 'lady in question' and had some pointed remarks to make about the safety of the tramway!

'We much regret to state that the services of the medical officers were required today in the case of a lady, the wife of Colour Sergt. Witham, of the 19th Middlesex, who met with a painful accident on the tramway. The frequency of such accidents makes it necessary to warn strangers of the danger attending this mode of conveyance.'

The severity of the tramway accident finally had an effect on the NRA Council and, belatedly, action was put in hand. On May 9, 'Thompson was to be instructed to report on the Tramway Plant, and Cars' and on May 19th the Council resolved that the Secretary contact Mr Gregory, President of the Society of Civil Engineers, for his advice on the subject of the Wimbledon Tramway.'

At this time some dissatisfaction with Thompson had shown itself in other areas of his responsibility. A further letter reflected the NRA Council's dismay at the state of the ground as left by him at the conclusion of the Meeting.

'20 November 1867

'Dear Mr Thompson

'I enclose a cheque for the amount of your account for work done at Wimbledon after the conclusion of the Meeting. I have at the same time to draw to your attention by the direction of the Council to the careless manner in which some of the work has been done - viz: Most of the Stopping up of the Holes made for the erection of poles; etc. as well as the trenches cut round the Tents - The Council direct me to request that you will at once see to the work being done in a more satisfactory manner without any charge to the N. R. Association.'

When Thomson sought renewal of his contract in 1868, which included laying the Tramway, Captain Drake recommended that that part of the contract relating to the Tramway should be removed. This was agreed by the Council resulting in Thompson being replaced at short notice by a new tramway contractor, Messrs John Aird and Son of Belvedere Road, Lambeth. Meanwhile Gregory had advised that the Tramway required new rails and, although these were assembled using the old wooden sleeper panels by Thomson, they were laid by Aird under Gregory's direct supervision.

Although Aird was initially employed on an emergency basis, solely for the duration of the 1868 Meeting, they made such a great success of the job that it was acknowledged in a letter, dated 15 August, from a very relieved NRA Secretary and led to the company being appointed as the tramway contractor for the remainder of the Wimbledon era.

'I have the honor to enclose a cheque, due to you by the Association, and I am to request that you will be so good, as to take back whatever rails have not been used, as it is not likely that we will require them another year.

'The Council have directed me to Convey to you the expression of their thanks, for the very kind manner in which you came forward to assist them and the liberality which you displayed on the occasion. They wish you to be assured, that it has been duly appreciated by all connected with Wimbledon. The work was admirably executed, and as proof of it, I may tell you that this is the first year that the Tramway was used from the first day till the last without it once being stopped from any accident.'

The track of the tramway having been replaced, the Committee was still dealing with the aftermath of the Witham case which included comments in the press casting serious doubts on the safety of the tramway. The Association needed to demonstrate that the tramway was now perfectly safe and what better way than to arrange for the wife of the Chairman, Earl Spencer, and other spouses from the Association's collection of aristocracy to ride on it in company with the usual passengers. A report having duly appeared in *The Times*, complete with an evocative description of the tramcars, full rehabilitation of the tramway in the eyes of the public appears to have been achieved.

'The Tramway was honoured today by some of the titled ladies just mentioned travelling by it. Like an American railway car, all of one class, and asking the moderate fee of twopence for its entire journey, the tram carriage is like a rough omnibus without cushions turned inside out. Travellers by it sit side by side on a hard wooden seat, and Lady Grosvenor, Lady Spencer, and the rest went up by it with a cargo of private soldiers, workmen, and volunteers, when tired of the Public Schools (who were taking part in the Ashburton Competition), this afternoon.'

It was not until late 1868 that the Council finally agreed to offer compensation to Mrs Witham, the victim of the 1867 tramway accident. A Council Minute of 6 November 6 summarised the resolution.

'Lord Spencer stated that he had requested Capt. Page and Surgeon Major Wyatt to see Mrs Witham, the person who had been seriously injured by an accident to the NRA Tramway in 1867, with a view to ascertain the extent of the injuries she had received and which it is said that she has not yet recovered; as it was desirable that some compensation should be offered to her, or to Mr Witham, for the expenses which they had been put to in consequence of the accident, Surgeon Major Wyatt was requested to offer some suggestion as to what he thought the amount of the compensation should be - Letters from Surgeon Major Wyatt and Capt Page bearing on the subject were read.

'It was resolved that the Secretary be directed to offer to Mr Witham the sum of £200 in full clearance of all claims, but that Mr Markby should be consulted previous to the offer being made to Mr Witham.'

Although this was accepted at the time by the Withams in the following year they attempted a further claim which was firmly rejected by the Council.

A letter, dated 22 January 1869, confirmed that Aird was to be awarded the annual contract to lay the Tramway for the July Meeting and to dismantle it and return it to store afterwards.

'I would esteem it a favour if you would let me know whether you would kindly undertake this year to lay down the tramway for us at Wimbledon - Sending your men down in time to convey the frames from the Store - then to the place where they are to be laid and also to remove them after the meeting and restack them at the NRA Stores behind the Butts - in case you kindly undertake this work you will oblige me by sending me an estimate of the cost of it.

'I am here every day and should be glad to see you or anyone whom you may like to send at any time which you would name.'

Aird produced an estimate on 22 March 22. and this was accepted by the Council.

'In reference to your letter of the 1st February last, containing an estimate of Cost of laying down the permanent way at Wimbledon, including the removal from the Stores and also taking them up and returning the same, the Cost being put down by you at

£45, I beg to inform you that the Council have much pleasure in accepting the Estimate and have at the same time directed to convey to you the thanks of the Council for the liberal manner in which you kindly have offered to undertake the work.

'I have to request that you will be so good as to place yourself in Communication with Captain Drake R.E. Milton Barracks, Gravesend, with a view to ascertain the day on which the work should begin. The permanent way must be in working order on the 2nd of July.'

Fires were not commonplace in the Camp but during the 1868 Meeting two fires were started which might have had serious consequences but for rapid action by bystanders and especially Drake who was in charge of the fire arrangements. The second of these was started by the careless disposal of a 'fusee' (pipelighter), thrown from a tramcar. A report appeared in *The Times* of 21 July.

'There was again an alarm of fire yesterday, and at one time the appearances were serious. Promiscuous throwing down of pipe-lights on the part of the Volunteers has been pretty nearly terminated, but it seems that a careless traveller by the tramway lighted his pipe or cigar as he was being drawn along, and cast away the fuse when he had done with it. It fell, unfortunately, not merely upon the dried and trodden surface of the Common, but among or in close proximity to some of the gorse which lies between the line and tramway and the lofty wooden paling that skirts the enclosure of the Association. In a few moments thick clouds of black smoke rose up into the air, and the Volunteers and bystanders becoming alarmed lest the fire should spread to the palings, and thence possibly to the houses opposite, tore down the wooden skirting, and with the fragments endeavoured to beat down the spreading flame. Little, however, in the way of effectual suppression was done till the arrival of Captain Drake, the Engineer officer in charge, with a party of the Guards,

THE HORSE CAR AT WIMBLEDON

A characterful study of the Tramway in 1872 depicting a full load of passengers complete with on-board entertainment from a group of minstrels. (*The Graphic*)

who, having first restored order, made a cordon with his men, and so kept a clear space within which the fire-engine could be brought to bear with effect. In this manner the flames were promptly subdued; but the incident afforded a fresh proof, if any such were needed, of the constant watchfulness over little things which is so peremptorily required at Wimbledon.'

About a month before the 1873 Annual Meeting, Mildmay was notified by the War Office that they were unable to supply the horses to draw the tramcars. They had provided this service on a routine basis since 1864 when the tramway was first constructed. On 5 June, the Secretary, wrote a memo to Stockman respecting tasks that needed to be carried out, and included comments on what was to be done about the lack of horse motive power for the tramcars:

'The W.O. cannot let us have the Tramway Horses this year - look out for someone who would do the job - six horses will be quite enough and the man can drive from the car.'

He also notified the Earl of Ducie, the Chairman of Council at the time, in a letter of the same date and in which he gave vent to his views rather more freely!

'The W.O. decline to give me the horses for the tramway - they say they have not got them - this shows great weakness in the Control Dept.* of a country to use this excuse not to be able to spare 15 horses for 19 days - a word from you to Mr Caswell would perhaps induce the Control Lords like the London Irish [i.e. to change their mind - the latter had recently given Mildmay some problems with fixing the dates of their attendance at Wimbledon which Mildmay referred to in the same letter!].'

*The Control Department was formed by the amalgamation of the Commissariat and the Military Train in 1869. In 1888 this became part of the newly constituted Army Service Corps which gained the 'Royal' prefix in 1918.

The War Office did not change their mind and the additional cost of horses and driver was quoted as £72 6s, a very substantial sum for the time. However, the tramway ran as usual and remained just as popular with the public as *The Times* of 8 July indicated. The ranges referred to were those nearest to the Wimbledon entrance:

'To those who enter by the main entrance, the tramway is the best way of reaching these ranges. A ticket which costs 2d, franks the traveller for the journey of three-quarters of a mile. Two long low cars travel on this road, passing each other by means of a loop in the middle part of the line. One horse ridden by a man draws each car at the end of a long rope, and anything more unlike the tramcars of the Metropolitan Companies it is impossible to conceive. The conveyance is none the less extremely popular, and the number of the passengers carried is only measured by the complaisance of those who occupy the seats.'

The following year the price of tickets had risen by a 1d caused by the Government being no longer able to supply the previously free motive power as the horses were required for the 'manoeuvres.'

The *Earwig* published this satirical set of Tramway bye-laws:

'BYE-LAWS AND REGULATIONS OF THE WIMBLEDON, BUTT-END AND WINDMILL RAILWAY COMPANY.

I. No person will be allowed to enter any carriage belonging to this Company without having first obtained a ticket. The Directors, however, in order to facilitate the traffic will not be particular as to its nature, provided only that, on being requested to produce it, the passenger observes, 'That's the ticket,' and tips the officer of the Company appointed for that purpose.

II. The train, in all cases, is to be started by whistle, the private of the Military Train who acts as engine will therefore keep his whistle wet, ready for any rum start that may be required of him.

III. In order to save the public from annoyance, two classes of carriages have been constructed, smoking and non-smoking. The passengers are therefore earnestly requested to smoke (if they must do so) in the non-smoking carriages, thus to equalise the atmosphere in both, and so enable the public to pass from one to the other without inconvenience.

IV. Bars will be erected at both ends of the line for the convenience of the passengers; and although the company has no spirit licence, the Military Train has kindly offered to provide cocktails, and sufficient Cognac will always be carried by the guard to make a brandy smash in case of accidents.

V. Any passenger letting off shells, breaking the windows, exploding nitro-glycerine, hamstringing the horse, carving his name on the back of the military train, swallowing the porter at either of the bars, or tickling the buffers (old or young), will be instantly removed from the Company's premises.

VI. Any person attempting to enter or leave a carriage when it is at full speed may enquire for his remains at the booking office.

VII. All dogs must be paid for, except the original Dog who, from his long connexion with the Volunteer movement, will be carried free.

VIII. Babies in arms will not be carried under any circumstances if loaded. Head-centres travelling with Greek fire will be taken at special rates on application (at the police office).

IX. No kissing allowed in the tunnel!!

X. In case of the carriages going off the line at the curve, passengers are strictly forbidden to leave their seats.

Approved, provided these Bye-Laws be published in the "Earwig".

For the Bored of Trade
H. Walker.'

The continued popularity of the Tramway caused the Council to enquire about additional cars to be used in emergencies. On 13 February 1877, the Finance Committee minutes recorded that a letter, containing an estimate for new Tramcars, had been received from the Metropolitan Carriage & Wagon Company of Birmingham through Aird.

'The letter enclosed an estimate for a new tramway car from tracings supplied by Messrs. Aird and had been left with the Secretary (of the NRA) by their manager, Mr. Soane. The Company state that they will undertake to supply cars, as per tracing, and loaded onto trucks at Birmingham for the sum of £24 each nett cash.

'The Committee recommend that two of these cars should be ordered with a view of using them on emergencies in addition to the two now used for each journey during the meeting. Mr Stockman, in connection with the subject, strongly recommended that the tramway should be opened during the dinner hour, and for one hour after gun-fire, also that it should commence running half an hour before morning gun-fire.'

The Finance Committee recommended the new Tramcars and on 16 February the Council formally agreed. Their decision was at once passed on to Aird. The letter from the MRCW Co. had been presented to the Council by Mildmay and he followed this with a communication to Aird informing them of the decision.

'Leave was given to order two new tramcars, for the Wimbledon Tramway, on a new plan submitted to the Committee by Messrs Aird & Son.'

'Feb 19 1877

'I laid before the Council on the 16th instant the letter from the Metropolitan Railway Carriage and Wagon Company of the 2nd instant addressed to you and enclosing a tender to supply open Tram Cars in accordance with your tracing, for the sum of £24.0.0 each nett cash loaded upon our Truck at Birmingham, and I am directed by the Council to request that you will be so good as to give our order for two (2) Cars to be constructed in accordance with the tracings and to be delivered in time for being used at the next Wimbledon Meeting which will be held in the month of July next.

'The Council have directed me to convey to you the expression of their best thanks for your kindness in taking so much trouble about the Tramcars, and at the same time to say that the tracings have in every respect met with their entire approval.'

These cars were designed to a conventional style with inward facing seating and safety rails all round. The original drawing shows that the entrances were at either end of the car. Two foot operated brakes, one at each end each operating on a single wheel only, were also provided, but the cars had no springs. The gauge was 3ft 4ins, not the 3ft 6ins of the Wimbledon Tramway.

The cars, however, were delivered to Aird's drawing which probably showed considerable variations from

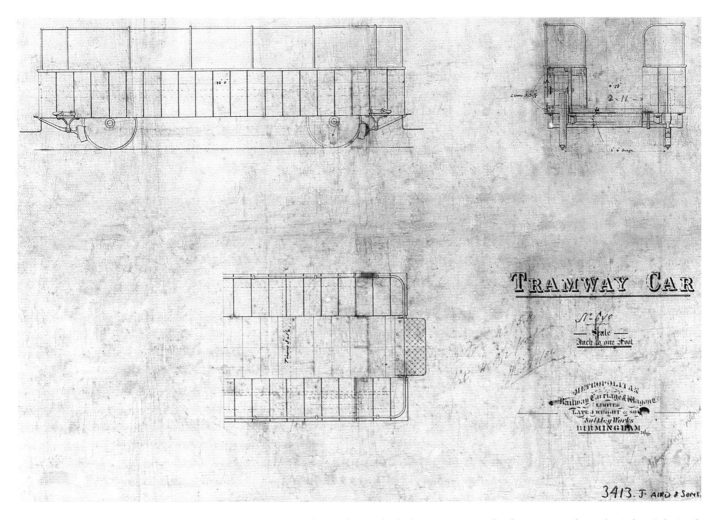

The original Metropolitan Railway Carriage & Wagon car design from which the 1877 NRA order for two cars through Aird was derived. Modifications to the drawing probably including the alteration of the gauge of the wheel sets to 3ft 6ins vice 3ft 4ins. The safety railings were altered at some stage to accommodate the single side-entrance. The redundant end-entrances and foot brakes were also dispensed with. (*Metro Cammell Collection – Birmingham Library*)

the basic design, including the gauge correction and removal of the foot brakes. One of these was to create an entrance on the middle of one side of the car only and do away with those at the ends. This also entailed the reconstruction of the safety railings in wood to a different configuration. Certainly, within two years, a number of modifications appear to have been made, some of which were almost certainly carried out by Stockman. Problems were also experienced with the lubrication of the axle boxes and Stockman had to replace the damaged solid wheels with similar ones to the spoked design used on the original tramcars. This gave the cars an archaic appearance.

An informative official notice, for the benefit of prospective Tramway passengers, was published in the *Volunteer Service Gazette* for 10 July:

'Official Notices (Wimbledon Meeting)
Tramway Regulations
1. The charge for each single journey is 3d.
2. No one will be allowed to travel who has not first paid the fare.
3 A ticket will be issued on payment of each fare, available for one journey only, and the ticket must be presented when demanded.
 N.B. - it is particularly requested that persons will tear up their tickets on leaving the cars.
4. An interval of 5 minutes is allowed between the arrival and departure of the cars.'

By 1883 the Council was offering Season Tickets on the Tramway for 2s 6d. These were valid for the duration of the Meeting.

Merryweather's Steam Tram Engine

The first mention of an 'engine' at the Wimbledon Meeting seems to have been a reference to a Merryweather fire engine hired for the 1865 Meeting at a hiring cost of £25. There is no indication that this was steam powered.

In 1872, Aird had drawn the attention of the NRA to the existence of a small steam engine that might be considered suitable for replacing the horses used on the Tramway. Mildmay responded to Aird on 4 of April indicating that he had also heard about one at Woolwich.

'Have you any news to give me about the little engine? If so a line from you will greatly oblige me - I hear that there is an 18 horse power engine at Woolwich but it would never do. 1st It would be much too large and noisy, and 2ondly it is made for a much narrower gauge than our's is. Your little one with coke will I am sure be the very thing for us.'

The requirement was given added impetus in 1873 when the military authorities were unable to supply horses for the Tramway and the Association were forced to hire their own at what they felt was an exorbitant price. It was not until the 1877 Meeting that Merryweather & Sons offered, on loan, one of their steam fire engines to the NRA and at the same time negotiated a trial of one of their early steam tram locomotives. Merryweather's, although well known in the business of fire engines and pumps, had only started the manufacture of steam tram locomotives in 1872 and it is evident that they saw this trial as an important business opportunity; the use of steam locomotives as tramway prime movers, especially in Britain, being still in its infancy.

The experiment with the tram engine was mentioned in the NRA Annual Report but no technical details were given. It can be assumed, however that the engine was already constructed to suit the nominal 3ft 6in gauge of the tramway.

'Another novelty on the ground was the Steam Tramway Engine, which Messrs Merryweather and Sons kindly placed at the disposal of the Council. It was perfectly successful, and being noiseless, did not in any way disturb the visitors or the shooters at the firing points. It should be noticed, that though the rails had never been intended for the traffic of an engine, no alteration whatsoever was required, and that they withstood the severe test during nearly the whole Meeting, without the slightest injury resulting to the tramway.'

The Merryweather Fire Pump, also offered for trial during the Meeting; was initially refused by the Council as they claimed that cases of fire were extremely rare in the Camp and the means of dealing with them were adequate. However having identified additional uses for it, they quickly changed their mind and proceeded to take up the offer with some enthusiasm!

'June 29 1877

'Gentlemen,

'The Council of the National Rifle Association are much obliged to you for placing one of your Engines at their disposal during the Wimbledon Meeting. The Officer who will take charge of it is Captain Salmond of the Royal Engineers, who, in the event of a fire occurring has command of the 'fire party'.

'The Council wish me to ask you whether you have any objection to the Engine being used for the purpose of throwing from time to time a jet of water on the grass in front of Lord Wharncliffe's Tents and those of the Staff. We have 2 Watering Carts from Messrs Braby, but in very hot and dry weather they hardly suffice for the watering of the grass as we keep them at work on the dusty roads - the engine being through your kindness lent to the Association the Council would not use it as proposed without your sanction.

I have the honor to be
Gentlemen
Your obedient Servant
Edmond St. John Mildmay
Sec. NRA

'The Office removes to Wimbledon on Monday next - then letters will be forwarded to the Camp.'

The *Volunteer Service Gazette* included some perceptive observations on the future use of steam tram locomotives in London. Contemporary street tramways there used horses exclusively although Merryweather had made available a tram engine equipped with a vertical boiler, but of standard gauge, for trials on the North

Metropolitan Tramway system earlier in the same year. It was tried out in the Leytonstone area of East London but, in the event, the Tramway Company was not persuaded to change over to steam locomotives until 1883 and was in fact the only London Tramway Company ever to use such locomotives.

'Saturday July 7th
'A beautiful steam fire engine, appropriately termed the "Volunteer," arrived this afternoon, and is housed in a tent near the Council. This engine, which is of the latest construction, is from the establishment of Messrs. Merryweather. It is fitted with the 'Field' tubular boiler, and it is said that it can be got into full working order in less than ten minutes after the fires are lighted.

'Thursday July 12th
'A new locomotive steam-engine has made its appearance on the tramway. It has been sent to Wimbledon by Messrs. Merryweather, who are the constructors of it, and if the rails are found to be strongly laid enough to bear it, it will be used instead of horses for the rest of the meeting. The engine, chimney, and all are boxed up in a metal carriage, and there is nothing in the appearance of the machine to alarm horses. It is said to work without either noise or smoke. It is to be hoped that it will be found possible to use it, for we shall certainly have to come to steam tramcars in London before long, and if Merryweather's engine succeeds at Wimbledon, some of the prejudice which at present exists may be overcome.

'Friday, July 13th
'The tramway steam engine has worked in a very satisfactory manner all day. It makes no smoke, and absolutely no noise, and runs at a very respectable speed over the slightly laid road on the common.'

The trial with the tram engine made a strong impression on the Council and Mildmay was able to make an enthusiastic statement at the end of the Meeting:

'The experiment made with the little traction engine was most successful and the Executive Committee have much pleasure in testifying to the zeal with which the persons in charge worked, and to their courtesy towards the numerous visitors who were all day crowding around the engine.'

In April 1878, Merryweather again offered to supply a Tramway Steam Engine and the Council instructed the Secretary to thank Merryweather and request the loan of the locomotive for the following two years.

At the following Council Meeting, which took place on 18 May, the favourable, albeit conditional, reply that had been received from Merryweather was presented by the Secretary.

'The Secretary stated that he had requested Messrs Merryweather and Sons to inform him whether they would be inclined to lend one of their Engines as they did last year to the NRA during the Wimbledon Meeting. Messrs Merryweather had called to say that they would do so but that they would have to alter the wheels to suit the peculiar gauge of the Tramway. The cost of this would be over £100, but that if the gauge of the Tramway could be widened to suit their Engine they would charge nothing for the loan of it. The Secretary wrote to Messrs Aird and Sons, the Contractors, to ask them what the cost of widening would be –'

'Dear Major Aird,
I am sorry to be so troublesome, but I must ask you to be so good as to give me the benefit of your kind advice in the following matter.

Messrs. Merryweather have again kindly placed an Engine at our disposal free of charge, but we must do on of two things, either widen our present Gauge to 4' 8½', or else ask them to narrow the width between the wheels of their engine to our present Gauge; the latter plan would cost about £100, but we have no notion of the cost of widening our Gauge - Will you then kindly let me know if you could ascertain for us which of the two plans would be the cheapest or most advantageous. If we increase the Gauge we shall have to increase also the width of our 6 Cars, which would entail a considerable expense, I presume.

The Committee have recommended that the Tramway should be extended 150 yards. I will submit this recommendation to the Council in a few days; will you let me know the latest date for sending you the order for the work.'

1878

May 18th.

Letter to 'mess" Aird & Sons - read	Mess". Aird and Sons, the Contractors, to ask them what the cost of widening the gauge would be and they replied that they were of opinion that the widening of the present gauge would be 'much in excess of the cost of altering the engine, and that they 'thought it would be open to great objection to interfere with the 'Permanent Way, as much of the Timber that is now good enough 'would become unfit for future use". Letter (9925) from Mess". Aird & Son's read.
Secretary communicates contents to Mess". Merryweather & Son. Their Offer.	On receipt of Mess". Aird's letter the Secretary communicated the contents to Mess". Merryweather who called to state that in going again into the question of altering the wheels to suit the narrow gauge they found that it would entail an almost total reconstruction of the Engine, and they therefore offered to supply one purposely made for Wimbledon at a price very much lower than their usual charge - The Secretary asked them to write him a letter embodying the terms of their Offer.
Mess". Merryweather's letter and Offer.	Read letter (10020) from Mess". Merryweather and Sons stating that they are willing to sell to the N.R.A. one of their patent Steam Tramway Engines altered to suit the Gauge as adopted at Wimbledon for the sum of £320; the ordinary price for such an engine being £600, but under the peculiar circumstances of the Case they are willing to make the reduction. They further state that they will let the N.R.A. have one of their Engineers to work the Engine during the Meeting at £2·14·0 per Week, the actual net cost to themselves.
Accepted with thanks.	Resolved that Mess". Merryweather's offer be accepted and that they be thanked for their liberality.
Cap Covers - pattern approved.	The Secretary submitted pattern of Cap Covers supplied by Mess". Silver & Co which were approved after a few alterations had been agreed to.

Letter

The Council minutes for 18 May 1878 indicating that Merryweather would supply the Association with a new locomotive at a very much reduced price.

The reply received from Messrs Aird, which was then communicated to Merryweather, stated:

'that they were of opinion that the widening of the present gauge would be much in excess of the cost of altering the engine, and that they thought it would be open to great objection to interfere with the Permanent Way, as much of the Timber that is now good enough would become unfit for future use.'

This was discussed at the next Council Meeting on 5 May, together with a further communication from Merryweather.

'On receipt of Messrs Aird's letter the Secretary communicated the contents to Messrs Merryweather who called to state that in going again into the question of altering the wheels to the suit the narrow gauge the found that it would entail an almost total reconstruction of the Engine, and they therefore offered to supply one purposely made for Wimbledon at a price very much lower than their usual charge. The Secretary asked them to write him a letter embodying the terms of their offer.'

'Read letter(100 20) from Messrs Merryweather and Sons stating that they are willing to sell to the NRA one of their patent Steam Tramway Engines altered to suit the Gauge as adopted at Wimbledon for the sum of £320; the ordinary price for such an engine being £600, but under the peculiar circumstances of the case they are willing to make the reduction. They further state that they will let the NRA have one of their Engineers to work the Engine during the Meeting at £2-14-0 per week, the actual net cost to themselves.'

Merryweather's exceptionally favourable terms on the purchase price of the locomotive and the offer to hire one of their engineers at cost were eminently acceptable to the Council and they also accepted the proposal to extend the Tramway to the Clock Tower by 150 yards, 'as the starting station is inconveniently situated.' Both decisions were communicated to Major Aird on 20 May. The cost of the extension work was £120 and this increased the length of the Tramway to about three quarters of a mile.

'The Council having agreed to purchase an Engine on very liberal Terms offered by Messrs. Merryweather and Sons, we shall esteem it a favour if the work required for the extension of the line was now proceeded with.'

On the same day, the Secretary confirmed the authority to purchase the locomotive in a letter to Merryweather:

'In reference to your letter of the 3rd of May, I am now directed by the Council of the National Rifle Association that they have pleasure in accepting your liberal offer to supply the Association with one of your Patent Steam Tramway Engines for the sum of £320 and I am further directed to convey to you their expression of thanks for your liberality.'

The *Volunteer Service Gazette* confirmed that the Tram Engine was available for the start of the Meeting in early July. The extremely short period of under two months from order to delivery, with negligible time for testing and running in, indicates that Merryweather already had a locomotive nearing completion for an existing order and diverted this to the Association. The Works Number 48, registered by the National Boiler Insurance Co. in 1908, falls into a sequence of orders, placed in 1877, for the Barcelona à San Andrés Tramway in Spain, the gauge of which was 1000mm – the metric equivalent of the 3ft 6in of the Wimbledon Tramway.

The purchase of the locomotive and the extension to the Tramway were duly noted in the 1878 NRA Report.

'Messrs Merryweather & Sons supplied one of their noiseless tramway engines made to suit the exceptional gauge of the NRA tramway, and as the firm offered it on very favourable terms to the Council, and it was found to work admirably and in some respects to have great advantages over the former expensive system of employing horse power, the Council purchased it.

'A great improvement was affected in the Tramway by lengthening the line 150yds, and thus bringing the starting point opposite the centre of the NRA Offices, and close to the clock tower which was

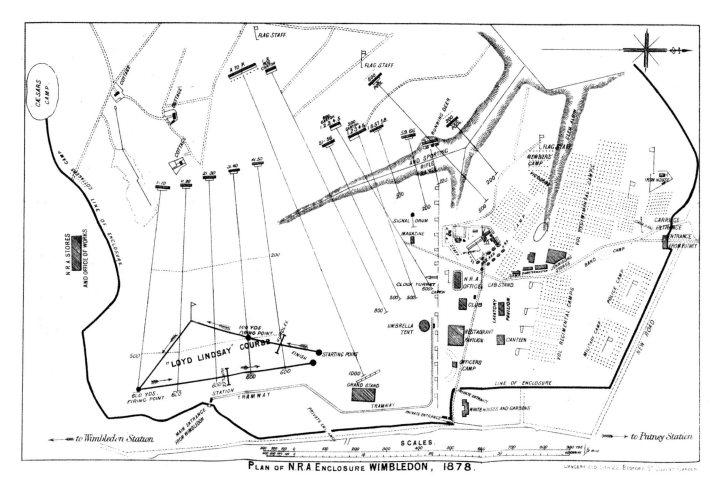

PLAN OF N.R.A ENCLOSURE WIMBLEDON, 1878.

The Wimbledon Plan for 1878. This was, in fact, printed too late to show the Tramway after it was extended to the Clock Tower. The half-way station, introduced in the days of horse drawn tramcars, had now been removed.

this year removed from its former place and erected in a line with the flag poles. It had always been considered that the point from which the cars started was inconveniently far.'

The following are the leading dimensions and other attributes, as far as can be ascertained, of the Tram Engine when new; however, the boiler and firebox dimensions are those for the post-1900 boiler whose pressure was 125lb per square inch.

Makers Class Type	Merryweather Type 1
Works Number	48 (Confirmed by Boiler Insurance Company in 1908)
Boiler Pressure	80lbs per square inch (125 psi from 1900)
Date constructed	1878
Gauge	Nominally 3ft 6ins (the actual gauge appears to have been 3ft 5⅝ ins – the Association were never quite sure!)
Weight (with water and coal)	4 tons
Maximum Height (to top of cab)	9ft
Power Rating	about 7 HP
Wheel Arrangement	0-4-0
Wheel Diameter	2ft 0ins
Length (over couplings)	8ft 11ins
Length (body)	8ft
Width of body	6ft 6ins
Cylinders (bore diameter x stroke)	6ins x 9ins
Firebox Length	2ft 9ins*

Boiler Barrel Length	3ft*
Boiler Barrel Diameter	2ft 7ins*
Number of Flu Tubes	94 (also in the earlier 80psi boiler)
Flu Tube Diameter (Outside)	1⅜ ins*
Boiler Heating surface	98 sq ft*
Total Heating Surface	132 sq ft*

*These dimensions are those for the reboilered loco-motive post-1900

'Monday July 8th 1878
'The tramway is greatly improved this year. Messrs. Merryweather's noiseless steam locomotive exper-imented on last year is now in full working order, and the trams run very smoothly. The only objec-tion to it appears to be that it is a little too noiseless. It may be well to provide the driver with a loud whistle, or other means of warning those riflemen who - absorbed in their mutual condolences as to the magpie that ought to have been an inner, or the miss that ought to have been a bullseye - stand, as we have seen them doing today, right on the track, and have only just time to skip out of the way of the engine. We should mention that the tramway now extends quite up to the front of the council building, which, if the weather is as hot as Mr. Gregory, the Manager of the Meteorological Department here, declares it is likely to be, will be of great advantage.'

The Accounts for that year showed the total cost of pur-chasing the tram engine as £331-2s-0d.

The *Gazette*, on 12 July, commented that 'The Tramway locomotive which performed so well last year, has, we believe, been purchased by the Association, and is now christened *The Wharncliffe*.' It was named after the Earl of Wharncliffe, the incumbent Chairman of the NRA Council.

In the following year the Gazette mentioned the Tram Engine again '…and the smart little locomotive, the *Wharncliffe,* was trying its paces on the Tramway in the afternoon. *Wharncliffe* turned out to be entirely to the NRA's satisfaction and on 11 January 1882, Mildmay wrote to Merryweather expressing the Council's appreciation.

'I am directed by the Council of the National Rifle Association to state that they have much pleasure in testifying to the very satisfactory working of the Steam Tramway Engine which has been in use at the Wimbledon Prize meetings every year since you sup-plied it in 1878. As to neatness and efficiency it leaves nothing to be desired.'

At this period, Merryweather was in the process of altering the design of their Tram engines. Originally equipped with the 'Field' vertical boiler, also used in the same manufacturer's fire engines, they were now of the 'standard type' with a conventional horizontal boiler. Merryweather also simplified the car body design to a much more open form with no glazing, providing sim-ple waste-height end doors and dispensing with the stylish ogive-shaped roof. *Wharncliffe* was constructed with the earlier body design, and thereby remained a unique hybrid.

In order to transport *Wharncliffe* and its cars from storage in the Association's workshops to the Tramway, Merryweather used a horse and trolley and also supplied two engineers and assistants to prepare the engine and operate it. At the end of the meeting they greased the engine and returned it to store. This contract was maintained until 1892, when the NRA had become firmly established at Bisley. As *Wharncliffe* was only used during the annual meetings in July lit-tle maintenance was required, however it is recorded that Merryweather supplied new brake blocks in 1885 and 1886. They also carried out £11 worth of repairs in 1888.

At a committee meeting held on 24 November 1879, the members approved the contents of a letter from Lord Wharncliffe, the Chairman of the Association, that 'the tramcars of the old pattern should be converted to match the new Metropolitan Carriage, Wagon & Finance Company (MCW&F) cars, at cost estimated by Mr Stockman at £7 each'.

By 1879 the Committee had become concerned about costs. 'The management of the Tramway must be gone into next year. The expenses must be reduced. General McMurdo suggested that men in uniform should not pay more than 1d. The pay of the boys 6/- per diem is excessive.' The boys mentioned acted as attendants on the Tramcars.

Wharncliffe at Wimbledon in 1879. The train consists of all four original cars in their original 'bianconi' configuration and the two MC&W cars of 1877. The locomotive gained its name in 1879 and the four older cars were rebuilt to a similar profile to the MC&W cars during early 1880. The photograph may have been especially posed, with a very full load of passengers, to celebrate the naming event. Behind, to the right, is the Pavilion, first erected in 1871. It is noticeable that the two MC&W cars still retain their original solid wheels.

By the beginning of 1880 all was not found to be well with the MCW&F pairs of cars and at the next meeting, held in February of that year, the Secretary notified the Committee of lubrication problems with their axles.

'The Secretary submitted letter No 2346 from Mr Stockman in reference to the Axle Trees and bearings of the two Tramcars supplied from Birmingham in 1877 and which he states must be renewed as having become unserviceable from insufficient lubrication.

'Mr Stockman produced as specimens one of the bearings referred to and explained the cause of the damage, and also that the wheels of the cars required renewing.

The Committee gave instructions to Mr Stockman to proceed with the necessary repairs to the Tramcars.'

In August of the same year the Committee raised some queries regarding Aird's Tramway account.

'The Secretary was requested to draw Messrs Aird's attention to several items in their account which were not included in the contract and to state that the Committee would suggest that in future these, where possible, should be included in the Contract. The amount of £1, charged for work on the 'level crossing', should have formed part of the contract.'

At the same time meeting they 'further instructed the Secretary to enquire of Messrs Aird whether they would undertake to work the tramway during the Prize meeting, paying the NRA a stipulated sum as a rent for the use of the tramway'.

Aird was unwilling to accept the proposed contract and the Council eventually decided to put it in the hands of a Mr. Biddulph, a member of the Council, and the Secretary. However Major Aird was then asked to comment on the excessive costs of the Tramway which had been noted in 1879.

'Tramway – Major Aird, of the firm of 'John Aird and Sons' attended after some conversation on the subject of the working and the management of the Wimbledon Tramway, and after going over the various items of expenditure Major Aird held out no hope of any substantial reduction in the expenses. He did not recommend any change in the management; but he promised to watch this year carefully the working

A 'Special' Train on the Range Tramway at Wimbledon c1880. This is possibly a publicity photograph for Merryweather taken at the commencement of the 1880 Meeting; 'Merryweather and Sons, Engineers, London' is stamped in the bottom right hand corner of the picture. The train is specially posed and seems to be carrying family parties with a few Volunteers in uniform. *Wharncliffe* is in its original livery, with Merryweather's logo painted at both ends whereas the cars appear in either plain white or cream. The 1st and 4th cars from the locomotive must be the MC&W cars of 1877. The other cars have been rebuilt from the original back-to-back configuration as a result of Lord Wharncliffe's suggestion, made in late 1879, that these cars be rebuilt to match the MC&W cars although they are certainly not identical. By the end of the decade all the cars had been re-painted in the house colours of blue and stone. All this work was carried out by Stockman, the Association's Clerk of the Works, and his successor, Hoey, at the Workshop on the Common. The wheels of the MC&W cars have now been replaced with spoked wheels similar to those of the older cars.

of it so that next year to be in a position to report whether any improvements which might reduce the expenditure could with advantage be introduced.'

'The Committee recommended that the arrangements for the Tramway management be left in the hands of Mr Biddulph and the Secretary and that Messrs Merryweather be requested to undertake that whoever they detailed to take charge of the NRA Engine should be considered pro: idem: as in the Service of the Association.'

In 1883 the Council received a report from Aird on the condition of the Tramway in which it was suggested that two modes of laying sleepers should be considered. This indicated that the extension to the Tramway in 1877 had been laid using longitudinal frames.

'Tramway. A report from Messrs Aird and Sons on the condition of the Tramway and suggesting 2 modes of laying sleepers where these schemes are required.

'One on longitudinal frames as already laid for the extension some years ago. They are easily laid & do not disturb the ground as they are laid on the surface – cost... £50-0-0

The other on ordinary sleepers – cost........ £23-0-0.'

Just before the 1883 Meeting the Wimbledon Committee made some changes to the issue of Tramway Season Tickets, originally issued through the Caterer;

'Tramway Season Tickets – 2/6 – may be obtained at the Secretary's Office.'

THE GRAPHIC

1. A Blow Out for Threepence.—2. Ammunition.—3. The Running Man (No. 1) : Friend A——, "Keep it up, Brown ; " Friend B——, "Give in Your Rifle, Old Man ; "
Friend C——, "Plenty of Room, Brown."—4. The Running Man (No. 2).—5. The Chiffonier Brigade.—6. Laying their Heads Together After
the Latest from Alexandria.—7. The Canadian Camp.

NOTES IN CAMP AT WIMBLEDON

The Tramway is included in a set of drawings of the Camp at Wimbledon in 1882 that also contains a depiction of the Running Man target. Given artistic licence the car appears to be one of the original cars rebuilt to 'match' the two MC&W cars. (*The Graphic*)

Wharncliffe and train at Wimbledon in July 1889. *Wharncliffe* runs round its train of cars at the 'Camp' terminus near the N.R.A. Offices. The 'Pavilion' in the background, moved to Bisley in 1890, had to be replaced in 1923 as it had become 'unhygienic and rat-infested'.

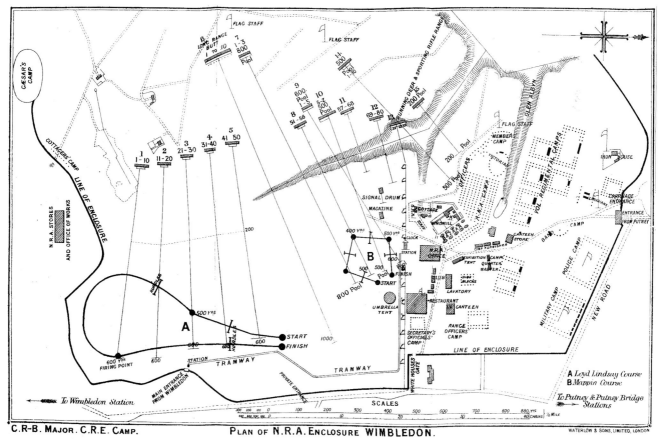

The Wimbledon Plan of 1889 – the last before the move to Bisley.

The Electro-Motor Syndicate

In 1883 the NRA was approached by a company called the Electro-Motor Syndicate with a view to using their electric propulsion system on the Tramway. Following Aird's report regarding the difficulties of reducing expenditure on the Tramway it can only be assumed that an enthusiastic Council really believed that this offered a potential way of saving money. The Syndicate's Managing Director was invited to attend a meeting of the Finance Committee, held on 8 May, to agree terms.

'Mr Macdonald the Managing Director of the 'Electric Motor Syndicate' attended and the terms on which the 'Tramway' was to be worked by Electricity in lieu of Steam, having been agreed upon, the Secretary was instructed to request Mr Markby to draw up the Agreement as directed by the Council.'

The Agreement placed the financial responsibility for this venture, including the costs pertaining to the laying of the tramway, on the Syndicate. This, of course, was in the very early pioneering days of railway electrification and the Council believed that they had minimised the risk to themselves and were well covered in financial terms. The Spring Meeting report bravely anticipated the success of the system.

'A novelty at the Meeting will be the working of the Tramway by the Electric Motor Syndicate, who have made an agreement with the Council to supply the motive power, using the NRA cars and rails.'

Although the equipment was duly installed it was not in working order by the first day of the Meeting, Sunday 8 July, and the *Volunteer Service Gazette* reported that -

'The electric engine is not yet in working order, and the tram-cars are still drawn by the steam locomotive, the *Wharncliffe*. An arrangement has been made by which awnings can be put over the cars, which will be a great comfort if the sun should be as hot again as it was last year.'

This report is also of interest at it appears to have been the only mention of some kind of 'roof' being applied to the tramcars.

By the following week the Syndicate was able to contemplate a trial run carrying a number of Council and other members of the Association. This produced a technically detailed but critical evaluation which was published in several journals of the day, including the *London Standard* of 4 August.

'An Electric Railway

The Electric Railway at Wimbledon, which it was expected would have carried passengers during the recent rifle association meeting, made a start on Friday, and a train, with Earl Brownlow, Sir Henry Halford and 18 other members of the association, ran the length of the line, about a mile, at a speed (six miles per hour) which earned for the engineer the congratulation of the party. The experiment has been, unfortunately, a rough one and the conditions under which it has been carried out are very detrimental to the reputation which the system is susceptible of attaining. The familiar track of light rails laid down 22 years ago, with carriages of the same date, the sleepers loose in the sandy soil, is not the kind of line for an electrically-driven train to be shown off upon, especially when the wheels of the cars are so much furrowed that their bearing surfaces bump on every chair of the rails they pass over. The system of propulsion is by current generated from a Weston dynamo, worked by a 12-horse power Robey engine and conveyed and returned by two flat copper bands about an inch broad, each laid at the bottom of a groove in long wood bearers stretched midway between the lines of rails, and supported on square wood blocks saturated with pitch. The insulation seems to be perfect, for when tested by a Galvanometer and a battery of five cells not the slightest deflection of the needle takes place. The motor consists of four external magnets coupled together in similar poles, and an armature formed of sixteen magnets, travelling in the interval between the external magnets and cutting all the lines of force. It is mounted on one of the ordinary carriages, and the current is drawn off and returned to the conductors by two trailing chains dropping within the conductor channels. The line was worked partially on Saturday and again for several hours yesterday. The system has been put under trial by the electro-motor syndicate,

The Clock Tower terminus of the Tramway at Wimbledon in the later 1880s as seen from the Windmill. *Wharncliffe* in the process of running round its train. All six cars are visible, one of which is parked adjacent to the Clock Tower at the end of the line. The original cars have now been rebuilt to resemble the two MC&W cars and are in their final Wimbledon livery of blue and white (the Association's house colours at the time). The prefabricated Council Offices of 1876 in the foreground and the ornamental Pavilion building of 1871 are visible, as is the Bell Tent, where the tramway originally terminated. and the Clock Tower to which the Tramway (seen from the Windmill) had been extended in 1878. All were moved to Bisley in 1890 but only the Council Offices now remain.

the motor being the invention of Mr. Brown. The line is not being worked to the full extent of the power furnished, the engine only making 40 revolutions and the dynamo 300, while the normal rate of the latter should be 900 revolutions. Much greater results, therefore, are to be looked for when the new motor is further developed.'

Unfortunately, although this pioneering experiment in electric traction was contemporary with the successful 'Volks Electric Tramway' laid along the seafront at Brighton (and still with us today), it was eventually reported as a failure. This meant, of course, that the 'old' system using the steam tram engine *Wharncliffe* had had to be substituted at short notice. This resulted in a considerable loss to the NRA who then naturally tried to reclaim their money from the Syndicate under the terms of the Agreement. The unsuccessful outcome appeared

in the minutes of the Finance Committee's meeting that was held on 14 November:

'The Secretary stated that in consequence of the 'Electric Motor Syndicate' not having taken any notice of the application for a settlement of the Claims for laying Tramway re as follows.

Aird and Co for laying Track	61-12-8
Merryweather working engine	39-10-0
Receipts Guaranteed to Association	15-0-0
	£116-2-8

Mr Markby had been directed to write to them and the reply was that the Syndicate had presented a petition for liquidation.'

In the circumstances nothing further could be done; the NRA, normally so prudent with its limited funds, had literally been taken for a ride!

'The Last Tram at Wimbledon'. (*Illustrated Sporting & Dramatic News*)

THE TARGET TRAMWAY

The Running Deer and Man Tramway

By 1862, mobile targets, commonly in the shape of a running deer, had been developed and introduced on various provincial ranges. However, the Council had only recommended the introduction of such a target when they received a communication from Alexander Henry, the noted Edinburgh gun maker, in which he offered to fund a prize for 'a running deer.' which was accepted by the Council.

The acceptance of the running deer prize gave Lord Elcho, the opportunity to introduce such a target, and at the Council Meeting of 16 May the Secretary read a statement of the various works. These 'works' were not specified but must have included the planned running deer range. These were the sole 'references' to the new Range and it seems reasonable to assume that it was, in fact, introduced as the result of a close collaboration between Elcho and Mildmay.

The new 'Running Deer' range consisted of an iron 'Deer' target mounted on a turntable and carried by a small four-wheel railway truck running over a short 'tramway' of approximately 67 yards in length. The 'Deer' was launched by its team of markers down a sloping section of track where it attained a speed of 12 miles per hour to pass an opening in the Butt that was visible to the rifle shooters at the firing point 111 yards away. It was slowed by the converse uphill section and brought to a halt by another team whose task it was to rotate it on its turntable and return it when signalled to do so.

To lay the track and keep the 'Deer' truck in adjustment the Association was fortunate in obtaining the services of Captain William Gooch of the 11th Wiltshire Volunteers (who was, in fact, the Superintendent of the Great Western Railway's Swindon Works). The Association also gained the assistance of well-known gun maker Lancaster, who had some experience with such exotic targets and was also in a position to lend the Association his own 'Deer', complete with its mounting truck, for the first season.

In May 1862 Mildmay had noted in his diary that 'we must have a plan of Running Deer Butts as Gooch can do nothing without one'. Gooch also brought along an assistant named Parks for whom Mildmay had high praise 'Parks from Swindon is such an intelligent fellow - and will arrange all about the Deer - he understands it perfectly.' On 24 May Mildmay noted to Elcho that

'I send you the plan of Running Deer - Gooch himself will be up on Monday at 12 - we had better take him to Wimbledon.'

On 14 June Mildmay noted that 'Gooch's foreman is gone to Wimbledon and on Monday must take up his residence at the Village - as he has to do the whole work' and on 26 June he observed that 'Gooch is not quite satisfied with the Deer - it does not roll fast enough - the wheels are too small.'

It is not known whether the Deer truck, as used at Wimbledon, incorporated the rocking mechanism shown in the diagram. If it did the extra friction of the 'rocking' eccentric may have been a factor. Later 'Deers' were not so equipped although a modification tested in 1878 failed for a similar reason. Whatever the cause it seems the problem was overcome by the time the Annual Meeting took place. The Report for 1862 described the arrangements for the Running Deer and also carried a comprehensive diagram.

'The greatest novelty however in this year's target arrangements was the running deer. The deer itself is the property of Mr Lancaster, the gunmaker, who kindly lent it to the Association. The rails, &c. were laid down by Captain Gooch of the Swindon Works of the Great Western Railway, and the Council have to express their thanks to him for the trouble he took in the matter, and for the efficient and successful manner in which everything was done. The preparing of the Butt etc, for the deer was a work of considerable labour and expense, as every possible precaution had to be taken to protect the markers, and guard against the splash of the lead. This there was great difficulty in doing, and the first day two of the markers, six being constantly employed in working the deer, were slightly cut. Additional means were however taken for their protection, and no further accident occurred. The running deer will it is hoped be a permanent institution at the Wimbledon Meeting, and it has been copied at several county meetings; the Council propose having a deer of their own made from a design by Sir Edwin Landseer, which they will be ready to let out to County and other Associations, and they likewise propose to have a moving figure of a man.'

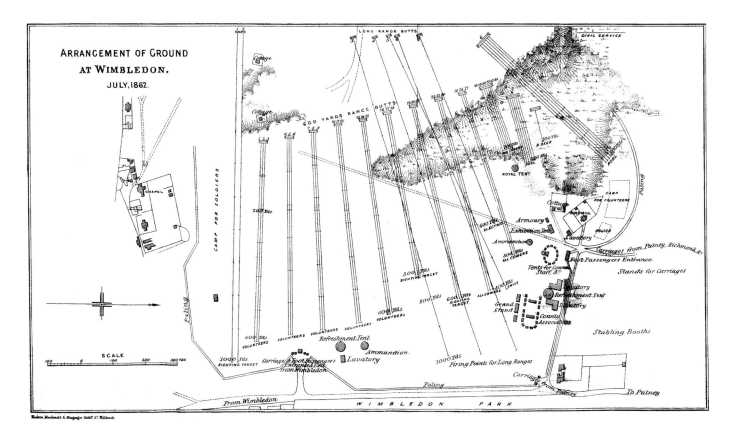

The Wimbledon Plan of 1862 showing the new Running Deer range located in the Ravine to the west of the Windmill and adjacent to the 200yd Pool Range.

The Times carried a full description of the Deer:

'The "Running Deer target", which has excited more curiosity among the inhabitants of Wimbledon, as well as the visitors to the camp, than any other feature of the arrangements is of Scotch extraction, and has been erected by the Association at considerable expense. The very look of the butt attracts attention; it is much wider than any of the others, and has a curved line running across its face. This line is, in fact, a second embankment which conceals from view the machinery by which a deer, life-size, and made of iron, is caused to pass rapidly across the face of the butt. The mechanism, which is highly ingenious, will afford a very good insight into the difficulties and excitement of deer shooting, and the zeal of the amateur sportsmen will be quickened by the fact that the game, for such it really is, entails forfeits as well as confers rewards. A bullet striking the deer in a vital part will entitle the marksman to share at the end of the day in the distribution of the pool; but, on the other hand, anyone hitting the haunch and 'spoiling

the venison' will not only forfeit his entrance fee but be muleted in a fine as well.'

The problems with lead splash were sufficient for further comments to be reported in *The Times*:

'The "Running-deer" Target was beginning to be in much request, but, unfortunately, at the expiration of a couple of hours a slight accident occurred, which put a stop to its further use during the day. The Council of the Association incurred great expense in the construction of this target, and believed that, by careful revetting externally and the erection of strong iron shield-plates inside, they had made it perfectly secure for the men who worked the machinery of the 'running-deer.' But, although they succeeded in guarding against injury from direct or glancing bullets, lead, when brought into contact with iron plates, has a tendency to 'splash,' and some of these fragments, unfortunately, struck two soldiers, inflicting upon them cuts, not at all serious, but sufficient to call attention to the fact that the target in its existing state was insecure. The men were promptly attended by Dr. Westmacott, of the London Scottish, and were able to walk away from the hospital tent to their own quarters. The 'Running-deer Target,' of course, will not be used again till it has been completely remodelled, and the Council have under consideration a plan for the construction of recesses, into which the men can retire and be out of harm's way, while barriers effectually prevent them from stretching out beyond a certain point, thereby obviating the danger to which there is some reason for believing the men exposed themselves in their anxiety that the deer should make a rapid flight.'

On 31 July, immediately after the Meeting, a very pleased Mildmay wrote a complimentary letter of thanks to Gooch

'My Dear Capt. Gooch
'I enclose with pleasure two cheques for the amount of our debt to you, and I seize this opportunity in thanking you for all the trouble you took in preparing the 'Deer' for us.

Please be so good as to thank Mr Parks on behalf of the Council for his share of labour in carrying out the arrangements of the Running Target. His services were most valuable and without them we should have been at a stand-still.'

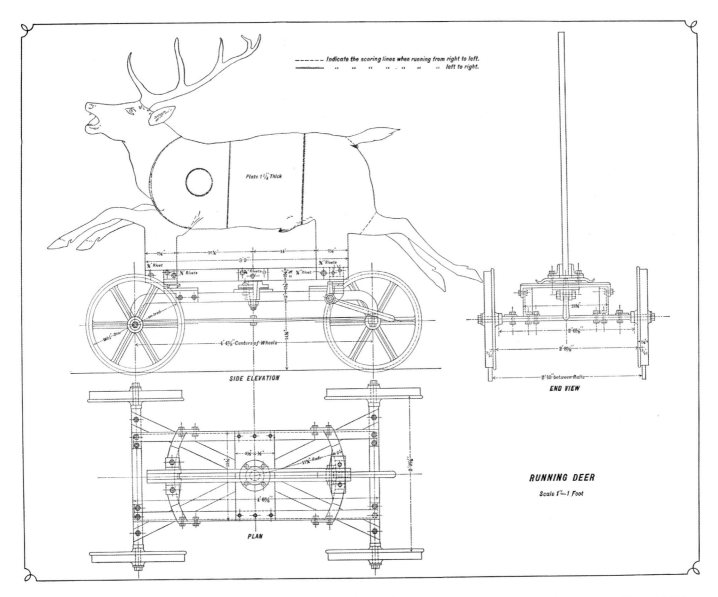

The N.R.A Running Deer of 1863 designed by Sir Edwin Landseer. This, with its 'truck', was constructed under the supervision of William Gooch at the Swindon Works of the Great Western Railway.

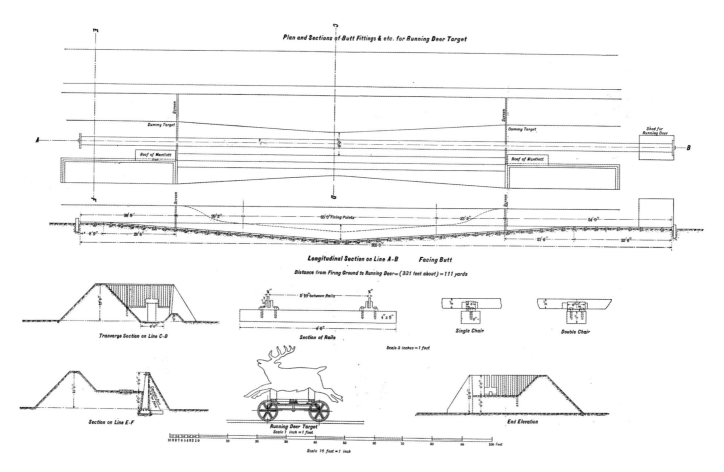

The Running Deer Range of 1863.

The undoubted success of the new Running Deer Range had persuaded the Association to order their own Deer and on 18 September Mildmay duly noted that 'Gooch will send an estimate for making a Deer - and undertakes the manufacture of it.' On 10 November, Mildmay noted to an unidentified party, 'I send you the Deer - could you get the Antler's in - take care how it is done as this is the copy to be traced on the stone.' The 'stone' referred to the contemporary lithographic printing method, a process that also permitted colour printing.

The NRA 'Deer', which had been designed by Landseer, at the instigation of Elcho, was made of wrought iron and constructed, along with its carrying truck, at the Great Western's Swindon Works under Gooch's supervision. It incorporated larger diameter wheels than Lancaster's and dispensed with the latter's 'rocking' mechanism.

The new Deer duly went into service at the 1863 July Meeting along with an alternative target, the 'Running Man', also constructed by Gooch and running over the same track. The 'Deer', however, always proved the more popular. The Running Man was from a design by George Frederick Watts. The new Deer again attracted a comment in *The Times* also indicating that both targets were originally painted.

'The Association now has a "running deer" of its own. That in use on the previous occasion was lent for the purpose by Mr. Lancaster; but since then one manufactured which is more than a mere target it is a work of art. The outline, life-size, was sketched by Sir E. Landseer, and from this drawing an exact counterpart in iron was made at the Swindon Works of the Great Western Railway, under the superintendence of Captain Gooch. To this plate an artist, who undertook the work at the instance of Sir E. Landseer, has added the necessary colouring with such fidelity to nature that it seems like desecration to spatter over this 'running deer' with the marks of rifle bullets. To vary the attraction, a 'running-man' will be substituted on alternate days. The figure is that of a Volunteer 'at the double,' and as one side is represented with a gray uniform, and the other with a scarlet tunic, there will be a favourable opportunity of testing the relative superiority of colour. The outline for this target, which is also of the natural size, was drawn by Mr. Watts.'

Both target designs were commented on in the year's Report.

'The only other point connected with the Wimbledon preparations requiring notice is the fact of a new iron deer having been made for the Association by Captain Gooch of the 11th Wiltshire Volunteers, from a design kindly furbished to the Council by Sir E. Landseer. Coming as this design does from his master hand, it is hardly necessary to say that it is full of truth, life and spirit. The original tracing has been carefully framed and preserved at the office.

'An iron figure of a Running Man was also made by Captain Gooch from a design by Mr. G.F. Watts, who first attracted public notice by carrying off the Second Prize in the great cartoon competition in Westminster Hall in 1843, and whose later works - amongst others his portrait of Tennyson - have made him justly celebrated.

'The Association is greatly indebted to these two distinguished Artists.'

On the day before the opening of the Annual Meeting the Prince of Wales visited the ground to inspect the arrangements and took the opportunity to try out the Running Deer Range.

'His Royal Highness also fired a few shots at the 200 yard Range and at the Running Deer, at which he was most successful. The rifle used on the occasion by His Royal Highness was a breech-loader made by Mr Smith, the Armorer of the Association.'

The visit of the Prince of Wales was also reported in *The Times* of 7 July and this also took especial note of his prowess on the Running Deer target.

'The next trial was at shorter range, but at a moving instead of a stationary target, and here the Highland experiences of the Prince stood him in good stead. Those who have not actually fired at the 'running deer'

can form no conception of the difficulty of hitting the mark. Appearing to move very slowly, it really travels with the velocity of a railway carriage, and, as in its course it describes an arc of a circle, the rate of speed at different points is necessarily various. The artist has made the deer of the dun instead of the red tribe, and there is consequently, little by which it can be distinguished from the bank behind, but for all that it rarely succeeded in crossing its 'corrie' scatheless. At one time the Prince succeeded in planting four bullets successively in the portion of the body forming the centre of the target. The members of the Association who were present concurred in declaring that the practice which had been made at this range, if not better, was at least equal, taking the general average of the shots, to that recorded of any single rifle at the meeting of 1862. His Royal Highness used a double barrelled rifle made by Mr. Smith, the Armourer to the National Rifle Association, and was so well satisfied with its performance that before leaving the ground he gave orders that one should be specially manufactured for him.'

The two mobile targets continued to operate satisfactorily, although, in 1871, the track sleepers required renewal and Aird was requested to carry this out in a letter dated 29 May.

'I hear from our foreman that the sleepers of the Running Deer range will have to be renewed and the rails re-laid - will you kindly undertake to have this done for us? Mr Stockman our foreman at Wimbledon is to be found any day on the Common, a person sent by you could see what has to be done.'

Unlike the passenger tramway of 1864 the track of the Running Deer tramway remained in position throughout the year. Attempts to give the 'animal' a more natural movement were revived from time to time but, in 1877, a 'Bounding Tiger' was tried out, the invention of a Mr. Hamilton.

'There was plenty of cracking at the Running Deer throughout the afternoon, in which Lord De Grey and Mr. Boswell, as usual, took a prominent part. Familiarity with this animal seems, however, rather to have bred contempt, and a change talked of for the last few days is now promised. The patient beast who has faced the rifles of so many deadly shots is now to be pursued by the likeness of a tiger, as we are told, which is to bound along after its prey in the sinuous mode of progression presumably adopted by the Royal original in the jungles of Bengal. It is an ingenious idea, and will create a new feature in the programme which will not be unacceptable.'

Having viewed the mechanism, the whole device was given a very favourable review by the *Volunteer Service Gazette*.

'We have been favoured by Mr. Hamilton, the inventor of the Bounding Tiger, with a view of the mechanism, which, though very ingenious, is of the simplest and cheapest, and will probably entirely supersede before long the iron rails for moving targets, not only at Wimbledon, but throughout the country. It can easily be worked by two men and almost any kind of motion can be given to the figure. We understand that it will replace the present deer at Wimbledon next year, but will probably not be brought into action during the present Meeting, though the figure of a deer, on Mr. Hamilton's system, has been several times tried before the firing had commenced and after it was over. The original 'Tiger', a spirited figure, executed by the inventor, now couches outside the mess tent of the London Scottish, in which regiment Mr Hamilton holds a commission.'

However, the bounding tiger did not re-appear the following year and the Council decided to experiment with a modification to the existing Deer in an attempt to emulate the galloping movement of the animal. The 'rocking' mechanism of the original was not incorporated into the new system, probably

ORDERS FOR MARKERS
AT THE RUNNING DEER
OR RUNNING MAN, 1886.

1. The deer will be run *head foremost*, or the man *face foremost*, from whichever side it happens to be on, by gong signal from the firing point.
2. On finishing the run the deer or man will be at once reversed on the turntable, so that it may be ready for the next run, and the hit or hits will be marked on the dummy as follows :—

Bull's Eye	..	..	.. White Disc.
Centre	..	..	.. Red „
Outer	..	..	.. Black „
Haunch (of Deer)	..	..	Black X.

   The disc will be shewn upon the dummy so as to indicate the spot struck on the target.
3. The men are on no account to expose themselves to danger by looking over the bank or passing the barrier.

A. P. HUMPHRY,
EXECUTIVE OFFICER.

EXECUTIVE 3, (B.)(25.)

The 1886 Orders for Markers on the Running Deer and Man Ranges

SKETCHES AT THE WIMBLEDON RIFLE MEETING.

The Running Man and Deer Range at the Wimbledon Rifle Meeting. It shows the Running Deer 'hors de combats' apparently damaged beyond repair. It survived however and is now a feature outside the NRA Offices at Bisley

'The sketches we now present are of an amusing minor feature of the Wimbledon Meeting, the moving target, in the shape of a *"running man"* which has superseded the "running deer", and which affords most useful practice for the military marksman.' (*Illustrated London News*)

because of the additional friction and weight it introduced. A similar problem seems to have afflicted the 1878 experiment.

> 'The Running Deer was by way of experiment made to imitate the movement of the animal at a gallop. The mechanism, however, by adding considerably to the weight of the carriage, had the effect of rendering its ascent into the butt too slow; at times the Deer stopped half way, and the old system of running it had therefore to be resumed.'

In 1883 Walter Winans, an American permanently resident in England, who was to become pre-eminent in pistol shooting at Bisley in the 1890s, and later a Vice-President of the Association, presented a Cup for a Running Deer competition. Winans was always a most enthusiastic supporter of the Running Deer and included copies of the original plans in his 1908 book 'The Sporting Rifle'.

In 1885 the iron Deer seems to have become unserviceable, it had probably split in the middle, and the *Illustrated London News* ventured to assume it had now been permanently superseded by the 'Running Man'. However the *News* included a drawing of it in the issue of 18 July, 'Sketches at the Wimbledon Meeting.' Although shown apparently abandoned the depiction seems to correspond well with the preserved wrought iron Deer we see today complete with its bolted-on substitute ear! In any case because of its undoubted popularity the Council saw fit to replace it, probably the following year, with a steel 'Deer' of identical design. Both Deers and the Running Man survived to be transported to Bisley where the steel version of the Deer and a sadly battered remnant of the Man (he had lost the barrel of his rifle) continued in service for a few more years.

CHAPTER 4

THE SEARCH FOR A NEW SITE 1887-1889

The viability of the Wimbledon Ranges had first been questioned during the 1860s, not many years after the opening, and there had been recurrent problems with tenants of the Duke of Cambridge's Coombe Wood Estate which lay directly behind the Target Butts of the ranges. Those most affected were small tenant farmers who had to be compensated during the Annual Meeting as they were unable to work their land safely. This came to a head in 1869 when the Duke's Solicitors demanded an absolute assurance that rifle bullets would not traverse his estate during the Meeting; failing which, firing would be stopped. A temporary resolution was reached in which a payment of £100 was made to the Duke's main tenant and this was followed up by an agreement dated 30 March 1870 between the Association and Cambridge that enabled either party to make a determination at short notice based on the 1869 issue which would require the Association to vacate the Common.

The popularity of the Annual Meeting was such that in 1887 further expansion of the Wimbledon Ranges was necessary and a request was made to the Duke of Cambridge as the owner of Coombe Wood to purchase that part of it on which the proposed extension to the Ranges would be situated. However this gave the Duke an opportunity to deliver notice of determination of the 1870 Agreement. He gave an explanatory statement at the Winter Meeting of the Association, held in March 1887, which he also chaired.

'They (the Association) were aware that though the Ranges were not on his ground they were backed by his ground. Considerable danger had arisen from the bullets going over the butts into his ground, and the question of giving notice to the National Rifle Association to discontinue their meetings had long been under consideration. But when he heard that it was proposed to expend a considerable sum of money on additions to the existing plant, he felt that he ought to give the notice at once so that the Council

might be enabled to set about finding a new shooting ground without any unnecessary delay. He need not assure his hearers that he had no desire to hurry the Association but the course taken was absolutely unavoidable for though every care had been taken his tenants were becoming seriously alarmed at the danger of stray bullets.'

This of course caused consternation in the ranks of the Association. However, the Council appointed a Special Committee to consider the issue. The first meeting of the committee was held on 1 June where it was resolved to request Cambridge not to allow the notice which he had given to terminate the agreement of 30 March to have effect until after the NRA annual Meeting of 1888 at Wimbledon, to which he readily agreed

Towards the end of 1887 the committee received permission from Cambridge to visit his land at Coombe Wood for the purpose of examining the safety issues for themselves. A report was placed before the Council meeting of 10 January 1888.

'The whole of this area is adequately protected during the Shooting by Police Constables, those in rear of the Butts (stationed in iron mantlets) being so placed to caution persons from approaching the line of fire; and so efficient are the precautions taken that during 28 years no accident has occurred from bullets flying beyond the butts

'Behind the Butts at a distance of about 1,500 yards, lies the property of H.R.H. The Duke of Cambridge, including the residence of General Clifton, called Cambridge Lodge, together with some cottages, farm buildings, etc. belonging thereto, and some 200 acres of agricultural land separated from Wimbledon Common by Beverley Brook. It is on a limited portion of this land that any appreciable danger from stray rifle Bullets appears to exist. The ranges were originally laid out so that the lines of fire, if produced beyond the butts would converge on a point a few yards from the Earl of Cambridge Lodge, this arrangement putting that residence and its outbuildings in the direct line of fire.

By a slight alteration in the direction of some of the ranges, the convergence of the lines of fire can be arranged so as to cover a much more limited area of the Duke of Cambridge's land than is case at present and solely on the South of Cambridge Lodge. Although it is not disputed that there may be some danger from stray shots to Cambridge Lodge and its dependant cottages, it would not appear to be very serious, for the occupants of the cottages attach so little importance to it, that they allow their children to pass freely to & fro between their homes and School during the Wimbledon Prize Meeting.

'The Report of Mr Metford (a very eminent authority) deals very exhaustively with the distance to which stray bullets will reach. The Committee are of the opinion that the fence dividing the farmland in the occupation of General Clifton from the Coombe Wood, is the limit to which stray bullets can reach; and this being so, they frankly admit that a certain portion of this land suffers some diminution in its value.'

The Committee drew the conclusion that lines of fire should be altered in order to confine the danger zone to a much smaller area south of Cambridge Lodge and finally to eliminate all danger through the Association acquiring this land, an area of about 120 acres. They additionally concluded that the land in question may continue to be used for agricultural purposes of good value, but that it appeared to be unsuitable for building purposes, and at the best only for an inferior class of residence!

However, Cambridge remained adamant in his opposition and caused his solicitor to write a strong letter to the Association reflecting this view, stating that the proposal to purchase about 120 acres of his Coombe Hill estate 'would be a most Serious injury to his estate, and might interfere very materially with its development hereafter.' He went on to dismiss an argument, used in this case, which quoted that 'the size and length of the butts are important factors in determining the safety of a range.' He stated that William Metford had not alluded to this at all dealing only with possible ricochets and he

also pointed out that Coombe Wood was 100ft lower than the Firing Points.

'... and as the range of a bullet from muzzle to first graze is, if fired from the first situation, greater over falling ground than over hard or rising ground, and as the extreme range of the Martini-Henry rifle is almost 3,240 yards, it follows that, according to Mr. Metford's measurements (as detailed in his report) Coombe Wood is within easy range from every firing point on Wimbledon Common, as a matter of fact bullets do now drop into the Wood beyond the boundary line of the land that it has been suggested the Association should purchase.

'There is, moreover, an immediate prospect of the general introduction of a Small bore military Rifle for practice, with which it is understood Wimbledon Common will be absolutely unsafe, and it appears, therefore, to His Royal Highness that under any circumstances the ranges can only continue to be used for a limited period.'

Cambridge remarked that he would quite understand if the Association decided in the circumstances not to re-elect him as President but of course it might be considered useful to have the Commander in Chief of the British Army in that position. He was re-elected unanimously!

It was now readily accepted by the majority of the Council that a new site must be found without delay as it was believed that 1888 would be the last year during which the Meeting could definitely be held at Wimbledon. In the urgency of finding a new site the nearby Richmond Park was proposed. This was supported by Queen Victoria but not by the Ranger, the Duke of Cambridge, for much the same reasons as he had stated in respect of Wimbledon Common! To this was added the vociferous objections from members of the public regarding the loss of valuable open space as well as concerns about the trees and, such being the opposition, the proposal had to be turned down by the Commissioners of the Park.

The Association now realised that they must urgently search for a new site outside the immediate London area. There were already two strong contenders, one at Cannock Chase, in Staffordshire, and the other on the Berkshire Downs at Compton, south of

Didcot, which had been offered by the Association's Chairman, Lord Wantage, on whose estate it was. A special meeting of the Council, attended by a deputation from Staffordshire representing the Cannock Chase offer, was convened on 22 September to decide between the two. Extensive discussions ensued, seemingly biased towards Wantage's Berkshire Downs site. Major Walker, a member of Council, had inspected both sites and had expressed himself in favour of the former. Capt. Pixley then moved a Resolution in favour of the Berkshire Downs site, seconded by Lord Bury. Everything appeared to be heading for a firm conclusion to the great satisfaction of Lord Wantage. The Resolution was put forward at a full Council Meeting held on 25 September.

The veteran Lord Wemyss, formerly Elcho, now stepped in with a statement which effectively put the whole issue back in the melting pot. Wemyss had by this time identified a site near Brookwood in Surrey and had gained influential allies outside the Council including Charles Scotter, the General Manager of the L&SWR, who had succeeded Archibald Scott in 1885

'Lord Wemyss then rose and in an exhaustive statement gave his reasons for objecting to a decision being given at this Meeting. There were but few Members of Council present at the Meeting of the 22nd when the Resolution as to deciding today upon one of the first sites was passed and several of the Members present today had not had an opportunity of discussing the question of sites – He was sure that Council felt as grateful as he did to Lord Wantage for his most generous offer, but he also felt that he could not vote in favour of Capt Pixley's motion to which he would propose the following amendments.

'Before finally adopting the Berkshire or Cannock sites it is desirable to give further time for enquiry as to the possibilities of obtaining a suitable site within a reasonable distance of the Metropolis, and that a Committee be appointed to communicate with the Government and ascertain whether they would assist the National Rifle Association to obtain a new Site for the annual Rifle Meeting.'

After discussions, Wemyss' amendment was decisively carried by a vote of 13 to 5 and a Committee was set up to look into all the sites afresh. In addition, there was

James Loyd Lindsay, Lord Wantage – Chairman of the NRA from 1887 to 1891. *Vanity Fair's* 1876 depiction of Lt. Colonel James Loyd Lindsay whom Queen Victoria elevated to the peerage in 1885 as Lord Wantage. Awarded a VC in the Crimea War, he was the prime founder of the British Red Cross and a philanthropic landowner. He also had significant railway connections having been a leading supporter and Chairman of the Didcot, Newbury and Southampton Railway as well as Chairman of the Wantage Tramway. (*Vanity Fair - Author's Collection*)

an important new proposal emanating from the major railway companies to consider.

'Now I find that managers of the leading railway lines have come to the conclusion that anything of the nature of competition would be against their own interest and they have agreed upon a scale of charge- namely, a single fare for the double journey from all parts of the country. This, I may observe, would be about 10s. to Cannock Chase and 5s. to Churn Down, and a similar sum to Brighton.'

At this point Cambridge wrote a letter to Lord Wantage complaining that he considered the action of the Council in making their decision was 'most unsatisfactory'. This immediately caused Lord Wemyss to make a reply in the strongest terms.

'Gosford
'Oct. 6th 1888
Sir,
'I regret to find by your Royal Highness letter to Lord Wantage that you consider the action of the Council of the NRA 'most unsatisfactory'. Your Highness says 'nothing but delay can result from the resolution adopted on Lord Wemyss' recom- mendation'. As the Council by a majority of 13 to 5 supported my amendment on the motion for the immediate adoption of either the Berks or Cannock Chase site I hope your Royal Highness will allow me on behalf of myself and those who supported me to explain the grounds of our action. It was undoubtedly with a view to 'delay' that the amend- ment was moved and carried. We sought delay in the hope of finding a more suitable site within rea- sonable distance of London which we believe to be essential to the future success of our Association. Acting on behalf of the Committee of the Council I have written to the Secretary of State for War set- ting forth our position and asking his help, and I now enclose a copy of my letter in the hope that your Royal Highness may be induced to use your great influence in our behalf with Mr Stanhope. I am encouraged to do this by the knowledge that your Royal Highness favours other sites than those which were alone submitted to our consideration at our Council meeting. Personally I would take this

opportunity of expressing my grateful sense of your Royal Highness' kindness in allowing us, if needs be, to remain one more year at Wimbledon – I hope however that it may not be necessary for us to avail ourselves of this friendly concession as our future will I doubt not, be decided before the end of '88.
I have etc.
Wemyss'

As mentioned in his letter Wemyss, with the firm back- ing of the Committee, had already put his case for the Brookwood site to Edward Stanhope, the Secretary-of- State for War. Cambridge now withdrew his opposition, and Stanhope replied

'War Office
November 20th 1888
'Dear Lord Wemyss
'I presume that I am right in addressing myself to you, as the spokesman of the recent Deputation, on the subject of the request made to Her Majesty's Government by the Council of the National Rifle Association.
'That request I understand to be as follows: At a meeting of the Council of the Association a Committee had been appointed to inquire into the practicability of obtaining a Site in the neighbourhood of London for the Annual Meeting, and also to communicate with the Government as to their willingness to contribute a sum of money towards that object. You, however informed me that in the opinion of the Committee the matter had assumed a somewhat different phase owing to the offer from more than one locality to place land, free of expense, at the disposal of the Association; and that in the circumstances you would not feel jus- tified in asking for the assistance of H.M. Government in purchasing a Site for this purpose.
'You further went on to say that the unanimous opinion of your Committee, after careful personal inspection, was that Brookwood, in the neighbour- hood of Pirbright and Aldershot, was a Site suffi- ciently near London to satisfy your requirements, while in other respects it seemed to offer special advantages.
'Your object, therefore, was to ask me whether the War Office would be prepared to grant to the Association the use of the land for the annual Meeting, and possibly also to provide a permanent

range for the use of the Metropolitan Volunteers; and also whether in such case, the Government would be prepared to contribute £25,000 towards the preliminary expenses of the Association in establishing itself at Brookwood.

'I have now had an opportunity of carefully considering this request and of communicating with H.R.H. The Commander-in-Chief: and I am happy to say that he entirely agrees with me in welcoming the presence of the National Rifle Association at Brookwood, if, on further examination, the Site is found suitable for the purpose.

'The Association being of opinion that this Site satisfies the condition of being sufficiently near to London, there can be no doubt that great advantage would result from bringing the Volunteers and the Regular Forces into closer relation with each other at Aldershot.

I am therefore quite ready to take the necessary steps for carrying out this object.

'But I am not prepared to recommend to Colleagues that a contribution of £25,000, should be made out of the Public Funds to repay the expenses, which, as you state, the NRA may have to incur. They have hitherto been independent of any Government interference; and it is open to very considerable doubt whether, in the interests of the Association, and of the objects we all have at heart, they would not be wise in retaining their independent position, and in deriving their main strength from the confidence and support of the great body of Volunteers in this Country.

Believe me

Dear Lord Wemyss

Yours very truly

(signed) Edward Stanhope'

No doubt Wemyss was greatly disappointed by the Government's refusal to help fund the enterprise but otherwise he had gained the firm backing of the Secretary of State for War and was now able to include in his report dated 3 December a very significant statement regarding the Bisley site which was reflected to the Sites Committee Meeting held in February 1889.

'Till within the last few days I was led to believe, from unofficial but apparently reliable information, that exceptionally favourable terms would be granted to Volunteers by several of the great railway lines, in competition among themselves to obtain the advantage resulting from traffic incidental to a 'New Wimbledon' etc.'

'… but the place which seemed specially to be desired was the tract of Government land adjoining the Brookwood Station on the London and South Western Railway.'

The Bisley site, near Brookwood, so strongly advocated by Wemyss, had been discovered by Captain Hoey when he was sent down to inspect other sites in the area. The Earl, in his seventies but still retaining his old energy and drive, was able to put forward a variety of excellent reasons for this choice including the proximity of the site to Aldershot and the help already offered by the military authorities there through the War Department. It was also adjacent to the existing Pirbright military ranges. Another important factor was the necessity for good railway communication, as minuted in the 1888 NRA Spring Meeting report that also noted the involvement of managers of leading railway companies in the discussions.

The L&SWR too was in no mood to lose the traffic that had built up at Wimbledon and the Board (then having the title of 'Court of Directors') had already directed Charles Scotter to do everything in his power to secure the NRA business at a new site on L&SWR 'territory'.

The Association now moved rapidly to reach a final conclusion. Six different sites were still in the frame in mid-February 1889 and these needed to be whittled down by the next Council Meeting.

'Statistics on forms prepared by Major Page were received relative to the following sites, and were read; the objections offered by Members of the Committee being separately noted:

Berkshire

Brighton

Brookwood

Cannock Chase

Dunstable

Lewes

It was decided that a visit should be paid to Brighton by members of the Committee on Monday next.'

At the same time three major railway companies came up with their proposals for fares to be charged from London and these were discussed at a further meeting of the Sites Committee.

'Letters were read from Managers of Railway Companies indicating that the following fares from London and back would be charged in the event of sites on their lines being selected.

London and Brighton Railway
    To Brighton for Volunteers in Uniform, Competitors duly vouched for, Members of Staff, re, 5/- 1st Class 2/6 3rd Class.

The decisive outcome of the vote for a new site. The Chairman of the N.R.A. Lord Wantage and the Secretary, Edmund St John-Mildmay sign the minutes confirming Brookwood (Bisley Camp) as the chosen site for the National Rifle Association.

London and South Western Railway
To Brookwood for Volunteers in Uniform and Competitors duly vouched for 1/6 3rd Class, for Members of Staff, re - 3/- 1st Class.

London and North Western Railway
To Cannock Chase - Volunteers in Uniform 7/6'

Finally, on 27 February, the Council took the decisive vote on the three most favoured sites, Brookwood, Cannock Chase and Churn Down on the Berkshire Downs, the latter being of course on Lord Wantage's land. The vote provided an easy majority for the Brookwood site. Although a rearguard action continued for a short time the Winter General Meeting of the Association finally confirmed Brookwood (later to be known as Bisley Camp) as the chosen location.

On 8 August, at the half-yearly meeting of the L&SWR, R.H. Dutton, the Chairman, noted with satisfaction the intended move to the new site in his statement on the opening of the new Wimbledon and Fulham line.

'The new Wimbledon and Fulham line had been opened since July, and the results so far had been equal to and, indeed, had exceeded their expectations. The line traversed a beautiful country for building purposes. Roads were being made and other measures were being taken to push forward the erection of houses. They believed that this extension would prove a valuable feeder to their main line.

'Referring to Wimbledon, he might state, although the shareholders were probably aware of the fact that the National Rifle Association had met there for the last time. He was, however, glad to be able to tell them that after inspecting various places in different parts of England the Association had settled on a site which would be known as Bisley Common, on the company's line. They looked upon this matter as one of national importance, and he assured them that nothing would be wanting on the part of the company to make it a success.'

PART 2
BISLEY
1890-1998

CHAPTER 5

THE NATIONAL RIFLE ASSOCIATION AT BISLEY

The Opening

Initial plans for the Ranges were published in March 1889. These showed that the intention was to establish the main range on a westerly alignment which would have had the unfortunate effect of requiring shooters to fire into a setting sun by early evening. By May this had been rejected in favour of another short lived northerly alignment roughly similar to that finally accepted but including the possibility of shooting to a maximum range of 2,500 yards. By the time construction started in August the final layout had been agreed modifying the longest range to 1,100 yards only.

The 1889 Report of the Association gave details of the new site and the final arrangements made to develop it for shooting purposes. This alluded to the fact that, while much of the land belonged to the War Office, private owners had also to be approached as it was found necessary to buy parcels of their land to make up the required area. Most of these owners had refused to sell on this basis unless the NRA were prepared to purchase all or a large part of this land, usually at an inflated price.

'After long and anxious deliberation, the Council, as was announced at the Winter General meeting, finally decided on the adoption of the "Bisley Common" site for the future Annual Meetings of the Association. A large portion of the land to be used is the property of Her Majesty's War Department, but lands necessary to the use of the site have been bought by the Association at a cost of over £12,000. By the favour of the War Office, the military authorities have been permitted to assist the Association, and the work has been energetically advanced by Lieut.-General Sir Evelyn Wood, commanding the troops at Aldershot. A Company of Royal Engineers and working parties from regiments quartered at Aldershot have been, and are, engaged in raising the butts, and in making the tramway line. Major J.L.(*sic*) Brown, of the Royal Engineers, has been placed in charge of the works by

the military authorities, and continues to act there at the present time.

'The provision of ranges is as follows: A range of twenty-four long range targets, of which sixteen will be available to 1,100 yards; a range of ninety targets available to 600 yards; a range of twenty-four targets available to 600 yards; a range of twenty targets available to 300 yards; and two running deer or man ranges. Sporting Rifle and Revolver ranges will also be provided for, as may be found necessary. Should it be desired for special purposes, long ranges up to 2,000 yards or more could at any time be laid out.'

On 25 July 1889 Lord Wantage written to Sir Evelyn Wood, the Officer Commanding at Aldershot, acknowledging that Major L.F. Brown and a Field Company of the Royal Engineers would be available to go into Camp at Bisley in early August for the purpose of starting construction at the site.

'I have the honour to acknowledge receipt of your letter No 446 of the 23rd inst, stating that Major L.F. Brown, Roy: Engineers, will go into Camp at Bisley with the 11th (Field) Company) R.E. on the 9th Proxn , and I beg to state that I am taking steps so that Major Brown may be in a position to commence work at once on arrival in Camp, also I arrange for him to meet me at Bisley tomorrow the 26th inst.

'With reference to the last paragraph of your letter as to the manner in which the necessary funds for the payment of the Military Working party are to be provided, I am unable at present to give an answer to the question without further consideration – I may, however, observe that application will be made to the Secretary of State for War to provide out of Public Money for the troops employed at Bisley.'

Lord Cottesloe, who, as T.F. Fremantle, had been the Assistant Secretary of the NRA during the move to

Bisley, described the development of the Camp and Ranges in a 1951 article for the NRA Journal.

'Well do I remember my first view of the ground at Bisley. It was early in 1889; I went from London by train on a Sunday morning, walking from Brookwood Station to the Common. The general site had been selected, but details were as yet unsettled. A row of white flags indicated a suggested site for the main butt, running along the eastern side of the Hog-Lees ridge, almost at right angles to the direction of the present ranges, but this scheme was quickly abandoned. From the ridge the Common seemed wild enough; near by I flushed a greyhen; she must have been one of the last of her species to remain on the wild Surrey heaths which had given black game a home for centuries, and I never saw one there afterwards. Many deep-worn tracks, no doubt of horses and mules, were noticeable on the heathy ground, where men had crossed the open heath as seemed to them convenient; these have disappeared since that time.

'When I saw the ground again, at the very beginning of 1890, the scene had entirely changed. Working parties were coming daily from Aldershot, and the Royal Engineers were making the butts. The railway line, officially a tramway, from Brookwood Station to the camp, was under construction, and the R.E. were making the bridge which takes the road over it.'

'There was then a little group of houses on the road opposite the entrance to Brookwood Station, but otherwise no buildings on either side of the road which leads from it to the camp; the working parties, detraining daily in the station sidings, had made their own track thence across the bare heathy ground towards the canal bridge, and beyond it towards the camp.

'The general arrangement of the various standing buildings in the camp had been settled, and the site for the camp railway station selected, as well as those for

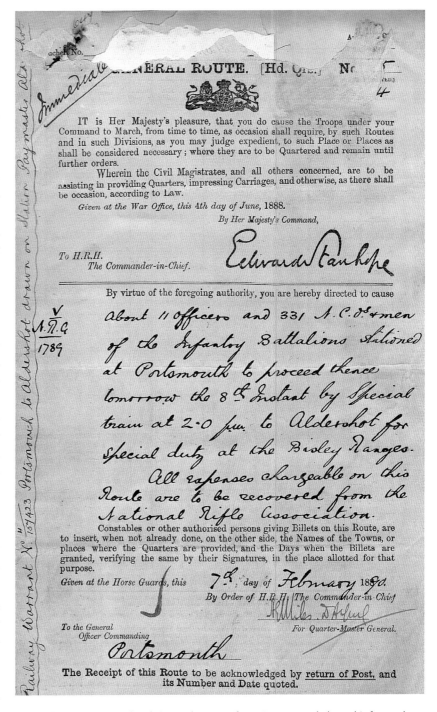

A travel warrant issued to bring volunteers from Portsmouth-based infantry battalions by special train to assist in the Bisley site development.

the offices and the refreshment pavilion. The buildings for these latter were the actual buildings which had for many years done service annually on Wimbledon Common; they were light constructions of timber, with roofing of stretched canvas, easily penetrated by rain; at Bisley they were re-roofed with a light temporary material. New buildings were necessary for many purposes.

'At Wimbledon the Victoria Rifles, the London Scottish, and other corps had had their own camps: these now established themselves on the new ground. The site for the Council Club, on the rising ground where it commanded a fine view across the valley to Chobham Ridges, was obvious. It was evident that the demand for accommodation for competitors would be large; at Wimbledon a great number of them had been able to lodge within a short distance of the camp, at Wimbledon or Putney, or to come daily from London for the shooting; at Bisley no lodging accommodation was available near the camp except the limited amount existing in the villages at a little distance from it. Blocks of wooden huts were therefore built to accommodate some forty competitors; clubs began to provide quarters for themselves; a few farsighted individuals erected their own huts; in such ways all made the best of the new conditions, with the cheerful co-operation to be expected from rifle enthusiasts.

'The first half of the year 1890 was a time of ceaseless hustle in the endeavour to complete all the arrangements for the meeting at the accustomed time in July. Much new equipment was needed, such as wooden chairs for register-keepers and for the great umbrella tent which had long been a feature of the meetings. A club building for the use of members of the Association was erected; a great improvement on the marquee they had used at Wimbledon. This building, like many others of the temporary buildings then erected, which were considered to be good for thirty years, is still serviceable enough. The umbrella tent reappeared, and for many years raised its high top opposite the club-house of the Army Rifle Association, but it was at least once blown away, and has long since been replaced by large marquees, which offer less temptation to the gales.

'The camp on Wimbledon Common was the model which it was natural to follow in making the layout for the new camp. There the Clock Tower, of great importance in giving the time for all the shooting, had always stood close to the office building, and, owing to the ground being flat and bare, it was in view from the firing points of all the ranges; it used to be said that the shooter did not need to carry a watch, as with his glasses he could always see the time. It was at first proposed to put the clock at Bisley in a similar position, but it was soon seen that it would be much better sited on the high ground between the long range and short-range butts, where it was visible from all the ranges, and there it stands to this day. The clock which had for so many years served at Wimbledon was superseded by a new one, which was the gift of Messrs. Gillett, of Croydon.

'The internal hedges of the camp enclosure were cut away except for a few hollies opposite the pavilion; the hedges in the perimeter of the camp which now remain were straggling, and the oak trees in them were small and looked scrubby, but in sixty years they have grown greatly and are becoming dignified. After the meeting of 1890, some shrubs were planted to hide the unsightly buildings of the lavatories; a row of trees was planted at the camp railway station, and by degrees more trees were planted and the lining of the roads with avenues began. The trees have prospered incredibly well, in spite of the sandy soil, and they have added much beauty to the camp in summer.

'The target accommodation at Bisley was nearly doubled as compared with Wimbledon. There were 24 targets on Stickledown, 16 of which were available to 1,100 yards; there are now 50, all used at 1,100, and about half of them at 1,200; at Wimbledon there were only 14 long-range targets. The fifty short-range targets of Wimbledon were represented by the ninety (since increased to 100) of the Ninety Butt. There were also the butts at Siberia, with their 24 targets available to 600 yards, and 20 to 300 yards. The small steam tram, as at Wimbledon, plied to and from the further ranges. There were ranges for the Deer and for the Running Man; for the latter there was also one on the top of Hog-Lees, but this disappeared very shortly.

'One rather difficult problem had to be dealt with. At Wimbledon it had been necessary to have in camp a large number of police from the Metropolitan Force, on account of the crowds which had free access every day after the hours of shooting, as well as for the whole of Sundays, and also to prevent people straying into danger on the ranges during the firing. There was vague talk of the possibility of the camp being invaded by roughs from Aldershot, and although there was unlikely to be at Bisley any such mass invasion by the public as had become habitual at Wimbledon, it was thought wise in the first year to have an ample force on the spot. Charge was for many years made for admission, but there has been little difficulty in the control of the camp, and the police required are now very few in number, although it is not possible to ensure the complete exclusion of undesirables.

'The long continuous firing points of the Ninety Butt at first caused some difficulty, since no range at Wimbledon had had more than ten targets, and now on the long firing point there was no conspicuous break to show the firer where he passed from one butt to the next. Also, at 500 and 600 yards, the lines of the poles carrying the wind pennants, which might be looked at diagonally as well as squarely to the butt, were apt to mislead the eye; this is still sometimes the case, for it is still not unknown for one new to the ground to fire at a target on the wrong butt. Going down to the 500 yards firing point on the Ninety Butt from which the Princess of Wales was to fire the first shot at Bisley targets a few days later from under a marquee, I found (for at that time I held temporarily the post of Assistant Secretary to the NRA) that the tent was being pitched diagonally to the proper line of fire, and was aligned on a target on a different butt; the mistake was, at that early stage, easy to correct.

'But it was evident that competitors might well be misled, and as they found error so easy to make, little signposts had for a time to be put on the firing points to indicate the targets proper to the firing points of each butt.

'There was a wet spell in the summer of 1890, and when I went down to live in the camp about a month before the meeting opened, the noise of the croaking of frogs was loud and continuous in the evenings. There were many wet places on the 500 and 600 yards firing points of the Ninety Butt, and heavy rain on one or two days of the meeting increased this trouble, which had not been unknown at Wimbledon. It looked as if it might be necessary to lay drains over much of the area, and guesses were made as to what the cost of doing this might be, some of which ran into very high figures. But fortunately, the solution of the difficulty proved to be unexpectedly simple. There is here, at a small distance below the surface of the ground, a formation known as the Bagshot Pan, a layer hard and impenetrable by water; this is only a few inches thick, and if it is pierced, any water it holds up escapes into soft soil underneath; the trouble was thus cured at very small expense.'

The new site at Bisley of course did not escape the attention of the major journals of the day and the *Illustrated London News*, published on 7 July described the scene.

'THE NEW WIMBLEDON AT BISLEY

'The National Rifle Association, which is so important as an auxiliary to the Volunteer Service, promoting skill in the use of the infantry weapon, holds its annual meeting, this year on the newly acquired camping-ground, with the ranges and offices there provided, on Bisley

A general view of the site in 1890 from the Running Man Range looking across the Ninety Butt Range. The Clock Tower and Camp can be seen on the right. In the right hand distance the embankment of the L&SWR main line can just be seen. The Running Man was moved to re-join the Running Deer in 1891. (*Illustrated London News*)

Common, near Brookwood, Surrey, instead of the old ground on Wimbledon Common.

'The Brookwood Station of the London and South Western Railway, a little over twenty-seven miles from London, is the first beyond Woking, and is adjacent to the extensive Cemetery of the London Necropolis Company, which lies to the left bank of the line. To the right, across the Basingstoke Canal, are Cowshot and Bisley Commons. with the tramway recently made to the new Bisley Camp station. The hills of Chobham close the prospect to the north-west. Our Plan shows the position of the Camp with the buildings. huts, and tents for offices, clubs, refreshments, police. bazaars. and exhibitions; the Magazine, the Clock Tower, the Signal Station, and the ranges and butts for shooting. The general view, represented in one of our Engravings, is taken from the Running Man Butt, looking in a south east direction towards Brookwood, and comprising only a rear view of the end of the great butts (at the 500 and 600 yds mid-ranges) a part of the railway, the Royal Engineers' Camp and other establishments, the Pavilion and the Clock Tower.

'The Great Butts, of which our artist gives a separate Illustration, are a quarter of a mile long, constructed of turf, with boards on the top, and are some 40 ft. high. They are divided into sections, numbered from six to fourteen, for the respective firing-parties. In front of the butts and parallel with them, runs the line of the Marker's Mantlets, a long covered gallery or verandah, open towards the Butts, and roofed with corrugated iron. Here the markers stand, in attendance on the targets, of which there are ninety-nine (sic). These are elevated, for the purpose of firing, on the top of the Marker's Mantlets, being raised or lowered by pulling ropes from below, similarly to the black boards used at stations of the Metropolitan to indicate the next trains. Whenever the target has been shot at, the man pulls it down, and pastes a bit of paper over the bullet-mark; he then raises it again, and everybody can see where the shot has hit the target. The firing-point for the long range of 1100 yards, and the Butts for that range, with targets numbered 2, 3 and 4, are shown in our plan; also the 200 and 600 yards ranges, the sporting and other short ranges, which need not here be particularly described.'

It had been hoped that Queen Victoria would agree to open the new Camp, just as she had opened Wimbledon thirty years before, but this time, much to the disappointment of the NRA, she declined. Lord Wantage reported this at the meeting of the General Purposes Committee held on 23 April.

'It was announced by the Chairman that Her Majesty would be unable to open the Meeting at Bisley. After discussion it was resolved not to have a formal opening but that the Prince and Princess of Wales should be asked to attend the Prize Distribution at the end of the Meeting.'

However, at the meeting held on 11 June, Wantage was able to report that the Prince and Princess of Wales had expressed their willingness to assist at an opening ceremony on the Saturday preceding the Meeting; a rough scheme was therefore prepared for the afternoon's proceedings. The official opening date was fixed at 12 July.

'Saturday was a day to be marked with a white stone in the annuals of the National Rifle Association. It was the day upon which the labour of many months was brought to a close, and the new camp, upon the laying out of which untiring industry, energy, and skill have been lavishly bestowed, was opened with all the ceremony appropriate to a Royal visit. The central point of interest in Saturday's proceedings was the arrival of the Prince and Princess of Wales, and that interest came to a climax when her Royal Highness, following the example set a generation ago by the Queen, pulled the silken cord attached to the trigger of a magazine rifle and scored an unquestionable bull's-eye. It was not until the ceremony was over that the mass of those who were present found time to make the circuit of the camp, and to form opinions with regard to its capacity. It will be convenient, therefore, to dispose of the Royal visit at once before attempting to describe the present aspect of the encampment. Waterloo Station was in a state of ferment all Saturday. Piles of luggage having a more or less military aspect. Volunteers in and out of uniform, and, if the truth must be told, endless confusion, were the signs of a great event in store; and those who were familiar with Wimbledon in the past will not be surprised to learn that above the babble

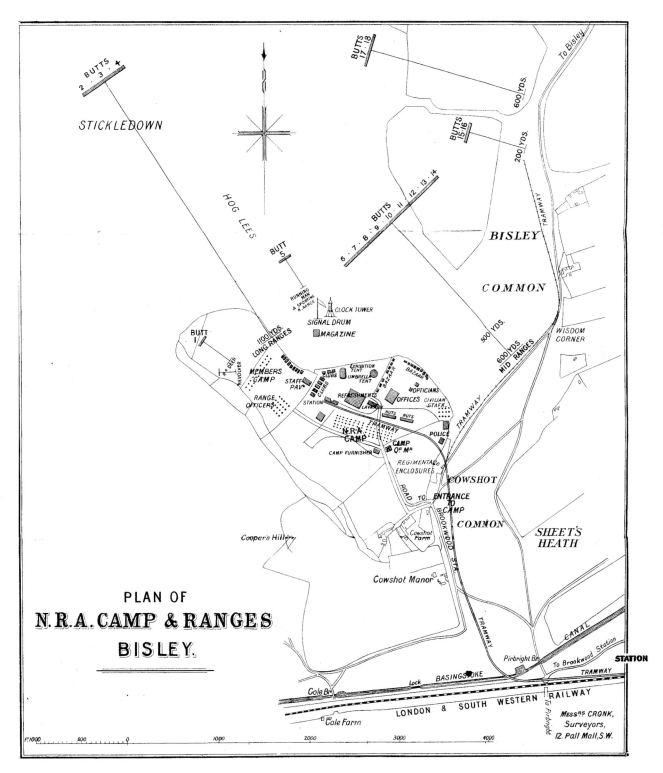

The 1890 Bisley Plan.

of voices the accent of riflemen from the land to the north of the Tweed was distinctly audible. Lord and Lady Wantage, with whom was Lady Jane Sanders, reached the camp shortly after 2 o'clock, and proceeded to the Cottage for the purpose of seeing that all was ready for the reception of the Royal visitors. Meanwhile, the pressure at Waterloo increased, for, in addition to the ordinary traffic, there were two special trains to be provided for shortly after 3 o'clock, however, the Royal train started, and made a

William Adams' Class O2 0-4-4 Tank Engine No. 185, especially named "Alexandra" and lavishly decorated, which brought the Royal Train carrying the Prince and Princess of Wales from Brookwood to Bisley Camp for the opening.

good journey to Brookwood, from which place it was brought by a gaily decorated engine, appropriately named 'Alexandra', to the Pavilion Station in the new camp. The other train, bearing a large company of guests, had arrived a short time before. The Royal party, followed by the distinguished guests, then proceeded to a temporary pavilion in a roped enclosure near the firing point opposite the great butt, 500 yards in length, which is the pride of the Association, and here it was possible to see who the visitors were. They were their Royal Highnesses the Prince and Princess of Wales, the Princesses Victoria and Maud of Wales, the Duke of Connaught, and the Duke of Cambridge. The Princess wore a dress of dark purple richly embroidered with flowers, and her daughters were dressed in fawn-coloured material.'

'The Princess advanced to a smaller awning at the 500 yards firing-point, in front of which was a rifle, well and truly laid by Sir Henry Halford and Captain Nathan, of the Royal Artillery, and fixed upon a rest. A bugle sounded, and the 90 targets at the great butt rose simultaneously. The Princess pulled the cord and the bullet sped upon its way to No. 12 target. All eyes

were turned towards the butt in expectation of the marker's signal, which, rising after a moment, showed that the Princess had made a bull's-eye. It would have been strange if she had not since Sir Henry Halford had fired more than one shot from the rest beforehand in order to make sure that all was right. The conclusion, foregone as it was, was received with prolonged cheers. In a few minutes Mr Hoey had the honour of presenting the carton to her Royal Highness, who was obviously pleased to find that it had been perforated almost in the centre of the black circle. To Mr Hoey the Prince addressed some kindly words of congratulation upon the excellence of the arrangements. The boys of the Gordon Home, well set-up lads, who promise to make good soldiers, were then signalled out for special honour, inasmuch as the Princess particularly requested that they might be brought up and presented to her.'

The Report for the year contained complete details of the opening of the Meeting and noted with much enthusiasm that the Queen had signed a Charter of Incorporation.

The scene shortly after Princess Alexandra, attended by Sir Henry Halford on her right and Captain Nathan (representing the Royal Laboratory at Woolwich and who had brought up the rifle used) on her left, had fired the first shot at Bisley from a .303 calibre experimental Lee Burton rifle provided by the Royal Laboratory. The Prince of Wales is standing within the tent behind Capt. Nathan. Halford holds the silken cord used to fire the rifle in his right hand.

'The Council have the pleasure of informing the Members of the Association that the steps referred to in the Report for last year as then being taken for obtaining a Royal Charter of Incorporation have had a successful result. Her Majesty signed a Charter of Incorporation on the 25th of November, 1890. This constitutes the Association a Corporate Body, in which all the property of the Association will henceforth be vested.

'Mr. Charles Scotter, General Manager London & South Western Railway, has been elected an honorary Life Member of the Association.'

The Early Years at Bisley

In the latter part of 1889, A.P. Humphry fulfilled the role of Acting Secretary, Mildmay having resigned after the 1889 Wimbledon Meeting. Humphry was offered the position but declined and it was then handed over to Lt. Col. Marsden, who had supervised the move from Wimbledon. However, after only a few months in the post, the latter resigned for personal reasons and the Association was forced to cast their net wider. They turned to their old colleagues at the Hythe School of Musketry and found a suitable candidate for the post in the then Chief of Musketry at the School, Col. William MacKinnon. He became the NRA Secretary in November 1890. In 1891, he awarded his Mackinnon Prize of £20 followed by his Challenge Cup in 1892. This was competed for by Teams of 'efficient' Volunteers from the home countries as well as several Colonies and is still one of the most important international competitions on the list. It is now open to any

Col William Mackinnon, Secretary of the National Rifle Association from 1890 to 1898, at Bisley in 1893.

other country whose shooting organisation is recognised by the NRA.

In 1891, Miss Winifred Leale of the Jersey Rifle Club became the first women to shoot in an NRA competition at either Wimbledon or Bisley. Having learnt from her father she now demonstrated that she could handle the fearsome kick of the Martini Henry rifle as well as becoming the object of curiosity and press interest after her considerable success in the *Daily Graphic* competition. Her efforts effectively opened the way for an increasing number of women to shoot competitively.

The Secretary of State for War, at the urging of the Council in 1891, approved a new competition with the object of letting the public see and practically test the

new .303 inch calibre Lee-Metford magazine rifle which had now been issued to the regular armed forces. Its use was permitted in the 1892 United Services Cup where the regulars, who were using the new rifle, won against the Volunteers who were still using the old Martini-Henry. Shortly afterwards the rifle was converted to a Lee-Enfield by substituting a new barrel with Enfield rifling, although this version did not come into general use at Bisley until 1896. This rifle became known as the 'Long Lee' after the introduction of the classic Short Magazine Lee-Enfield (SLME) in 1904 (In 1906 examples were test-fired at Bisley by members of the Council). The iconic Mark III version was introduced in 1907 and became the British Army's standard infantry weapon during the first half of the twentieth century. Volunteers, and later Territorials, shooting at Bisley continued to use the Long Lee up to the First World War however.

Just after the Annual Meeting of 1898, Col. W Mackinnon fell seriously ill. He resigned in November being unable to continue in office, and died in early 1899. His position was filled on a temporary basis by Capt. Matthews, the Assistant Secretary, but he was unwilling to take on the job of Secretary on a permanent basis due to other commitments. The Council then chose Captain Mayne, who had already been accepted as Chief Constable of Suffolk. The Council now had to turn to their second choice, Lt. Col. C.R. Crosse, who had acted as the Chief Range Officer for the previous eight years. Crosse quickly proved to be an outstanding Secretary in the twenty one years that he was to hold the post. He saw through the high noon of the Edwardian period and the lows of the Great War with great skill and diplomacy and he built up an excellent relationship with the London & South Western Railway, so important to the success of Bisley in those years.

Among other notable losses to the Association during this period were J. Rooke, the NRA's long serving Accountant who died at his desk on 1 June 1898; having been with the Association since the beginning and, in 1899, Captain Stewart Pixley, winner of the Queen's Prize in 1862 and an able Council Member for many years.

The outbreak of the South African, or 2nd Boer War as it became known, in 1899 rapidly exposed shortcomings in the British Army, including outdated training methods, some of which reached back to the Napoleonic Wars. The military authorities were still advocating the old 'Hythe' positions – firing from the kneeling or

PRIVATE D. DEAR, QUEEN'S EDINBURGH RIFLE VOLUNTEER CORPS.

THE WINNER OF THE QUEEN'S PRIZE AT BISLEY.

MISS LEALE,

THE LADY RIFLE-SHOT AT BISLEY.

NATIONAL RIFLE ASSOCIATION MEETING AT BISLEY.

The winner of the Queen's Prize, £250, with gold medal and yearly champion's badge, is Private Dear, of the 5th Company of the Queen's Edinburgh Volunteer Rifle Battalion. On Tuesday, July 21, in the final competition at long range, he gained the victory by one point, having scored altogether 269 out of a possible 330—namely, 188 in the first and second stages, 42 at 800 yards, and 39 at 900. Sergeant-Bugler Hill, of the 19th Middlesex, with a total score of 268, won second honours. Mr. Dear is thirty-one years of age, a native of Forfarshire, and is cashier and book-keeper to a firm of solicitors in Edinburgh. He joined the Queen's Edinburgh Volunteer Corps in 1885, shot at Wimbledon next year, and gained some prizes in 1888. Another member of the same corps—Sergeant Menzies—was winner of the Queen's Prize at Wimbledon eighteen years ago. It has not been, altogether, a very brilliant meeting at Bisley this year. One minor incident of novelty was the presence of a young lady, Miss Winifred Louise Leale, with the Jersey team of riflemen, taking her turn to shoot. When the Duke of Cambridge visited the camp, on Wednesday, July 22, and met Colonel Robbin, the captain of the Jersey team, his Royal Highness asked to be introduced to the young lady who had been competing with trained marksmen, complimented her on having done so well, and congratulated her on her shooting record. The Jersey team, with the Canadian, a Welsh, and an English team, on the previous Saturday, competed for the Mackinnon prize, at a figure target 400 yards distant, but were unsuccessful.

The Queen's Prize Winner for 1891, Private D. Dear and the first women to shoot in the Annual Meeting, Winifred Leale of the Jersey Rifle Club.

standing position – and the value of camouflage was generally disregarded. The 'untrained' Boer farmers, with their modern German Mauser rifles, who had honed their marksmanship skills from boyhood, were able to take on this professional army and inflict serious reverses on it in the field. The quality of their marksmanship made a deep impression on observers and the lessons were not lost on the NRA. On 3 January 1900, the General Committee agreed to an ultimately far-reaching Resolution that lead the way to a massive expansion in the number of Civilian Rifle Clubs in Great Britain.

'A discussion on the subject of Rifle Clubs then took place, and it was resolved on the motion of Major Fremantle, seconded by Mr. Whitehead,

'That the War in South Africa, having proved the great value of an irregular force of skilled marksmen for purposes of National Defence, the Council consider it very important that the formation of Rifle Clubs should be promoted throughout the Kingdom, with the special object of making rifle practice accessible to the general population and will be glad to afford every assistance in the formation of such Clubs and will welcome any suggestions in furtherance of this object.

'It was also ordered that this Resolution be notified to the public press at once.'

Towards the middle of 1900, Arthur Conan Doyle, the doctor turned writer who had become famous through his creation of Sherlock Holmes, returned from his voluntary mission to South Africa where he had not only re-honed his medical skills but managed to observe the successes of the skilled Boer marksmen against the British. His enthusiasm and support for the training of civilian marksmen in rifle shooting ran entirely in harmony with the aims of the NRA and he was invited to serve on the newly formed Rifle Clubs Committee, becoming instrumental in the setting-up of civilian rifle clubs. In the following year, he formed his own rifle

Lt. Colonel Charles Robert Crosse, Secretary of the National Rifle Association from 1899 until 1921. Photographed at Bisley during the July 1900 Meeting.

club based at his Hindhead home, Undershaw, which became affiliated to the NRA in 1901.

In 1902, Conan Doyle produced a paper on the formation of Civilian Rifle Clubs – 'Why you should form them & how you should form them' – and sent his hand-written draft to Crosse. In 1903, he held a rifle competition at his 'Undershaw' range which was eventually won by a strong team from the L&SWR. This event was regarded as of sufficient moment to be reported in *The Times*.

'Rifle Clubs and Sir A Conan Doyle
'The title which I have chosen deliberately is certainly not one which would have been selected by Sir A Conan Doyle himself. Yet the character of the interesting and important little scene that was enacted on Saturday on both sides of the ravine of Hindhead which leads up to Undershaw, Sir A Conan Doyle's house, was such as to show that credit is due mainly to his untiring energy for the practical success of a movement of considerable value to the nation. On the one side of the ravine was a rough and ready firing point, a little platform of turf sheltered from the rain, which seemed imminent but never actually fell, by a makeshift awning of canvas. Across the ravine, on ground the property of Mrs Tyndall, the widow of the late Professor John Tyndall, were four targets and a mantlet, distant 100 yards from the firing point. The targets were the well known Morris targets, with 4in. bull's eyes, so graduated in point of size that, to riflemen armed with weapons fitted with Morris tubes 100 yards were as 600 yards are to men using the service rifle and a full charge at Bisley targets; and the strong breeze which swept up the ravine from the right of those who fired, a 'three o'clock wind' in Bisley language rendered shooting difficult enough in all conscience. In scattered groups among the bracken and the heather behind the firing point were to be seen the champions of some 20 rifle clubs of Surrey, Sussex and Hampshire who had come to compete for the handsome challenge trophy, a silver statuette of a typical civilian rifleman, presented by Mr. Langham, whose hospital did yeoman service during the South African war, and for medals and extra prizes presented by the Morris Company. They came from Undershaw – where the club has a 100 members, most of whom had never handled a rifle before until Sir A. Conan Doyle founded the club, which he calls with honest pride, the 'Mother Club', - from Beefolds, where Mr. Brian Hook has done similar service – from Byfleet, Brightstone, Haslemere, Boyatt, Guildford, Albury, Merrow, Newlands Corner, Wotton, Shere, South Fulham, Epsom, Leatherhead, Blackmoor, Grayshott-Hall, and Portsmouth. Also the London and South-Western Railway sent on a team. The sharp detonations of the adapted rifles, some of them .303, others Martinis, most of them fitted with Kynoch's adapters, were heard all day. The teams, on the other hand, were not on view simultaneously – in fact, there would hardly have been room for them and the small gathering of interested

spectators – save at a luncheon provided in a neighbouring building by Sir A. Conan Doyle, where he addressed a few words to about 100 riflemen. The Undershaw team, consisting of Sir A. Conan Doyle, the landlord and the barman of the village inn, and a working electrical engineer, shot early in the competition and headed the list for some time. Firing two sighters each, and ten shots to count, they amassed the very creditable score of 162 without a miss or an 'outer'. Afterwards the Beefolds team, who at one time looked very like winning and shot remarkably well, reached the score of 161, and it was until later in the afternoon that the four champions of the London and South-Western Railway Rifle Club, one of whom made 48 with two inners, secured the custody of the trophy with a fine score of 163.

'But if the world at large is likely to be but faintly interested in the individual fortunes of these modest clubs, it is none the less undeniable that their existence, and the general average of the shooting, which was excellent, are matters of national and of even Imperial moment.'

In 1906, his first wife died and Sir Arthur Conan Doyle, as he had now become, made a decision to move from Undershaw making this competition redundant. He now presented the silver statuette to the NRA to be shot for in conjunction with a competition to which he had been asked to lend his name the previous year. This was duly acknowledged by the NRA Secretary.

'March 29th 1906

'My dear Conan Doyle,
'I am directed to acknowledge your letter of 19th inst., and to express the thanks of my Council for your kind offer, which they gladly accept, of a Silver Statue of a Civilian Rifleman to be shot for annually in the Competition which bears your name.
   Sir Arthur Conan Doyle
   Undershaw
   Hindhead
   Haslemere'

The Conan Doyle competition with the prize of the original silver statuette, as well as the Association's Silver Medal and a sum of money, still appears in the competitions list of the annual Meeting to the present day.

In 1903 the Palma Trophy competition was held at Bisley. Originally presented by the NRA of America to be shot for by international teams, it was won by the United States. However the American press published a story alleging that the American team had been equipped with more than one rifle for the competition. One of these was not the standard military weapon required under the rules of the competition as it had a special barrel differing from the military version, in having an increased number of rifling turns. This was the one used by the team. The NRA of America, after extensive investigations, found the allegations proven and forthwith declared the result null and void. The Trophy was returned to the Association who, however, only accepted it as custodians rather than as the winners by default.

The lessons learnt in the South African War had resulted in the complete abandonment of the Hythe standing and kneeling positions for riflemen. Lord Roberts of Kandahar, who had succeeded General Sir Redvers Buller in South Africa, had brought that war to a victorious conclusion by the application of new fighting techniques to match and overcome the considerable skills of the Boers. He was now a strong advocate of the use of accurate rifle fire over short distances from behind cover and proved to be a great supporter of shooting at Bisley and the Amateur Rifle Clubs which shortly sprang up all over the country. He also presented a Challenge Cup to the Association.

After his return from South Africa in November 1900, Buller had been put in command of Aldershot District where he had noted and complained of the 'unsoldierlike bearing' of Volunteers attending the Meeting that year. The Council now reluctantly agreed to make uniforms optional in competitions restricted to Volunteers but were able to reach a satisfactory compromise with the Commander-in-Chief, Lord Roberts, in that such uniforms were to be worn correctly.

Lord Cheylesmore, who had acted as an Association official at Wimbledon for many years, became a very active Chairman in 1903 and saw the Association right through to the outbreak of the Great War in 1914 when he took over as the Officer in Command of the School of Musketry which was established at Bisley Camp. He was also instrumental in rebuilding the fortunes of the Association after the end of that conflict. During his tenure of office, in 1906, he was able to realise his plan for the introduction of a Boys Camp to take place at the end of the Annual Meeting. This was designed for schools without cadet corps effectively opening competitive shooting on a much wider scale than the Ashburton Competition which was largely restricted to Public Schools.

During the same year Captain Barlow presented a pair of magnificent wrought iron gates to adorn the main entrance to the Camp. These were unfortunately removed in 1940 to assist the insatiable scrap-metal drive of the Second World War leaving their brick supports in lonely isolation to this day.

In 1904 the Duke of Cambridge died. He was succeeded by the Prince of Wales. There was, however a cause for great celebration that year when Edward VII made an official visit to the Camp on 22 July where he made an extensive tour including meeting many competitors from the Empire and presented the prizes.

This was the first visit of a sovereign since Queen Victoria opened the first Meeting of the Association on Wimbledon Common in 1860, which the king as a young boy had also attended. As Prince of Wales he had visited Wimbledon on many occasions since that date and had also, of course, opened Bisley Camp with Princess Alexandra firing the first shot on that occasion.

In the following year, at the suggestion of Cheylesmore, the Ranges were opened to boys from schools not having uniformed Cadet Corps. The Camp was run on military lines with the boys being exercised in drill as well as shooting. This camp took place in the week next but one after the closure of the Bisley Prize Meeting and twenty-four schools took part. It was inspected by Lord Roberts who expressed his decided approval and congratulations. The costs were largely covered by private subscriptions which included the King, the Prince of Wales and the Duke of Connaught.

King Edward VII at the Council Club on the occasion of his visit to Bisley Camp on 22 July 1905. On the left of the King is the Duke of Sparta, afterwards King of the Hellenes, and Earl Roberts of Kandahar respectively. Lord Cheylesmore, the NRA Chairman, stands at front on the right.

Towards the end of 1907, the War Office had produced a document which advocated the adoption of snap shooting and rapid fire in training for war. These principles were to govern conditions at Meetings where assistance was given from public funds. The principle of bullseye shooting was dismissed as of little use in spite of the lessons learned in the recent South African War. This decision was very strongly opposed by the Association who felt that this would grievously undermine the integrity of rifle competitions. Fortunately, the strong arguments put forward forced the War Office to retreat from this extreme position by agreeing a number of beneficial compromises.

A perceived threat to the very existence of the NRA occurred when, under the Army Reforms introduced by Secretary of State for War, Richard Haldane in 1907, the existing auxiliary forces (the Yeomanry and Volunteer forces) were to be combined (with effect from 1 April 1908) as a new organisation to be known as the Territorial Force. However the tact and diplomacy of Cheylesmore was of great assistance in overcoming these difficulties. This Force was re-designated as the Territorial Army in 1921 and Territorial Army and Volunteer Reserve in 1967.

The Rifle and Shooting contests of the 1908 Olympics were held at Bisley occasioning the opening of the Camp Tramway for the event. In respect of the competitions one still required standing and kneeling as well as lying down positions, the former two shooting positions had not been used in Great Britain for many years although the latter managed to achieve a credible sixth position.

Cinematograph photography had now come of age and several companies, from 1908 onwards, made application to the NRA to shoot commercial newsreels at Bisley, mainly in connection with the King's Prize.

The death of Edward VII on 6 May 1910 led the NRA to send an address of condolence to Queen Alexandra and the new king, George V. The late king had been

The Final Stage of the 1913 King's Prize on the Stickledown Range. The Clock Tower, transferred from Wimbledon, is centred on the ridge in the background. On the right a Cinematographer manipulates his bulky camera while behind a group of soldiers use a cart as a grandstand.

Patron of the Association from 1863 until his death and always took a keen interest in its affairs. Queen Alexandra replied with a short note of appreciation and an official Government response was received signed by the Home Secretary, Winston S. Churchill. Just a few years later, in late 1914 the Association mourned the death, at just under the age of ninety seven, of Lord Wemyss.

The Period of the Great War

On the outbreak of war in August 1914, the entire Camp was handed over to the military authorities for the duration. At the request of the War Office a School of Musketry was established primarily staffed by a Corps of Instructors who had been expert shots at Bisley in pre-war days and were not otherwise eligible for war service. They wore army uniform, and became the 'Bisley Wing' of the School of Musketry. Over the period of the War they imparted their skills to hundreds of Army personnel who became instructors in their turn, ultimately training several million men. Cheylesmore was appointed as Camp Commandant, with Crosse as his Staff Officer. Nearly all the peace time competitions were cancelled but a few new ones, directed towards the war effort, were introduced. The Camp also came to be occupied at various times by The Motor Machine Gun training centre, incorporating the Heavy Machine

A. Stone.   J. R. Barber.   N. J. Marriott.   J. King.   F. A. Biddle.   L. S. Davies.

F. A. Gould.   J. P. Somers.   P. W. Richardson.   J. Bostock.   B. Harmer.

The School of Musketry Staff at Bisley in September 1914. The Commandant, P.W. Richardson, later became Chairman of the NRA.

Gun Service, the Motor Machine Gun Service and a Machine Gun Cadet Battalion, as well as an Officer Cadet Battalion and various army units. A major result of all this activity was the construction of a large number of new huts in the main Camp area for training and accommodation. Some of these, however, appeared without proper authorisation leading to Crosse having to fight unwanted battles with the authorities. Another major addition took place in 1917 when an extension of the Camp Tramway line to serve the nearby Pirbright, Deepcut and Blackdown military camps was constructed. It was thought that this would bring great advantages to the Camp but unexpected difficulties arose in dealing with the military authorities and particularly the War Office. This resulted in some of the demands made on the NRA having to be legally challenged with the actual 'ownership' and distribution of revenue coming under close scrutiny.

The Great War took a heavy toll of Bisley shooters, probably the best known being A.N.V.H. Ommundsen, one of the most distinguished marksmen of the Edwardian era. He had won the King's Prize and St George's and was twice winner of the Grand Aggregate and is now regarded as one of the finest shots at Bisley. He was commissioned as a 2nd Lieutenant in the Honourable Artillery Company and was killed by shell fire near Ypres in 1915.

One of the units that set up a training camp at Bisley was the Heavy Section of the Machine Gun Corps, originally established in 1915, which became a major training facility for the weapons used by the new Tank Corps. In 1916 this unit, which was based on the Siberia Ranges, decided to use Stickledown for practice shoots using 6 pounder shells (for the type of gun used in the 'male' Mark 1 tank), albeit without explosives. This was without doubt the largest calibre that had ever been used on the Bisley Ranges and naturally caused Crosse considerable concern when these activities began to inflict damage to the Mantlets and Butts!

'May 27th 1916

'O.C.

'H.S. M.M.G.C.

'I note that you have erected on the 1000 firing point at Stickledown, platforms for firing your 6-pounder guns. I have not objected so far, but after yesterdays experience of your shell firing, I must draw your attention to the damage you will probably cause to our Mantlets. I have in our Office two shells taken out of the front of the Mantlet where they had penetrated nearly 3-feet.

'Would it not be better to move these guns to Siberia; it would be nearer your own Camp and on the Range allotted to you.

The Classic Buildings at Bisley

No new buildings, other than huts for accommodation, were constructed for the opening of the Camp but the three NRA prefabricated buildings that had graced the Wimbledon scene were brought to Bisley where they were re-erected and modified as necessary to make them 'permanent'. These were the Pavilion (1871), the Council Offices (1876) and the Staff Pavilion (1885). The last was renamed the 'Council Club' when re-erected at Bisley and was later greatly extended to offer additional accommodation. The Clock Tower was also re-erected, lasting until 1935 when it was replaced. A new Council Office building, which was to become the headquarters of the NRA, was constructed of brick in 1903 and the now redundant old building was made available for tenant use and still houses the famous firm of G.E. Fulton and Son as well as rifle clubs. George Fulton's son, Arthur, won the King's Prize on three occasions.

During the early 1890s Club Houses of a more permanent nature as well as so-called prefabricated 'huts' began to appear. Of all these 'huts' probably the best known was that of Walter Winans, the great American pistol shot, who had purchased it from the Ducker Company of New York. This was delivered and erected in 1891 at the same time as one for the English VIII Club which was supplied by the Wire Wove Waterproof Roofing Company. All the above still exist except for the Pavilion which had to be replaced in 1923 with a brick building on the same site.

Other noteworthy buildings included the Ladies & Members Club, later the Exhibition Hut, that appeared in 1891, possibly also of prefabricated construction. In 1908 the Dukka Hut (also by the Ducker Company) appeared and, in 1911, the Sit Perpetuum Hut which originated as a church in Byfleet. This building is probably of late nineteenth century construction when such corrugated iron churches were popular. In 1897 the Canadians erected their own club house.

The Council Club, previously known as the Staff Pavilion in Wimbledon days, newly erected at Bisley in 1890. It had been originally designed by a Member of Council and constructed on Wimbledon Common under the supervision of Capt. John Hoey, the Clerk of the Works, in 1885.

In 1898, during the July Meeting, the Association suffered a near catastrophic failure of the Camp mains water supply. The timely intervention of the L&SWR in supplying old engine tenders saved the day but the Council immediately put in hand measures to alleviate further problems. They asked a notable civil engineer, Arthur C. Pain, to advise on the best course of action. This resulted in the procurement of a large water tank, of 60,000 gallons capacity, from the Farnham Water Company, mounted on the top of a specially constructed brick base that was also designed to function as a store-room but is now occupied by a firm of Gun-makers. The tank was completed well in time for the 1899 Meeting and it now appears on maps of the Camp as a 'reservoir' and remains a feature at the northern end of the Camp.

Of all the Club Houses, probably the most notewor-thy is the present Macdonald Stewart Pavilion, the Club of the Canadian Teams to Bisley (also known unofficially as 'the Canadian Palace'). This was originally called the Canadian Hut when it was erected in 1897 and was built using mainly Canadian materials. The construction phase was unfortunately marred when Major Perley, a Canadian who had especially come over to supervise the project, died. The original pergola that dominated the centre of the roof has since been removed.

Originally all the buildings were owned by the NRA and leased to tenants. This was later changed so that the Association retaining the freehold of the land with tenants, mainly rifle clubs, erecting and owning their own buildings but leasing the land on which they stood. Most of the early buildings are now listed and form an interesting colonial 'village' with many of them retain-ing their original features including the characteristic external galleries.

The NRA at Bisley after the Great War

In November 1918, the Armistice had effectively terminated the Great War, thus permitting the annual Meeting to resume in 1919 with all the ranges re-opening except for Long Siberia. Of great significance was the decision to open the King's Prize to all comers, who had served in the Armed Forces, instead of being restricted to Volunteers and Territorials. Otherwise there was a very large reduction in competitors, compared with those attending prior to the war, partly due to a general revulsion against firearms but aggravated by a decision by the Railway Executive, though quickly revoked, not to allow reduced fares which were already subject to massive inflation as a result of the war. The Camp Tramway, along with the 1917 extension to the military camps at Pirbright, Blackdown and Deepcut, remained under War Office control until 1921, although the Camp Tramway service was restored for the duration of the Meeting, but the Range Tramway remained closed.

The vast quantity of redundant firearms left over by the War had forced the Government to bring in legislation controlling their use due to fear of revolution by the 'lower classes' who had now been trained to use them. This resulted in the Firearms Act of 1920 which required anyone keeping or carrying a firearm or ammunition to obtain a Firearms Certificate. For the purposes of the Act the NRA was considered to be a Club which enabled it to extend umbrella coverage to all Members of the Association and affiliated Rifle Clubs, who then only had to be in possession of their cards or badges certifying that they were bona fide members when in possession of or carrying firearms for target practice. This did not extend, however, to keeping firearms in their homes, which now required personal certification. Towards the end of the same year the Association officially recognised that the conditions under which they operated had greatly changed and a meeting of interested parties agreed that the Council should consist of ten members of the NRA as well as ten from the armed services (known then as the Imperial Services) and one each from Canada, Australia and South Africa respectively.

The Association suffered a great loss towards the end of February 1921 when Crosse died suddenly. Major C.E. Etches, who had been a prominent shooter before the war, was appointed in his place and was largely responsible for restoring much of the Association's fortunes after the low points experienced following the Great War and extending well into the 1920s. He retired in 1938 to be followed by Sir Alan Hunter. In 1925 Lord Cheylesmore tragically died in a motor accident.

In 1923, the over 120 railway companies that existed at the time in the United Kingdom were amalgamated into four new companies. The old L&SWR, that had given so much assistance to the NRA from its earliest days at Bisley, now became a constituent of the new Southern Railway but, fortunately for the Association, its General Manager was their old friend, Sir Herbert Walker, who had occupied the same appointment in the L&SWR. He was extremely keen on rifle shooting, always encouraging his staff to take up the sport. The old L&SWR prize was now replaced by the Southern Railway prize from 1924 but was shot for under very different conditions and Walker also awarded his own prizes to be shot for by railway staff.

During the same year it was decided to replace the old 'unhygenic and rat-infested' Pavilion with the red brick building on the same site opposite the Council Offices.

In 1926 a suggestion by Sir Lionel Fletcher for the re-opening of the Long Siberia Range and the repair and extension of the Range Tramway was considered. Rough estimates of the possible cost of such an undertaking were discussed and in view of the accommodation which would be available for 'unlimited' shooting on other ranges it was considered that the time had not yet arrived to take action in the matter. Long Siberia had only ever served as a 'Pool' Range and for Rifle Club and secondary competitions and lead a nebulous existence throughout its life. Although it was brought back into use during the 1930s and refurbished again after the Second World War, it then seemed to have gradually fallen into disuse and was finally abandoned in 1968. One of the reasons for its final demise seems to have been that it was no longer regarded as safe when some of the land in its danger zone was sold to a private buyer by the Ministry of Defence. However, part of the Range has since been re-opened as a sporting shotgun shooting ground.

The British Broadcasting Company, the direct predecessor of the present day Corporation, was formed in October 1922. By the following year wireless broadcasting was being demonstrated at the Annual Meeting of the Association which, thereby, came in on the 'ground floor' of this new technological development.

'We have to congratulate Messrs Malcolm and Joyce on a series of most excellent wireless demonstrations given during the course of the fortnight. During the first week their work was most troubled by 'statics' due to the high electrical state of the atmosphere – so much so that on one evening they were forced to forego an advertised concert. During the second week, however, conditions were good, and their demonstrations gave a great amount of pleasure to a large number of competitors and their friends. By the kindness of the British Broadcasting Company, your Editor was enabled, on the Wednesday evening of the first week, to broadcast a chat on Bisley from the London station, and it is hoped that this short talk enabled many thousands of 'listeners-in' to take a real and understanding interest in the reports that were appearing in the daily press. Bisley results were a part of the news items broadcasted from the whole of the stations during a greater part of the meeting, and there is little doubt that this most popular form of propaganda has helped materially to speed up the rapidly growing interest of the general public in marksmen and their doings. We trust we shall be able to make similar arrangements during the great Imperial meeting next year to keep all our distant friends informed of our doings.'

In 1928, the BBC inaugurated a regular commentary on the final stage of the King's Prize. Their outside broadcast van was connected to a temporary telephone line near the 1000yds firing point of Stickledown Range where the winner, A.C. Hale, was interviewed by Capt. E.H. Robinson, a Life Member of the Association, with both being perched precariously on the top of the van! This annual commentary on the final of H.M. The Sovereign's Prize became incorporated into the Empire Service which started in 1932, with a regular entry in the Association's Annual Report appearing thereafter for many years.

'The British Broadcasting Corporation very kindly arranged to broadcast a running commentary of the

The first outside broadcast from Bisley by the BBC. A.C. Hale being interviewed by Capt E.H. Robinson after winning the King's Prize in 1928. Robinson became the Editor of the NRA Journal when it was restarted after the War.

final stage of the King's Prize, on a wavelength which was audible throughout the Empire.'

In the 1950s there was some television coverage but only of the prize giving at the end of the Annual Meeting.

The year 1930 came to have some significance in the history of the NRA. Particularly noteworthy was the success of Marjorie Foster who became the first woman to win HM The Sovereign's Prize. Before the War shooting had become very popular with women however, at the 1919 Meeting there was only a single representative but Miss Foster's success re-kindled much of the old enthusiasm. Already highly regarded as a crack shot she went on to win more prizes and captain teams into the 1950s. Her success in the King's Prize attracted the personal congratulations of King George V in a telegram to Lord Jellicoe, the NRA Chairman. In the Report for the year the death of Conan Doyle was given some prominence, with an obituary recording his efforts in forming Rifle Clubs before the War. Lord Jellicoe resigned as Chairman at the end of the Meeting and Lord Cottesloe was appointed in his place. Another former Chairman, Lord Waldegrave who first attended Wimbledon in 1868 also died. In the following year, 1931, the distinguished shot, Arthur Fulton, who had won a DCM during the war, achieved a new record by winning the King's Prize for the third time. His first win dated back to 1912 and his second was in 1926.

Throughout the 1930s major developments were recorded with new target sheds being constructed to serve both Stickledown and the Long Siberia Ranges together with improvements to the telephones there. During the closed season from 1938 to 1939 construction of a new Sniping and Sporting Range took place on Hoglees, behind the Butts of the 200 yard Range, which included an automatic Running Bear facility. However use of this Range was not included in the list of competitions for the year and in any case its use was quickly curtailed by the declaration of war on 3 September 1939 and it was not until 1947 that it was eventually opened.

Major C.E. Etches retired in 1938. A tribute to him by the Council, recorded in the 1938 Report, noted that 'His tenure has extended over a long and difficult period of reconstruction after the Great War, and his unsparing efforts have contributed very largely to the restoration and increase of the Association's prosperity.' Throughout this period the Southern Railway, aided

and abetted by its General Manager Sir Herbert Walker (who retired in 1937), continued the fare concessions and sponsored shooting competitions at Bisley for the armed forces and for members of its staff. By the end of the decade Bisley had regained something of its pre-war character. In 1933, a poster proclaimed that the final of the King's Prize would be shot for by the hundred best shots from all parts of the Empire and that the massed bands of no less than four Regiments would entertain the crowds, with the Southern Railway offering cheap fares to all comers by all trains for that day. Throughout the 1930s large contingents of military personnel were brought in by train for Range duties during the Annual Meeting, quite often over substantial distances, reflecting the distinct revival in fortunes by the Association.

The winners of the 1938 China Cup parade their heavy trophy round the Bisley Ranges. This solid silver cup was presented to the NRA by the Shanghai Volunteers in 1864. In 1938 it would have been shot for by teams of Territorials each made up of six Riflemen and two Lewis Gunners in uniform. The trophy is now kept permanently in the NRA Museum at Bisley.

In those days, the Range Officers were made up of officers and senior NCOs selected from all three of the military services. At the July 1939 Meeting, however, the War Office had only been able to supply a fatigue, rather than the full working party normally used to assist in range and other duties, owing to the threat of war. At the outbreak of the war the Camp was once again handed over for military use.

A Small Arms School was immediately established at the request of the War Office and it was also found that the site offered excellent facilities for Home Guard training when this body was formed in 1940. The Small Arms School only lasted for a single year but the formation of a 'Local Defence Force' had been announced on 4 May and by June the familiar name of 'Home Guard' had been substituted. By 25 May, over 400,000 had been enrolled with almost 100,000 passing through Bisley Camp during the course of the year; by October the roll stood at 1,750,000. The Association itself would benefit when a proportion also took out membership. In the early days questions were asked in the House of Lords about why many of those who had gone to Bisley for training were being forced to pay for their own railway tickets, but this was quickly addressed. In that year the Bisley Tramway was again taken over by the War Office who proceeded to re-instate part of the old First World War military extension, but this time only as far as Pirbright Camp. A miniature Anti-Tank Range was also erected on the Running Deer Range. Although the Home Guard was disbanded in late 1944 the NRA were able to reap a valuable legacy from that organisation as they had now gained a large number of members with many more subsequently joining in order to maintain their old comradeships.

At the war's end, the Camp was in a rundown state with the debilitations of the war years resulting in a large backlog of maintenance. However, it was found possible to hold a token one day Meeting on 21 July 1945. In 1946 the full Meeting was held and the Tramway facilities were re-instated by the Southern Railway but without the pre-war fare reductions. By 1949 a start was made with the refurbishment of the Long Siberia Range whose targets and other butts furniture had been shot to pieces by machine gun fire during the war. By the following year, however, it was reported as being in full working order. In 1950 the Second World War military extension to the Bisley Camp Tramway was dismantled but the Tramway itself only lasted a further two years, being closed in 1952, with the replacement bus service lasting a few years thereafter as the bus company soon found it uneconomic, private transport and restrictions on the carrying of firearms having taken their toll.

The Southern Railway had become the Southern Region of the nationalised British Railways organisation in 1948 but the name of the Southern Railway competition remained and continued until 1962. However, a member, Major T. Anstey, who had been in charge of the Tramway closure ceremonies in 1952, sponsored a replacement competition in 1963 which was named 'The Bisley Bullet' after the old Camp Tramway.

Another link with the past finally came to an end in the 1970s. As the origins of the NRA lay in the Volunteer movement it had always been the custom to use the military titles of the competitors although there were civilian shooters from the earliest days. In the First World War, the vast majority had seen military service and the custom was continued after the Second World War which reinforced it for the same reasons. However, by the seventies, far more civilians with no military background were taking part and the practice ceased.

The Queen, the Patron of the NRA, visited the Camp on 15 July 1960 to celebrate the 100th anniversary of the first Meeting. She was met by the Chairman, Lord Tedder, (Marshall of the Royal Air Force Sir Arthur Tedder) and members of the Council. She was given an extensive tour of the site and Ranges where she was introduced to many of the shooters, including teams from the Commonwealth taking part in the Annual Meeting. She also took the opportunity to renew the Royal Charter of Incorporation that had originally been signed by Queen Victoria in 1890.

With the development and issue to the Armed Forces of the semi-automatic rifle in the new 7.62x51mm NATO calibre in the 1950s, and the resultant cessation of manufacture of the .303" cartridge, it became obvious to the NRA Council that at some point in the not-too-distant future the supply of .303in. ammunition would cease, and therefore it would be necessary to start using the 7.62mm NATO cartridge. As it was considered that the new military rifle was unsuitable for the style of target shooting that was popular throughout the former British Empire, strenuous efforts were made, not only in Britain, but also in Australia and Canada, to convert the existing rifles used for target shooting to take the

HM The Queen, inspects the Ranges at Bisley in the company of (l to r) a Council Member Major J. Crawford, the Chairman, Lord Cottesloe and the President, Lord Tedder on 15 July 1960.

new cartridge). These being the No.1 Rifle - the Short Magazine Lee-Enfield, the SMLE of the First World War; the No.4 rifle, the Second World War descendent of the No.1; and the No.3 Rifle, the P14 as made for Britain by several companies in the USA during the First World War.

Initial results were not encouraging. It was not just a case of removing the old .303in barrel and replacing it with one chambered for the new round, but otherwise identical in form to that being replaced. The new ammunition had different characteristics, both in pressure and velocity, which considerably affected the inherent accuracy of the rifle. In addition, it was found that the lighter bullet, with its very short length of 'parallel' to take the rifling, had to be made to tighter tolerances

to produce good accuracy. As the ammunition factories gained experience in the manufacture of this round and replaced old machinery this problem was eventually overcome to a great degree. Ammunition from various foreign manufacturers was tested, along with various designs and makes of barrel.

The eventual result of this experimentation was that for the 1969 Annual Meeting the 'Service Rifle Class b' in .303in. disappeared, and in its place was 'Target Rifle', in 7.62mm NATO calibre, with the Rules being amended to allow any bolt action rifle in this calibre, provided it was available in quantity, did not weigh more than 11½ lbs, and was approved by the NRA Council. So in addition to the converted .303s, there were now to be seen on the ranges rifles built on Mauser and various other actions, both of military and commercial design. Also, new purpose-built actions appeared, such as the Australian 'Sportco', the British 'TX1200' by Parker-Hale, and the eventually predominant 'Swing' rifle (and its derivatives), designed by George Swenson (an American), and his colleague Laurie Ingram. Swenson had started development of the 'Swing' rifle in 1970 with the first prototype becoming available in 1972. Geoff Cox used it to win the H.M. The Queen's Prize in 1986.

In 1975 Prince Charles became the Association's sixth President. He visited the Camp on 21 July 1978, where he shot on some of the ranges including the Running Deer and the 1,200 yards Stickledown Range where he received instruction in the use of the 'back position.' In 1980 he also shot for the House of Lords against the Commons in the 'Vizianagram' match, another competition dating back to the early 1860s.

By the 1960s, the practice of using the military ranks of shooters was fast dying out and the change over by the Army to the semi-automatic FN rifle effectively severed the military rifle links with the Association that dated back to 1860. Cutbacks in the armed services meant it was becoming more and more difficult to obtain range officers and other details including military bands for the Annual Meeting and these were replaced by paid civilian volunteers and shooters taking part in the various competitions. The competitions specifically for the armed forces continued however; one notable one, the China Cup dating from 1864, is still shot for by the Territorials. This involves teams of eight, six armed with military rifles and two, originally with Lewis machine guns, but replaced with light machine guns in later years.

The Centenary of the NRA at Bisley was celebrated in 1990 and this was marked by a special issue of the Journal which included supportive messages from Prince Charles and the Minister for Sport, Colin Moynihan. Special arrangements to celebrate the event were also made during the Annual Meeting.

The Camp Tramway from Brookwood had closed in 1952; however two main features of the line remained. These were the Cowshot Bridge and the substantial steel truss bridge across the Canal. The Cowshot Bridge, which belonged to the NRA, proved to be something of an albatross round the Association's neck until the early 1960s when it was taken over and then removed by Surrey County Council, partially at the Association's expense. The bridge over the canal, now owned by British Railways, was not removed by them until 1979. However the tramway was not finished with quite yet for in 1998 the Army commissioned a report into the feasibility of re-opening it along with the old military extension into the Camps at Pirbright, Deepcut and Blackdown. This noted that it would not be possible to re-open large parts of the original route resulting in the matter being dropped.

CHAPTER 6

THE GENESIS OF THE BISLEY COMMON TRAMWAY 1888-1890

At the Annual Winter General Meeting of the National Rifle Association, held on 28 February 1888 Lord Wantage, while addressing the reasons behind the required move to a new site, gave strong emphasis to the importance of good railway access.

'... One point ought, in my opinion, to be deemed essential, namely, that the meetings should be held on land owned by the Association. The immediate proximity of open land sufficient for Volunteer encampments on an extensive scale, and complete access by rail, are also, in my estimation, matters of vital importance...'

In the same year the Board of the L&SWR, acutely aware of the NRA's imperative needs, implemented exceptional measures in order to retain and develop the lucrative business that they had built up over the previous twenty eight years at Wimbledon. On 7 June, they passed a resolution that 'the General Manager be authorised to offer the most favourable terms to the Volunteer Rifle Association in case an application is made to the Company to establish a Camp at any place on this railway.' In order to actively promote this, Scotter skilfully prepared his ground by establishing an immediate alliance with Wemyss.

Obviously, nothing could be done in this consideration until possible sites on 'L&SWR territory' were identified. This was duly rectified in late October 1888 when Hoey was sent to investigate sites in the Pirbright area that had already been recognised. None of these proved satisfactory but he discovered nearby a suitable tract of Government land situated just to the north of the L&SWR main line and a short distance from Brookwood Station, some twenty seven miles south west of London. This was quickly reported to Wemyss and Scotter who met at Waterloo Station a few days later where they agreed a strategy that proved crucial to the selection of the Bisley site.

Scotter immediately followed this up with a letter laying out the return fares for Volunteers travelling to Brookwood. This proved to be a communication of the

The Spy Cartoon from Vanity Fair of Charles Scotter, General Manager of the London & South Western Railway at the time of the opening of the Bisley Camp branch who gave so much assistance to the NRA in establishing the Bisley site and tramway. (*Vanity Fair – Author's Collection*)

utmost importance as it laid down a fare which was maintained right up until the First World War.

'November 8th 1888
'L&SWR General Manager's Office
'My Lord,
'With reference to your Lordship's call here the other day.

'I think I may now state that provided the National Rifle Association select the site near Brookwood as their future encamping ground we should be prepared to carry the Volunteers in uniform at a fare of 1/6 each from London to Brookwood and back.

I have the honour etc.
Chas. Scotter

The Right Hon:
The Earl of Wemyss and March
23 St James' Place
S.W.'

This was followed up by a further letter from Scotter, dated 15 February 1889, to the Sites Committee of the Association which stated that:

'With reference to your letter of the 13th instant, I beg to inform you that we should be prepared in case the National Rifle Association select the Brookwood site for the annual Rifle Meeting to convey (i) volunteers in uniform, return ticket London to Brookwood, third class 1s. 6d. each; (ii) competitors duly vouched for, but not in uniform, on production of the Association Voucher, return ticket third class 1s. 6d. each; (iii) Members of the Council and Staff on production of Voucher, return ticket first class 3s each. In like manner tickets would be issued at these rates from London to Brookwood and back during the time of the Meeting.'

At this time the Council had also received notification from two other major railway companies, the London, Brighton & South Coast and the London & North Western, regarding the fares that they proposed to offer to Volunteers. Comparing them left little doubt about the preferred choice of site with the offer by the L&SWR being by far the lowest.

Minutes of NRA Committee Meetings at this period indicate that the L&SWR, when the Bisley decision was confirmed, had agreed to build a new station on the high embankment of the main line about three quarters of a mile due south of the chosen site and about a half mile west of Brookwood Station. At a meeting with Scotter on 4 April, Wemyss raised the prospect of a branch line to connect the proposed station with the new site.

'Mr. Cronk reported that he attended at the South Western Railway Office at Waterloo Station on Thursday the 4th inst, by appointment, to meet Mr. Scotter at 4 o'clock. Lord Wemyss also attended. Mr. Scotter however was detained at the House of Commons before a Committee, and Lord Wemyss and Mr. Cronk then went on to Messrs Bircham & Co's Offices, where Mr. Scotter was.

'Lord Wemyss brought the matter of the laying of a branch line from the Railway to the Ranges in view of the new Station. Mr. Scotter however seemed to think it was impossible to do it, as not only were there engineering difficulties, but the cost would be very great, and the line would be of no use to the General Public, as the Company could not run their Main Line Trains into the Ranges and that the General Public would have to stop at Brookwood Station.

'Mr Scotter also stated that if they were to make a line, suitable for carrying Passengers, the Board of Trade would compel them to have expensive signals and accessories and to make the line altogether the same as an ordinary line.'

Scotter however, after this apparent dismissal of Lord Wemyss' proposal, had immediately applied his team to the development of an alternative scheme that would come to fulfil the objectives of both parties in a mutually satisfactory manner. This new proposal, produced in less than four weeks, made unique use of the Tramways Acts in order to avoid the necessity for 'having expensive signals and accessories', and became the basis of the plan essentially adopted; in the process effectively defining a 'Light Railway' in all but name seven years before the Light Railways Act of 1896.

In the middle of these negotiations the L&SWR arranged a special train for the carriage of senior officials of both the Association and the railway company to visit the site. This was fully reported in *The Times* of 20 May.

'Bisley Common

'Although for various reasons the National Rifle Association will this year return for the last time to Wimbledon in order to hold its annual meeting, the character of the site which has been chosen for future operations has already become a thing of public interest. It was therefore in no unhappy moment that the general manager of the London and South-Western Railway conceived the idea of inviting a party of visitors to go down, as the guests of the company, and survey with their own eyes the Wimbledon of the future. Saturday was the day chosen for the expedition, and the invitation given was generally accepted. A special train left Waterloo at 10.45 a.m. bearing the chairman of the company, the Hon. R. Dutton, the deputy chairman, Lord Wantage, the popular chairman of the Council of the National Rifle Association, Mr. Hoey and other officials capable of explaining the exact nature of the proposals made by the company on the one hand and the National Rifle Association on the other. The first practical question to which an answer will be expected has regard to the time expended on the journey under existing conditions. From Waterloo to Brookwood, proceeding at a pace by no means hazardous, the special train ran in 45 minutes. From Brookwood Station to Cowshot Manor, in the neighbourhood of which the centre of Bisley camp will be, a visitor can walk in about 20 minutes. It was explained however that even this slight exertion will not be required of those who attend the meeting. A supplementary station will be built a little lower down the line than Brookwood, and a tramway will receive the Volunteer as he detrains, and will carry him to the bottom of the hill, upon the summit and slopes of which will stand the offices of the association and some of the principal lines. In short, there is no question but that, as far as time is concerned, the new Wimbledon will be at least as accessible as the old.

'After the nature of the proposed arrangements had been explained with equal courtesy and care, the individuals composing the expedition returned to Brookwood where they were hospitably entertained at luncheon by the South–Western Railway Company. Various toasts were proposed, and speeches were made by the chairman of the company, by Lord Wantage, by the deputy-chairman, and others, after which the party returned to London.'

Although it was being stated publicly that a new station would be provided on the embankment near Brookwood Station, with a tramway to the Camp running from the bottom, things had already moved forward significantly and, at a meeting between the NRA and the L&SWR, held at Brookwood on 3 May, Scotter personally drew up a summary of the latest proposals and this was included in the minutes of the Bisley Common Committee Meeting held on 21 May.

'The following Minute of a Meeting with Directors (sic) of the London and South Western Railway was reported; the Minutes having been drawn up by the General Manager of the Line.

May 3rd 1889

Lord Wantage	}	
Mr Hoey	}	National Rifle Association
Mr Cronk	}	

Mr Scotter (General Manager)	}	
Mr. Macaulay (Secretary)	}	
Mr. Galbraith (Consulting Engineer)	}	South Western Company
Mr. Andrews (Resident Engineer)	}	
Mr. Verrinder (Superintendent of the Line)	}	
Mr. Haines (Solicitor)	}	

'Attended at Brookwood today and considered on the Ground the best mode of effecting interchange both for Passengers and for Goods between the Company's Railway and the Tramway proposed to be made by the National Rifle Association, when after considering various schemes which were proposed, it seemed to be agreed on all hands that the most convenient plan would be that the Association should enter into negotiations with the various parties interested, with a view to bringing the Tramway by a bridge over the Canal and across the Public Road on the level, and then to carry the Tramway up and as near to Brookwood Station as possible and as far as may be on land belonging to the Company, the intention being that the terminus of the Tramway shall be as nearly as possible on a level with the Railway, so as to afford the readiest means of interchange and of effecting a physical junction between the Railway of the Company and the Tramway of the Association.

'With a view of getting the necessary Survey sections, plans and estimates made, the Company promised to assist the Association with an experienced Engineer for the purpose, free of cost.

'A separate Estimate to be prepared as to the cost of the Tramway from a point immediately on the Northern side of the Canal to the Brookwood Station, and the Company would be prepared to consider their contribution towards such cost from a liberal point of view, and with the object of relieving the Association of any cost in respect of construction or in respect of acquisition of land whether belonging to the Company or under offer to them by the Necropolis Company. The Association would at once get into communication with the necessary Authorities as to crossing the public road with their Tramway on the level'

At the same meeting, the Chairman read a letter from the War Office which confirmed that Royal Engineers would be made available to assist the Association in laying out the Ground which included that part of the Tramway belonging to the Association.

At a meeting of the Committee, held on 20 June, the L&SWR's completed plans were tabled by Cronk.

'Mr Cronk attended with the plans submitted by the London and South Western Railway Co for the proposed tramway. The General Line as proposed, but without branches, was approved and Mr Cronk was asked to take all necessary steps for the acquisition of such lands as were required.'

The Bisley Common Tramway Order

In October 1889, belatedly, the Council, advised by their Solicitors, Messrs Markby, Wilde & Johnson, moved to secure a Provisional Order for construction of the Tramway. On 30 October, Humphry wrote to the Solicitors requesting that the necessary steps be taken to obtain the Order. – 'Lord Wantage authorises me to request you to take the necessary steps for obtaining a Provisional order for the Tramway at Brookwood, as to

the details of which Mr Cronk will no doubt be able to give you all the requisite particulars, or to obtain them shortly.'

It was not until late into the first half of 1890 that any progress was made in obtaining the necessary Parliamentary Order authorising the construction of the Tramway and in fact the provisional National Rifle Association (Bisley Common Tramway) Order was not received by the Board of Trade until 21 June, a mere three weeks before the opening!

On 7 May, Major F.A. Marindin, the Inspecting Officer for the Board of Trade, wrote an interim inspection report on the L&SWR works at Brookwood in connection with the new Tramway, including various alterations to the main line station, and he also took the opportunity to observe progress on the latter.

'Secretary of Railway Dept
'Board of Trade
'When inspecting today a new Siding at Brookwood on the London & South Western Railway I was shown the works in progress for the new Tramway or Railway to the Camp of the National Rifle Assn at Bisley. –

'This Tramway has no facing junction with the main line of the L & S West. Rly, but it terminates at the back of a new platform which is being constructed at the west end of the up main line platform.

'A footbridge is being erected between the up and down platforms, and other alterations and additions are in progress at the Station.

'The Tramway, which upon the South side of the Basingstoke Canal, is the property of the L.S.W Rly, is joined and consists of several sidings, as it passes through the Railway Company's Goods Yard, and upon the plan which was shown to me, no provision has been made for signals, safety points, and other safety appliances which are considered necessary upon a passenger line –

'I understand that the line is to be worked by an Engine, but I am not aware whether it is to be considered as a Railway or a Tramway.

'It is desirable that this point should be settled as soon as possible, for if it has to be passed as a Railway for passenger traffic, then considerable alterations to the plan shown to me will be necessary.

'The Bridge carrying the line across the Canal is an important work being a girder bridge of over 100ft span.

F.A. Marindin
7/5/90'
Board of Trade - Bisley Common
Tramway Order

This was quickly passed on to Charles Scotter, who then returned a plan of the terminal arrangements at Brookwood. The new line might have been classed as a Tramway but it was not that straightforward, apparently!

Shortly afterwards Messrs Cronk, the NRA's Land Surveyors, wrote to the Board of Trade stating that the new line should be ready by the beginning of July while an internal memo at the Board of Trade confirmed that the Order authorising the line was before Parliament. Just after this Scotter sent a plan of the point locking arrangements installed at Brookwood accompanied by a technical letter of explanation. The Board of Trade was not familiar with this style of locking and made some pertinent comments in an internal memo.

In respect of the legal aspects things were moving rather slowly. A Council Minute of 11 June noted that a draft lease from the War Office of their land crossed by the NRA Tramway had been submitted and that Lord Wantage had promised to see Sir R. Thompson on the subject.'

This was the month before the Tramway was due to open and it contained paragraphs that needed to be contested! Wantage, therefore, found it necessary to write to the War Office seeking clarification on these points.

'To the Permanent Under Secretary of State for War
'Sir,
'I have the honor to refer you to the draft of a Lease of Easements for a Tramway proposed to be laid down over the War Office land near the Brookwood Station.

'I would respectfully point out that the term of six months notice for terminating the lease might prove highly inconvenient to the National Rifle Assocn and I would venture to ask that the term be extended to twelve months at least.

'I would also venture to point out that the clause which provides that the Tramway should not at any time be worked save by steam power may also prove

inconvenient - the provisional order now in course of sanction by Parliament and which has been adopted by the Board of Trade provides for the use of animal power, the use of other power being dependent on authority from the Board of Trade. I submit that the question of motive power may be left to the Board of Trade. With regard to the Clause requiring the consent of the Secretary of State for War being given 'to carry goods or merchandise', I beg to submit that the purposes of the Assocn will require sound carriage of Goods and supplies for the Camp, and it would therefore be desirable to have this provided for.'

The lease was finally dated 17 November 1890 but backdated to 1 January 1890. In the lease, the War Department granted the National Rifle Association the right to build, maintain and use a Tramway between Brookwood Station and Bisley Camp. The part of the Tramway between the Basingstoke Canal and a point just short of the camp station was constructed built on land leased by the War Department to the Association for a term of 99 years. During the lease, it was required that the tramway would be maintained and worked in accordance with the National Rifle Association (Bisley Common Tramway) Order, 1890. The lease was at a nominal rental, with a provision that either party might be determined on the one giving the other 12 months notice.

In 1952, in order to close the Tramway, Solicitors acting for British Railways had to unravel the agreements and legal aspects under which the Tramway had been originally constructed. A short paper was produced which sought to clarify the position (The reference to the area of land *'shown in red on the plan'* refers to the land transferred in 1895 from the NRA to the L&SWR under the terms of the 1895 Agreement).

'The Branch, which was known as the Bisley Common Tramway, was constructed under powers contained in the National Rifle Association (Bisley Common Tramway) Order, which was confirmed by the Tramways Order Confirmation (No 1) Act, 1890.

'By a Deed, dated 17th November, 1890, The War Department leased to the promoters for 99 years an area of land, shown edged green on a plan attached to the Deed, for the purpose of constructing the tramway on terms which included the payment of a yearly rental of 10/- and provides for the determination of the Lease by 12 months notice on either side.

'By a conveyance dated 15th March 1890, from the Trustees for the Holders of Debentures of the London and Hampshire Canal and Water Company Ltd. to the promoters of the Bisley Tramway Order the Promoters were authorized to construct a girder bridge over the Basingstoke Canal to carry the tramway. In addition, an area of land, shown in red on the plan attached to the Conveyance, was conveyed to them, the Promoters paying £400 in respect of the terms of this conveyance.'

(*Peter Harding - Dennis Cullum Papers*)

On 12 July a letter from Andrews, the L&SWR Resident Engineer, to Cronk was read to the Committee giving estimated costs of the proposed light railway. That from the North side of the Canal to the terminus in the Camp was estimated at £2300 (the portion assigned to the Royal Engineers), and that of the L&SWR's portion from Brookwood Station to the North side of the Canal was £1800.

There now arose some concern about who was to pay for the Tramway as the meeting with the Railway Company on 3 May had only secured a vague commitment from the latter 'to consider their contribution towards such cost from a liberal point of view.'

'It was agreed that Mr Cronk be requested to see Mr. Scotter, and let him understand that the NRA consider that the Railway Company mean to pay for the whole expense of the light railway in consideration of the NRA not holding the Company to their engagement to erect a station on the high embankment and to contribute £2000. Also to tell Mr. Scotter that we think that the organization of the Railway Company had better be used for arranging for and making the Line, the NRA appearing as principals so far as may be required.'

On 24 July Cronk reported that 'A provisional order from the Board of Trade would be necessary before the light railway could be constructed. Lord Wantage undertook to write to General Hutchinson to expedite his passing the plans with a view to such order.'

He also reported that 'there were certain doubts as to the ownership of certain land in the course of the light railway.'

However, this brought from the Board of Trade a quite unexpected point-blank refusal regarding the planned level crossing; surprising in view of the 'Tramway' status of the proposed line.

'The Committee were informed of the refusal of the Board of Trade to sanction the crossing of the public road near to the Canal by the proposed light railway on a level crossing. They also learned that the Engineers of the London & S.W. Railway were engaged in laying out another plan for the portion of the line affected by the above refusal.'

The new plan involved the construction of a bridge over the road although the Railway Company refused to accept the cost as this part of the Tramway was the responsibility of the Association. Such an expensive development was unwelcome to say the least as the finances of the Association were already stretched to the limit!

On 23 October a Meeting of the Bisley Common Committee reached agreement on paying the cost of the military working parties on the Bisley site and a report was made on the division of responsibilities that had been finally agreed at a meeting held at Waterloo Station between the Committee and the L&SWR's Board, which included the General Manager and his team.

'The general position of the Association with reference to the London & SW Railway Company as regards the construction of the tramway from Brookwood Station to the Camp was discussed.

'Lord Wantage stated that 2½d per man per day would have to be paid for Working parties henceforward, to induce the men to volunteer, and that the Secretary of State for War had stated his inability to defray this charge. The number of men now offered by Sir Evelyn Wood is such as to bring the total of this payment to about £25 per week up to the end of January -

'It was agreed that the Association should pay this charge.

'The Committee proceeded to Waterloo Bridge Station to discuss the subject of the construction of the Tramway, at Bisley Common with the Board of the London and South Western Railway.

'It was ultimately agreed on both sides that the Railway Company should construct the tramway from Brookwood Station to the north side of the Canal, the requisite land from the point at which the tramway diverges from the Railway line up to the North side of the Canal being provided by the Association; and that the Association should construct the tramway from the North side of the Canal to the Camp, the Railway providing the road materials (but not ballast) for this portion of the tramway and contributing further the sum of £1000, to the Association. A written agreement carrying out these provisions was drafted in the room, which it was agree should be signed on behalf of both parties.'

The L&SWR Terms of Construction & Maintenance of the Tramway were agreed at a Meeting held at Waterloo Station on 23 October 1889:

'Meeting at Waterloo Station
23rd October 1889

Lord Wantage	}	
Lord Wemyss	}	
Major Flood Page	}	National Rifle Association
Major Knox	}	
Mr. Humphry	}	
Mr. Cronk	}	

Mr. Portal	Director	}	
Mr. Guest	Director	}	
Mr. Mills	Director	}	
Captn Johnson	Director	}	
Col Campbell	Director	}	South Western Railway
Mr. Scotter	General Manager	}	
Mr. Macaulay	Secretary	}	
Mr. Bircham	Solicitor	}	
Mr. Galbraith	Consulting Engineer	}	
Mr. Andrews	Resident Engineer	}'	

'The Railway Company
To make Tramway from a point as near as practicable to the Brookwood Station and to be defined by the Railway Company to a point immediately north of the Canal as shown the line colored blue on the Ordnance Sheet – submitted and thereon marked Scheme B.

'The Association
To put Railway Company in possession of land necessary for purpose from the northern boundary northwards to the point immediately north of the Canal and shall free of cost to the Railway Company arrange with the Canal Company for power for the Railway Company.

'The Railway Company
To contribute £1000 & to provide permanent way materials (exclusive of ballast) for the Tramway up to the point D on the plan for one line of rails. The Tramway from the northern boundary of the railway to its termination to be the property of the Association & to be maintained by them, as much of the Tramway as is constructed on the Railway Company's property remaining the property of the Railway Company and to be maintained by that Company.

'The Railway Company
To be at liberty to deviate the Tramway so far as the same may be on their land if at any time they should find it necessary to do so, making good the connection.'

On 30 October Humphry wrote to Frederick Macaulay, the L&SWR Secretary, regarding the charges for carrying the military working parties, who were to construct the Ranges and much of the Brookwood-Bisley 'Tramway', between Aldershot and Brookwood.

'I should be much obliged if you would be good enough to obtain for me a statement of the rate which will be charged by your Company for carrying the military working parties to and fro between Aldershot and Brookwood; the information being necessary to enable us to estimate our probable outlay for works.
'I take it that the total charge will be treated as matter of account as against the contribution of £1000 which your Company was good enough to give to this Association.'

On the same day Humphry wrote another letter to the L&SWR, this time to their solicitor, Sam Bircham, expressing some concerns about the routing of the 'Tramway.'

'I am asked by Lord Wantage to write to you with reference to the fact that this agreement which it is proposed should be entered into as regards the tramway from Brookwood station to the Camp contains nothing to the effect that a physical junction is to be

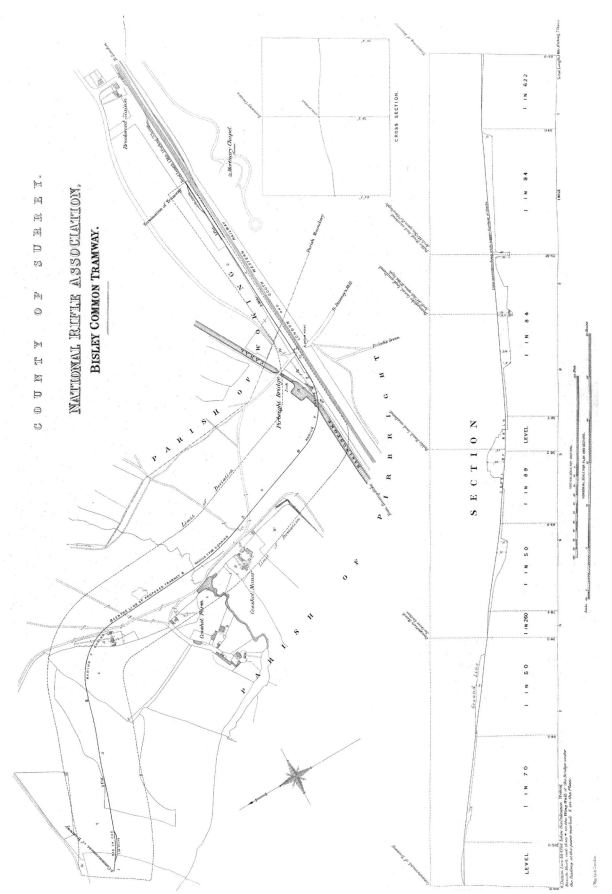

The Parliamentary Plan for the Bisley Common Tramway. The route is shown as stopping short of Brookwood Station and this lead to a letter from the N.R.A. to the LSWR expressing their concerns. (*Parliamentary Archives*)

made between the tramway and the railway of the L&SWR Co. Such a junction was contemplated by the Railway Company, as shown in the minute of a meeting between representatives of the Railway Co. and of this Association.

'Lord Wantage thinks this point of importance as it affects the possibility of running from the railway line over the tramway into the Camp without breaking bulk.

The ordnance sheet, which I have to thank you for sending me is not explicit in this; the tramway as there shown stops considerably short of Brookwood station.'

This was followed by another letter to Bircham dated 8 November which sought clarification of the Tramway Agreement between the L&SWR and NRA.

'The agreement respecting the proposed Tramway at Bisley together with the Ordnance Map, and your letter of 2nd November has been submitted to the Council of this Association. They have no objection to the general terms of the agreement as further explained by your letter, but they think that the map should contain some indication of the course of the Tramway to the Brookwood Station and of the junction which it is proposed to make there with the railway line; also of the proposed subway. These matters might if necessary be drawn on a plan of larger scale; at present we have no very clear knowledge of the details of the connection to be made between the railway and the tramway.

Otherwise we have no wish to delay the completion of the agreement.'

Things were now approaching the stage when larger military working parties from Aldershot would be needed. Major R. E. Brown, the Officer who was in charge of the work at Bisley including construction of the Tramway north of the canal bridge, wished to increase the size of the site working parties and had presented his opinion to Humphry who, in turn, passed them on to Scotter in a letter dated 4 December.

'Major Brown thinks he may want larger military working parties shortly to be carried between Aldershot and Brookwood, but says '900 men will require two engines to the train, more men than that will require two trains for which there is not siding accommodation at Brookwood.

'I suppose that the necessity for 2 engines would not be an obstacle; as regards the feasibility of running two trains, perhaps you will kindly let me hear what can be done.'

On the same day he wrote to Major Brown regarding both this and materials for the Cowshot Bridge.

'I am communicating your wishes as to bricks and the time for their arrival to Mr Cronk; and am writing to Mr Scotter, the General Manager of the L&SWR, to ask what can be done by way of trains for increased working parties.'

The NRA Report for 1889 carried a brief account of the activities.

'By the favour of the War Office, the military authorities have been permitted to assist the Association, and the work has been energetically advanced by Lieut-General Sir Evelyn Wood, commanding the troops at Aldershot. A company of Royal Engineers and working parties from regiments quartered at Aldershot have been, and are, engaged in raising the butts, and in making the tramway line. Major J.F. Brown in charge of works.

'The London and South Western Railway, who are constructing a portion of the tramway, and providing permanent way material for the remainder, are making important enlargements at their Brookwood Station, and have promised to contribute £1,000 to the general expenses of the Association.'

Civilian contractors had, in fact, taken a large share of the work and especially on the more specialist parts of the tramway such as the laying of the track. In such cases it had been arranged that NCOs under Major Brown would supervise their civilian counterparts and the tramway was in fact laid by a Basingstoke firm, Messrs Buchanan and Richards, who brought up materials in horse drawn wagons over the completed sections. John Faggetter, a well-known local builder, constructed the platform wall for the original Pavilion Station in Bisley Camp.

Canal Wharf, Basingstoke,

15 *March* 1890

Engineers Dept

**Dr. to The LONDON AND HAMPSHIRE CANAL,
AND WATER COMPANY (Limited).**

Folio _____

March 8	To freight on	65	tons	Ballast	1/	3	5
10	" " "	40	"	"	1/	2	
12	" " "	66	"	"	1/	3	6
13	" "	65	"	"	1/	3	5
18	" "	50	"	"	3/6	8	15
		28 6				20	11

Rec April 25 1890

Canal Manager

The Invoice from the London and Hampshire Canal and Water Co for the freight of ballast over the Basingstoke Canal for the Tramway.

12, PALL MALL, LONDON, S.W.,
AND SEVENOAKS, KENT.

No 141   24 Apr 1890

Certificate *of Advance in*
respect of Bisley Common
at Woking *in the County of* Surrey.

We hereby Certify *that the Sum of* Twenty Pounds
eleven shillings
is due to The London & Hampshire Canal and Water Co Ltd *of*
Basingstoke *in the County of* Hampshire
in settlement of
~~Builder, on~~ *Account for* ~~Building~~ Freight of Ballast *for the*
~~according to Plans and Specification prepared by me, and approved of by~~
Tramway &c at Bisley Common ~~and subject to the Terms and~~
~~Conditions of Contract entered into the~~ ~~day of~~ ~~188~~

£ 20 = 11 = 0   Cronk

Cronk's Certificate regarding the freight of ballast, via the Basingstoke Canal, for the tramway.

Local Builder John Faggetter's Invoice for construction of the platform wall for the original Pavilion Station.

The Invoice from Messrs Buchanan & Richards of Basingstoke for laying the Tramway track.

The ballast for the tramway, and other materials of a similar nature, were brought up on barges along the Basingstoke Canal directly to the wharf adjacent to the site of the tramway canal bridge.

The move of plant from Wimbledon was also being dealt with by the L&SWR. The planned dates were contained in a letter dated 7 February from Humphry to the L&SWR Goods Manager, Charles Owens (who was later to become General Manager of the L&SWR in succession to Scotter).

'With reference to your letter of 5th inst. I am afraid we cannot begin immediately to move our plant from Wimbledon, but I am endeavouring to push matters on, and hope we may be able to effect the move between the 24th inst. And 15th March.'

Rooke, the NRA Accountant, confirmed these dates to Owens in a following letter dated 10 February and by May, Humphry was asking the Railway Company to define the terms for operating services to the Camp, including setting up the necessary fare arrangements.

At the 27 March meeting of the Bisley Common Committee a letter was read from General Hutchinson which insisted upon the tramway line being fenced. Lord Wantage also reported that the General Manager of the L&SWR undertook to provide an engine and carriages fitted with continuous brakes. During the following meeting, on 9 April, it was agreed to award the fencing contract to Messrs Bayliss & Co.

'Agreed that Bayliss & Co's tender, No 3, for wire fencing at 9½d per yard for materials, less 2½d discount, and 3½d per yard for fixing, be accepted.'

On 20 May Humphry wrote to E.W. Verrinder, the L&SWR Traffic Superintendent, an optimistic letter regarding the possibility of running direct trains to Brookwood or Bisley Camp from other parts of the country.

'I am obliged for your letter respecting fares from stations in Hampshire which I am forwarding to Major Holbrook.

'It has been suggested that it would be a convenience to competitors coming from the North, if it could be arranged for carriages for them to be run straight past London to Brookwood - or better still right into the Camp - without the necessity to change and drive across London from their terminus of arrival to Waterloo. Probably a large enough number of men would travel from, say Glasgow and Liverpool to make this worthwhile, if it can be arranged, and others doubtless would join at stopping stations on the way. Perhaps you would let me know if anything of this kind is feasible. The date of travelling would be Sat 12th July. Something of this kind might also be useful for the return journey, but the men will return at more varying dates.

'I should be glad also if you would let me have an idea of the times of running of trains which you propose for the time of the meeting between London and Brookwood.'

On 28 May he was also asking the L&SWR, through Scotter, the terms for working the new Bisley Camp Tramway.

'I am desired to ask you upon what terms the London & South Western Railway would undertake to provide the necessary Engine or Engines and Carriages and generally work the tramway line connecting Brookwood Station and the Camp, so arranging to meet every train arriving at and departing from Brookwood.

'I am also desired to request you to arrange if possible for persons to be able to book for the tramway journey and also for admission to the Camp from any station on the London & South Western Railway or at least from Waterloo Station, at the same time as they pay their fares for the railway journey.'

This resulted in a meeting being called at Waterloo Station on 9 June which was chaired by Scotter and supported by Verrinder and Andrews. A 'Memorandum of Interview' was drafted and discussed at the Council Meeting held on 11 June.

'Railway and Tramway:
'A memorandum of the arrangements made at an interview with the General Manager of the London

and South Western Railway, at which Col. Marsden, Mr. Humphry, Mr. Fremantle, and Mr. Cronk were present, was read.

'It was proposed by Sir H. Halford,

'Seconded by Sir H. Wilmot, and carried,

'That the arrangements entered into with the London and South Western Railway of which notes have been read, for working the tramway and as regards train service, be approved.'

'The Text of the Memorandum of Interview

'The question of working the Tramway at Brookwood was discussed and it was agreed as follows.

1. Only one class for passengers on the Tramway.
2. One fare 3d each way.
3. London and South Western for this year to supply Engine and Carriages to work the Tramway traffic at half the gross Receipts.
4. L.&S.W. will supply Booking Box for Brookwood Station.
5. National Rifle Association to supply Booking Box or Offices at their Station on the ground.
6. The fares to and from London and South Western Stations to include Railway journey only to and from Brookwood.
7. National Rifle Association to arrange for issuing and collecting tickets for the Tramway at their Station and the South Western Compy to arrange for the issue and collection of Tramway tickets at Brookwood Station.
8. South Western will supply train of not less than five coaches and van.
9. Tramway to be worked so as to meet, as far as possible, all the up and down London trains.
10. Tramway to be worked between the hours of 8am and 8pm.
11. Suggested that fares to the public should be from London
    5/- First Class Return
    2/6 Third Class Return
12. London and South Western will arrange for a Special train to run through from London to Brookwood between 2 and 3pm and to return between 6 and 7pm.
13. London and South Western will supply tickets for the Tramway printed

Brookwood to Camp
Camp to Brookwood
And numbered consecutively.

14. London and South Western will lend for this year to the National Rifle Association two ticket dating stamps.'

Before this meeting, on 4 June, Mr Cronk had been instructed to ascertain what signals were necessary for the trains, and to arrange for their provision; however this proved unnecessary owing to the tramway status of the line. On the same date, he was also able to tell the Board of Trade when the Line was expected to open.

'4th June 1890
The Secretary, Board of Trade
Whitehall,
S.W.
Sir,

<u>National Rifle Association</u>
<u>Bisley Common Tramway</u>

'We beg to inform you that we hope to have the Line completed and ready for opening by quite the beginning of next month and we shall be glad if you will kindly arrange for the inspection about that date.'

On 25 June it was minuted that the Princess of Wales had consented to come to Bisley with the Prince on Saturday 12th and to open the Camp by firing the first shot; a rough scheme had been completed and the NRA became extremely anxious about the necessary inspection so that it would be ready for the visit of the Prince and Princess of Wales. A letter, dated 28 June, was sent to Captain Maxwell of the Royal Engineers who had responsibility for the Tramway with a similar letter to Cronk.

'The Chairman is informed that the Tramway has not yet been passed by Colonel Hutchinson and Colonel (sic) Hutchinson is waiting to be informed by the National Rifle Association when the Tramway from Brookwood to Bisley will be ready for his official inspection

'Are you in a position to name a day for Colonel (sic) Hutchinson's inspection of the Tramway, with a view to it being used by the Prince and Princess of

759

12 Pall Mall East
London SW.
& Board Room,
Waterloo Station L&SWR.
London SE.
30th June 1890

We hereby undertake that the single Line between Brookwood and Bisley Station shall be worked with only one Engine (or two coupled together) such Engine or Engines to carry a Staff.

Wantage.
Chairman N.R.A.

G. P. Humphry
Secretary N.R.A.

Ralph H. Dutton. Chairman of the London & South Western Rly Co.

Geo. T. Macaulay. Secretary of the London & South Western Rly Co.

The NRA and LSWR jointly sign the undertaking to operate the Bisley Camp Tramway under the 'one engine in steam principle'. (*National Archives, Kew*)

Wales on Saturday the 12th July? Lord Wantage has an appointment with Mr Scotter at Waterloo Station on Monday at 1 o'clock.. (Hutchinson's rank was in fact Major-General !).'

'June 28th 1890

'Dear Mr. Cronk,

'Lord Wantage has a meeting at Waterloo Station on Monday at 10 o'clock with Mr. Scotter in reference to arrangements for the 12th of July. I was directed by his Lordship to enquire today to Capt. Maxwell to know if the Brookwood Tramway is in a position to be officially inspected by Major-General Hutchinson with a view to it being used by the Prince and Princess of Wales on the 12th. If you

have any information you had better come here on Monday and see Humphry.'

It was not until October 1890, long after the Tramway had opened, that the outstanding problem of the right to cross Government Land was resolved. This was announced at the first meeting of the Bisley 'Ways and Means' Committee held on 10 October.

'Lease from War Office of the right to traverse Government Land settled. The sum of £442 deposited in Court will be recovered as soon as the offices of the Court are open. Accounts will be completed as soon as possible.'

Major-General Hutchinson was able to carry out his inspection almost immediately, dating his report 9 July, just in time for the Royal visit. The report sanctioned the issue of a Provisional Order with a re-inspection to take place when certain conditions had been fulfilled.

'Railway Department
Board of Trade
Whitehall
London SW
9th July 1890

'Sir,

'I have the honour to report for the information of the Board of Trade that in compliance with the instructions contained in your Minute of the 19th ultimo I have inspected the Bisley Common Tramway for the construction of which the National Rifle Association have applied for a Provisional Order now waiting for confirmation by the Legislature.

'This tramway (or more correctly speaking Tramroad) commences on Pirbright Common on land held by Trustees on behalf of the National Rifle Association & thence passes across the common over the London & Hampshire Canal and over the Road from Pirbright to Brookwood into land belonging to the London & South Western Railway, whence it is continued parallel and close alongside the Railway to Brookwood Station, where it terminates at the back of the up Platform, which has been enlarged to afford the necessary accommodation.

'The total length of the line shewn on the deposited Plans is 1 mile 17 chains but it has been lengthened at the end by 10.3 chains to extend it up to the Platform at Brookwood Station so that its total length as constructed is 1 mile 27.3 chains.

'The line is single throughout, with the exception of a loop at the Camp Station for the engine to run round its train, and of another loop at Brookwood station, where also there are siding connections. There is likewise a siding connection near the Camp station for the conveyance of Stores into the Camp.

'The steepest gradient on the line has an inclination of l in 50 and the sharpest curves (of which there are two) have radii of 7 chains each.

'For the first 1 mile 1.89 chains, the permanent way is laid with flat bottomed steel rails in 24ft lengths, weighing 68lbs to the yard, fished at the joints and secured to rectangular creosoted fir sleepers 9ft by l0in by 5in (of which there are 10 to each rail length) by dog spikes and fang bolts, one of each, on each side of the rail at each sleeper.

'The ballast is of sand with a topping of gravel.

'For the last 25.41 chains, the permanent way has been laid with the London & South Western Company's Standard Pattern.

'The works on the line consist of

(1) An over bridge in brickwork of sufficient width between the abutments for a single line.

(2) A bridge over the London & Hampshire Canal of 108.5 ft, on the skew, the square span being 54½ feet; each abutment consists of two cast iron cylinders, 5 ft in diameter, filled with concrete and brickwork connected at the top by a wrought iron stringer girder; the main girders are of wrought iron with top and bottom booms connected by triangular bracing with wrought iron cross girders and rail bearers, the latter being in the form of troughs. Behind the cylinders brick retaining walls have been built to support the embankment.

(3) A bridge over the Pirbright & Brookwood road of 29ft maximum span, constructed with brick abutments carrying wrought iron main and cross girders.

'The works appear to have been all substantially constructed and to be standing well. The girders have sufficient theoretical strength and gave moderate deflection when tested.

There are no tunnels and no level crossings of public roads. The fencing is wire.

'A small station has been put at the Camp Terminus and another one at a short distance from it close to an occupation Crossing.

'Additional siding accommodation has been provided at Brookwood station and a footbridge has been provided to give access between the down platform and that portion of the up Platform which will be used by the Camp Trains.

'The locking of the points at the Camp Station and of the siding connection near it is done by means of the key forming part of the staff to be carried on the engine by which the line will be worked.

'At Brookwood station a new cabin has been erected in connection with the new line. It contains 16 working levers and 3 spare ones. The principle of route locking has been introduced into this cabin as a means of diminishing the number of levers and for securing facing points. In this case there are 4 sets of facing points, 2 sets in each direction and in place of 4 locking bar and bolt levers, as would be usually required, 2 route locking levers and 2 locking bars only are needed. There are treadles used in connection with the arrangements and until these treadles have been passed over by a train for which a Signal has lowered, no change of points can be made. This may prove inconvenient in the event of a Signal having been lowered in error, as it would involve sending a man to actuate the treadle before the error could be corrected otherwise I see no fault to find with the system which is well worthy of a thorough trial.

'The only requirements I observed in the course of the Inspection are as follows.

1. The planking between the rails of the under bridges should be covered with ballast as a protection against fire.

2. The wire fencing should be properly completed.

3. The occupation Gates should be hung so as to open only outwards except when the line is closed for the season when they should be shut across the line.

TELEGRAPHIC ADDRESS :
"SIGNALMEN," LONDON.
TELEPHONE No. 7068.
1885.
GOLD MEDAL.
INTERNATIONAL INVENTORS EXHIBITION,
LONDON.
GOLD MEDAL & SILVER MEDAL,
INTERNATIONAL EXHIBITION.
ANTWERP.
FOR RAILWAY SIGNALS AND SAFETY
APPLIANCES.

L. & S. W. R.
8612
19.8.90
ENGINEERS OFFICE, BISHOPSTOKE

London, 5th August 1890.
N.W.

Messrs Cronk.

12 Pall Mall S.W.

TO SAXBY & FARMER.

1890.	Bisley Common.					
	Tram Station & Victualling Siding.					
	To					
2	Ground Locking Apparatus,					
	Each with 2 levers = 4 Levers @ 4/10/		18	.	.	✓
2	Annetts Locks	7/5/		5	10	.	✓
1	Staff with key attached			1	.	.	✓
2	Large special timber						
	Frames.	7/10/		5	.	.	✓
	Flooring 6' 5 x 4' 6 x 1½ thick						
	with handrail & standards.			2	17	9	
	Flooring 6' 0 x 6' 0 ditto			3	12	3	
	Excavations 6' 0 x 6' 0 x 1' 6 deep			3			
	= 2 5/10 Cube	4/		14	8	
12	yds. Point Connections						
2	Facing point Locks						
	with 21 ft. Bars.	8/8/9/		17	17	6	
2	Tie plates 7' 0 x 12 x ½	30/		3	.	.	
7	Point adjusting screws	10/		3	10	.	
6	W. I. flat cranks 9" x 10"	12/		3	12	.	
2	Flat Compensators						
	each 18" long.	14/		1	8	.	
	Carried forward £		80	1	3	
				79	18	3	

Messrs Saxby and Farmer's Invoice for the interlocking at Bisley Camp Station that Scotter refused to pay.

COWSHOT FARM.

Train heading towards Bisley Camp with the Cowshot Bridge in the distance. (*Illustrated London News*)

4. The platform at the Camp station should be lengthened so that the whole of the loop may be utilized for loading and unloading trains without moving them backwards or forwards.

5. The ballasting of the line requires completion.

6. Gauge ties should be supplied round the sharp curves of 12 chains radius.

7. The interlocking of some of the levers in the Signal Cabin requires correction.

'The line is to be worked by only one engine in Steam or two coupled together at one and the same time; such Engine or Engines to carry a Staff. An undertaking to this effect signed on behalf of the National Rifle Association and of the London & South Western Railway Company (who are to work the line), was handed to me, but I gave it back in order that it might be sealed with the Company's seal (the National Rifle Association have no seal).

Subject (1) to the above requirements being at once complied with (2) to a re inspection taking place when they have been reported to have been complete (3) to the receipt of the undertaking as to the mode of working the line; and (4) to a speed not exceeding 15 miles an hour being observed in running round the curves of 7 Chains radius, I can recommend to the Board of Trade to sanction the Bisley Common Tramway being opened for Passenger Traffic.

I have etc.
(sgd) C.S. Hutchinson
Major General
R.E.'

Messrs Saxby and Farmer had provided the levers and general point apparatus at the Pavilion Station but the L&SWR refused to accept a proportion of the charge for this equipment presumably as this was regarded as part of the section of line belonging to the Association, being within the Camp. Col. W. Mackinnon, the newly appointed NRA Secretary, duly notified Messrs Cronk of this decision.

'13th November 1890

'Dear Gentlemen

'In reply to your letter on your application to the Manager South Western Railway for payment of a portion of Messrs Saxby and Farmer's bill. It would appear that nothing further can be done in the matter; as Mr Scotter declines to accept the charge. We have paid Saxby and Farmer's account on your certificate.'

On 9 July Hutchinson reported favourably on signal alterations carried out at Brookwood Station in connection with the Bisley Tramway and recommended their use. The following day a Board of Trade internal memo confirmed Hutchinson's view that the Tramway might be sanctioned for opening. The memo also confirmed a speed limit of 15mph on two sharp curves. (In later years the speed limit was reduced to 10mph throughout with a further restriction to 5mph at the Cowshot Crossing).

Hutchinson carried out a further inspection at the beginning of September noting that, although the station platform had been lengthened in line with his requirement, it needed the addition of a ramp. In early November Cronk wrote to say that this had been completed.

The Order confirming that the Tramway had been certified as fit for public traffic was finally issued in September.

The Cowshot Bridge.
The Bridge erected at the behest of the Board of Trade to avoid a level crossing. In the background the Tramway can be seen inclining up the embankment of the L&SWR main line towards Brookwood Station. The tiny 0-4-0 locomotive, truly a figment of the artists imagination, should have represented an Adam's 0-4-4 Class O2 Tank Engine! The ownership and maintenance of the bridge was to have repercussions for the N.R.A. over seventy years later and long after the Tramway was dismantled. (*Illustrated London News*)

DRAFT.

R. 8986

The Board of Trade hereby certify that the undermentioned [portion of the] Tramways authorized by the *National Rifle Association (Bisley Common Tramway) Order 1890*, which was confirmed by the Tramways Orders Confirmation (No. 1) Act, 1890, has been inspected by Major-General Hutchinson, R.E., C.B. the officer appointed for that purpose by the Board of Trade, and that the said [portion of] Tramways are [is] fit for public traffic (that is to say)

A Tramway 1 mile 17 ch. or thereabouts in length, commencing on the portion of Pirbright Common, known as Hoglees, passing thence across the said Common, over the London & Hampshire Canal, & over the road from Pirbright to Brookwood, & alongside the London & South Western Ry., & terminating at the Brookwood Station of the London & South Western Ry. Co.;

And the B. of T. also hereby consent to the use of steam power on the said Ry. for a period not exceeding seven years from the date hereof; provided that the speed of trains travelling at the two curves of seven chains radius shall not exceed 15 miles an hour

Signed by order of the Board of Trade this 10. day of Sep 1890.

Sd R. Giffen
Assistant Secretary
to the Board of Trade.

J. & M. 200 9—84
9785

The draft authorisation of the Tramway by the National Rifle Association (Bisley Common Tramway) Order 1890 confirmed by the Tramways Orders Confirmation (No 1) Act 1890. (*National Archives, Kew*)

CHAPTER 7

THE BISLEY CAMP TRAMWAY AND THE LONDON & SOUTH WESTERN RAILWAY 1890-1922

The opening of the Camp gave the *Volunteer Service Gazette* much to report and it laid considerable emphasis on the tramways. The issue of 28 June 1890 contained an article on the new Camp and Ranges with the new 'tramways' being described in some detail.

'A branch railway from Brookwood Station will run right up to the middle of the camp enclosure, close to the Pavilion, and one is here close to everything except the Queen's ranges and the 'permanent ranges', which during the NRA meeting, will only be used for the Mullens' and other 'field firing' competitions. And to these (the Queen's and permanent ranges) the old Wimbledon Tramway will take the competitors

and visitors from the entrance to the camp in a very few minutes.'

In the Issue for 12 July the *Gazette* commented on the 'Tramway' status given to the Bisley Camp branch.

'….the branch from Brookwood to the Camp is called, we observe, a 'tramway', but to the untechnical eye it appears to be a carefully constructed single-line railway of the ordinary type.'

Although the general arrangements for the opening Meeting seemed to have gone well there was a problem with reconciling the tickets sold and fare collection at

Adam's O2 0-4-4 Tank Engine Number 185 *Alexandra*, taking water at the original Bisley Camp Pavilion Station in July 1890. Especially named for the opening of Bisley Camp by the Prince and Princess of Wales the locomotive is shown in regular service, now shorn of its decorations for the occasion but retaining the wooden nameplates.

THE CAMP STATION.

The Station at Bisley Camp, known as The Pavilion Station. The Pavilion itself, with its rotundas, can be seen beyond the station. This station together with the platform near the Cowshot crossing, were both replaced in 1891 by the more central Bisley Camp Station on the other side of the Camp level crossing, most probably using the existing shelter The dubious saddle tank engine of vaguely Great Western origin together with its nondescript train seems to have come straight from the artist's imagination! (*Illustrated London News*)

both the Pavilion Station in the Camp and Brookwood. Mackinnon had just taken up his position as the new NRA Secretary (probably not being fully aware that he would be also fulfilling the position of 'General Manager' of the NRA's Bisley Tramway) and he now had to write to Verrinder explaining these difficulties in a letter not exactly characteristic of his recent employment as the Chief Instructor of the Hythe School of Musketry!

'August 6th 1890

'The number of tickets issued from both Stations at Bisley and Brookwood was 11,080, this however will be considerably below the number used at the Brookwood end of the Railway as, by a fault in placing the egress door at the Pavilion Station too far from the Booking Office, many passengers took their places on the train without providing themselves with tickets. This was remedied during the Meeting and in a Communication issued from your Office it was mentioned that the issue of tickets from the Brookwood end would be considerably in excess of ours, tickets having been drawn to replace those omitted to having been taken at Bisley.

'The residue tickets were left at Bisley, but I will give instructions for them to be returned for your inspection - in the mean time perhaps you will kindly

inform one the number of tickets issued by your Company.

'E.W.Verrinder Esq
'Traffic Superintendent L&SWR'

The two station layout had proved to be impracticable and the situation of the Pavilion Station was also inconvenient. Major General Hutchinson had noted in his report that the platform would have to be lengthened so that trains did not need to be moved forward or backward for loading and unloading and every train movement obstructed the main Camp Road at the adjacent level crossing. From the few photographs it is apparent that the run-round loop did not encompass the whole of the available platform length, hence General Hutchinson's comments.

At a meeting of the Sub-Committee on 16 October it was agreed to combine the stations into one more centrally placed near the huts east of the Pavilion. At the same meeting, Hoey undertook to repair the tramway embankment. No further details were given but this must have been on a section of the Tramway outside the immediate Camp area. The responsibility for such repairs would be handed over to the Railway Company in due course.

Regarding the Stations Lord Wantage personally noted under the minute 'that this to stand over for

SOUTH WESTERN RAILWAY.

NATIONAL RIFLE ASSOCIATION MEETING AT BISLEY (BROOKWOOD).

Saturday, July 12th to July 28th.

Trains leave Waterloo, Clapham Junction, and Wimbledon, for Brookwood as under :—

		a.m.	a.m.	a.m.	a.m.	a.m.	a.m.	a.m.	a.m.	a.m.	p.m.	p.m.	p.m.	p.m.	p.m.	p.m.	p.m.	p.m.	p.m.	p.m.	p.m.
Waterloo	dep.	5.50	6.50	7.10	7.50	9.10	9.30	9.45	10.15	11.35	12.15	12.45	2.45	4.10	4.20	5.5	5.50	6.20	7.5	9.55	11.50
Clapham Junc.	,,	5.41	7.1	7.22	8.1	—	9.39	9.58	10.26	11.45	12.27	12.55	2.58	—	4.30	5.15	—	6.29	7.15	10.5	—
Wimbledon	,,	5.48	7.8	7.31	—	—	—	10.6	—	—	12.35	—	—	—	—	—	—	—	—	—	—
Brookwood	arr.	6.48	7.52	8.25	8.43	9.55	10.30	11.2	11.15	12.27	1.32	1.45	3.43	5.0	5.49	5.54	6.42	7.27	8.5	10.54	12.47

Up Trains.

		a.m.	a.m.	a.m.	a.m.	a.m.	p.m.	p.m.	p.m.	p.m.	p.m.	p.m.	p.m.	p.m.	p.m.	p.m.	p.m.	p.m.
Brookwood	dep.	8.19	8.42	9.23	10.50	11.2	12.8	12.49	2.17	3.12	4.12	5.2	6.9	6.24	7.23	8.20	9.14	10.49
Wimbledon	arr.	—	—	—	11.57	—	—	—	—	4.8	—	—	—	—	—	—	—	11.42
Clapham Junction	,,	—	—	—	12.7	—	12.46	—	2.55	4.15	4.54	—	6.58	7.27	8.10	9.23	9.58	11.50
Waterloo	,,	9.15	9.44	10.24	12.19	11.50	12.57	1.32	3.7	4.28	5.7	6.12	7.9	7.38	8.23	9.35	10.10	12.2

Special Fast Trains will run from London to Brookwood and back as the traffic may require.

Special Fares—Waterloo to Brookwood and back, during the Meeting only : First Class, 5/ ; Third Class, 2/6.

Volunteers in uniform, upon production of a Certificate from the N.R.A. : Third Class, 1/6.

Trains leave Kensington (Addison Road) for Clapham Junction at 6.5, 7.7, 8.29, 8.42, 9.12, 9.33, 10.15, 10.40, 11.15, and 11.40 a.m. ; and 12.9, 12.49, 1.26, 1.50, 2.37, 2.50, 3.41, 4.10, 4.53, 5.8, 5.40, 6.12, 7.0, 7.15, 7.50, 8.5, 8.47, 9.22, 9.44, 10.18, 11.0, and 11.35 p.m.

Trains leave Ludgate Hill for Clapham Junction at 7.58, 8.35, 9.23, 10.16, and 11.36 a.m. ; and 1.23, 2.1, 2.39, 3.13, 5.1, 5.32, and 6.51 p.m.

Trains leave Ludgate Hill for Wimbledon at 8.43, 9 47, 11.16, and 11.39 a.m. ; and 1.18, 2.55, 4.2, 5.8, 6.7, 7.6, 8.0, 9.6, 10.19, and 11.35 p.m.

A Tramway Service has been arranged from Brookwood Station direct to the Camp, connecting with all the principal trains to and from London—Fare each way, 3d.

The Railway Timetable for the first Bisley Meeting in July 1890. Note the reference to the new Tramway connecting the Camp with Brookwood.

The Pavilion Station. A tantalizing glimpse of the short-lived Bisley Camp Station of 1890 shortly after the opening of the Camp by the Prince and Princess of Wales on 12 July. The Class O2 0-4-4 Tank Engine leaving with its train for Brookwood is the 'Royal' Engine no 185 *Alexandra*. The two Luggage Vans in the foreground are, on the left, a 24ft Van of 1887 (lettered 'L&SWR 76 Luggage Van') and, on the right, an unidentified 22ft luggage van of 1883. Pirbright Camp can be seen in the distance.

The throat of the original Pavilion Station. The Camp level crossing is at the left of the picture at the head of the track into the Camp. This remains the main access.

The Gentlemen of the Press pose close to the original Pavilion Station at the 1890 Bisley opening Meeting. Another glimpse of the Pavilion Station platform taken from the western side. One of the gables of the Pavilion itself is visible at the right background together with a section of Faggetter's station platform wall. The carriage in the station is probably the same archaic 4-wheel Passenger Brake as seen in the picture of 'The Pavilion' Station taken from the opposite direction.

further consideration' probably on the grounds that no costs had been taken into account and the L&SWR would have to be consulted in any case. This issue was again raised at a meeting of the Sub-Committee dated 8 April 1891 and this time it was passed with the proviso that it could be done for £300.

In discussions with the L&SWR the latter proposed to rebuild the Camp station on the eastern side of the level crossing as well as providing a Goods platform opposite (and to the west of) the site of the original station. However the Council found the estimate for the work excessive and requested the Company, through Andrews, to reduce it.

> '24th April 1891
> E. Andrews Esq.
> Engineers Office
> Waterloo Station S.E.

'In reference to your letter No 5435 of 21st inst. forwarding plans for proposed alterations to the existing system of Stations on the Tramway at Brookwood at a cost of £400. I am directed by the Council to explain to you that they do not feel justified in spending so large a sum; but, could the estimate on reconsideration be reduced to £300, they would be glad to have the work commenced at once; they would be content with a Goods Platform one fourth the length shown in the plan.

'The Council hope that the L&SWR will find it possible to oblige them in this matter, the work being one that cannot fail to benefit the Railway as well as the Association.'

Wantage, accompanied by the NRA Secretary, met Scotter towards the end of April to discuss and consolidate the new station proposal as well as improvements to the train service and ticket arrangements. The outcome of the meeting was noted by the Sub-Committee on 29 April.

'Alteration of Stations - It was arranged that the L.& S.W.R. Company would undertake the work of making a new Station at Bisley, removing the two present Stations, for £300; but substituting for the large unloading dock on the plan a landing sufficient for unloading one truck at a time.

'Through Tickets - Mr Scotter stated that the L.& S.W.R would arrange to issue through tickets.

'Running of Trains - A double set of officials to be employed this year which will allow trains to be run more frequently and up to the time of the last 'up' train; on any plan proposed by the Association.

'Whit Monday - A special will be run between 7 and 9 a.m. returning between 6 and 8 p.m.

'Additional trains to stop at Brookwood - Consider to arrange for a 'down' train to stop at Brookwood when required between the ordinary arrivals 1.45 and 3.43.'

The L&SWR agreed to this modification and work commenced with the aim of opening the re-sited station in time for the Annual Meeting. The new Goods platform, on the western edge of the goods yard opposite the site of the original station, was primarily of banked earth construction and was provided with a small wooden office. Although the new station platform was constructed by the L&SWR the combined waiting shelter and ticket office seems to have been that used at the Pavilion Station. Later a smaller wooden building was also constructed to house the set of turnstiles giving controlled access to the platform.

The alterations necessitated an official Inspection and so, on 3 June, the newly appointed NRA Secretary, Col. W. Mackinnon, wrote a request to the Board of Trade for this to be carried out as soon as possible.

'I am directed by the Council to inform you that certain alterations are being made in the Bisley Tramway. Our new Station is substituted for the two Stations, and the level at this point is altered making the gradient less.

'The work is being done by the London & South Western Railway, and is expected to be completed by the 1st July; and I am to request the favour of an early re-inspection of the line with a view to authority for its use when completed, subject to any requirements of the Inspecting Officer being complied with.'

At the request of the L&SWR, in order to facilitate the opening in time for the Meeting, Mackinnon wrote a personal letter to Hutchinson.

> '17th June 1891

'Dear General Hutchinson
'Would you make an early opportunity to inspect our altered Bisley Tramway; though not finished,

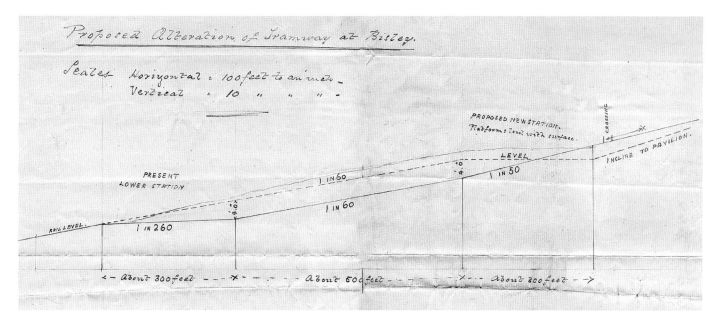

Plan of the new Station levels. The new central Station necessitated some considerable alteration to the levels. This plan would have been drawn up under the direct supervision of Edwards, the L&SWR Resident Engineer, and indicates the substantial amount of earth moving that was necessary in order to level the site for the new station.

the L&SWR would like you, as time presses, to see it in view of any work not in hand but which you may consider necessary

'Yours very truly
W. Mackinnon Col.
Sect NRA

Major General C. Hutchinson C.B.
8 Richmond Terrace
Whitehall
S.W.'

Hutchinson inspected the relocated station almost by return, dating his report 22 June.

'I have the honour to report for the information of the Board of Trade that, in compliance with the instructions contained in your minute of the 10th instant, I have inspected the new terminal station of the National Rifle Association Tramway at Bisley Camp.

'The Station has been constructed to take the place of the original terminal station and of another a short distance from it, the two having been found unnecessary and the position of the former inconvenient.

'The new station has been placed rather nearer Brookwood than the former one; the line has been made level along the platform and along the sidings on the down side of it, the gradient of the line from the up end of the platform towards Brookwood having had in consequence to be steepened for a short distance.

'The points have been locked in to 2. Lever frames, the Key of which is the staff carried by the Engine which works the line.

'The only requirements I noticed were that an interlocked safety point should be provided at the up end of the Engine loop, and that the normal position of the points at the down end of this loop should lie for the loop.

'These matters are to receive immediate attention and upon this understanding I can recommend the Board of Trade to sanction the use of the new Terminal Station at Bisley Camp.'

The *Volunteer Service Gazette* of 18 July confirmed the changes.

'The Bisley Meeting 1891
'Saturday, July 11
'The station of the branch railway (or 'steam tramway'), at the entrance of the Camp, has been done away with, and the Bisley terminus is this year immediately opposite to the Council Building. ......'

'We have already mentioned the change in the locality of the Bisley terminus of the steam tramway. The trams on this tramway now run from each end at half hour intervals during the day.'

On 4 August 1892, the Secretary wrote to the War Office regarding the consolidation and sale of lands surplus to the Association's requirements, with the exception of the piece of land adjacent to the north side of the Basingstoke Canal containing the north pier of the Tramway Canal Bridge as it was intended to make it over to the Railway Company.

'and excepting a small patch of about half an acre bought from the Basingstoke Canal: on which their tramway is laid and which they may wish to make over to the London & S.W. Railway. The extent of land which the Council desire to sell is given in the accompanying Schedule and other property of the Association therein, excepting the small piece occupied by the tramway, should the Association at any future time desire to sell it.'

On 13 February 1893, Mackinnon wrote to Scotter stating that the Association was prepared to convey the area of land on the north side of the canal to the company.

'I am directed to inform you that the Council of the National Rifle Association are prepared to convey to the L.&S.W. Railway Co all the land bought from the Basingstoke Canal Company on condition that the Company will undertake to keep the Tramway in working order throughout, so long as Meetings are held at Bisley. Also; to enable the work to be done, to give the Company, so far as it lies in their power, the full right of entry over all the land on which the Tramway is laid which they cannot convey.

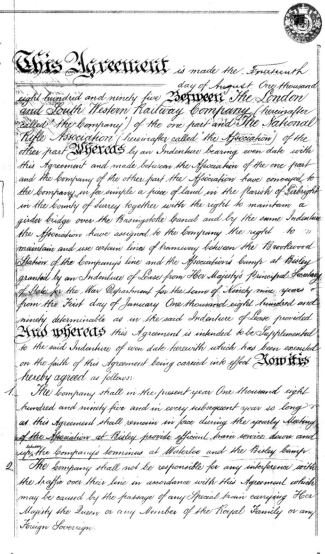

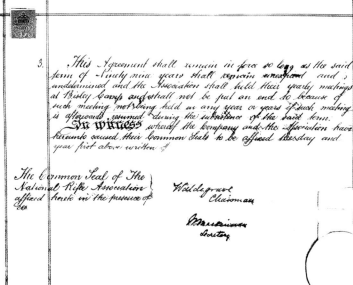

The 1895 Agreement between the NRA and LSWR which effectively enabled the latter to take over the operation of the Tramway. At this time the L&SWR took the opportunity to substitute their standard chaired track for the lightweight flat bottom track originally laid.

'The Council understand that the Company's Solicitors will prepare the conveyance; they would like it to be examined by their Solicitors, Messrs Markby, Wilde & Johnson before execution.'

However, it was not until 1895 that an Agreement was finally signed; the Association had tried to insert a clause regarding fixed fares into it but this was not surprisingly rejected by the company.

'A letter was read from Messrs Markby, Wilde & Johnson, who ask for further instructions in which they represent that the General Manager L.&S.W Railway objects to binding the Company to provide access to the Camp at specified fares in accordance with one of their timetables attached as a Schedule to an agreement, which agreement to provide access to the Camp is to be presented simultaneously with the Deed of transfer of land and of the War Office concession for the use of their land for purposes of the Tramway, on the ground "that the Association may well leave it to the Company to provide a sufficient and efficient service of trains while the fares are so well understood that no agreement in this respect is necessary".

'After discussion it was decided that the Solicitors be authorised to conclude the agreement omitting the clause objected to by the General Manager.'

Operating the 'Network' 1890-1899

From the opening of Bisley Camp, NRA Secretaries found themselves in an unusual position. Their responsibility for managing all aspects of the shooting activities of the NRA as well as maintaining the site were now suddenly expanded to include the duties of a General Manager of a small but, on occasion, very busy railway network. The core of this operation was, of course, the newly built Tramway from Brookwood to the Camp. But this relied on an efficient service of trains on the L&SWR mainline through Brookwood as well as through trains and saloons directly into the Camp itself. The idea of an 'efficient service', which sometimes differed from the Railway Company's views, exercised the minds of several generations of NRA Secretaries, and especially those who held the post before the Great War. There came a time too when individual members discovered that their complaints and comments about aspects of the train services could be channelled through the Secretary with a fair chance of action being taken by the Railway Company.

The first major task facing the NRA was to ensure that the large number of Volunteers who had attended the Meetings at Wimbledon would continue their patronage. Elcho had largely resolved the attendance problem at Wimbledon by negotiating cheap fares with the major railway companies, but this had been to an area of London that, over the years, had become relatively easy of access. At Bisley, out in the country to the south west of London, the main task now was to attract those from East Anglia, the Midlands and North of the United Kingdom, especially Scotland, who would generally have to cross London in order to reach the L&SWR's Waterloo Terminus. A major part of this strategy was to ensure efficient train services to Brookwood and the Camp itself and, although the L&SWR was prepared to go to considerable lengths to achieve this it was left to the N.R.A, through its Secretaries, to suggest and negotiate improvements.

An attempt to resolve the 'London' problem had been made by Humphry, in 1890 when he had put forward a radical idea – avoid London altogether! This suggestion, although specific to the opening Meeting, was partially acted on by the provision of special saloons, mainly for foreign and colonial competitors and quite often at short notice, the L&SWR normally making the necessary arrangements with other railway companies. Through trains from Waterloo directly into the Camp also became a regular feature of the timetable during the Annual Meeting and also at other times as required.

In 1891 there were some complaints about the train service and the Council made personal representations to Scotter. They also hoped to arrange additional special trains to and from London during the evening for the convenience of those in the Camp

'The Council have represented to the London & South Western Railway the complaints that were made to them regarding the train service, which was certainly affected by exceptional demands upon the Railway at the time; they have been assured by Colonel Scotter that he will do all in his power to facilitate the travelling between London and Brookwood. The Council hope to arrange for certain special trains to run to London after 6 p.m. returning about 11 p.m.

SOUTH WESTERN RAILWAY

NATIONAL
RIFLE ASSOCIATION MEETING
AT BISLEY.

From MONDAY, July 11th, until SATURDAY, July 23rd, inclusive,

LATE TRAINS for LONDON

WILL LEAVE AS FOLLOWS:—

		p.m.	p.m.	p.m.			p.m.	p.m.	p.m.
BISLEY CAMP	abt.	10 0	10 30	..	WIMBLEDON .... arr.		10 52	..	11 45
BROOKWOOD	dep.	10 15	10 49	11 12	CLAPHAM JUNC. "		10 59	11 50	11 53
WOKING......	arr.	10 22	10 55	11 17	VAUXHALL .... "		11 6	11 55	11 59
SURBITON	"	10 44	11 34	11 37	WATERLOO .... "		11 12	12 0	12 5

On SUNDAYS, JULY 17th and 24th,
LATE TRAINS WILL LEAVE

BROOKWOOD for LONDON

AS FOLLOWS:—

		p.m.	p.m.			p.m.	p.m.
BISLEY CAMP	dep.	9 0	9 0	SURBITON .... arr.		9 40	10 20
BROOKWOOD	"	9 15	9 50	CLAPHAM JUNC..... "		9 50	10 32
WOKING...........	arr.	9 20	9 56	VAUXHALL.......... "		10 3	10 38
WEYBRIDGE	"	..	10 7	WATERLOO.......... "		10 9	10 44

CAMP TRAMWAY.

BROOKWOOD STATION to BISLEY
AND BACK.

From Monday, 11th, until Saturday, July 23rd inclusive, the Trams will start from Brookwood Station every 30 minutes, commencing at 7.45 a.m., and from the Camp Station commencing at 8.0 a.m.
The last Tram from Brookwood Station to the Camp will start at 10.10 p.m., returning at 10.30 p.m.
The Tram will not run on the Camp Tramway on Sunday, July 10th, but will run on Sundays, July 17th and 24th, from about 9.30 a.m. until 9.0 p.m.

CHAS. SCOTTER, General Manager.

Waterlow & Sons Limited, Printers, London Wall, London.

760/

CAMP TRAMWAY.

BROOKWOOD STATION TO BISLEY AND BACK.

From Tuesday, 13th, until Saturday, July 24th inclusive, the Trams will start from Brookwood Station every 30 minutes, commencing at 7.45 a.m., and from the Camp Station, commencing at 8.0 a.m.

The last Tram from Brookwood Station to the Camp will start at 11.15 p.m., returning at 11.30 p.m.

The Trams will run on the Camp Tramway on Sunday, July 18th, from about 8.45 a.m., until 11.15 p.m.

By Order,

W. MACKINNON, Col.,
Secretary, N.R.A.

The 1893 Bisley Meeting Timetable.

daily, with the object of enabling residents in camp to visit London after the day's work, either for business or amusement.'

An evening train ran between Brookwood and London in 1892 and the Council extended their thanks to Scotter and Verrinder, for the improved train services.

In 1893, the Report gave a breakdown of the number of passengers and amount collected of passengers arriving by rail at Bisley Camp Station. It also mentioned new arrangements with both the L&SWR and District Railway in which passengers could book through to the Camp. The turnstiles mentioned were located within the small building at the Camp station. Through trains to the Camp had been introduced at great convenience to both members and the public.

However, through trains were arranged at other times than during the July Meeting. For example, in May 1894, Mackinnon wrote to the Superintendent of the Line of the L&SWR accepting a proposal that through trains could be arranged respecting teams competing in a competition at Bisley on 2 June.

At a meeting of the Council held on 5 June, the possibility of obtaining tramcars from Glasgow to run over the Tramway was discussed and the Secretary was requested to ascertain if the L&SWR would carry passengers from Brookwood to Bisley on days when there is a large attendance. The Chairman was authorised to take any necessary measures if purchase of

The 1897 Timetable for the Camp Tramway.

 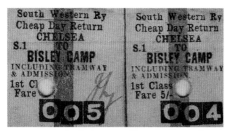 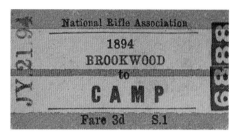

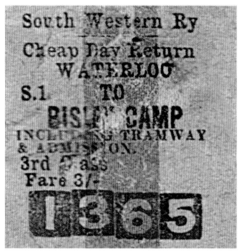 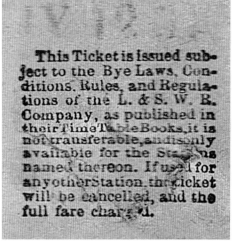

Early NRA & LSWR railway Tickets. The NRA tickets, actually printed by the LSWR, were superseded by those of the Railway Company when the latter became responsible for operating the line. This transition commenced in 1894 although the Agreement was not signed until 1895. (*NRA Museum & GWS Collection*)

tramway cars became urgent.' In the following year, Mackinnon wrote to the new L&SWR Superintendent of the Line, G.T White, regarding a graduated reduction of fares for Volunteers. However, nothing seems to have come of these proposals.

'10th January 1895

'Volunteer Fares to Bisley

'With reference to our conversation on this subject an idea has occurred to me which it may be worthwhile to mention again

'I understand the return fare 3rd Class to be at present 1/6 decreasing as a graduated scale at certain Stations, Wimbledon for example, to 1/- at Surbiton; could a concession be made of a uniform fare of 1/3 from all stations east of Surbiton. This would be a great boon to the Metropolitan Volunteers and would I feel sure materially affect the number of Volunteers coming to us from London to our mutual advantage.

'G.T. White Esq.
Superintendent of the Line
London and South Western Railway
Waterloo Station'

By 1899, the L&SWR mainline was becoming increasingly congested and plans had already been made to widen it from the existing two to four tracks. However, in that year the Volunteers had cause to complain about the special trains taking them to the Bisley Ranges for the annual Meeting as they were always given lower priority than other passenger traffic, especially during race days at Sandown Park close to Esher station. On many occasions, their trains were shunted into sidings to await a path. A typical letter of complaint appeared in the daily edition of the *Volunteer Service Gazette* for 17 July.

'When racing takes place at Sandown, Bisley men must go to the wall – or, to be strictly correct, to the siding – in many instances. The way in which the trains both to and from London, were run on Saturday beggars all description. Whether leaving London for Brookwood, or Brookwood for London, Bisley men would be well advised to travel by train at least two hours earlier than would be necessary if punctuality were the rule. For few of us, however, is this mode of travelling convenient and we would impress upon the Railway Company the desirability of limiting the delay to, let us say, half-an-hour during the remainder of the Meeting, Sandown or no Sandown. Cannot the Council of the NRA make its voice felt in the matter?'

The Vanity Fair cartoon of Sir Charles Owens, General Manager of the L&SWR 1898-1912. (*Vanity Fair – Author's Collection*)

During the same Meeting to add to their woes there was another considerable delay, this time due to a derailment in Bisley Camp Station which occurred on 16 July.

'Travellers to Bisley yesterday morning were gratified to find that between London and Brookwood no serious delay occurred. This is to be explained by the fact that there were no racing fixtures to cause the traffic to be disorganised, but those who were congratulating themselves on a fast run from London as they steamed into Brookwood little knew what was in store for them. An accident had happened at the Camp Station, which was calculated either to annoy them seriously or teach them that patience is a virtue. After remaining on the up platform for some thirty minutes however, a move

was made for Camp, where, at the station, was to be seen an engine which had left the metals. It was impossible for the 11.25 train from London to reach the platform, and a number of ladies and others had to climb down by the aid of forms, &c. Among those who were thus delayed was the Chairman of the Council.'

Sir Charles Scotter retired as General Manager of the L&SWR in 1898 and immediately moved on to the Board of the Railway Company, becoming the Deputy Chairman in 1899 and Chairman in 1904. He was succeeded by Charles Owens, formerly the L&SWR Goods Manager, who had arranged the move of plant from Wimbledon to Bisley.

The 1898 Accident at Bisley Camp Station

On 11 April 1898, a serious collision took place at Bisley Camp Station between a locomotive and the train that it had been scheduled to collect. The train was full of Volunteers who, having spent the day in shooting practice, were waiting to return to London, and the serious nature of the accident was compounded by rifles, stacked in the overhead luggage racks, falling on to the men after being dislodged by the violence of the collision.

Both *The Times* and the local paper, the *Woking News and Mail*, reported the incident on the following day in similar terms.

'At 6 o'clock last evening an accident occurred on the London South Western-Railway at Bisley Station, by which between 20 and 30 Volunteers were more or less injured, some half a dozen cases being regarded as very serious. In connexion with the Easter Volunteer Manoeuvres the 15th Middlesex (Docks and Customs House) Volunteers, commanded by Colonel Chambers, went down from London yesterday morning and were exercised in class firing. At the termination of the day's proceedings the corps, headed by the bands, marched to Bisley Station to take train for London. They arrived at the station shortly before 6 o'clock, and the entraining was speedily completed. At this time it appears that the engine that was to bring the men to Waterloo was not attached to the carriages, but suddenly the train was crashed into and great excitement and commotion occasioned. The engine had arrived with an unexpected impact that was quite unaccountable to those at the station. Whether distance was misjudged or control of the engine lost is not known, but the violence of the impact partially wrecked the guard's van and also the first coach, in which some of the Volunteers were sitting. The carriage of the guard's van was detached, and the force of the collision knocked the buffer stops off the engine and otherwise damaged it. The guard was, fortunately, standing on the platform and thus escaped injury. A drummer of the Regiment was looking out of the window of the first carriage; but, although he saw the engine approaching, and realised that a collision was about to take place, he had no time to leave the carriage and had only just shouted to his comrades "Look out," when the collision occurred, This drummer escaped injury, but the other drummers in the compartment were injured. The occupants of carriages further from the engine were also injured by broken glass, sustaining bruises and cuts. The corps itself from its uninjured members was able to provide ready assistance to the injured, and Colonel Chambers lost no time in superintending the arrangements for the necessary attention. The camps of the Artists Corps and 14th Middlesex Volunteer Corps being situated almost adjoining the station were quickly apprised of the accident, and the men turned out and conveyed those most seriously hurt to their huts and tents. The injured were mostly bandsmen of the corps and included Drum-Major Kelly. Drummer Walsh, who was in a compartment about the third removed from the guard's van, was, with others, injured, but two lady friends of some of the occupants of this compartment escaped unhurt. The engine having been partially derailed and this section of the line being a single road, there was no help but to send the uninjured members of the corps by road to Woking, where a special train was made up to convey them to London. The majority of the injured were able to accompany their comrades to Woking in vehicles provided at Bisley, and proceeded to London, where their comrades accompanied them to their respective homes. Some half a dozen men, however, detained at Bisley. At the time of the accident there was a heavy downpour of rain.'

'The Railway Accident at Bisley

'Over 20 of the passengers by the volunteer train to which a serious accident happened at Bisley on Monday were conveyed on arrival in London to St. Thomas's Hospital. Only four, however, were detained, the names of these being William H. Ball, John Sweeny, Richard Henderson, and a man named Easterbrook. The injuries to the three first-mentioned are not considered of such a nature as to cause any anxiety but the condition of Easterbrook is more serious, and the full extent of his injuries have not yet been ascertained. The more seriously injured men, who were removed to the Guard's hospital, Pirbright, are all progressing favourably. Their names are Drum-major Kelly, Colour-Sergeant Davies, Lance-corporal Hudson, Private Leary, Private Hall, and Private Connor. Davies was picked up insensible and Kelly had a very deep cut over the eye. Altogether 23 men were badly hurt. Colonel A.W. Chambers, in command of the 15th Middlesex, says that of 200 men quite 150 were more or less cut about.'

The driver, Robert Joy of Nine Elms, was initially suspended and placed on duty in the running shed there, pending receipt of the Board of Trade report.

Major F.A. Marindin, the Inspecting Officer of the Board of Trade, dated the report of his investigation into the accident on 25 April, in the process throwing some interesting light on operations over the Tramway in the early days.

'London and South Western Railway.
Railway Department, Board of Trade,
8, Richmond Terrace, Whitehall, London, SW.,
April 25th, 1898

'Sir,

'I have the honour to report for the information of the Board of Trade, in compliance with the instructions contained in the Order of the 13th inst., the result of my enquiry into the causes of a collision which occurred at Bisley Station, on the London and South-Western Railway, on the 11th inst.

'In this case a light engine (No. 175), running tender first, and coming from Brookwood Station to Bisley, came into violent collision, at about 6.10pm., with a loaded special train of 11 vehicles which was standing at Bisley platform, and to which the engine was to have been attached to take it back to Waterloo, whence it had brought it in the morning.

'The train, which was a block train with a brake-carriage at one end and a brake-van at the other, was driven back for about 40 feet, the brakes in both the van and the brake carriage being on, and it was considerably damaged. The brake-van, the vehicle which was struck by the engine, was smashed, the end of the carriage next to it was broken in, and the bodies were shifted, headstocks broken, or some windows broken in all the other vehicles. The tender of the engine was slightly damaged.

'Twenty-three of the passengers, volunteers of the 15th Middlesex Regiment, were injured so much as to prevent them from walking to Brookwood to be entrained, some of the injuries being severe; and altogether no less than 130 complaints of injury have been received. Most of those complaining, however, have probably been only slightly injured.

'Description

'Bisley Station is at the terminus of a short branch 1¼ miles in length, from Brookwood Station, and it is only used occasionally when required for the convenience of volunteers going to Bisley Camp for practice or manoeuvres.

'It falls from the main line to the crossing of the Basingstoke Canal, and then rises to the terminus, on gradients of 1 in 50 and 1 in 60.

'Approaching the station it is on a sharp curve to the left and on a gradient of 1 in 50 to within 30 yards of the point of collision, which was just opposite to the end of the platform ramp.

'The last 30 yards are on gradients of 1 in 60 and 1 in 119, the line along the platform being on a gradient of 1 in 250.

'A brake van standing at the point of collision is plainly visible from an approaching engine for 250 yards.

'Evidence

'Robert Joy states : I have been 17 years in the service, and a driver for four years four months. On the 11th inst. I came on duty at 7.45 a.m. at Nine Elms for special duty. I went to Waterloo, left with special train at about 9.20, arrived at Bisley at 10.23, left at 10.34, and arrived at Woking at 10.44. I was then instructed to work a special coal train from Woking to Basingstoke. I left Woking at 12.10 and arrived at Basingstoke at 1.17. After turning and taking coal, I left Basingstoke at 3.20 and arrived at Brookwood at 3.50; I stood at Brookwood from 3.50 to 6 p.m. My engine (No 175) is a six-wheels-coupled goods engine, with a six wheel

tender. There is a steam-brake working blocks on all the engine and tender wheels; there is also a hand-brake which applies the tender brake, and there is the apparatus for working an automatic vacuum-brake on the train. The steam-brake and the automatic brake are applied by the same action. The brake was in good order, and worked satisfactorily whenever I had occasion to use it during the day. I had used it up to 3.50 p.m.; I had no occasion to use it again until I was approaching Bisley just before the accident. I left the special train at Bisley platform at 10.23 a.m. The train was due to leave Bisley for Waterloo at 6.25 p.m. I left Brookwood at 6 p.m. to come to Bisley to be attached to the train; I was running tender first, and I had on the foot-plate, besides my fireman, Mr. Tompkins, the station-master at Brookwood, who was on duty, and a porter also on duty. I had 100 lbs. Pressure of steam, my proper running pressure being 150 lbs. The pressure of 100 lbs. was ample for me to take the light engine to Bisley, and I would have had no difficulty in getting the pressure of 150 lbs. before starting with my train. It is about a mile from Brookwood to Bisley. I had never driven a train on the branch before that morning, but I had acted as firemen to trains on the branch on one day previously; I was well aware of the gradients, and I knew about where I had left the train. On leaving Brookwood it commenced to rain; I shut off steam after leaving Brookwood, until passing over the canal bridge, on which the order is to go at walking pace. On passing the bridge I applied steam again sufficiently to come up the bank at a speed of about seven miles an hour. I shut off steam at or near the level crossing, 300 or 400 yards from the station. My speed at that point was about seven miles an hour. After passing the level crossing I could see the train, perhaps then about 200 yards away. I at once applied the steam-brake and told my fireman to apply the hand-brake. He did so, but was not able to get it on as quickly as if there had been on one but ourselves on the foot-plate. The brakes did not have the desire effect on application, owing to not having been applied for some time previously; I think this is because there was water in the cylinder. It is my experience that the steam-brake does not act so well on the first application after standing for some time; some brakes act better than others, no doubt. The brakes did not pull up the engine, and I came into collision with the standing train at a speed of about four miles an hour. I was not knocked over; in fact, the collision had no effect on me personally. When within about two lengths of the train I tried to reverse my engine, but could not put my lever over in consequence, I believe, of the sharp curve. It is an order that engines are to set back on to their trains at hand-brake speed, that is, at such a speed that they can be stopped by the hand-brake only. I did not sound my whistle except when approaching the crossing. The rails were wet and greasy. I think the collision was due to a miscalculation of speed, and to an error of judgment on my part in not applying the brake earlier. The steam-brake acts with more effect when there is a good pressure of steam. My reason for having resorted to the steam-brake was that I thought I was going a bit too fast.

'No.25403 Second-Corporal Walter Harris, R.E. states : I am being trained as a driver at Nine Elms, and have been at work with engines of the London and South Western Railway for three months. I have worked with driver Joy for about a fortnight; I have been working on different parts of the line. I have worked as driver with traction engines and small military engines before coming to the London and South Western Railway. I came on duty with driver Joy on the 11th inst. and worked through the day with him. So far as I can recollect, the driver did not shut off steam after leaving Brookwood until approaching the level-crossing outside Bisley station, when we were running at about seven miles per hour. He applied the steam brake when over 100 yards from the tail of the train, and he told me to apply the hand-brake. I went to do so, but made nine or ten turns before I felt it; this was when we were getting near the train - perhaps 30 or 40 yards from it. I think our speed when we struck the van was between four and five miles an hour. The shock did not knock me over.

'Charles Tompkins states : I am station-master at Brookwood, and when there are trains on the branch I am in charge at Bisley. I have been 34 years in the service. On the 11th April there was a special train to Bisley with the 15th Middlesex Volunteers. This train arrived at Bisley at about 10.23 a.m., and was due to go back to London at 6.25 p.m. Driver Joy, who had brought down the train, was on other duty during the middle of the day, and came back to Brookwood in the afternoon. He came to me at about 4 p.m. to ask when he

would be required and I told him at about 6 p.m., and he went away to his engine. He was in a proper state and fit for duty At 6 p.m. I went to the engine, which was in the siding, in order to go to Bisley. It is my duty to go with the staff to the driver, and to go to Bisley when there is a train there to be attended to. There were also two porters on the foot-plate, one, a Brookwood man, who was coming to assist me with the train, and another, a Waterloo man, whose duty it was to light up the train. There were altogether five men on the foot-plate. Driver Joy was quite fit for duty and showed no sign whatever of having been drinking. It began to rain smartly at about 6 p.m. We came steadily down the hill, and over the canal bridge with a little steam on, but not much. The brake was not on. After crossing the bridge I asked the driver to sound the whistle for the level crossing, and he did so. He put on steam after crossing the bridge, and he came up the bank at a speed of about 10 miles an hour. We approached the crossing at the same speed. I called his attention to the train when we were about 200 yards from it, and asked him if he was not going to shut off steam, showing him the train. He did not shut off steam until he was within a few yards of the coaches, although I shouted to him two or three times. He then reversed the engine, and put on the steam brake, but it was too late, and we came into collision with the train at almost the same speed as we were running at over the level crossing. I did not hear the driver tell his fireman to apply the hand-brake, and I do not know whether he did so or not. I do not think he took any steps to stop the engine until we were the length of a coach from the van of the train. I felt a considerable shock from the collision, and was nearly thrown over. I was slightly injured. The guards van was knocked to pieces; it was lifted up and dropped. The whole of the carriages sustained damage to some extent. It drove the train forward about a coach length. The train was pretty full, and a number of men were injured, principally from cuts to the head. I do not know that any were seriously injured. Many of the injuries were from the rifles falling from the racks.

'Driver Joy denies that the station-master spoke to him during the journey at all, and says he was leaning over the tender sheltering from the rain. Fireman Harris agrees with the driver.

'Christopher King states : I have been nearly a year in the service as porter at Brookwood. On 11th April I came on duty at 6 a.m. to work till 6 p.m. with nearly two hours for meals. I did not get off duty that day till midnight, owing to the accident. I came by order of Mr. Tompkins to Bisley on the light engine to attend to the train which was at Bisley. We came down to the canal bridge from Brookwood pretty fast, but I do not know whether steam was on or not. We came up the bank to Bisley at about the usual speed, but I cannot say what the speed was. I was standing at the right side of the foot-plate, as we were running and I believe I was looking over the side. The station-master was next to me. I do not know which way he was looking. After we came over the level crossing I heard the station-master tell the driver to go steady. I did not notice him do anything else. I did not hear him speak more than once. I think we were then 100 yards from the coaches. The driver reversed his engine and applied the steam-brake when the station-master spoke to him. I do not know whether steam was on or not. I do not know much about engines. I was not hurt by the collision. When the station-master spoke to the driver he pointed to the train and said "There's your train up there."

'James Larwood states : I have been nine years employed in the service as a porter, and employed at Waterloo for three weeks. On the 11th April I came from Waterloo to Brookwood by the 4.10 p.m. train, with orders to go to Bisley to light up a special volunteer train. I came from Brookwood to Bisley on the engine; I came up holding on to the end of the tender, with my face in the direction to which we were going, but stooping to keep out the rain. The station-master was standing behind me, but as I did not turn round I do not know which way he was looking. I think our speed up the bank was between 10 and 12 miles an hour; the speed was checked when we were about 300 yards from the train. I do not know where steam was shut off, but it was reduced to about half what we had been running when we were about 300 yards from the train, as near as I can guess. I have never been on the road before, so do not know the level crossing. I heard no conversation of any kind on the journey up, except that when we were pretty close to the train I heard the station-master call out "Woa!" or something; that was immediately before the collision. I was not hurt by it; I think the speed at the time was from four to six miles an hour. I did not feel the application of the brakes at all; I was cold and wet and

was not taking much notice. I heard nothing else said by the station-master on the journey but what I have stated.

'James Slade states : I have been 28 years in the service, and a guard for 16 years. On the 11th April I came on duty at 9 a.m. for special duty. I came with a special train of volunteers to Bisley, arriving at 10.22. The train was made up as follows : third-class brake carriage, nine coaches, and third-class brake-van; a block train. The train was pretty full. I remained at Bisley all day; the train was due to leave for Waterloo at 6.25. The men on arriving at the station took their seats in the train, as it was raining fast; the train stood in the same position as it had been left in the morning. I had been in my van arranging the band instruments, and got out just before the collision took place. When I got out I saw the engine approaching a few lengths off; I thought it was running too fast and that there would be a collision, so I ran out of the way. When I first saw the engine steam was off, but I cannot say whether or not the brakes were on. I think the speed at which the engine struck the van was about six miles an hour. I think the engine was five or six lengths away when I first saw it, but I was rather alarmed, and cannot be sure.; I had not time to warn the passengers. My brakes were both on; the train was driven back about 40 ft. There were a number of the men hurt. But I do not know how many. My van was badly damaged, and the next coach was a good deal damaged; most of the carriages had only windows broken.

'Conclusion

'This collision, which was quite inexcusable, and caused injury to a great number of persons, was due entirely to the omission of driver Robert Joy to get his engine under proper control, and he admits his error.

'He had brought the special train from Waterloo to Bisley in the morning, and had left it standing at the platform exactly where it was when he allowed his engine to run into it at a speed of some six miles an hour, when returning in the evening to couple on to it, and to take it back to Waterloo, and, although he had not driven on the Bisley branch before that day he states that he was quite well aware of the gradients, and that he knew that, according to the rules, he ought to have approached the train to which he was to be attached at hand-brake speed, that is, at such a speed that he could stop by the use of the hand-brake only. He left Brookwood at about 6 p.m., and there is no reason to think that his speed when coming up the incline was in any degree excessive, although it was probably more than the speed of seven miles an hour at which he estimates it, and he simply ran too far before taking the proper steps to reduce his speed. If, when running at seven miles an hour, he had applied his steam-brake, as he says he did, when 200 yards from the train on a rising gradient of 1 in 50, he would not have reached the train at all, instead of striking it with violence as he did, and I believe that the real reason for the collision was that the driver, with the other men on the engine, was sheltering himself as he best could from the sharp storm of rain which came on just at that time, and did not realise where he was until close to the train, when it was too late to pull up.

'The station-master from Brookwood, who was on the foot-plate, states that he warned the driver several times in the last 200 or 300 yards to pull up, but the driver denies this, and I think that the story told by porter Larwood is the true one, and that it was only at the last moment that the station-master or anyone else perceived the danger.

'The driver does not think that the steam-brake acted as quickly and effectually as it should have done, and very possibly, as he had been standing at Brookwood for some hours, and, moreover, had a low pressure of steam, this may have been the case, but there should have been no occasion to have resort to the steam-brake at all. There may, however, have been some impediment to the quick application of the hand-brake by the fireman, as there were five men on the foot-plate, which is certainly too many under ordinary circumstances. Still, as all the men were going to Bisley on duty, I do not think that there was any particular objection to their going up on a light engine, and the crowded state of the foot-plate was not sufficient excuse for the collision. The reason that so many persons were injured seems to have been that all the men had got into the train to shelter from the rain, instead of waiting till the engine had been attached, and that a number were cut by their rifles being jerked out of the nets of the carriages on to their heads.

'At the time of the collision Driver Joy had been on duty for about 10½ hours, and for the last 2 hours he had been standing at Brookwood.

I have, &c.;

The Assistant Secretary,   F. A. Marindin,
The Railway Department,
Board of Trade   Major, R.E.

'Appendix

'RETURN OF DAMAGES TO ROLLING STOCK
'Damage to Engine and Tender
'Both tender buffers broken; three lamp-irons broken; vacuum-pipe broken; back of tender slightly damaged.
'Details of damage to Stock
'No. 168 passenger brake-van. – Pair of wheels knocked from under; two sole bars, two headstocks, axle guards, under frame, brake-work and body badly broken.

'No. 155, third. – End broken in; roof raised; and eight quarter-lights broken.

'No. 536, third. – Body shifted; side panels sprung and damaged; and three quarter-light broken.

'No. 94, composite. – Two headstocks and eight quarter-lights broken.

'No. 97, composite. – Six quarter-lights broken.

'No. 211, composite. – Buffer-rods bent; and buffer pads damaged.

'No. 41, composite. – Side panel broken; buffer-rods bent; and buffer pads damaged.

'No. 566, third – Under frame timber damaged; and quarter-light broken.

'No. 113, composite. – Door glass and two quarter-lights brken; body shifted; and two end step irons bent.

'No. 207, third. – Five quarter-lights broken; and body shifted.

'No. 538, third-brake. – body shifted; quarter-light broken; crib rail, beading, and step-board damaged.

Printed copies of the above report were sent to the Company on 16 May.

The transcript of the decision regarding Driver Joy, signed by Drummond, the Chief Mechanical Engineer, and Macaulay, the Company Secretary, reads as follows:-

'Train Accident at Bisley
11th April 1898
'Referring the minute of 27th April the Board of Trade Inspector's report on the above accident was submitted.

'The Driver 'R. Joy' to be reduced to a Goods Driver for 12 months and after this period his case to be brought up again for further consideration.'

It is recorded that Driver Joy was reinstated when his case was re-examined one year later.

The class of the locomotive involved in the accident was not previously known to have been authorised over the Bisley Camp Tramway. Number 175 was an Adams 0-6-0 tender locomotive of Class 0395; originally designed as goods engines they proved themselves to be competent, albeit rough riding, mixed traffic locomotives. Number 175 only lasted until 1916 but a few of the class, equipped with Drummond boilers, were still in use well over fifty years later. One was in fact used to haul the Railway Correspondence and Travel Society's special train from Waterloo to Brookwood in November 1952 on the occasion of their excursion over the then recently closed Bisley Tramway.

The Water Crisis of 1898

In 1898 concern was expressed that, in case of a shortage of water in the Camp, there was no safeguard for the boiler. This led to the NRA enquiring through Pain whether a suitable tank which they had located in Woking would be adequate for the purpose. The Council did not know that at the height of the July Meeting such a shortage would occur when the water company's supply to the Camp failed.

'Secretary supported purchasing an iron tank for sale at Woking, 1600 gallons, as a safeguard against scarcity of water for boiler.

'Recommend that Secretary be authorised to purchase the tank if in the opinion of Mr. Pain of Woking it is sufficiently good for our purpose.'

On 16 July, during the Annual Meeting, there was a major breakdown in the water supply to the Camp which would have proved disastrous if the L&SWR had not come to the rescue by providing old locomotive tenders as water carriers. This was reported in *The Times* of 17 July.

'There was the threat of a water famine yesterday and the threat was not entirely unfulfilled. For a time the water was off, but prompt measures were taken and

NOTICE!

In consequence of the failure of the Woking Water Co., to Supply Water

The Shooting Man's Hot Shilling Dinner is Suspended

until further notice, and in lieu thereof A LARGE PLATE OF COLD MEAT AND BREAD WILL BE SERVED AT 10d.

By Order,

W. MACKINNON, Col.,

Camp, Bisley,   Secretary, N.R.A.
[25]   July, 1898.

One alarming consequence of the failure of the Camp water supply!

the general manager of the South Western Railway came to the rescue with special tanks, and little or no serious inconvenience was felt. But today the water was off again, fortunately long after the hour of baths, and it is to be feared that the resulting discomfort will be considerable. It is on again now but confidence is destroyed. Certainly severe things have been said, and will be said, concerning the water company at Woking to which the breakdown is due.'

Capt. M.C. Matthews, the Assistant Secretary, wrote to the General Manager of the L&SWR to see if the 'special tanks', which were old locomotive tenders, could be retained for the time being.

July 18th 1898

'Dear Mr Owens,

'I am desired by the Council to express their hope that you will allow us to retain the two tenders during the uncertainty in the water supply, with authority to get them fitted when wanted at such places as may be ordered by you. Also that you will give instructions so that we can obtain water on telegraphing in case of emergency, which we trust will not occur.

Matthews had also written to Pain requesting his professional advice on the matter and had followed this up two days later with a letter to the Chairman of the Association, Sir Henry Fletcher, regarding the Water Supply to the Camp and also the new Tramcars for the Range Tramway.

'16th November 98

'Dear Mr Pain

'In case I do not see you in the train this evening I write to say I should be glad to have a chat with you about the Rifle Association Water Supply. I am not definitely authorised to ask you to advise the Council on the subject but am instructed to see you about it and to 'sound' you as to fees etc. What the Council wants is someone who is well up in such matters to advise them – they don't know if any works will be necessary nor do they know at all what may be required to be done but they want someone of experience to advise them on the whole subject. With an Association such as ours where practically all expenses mean a corresponding reduction in our prize list the question of expense is an item of considerable consideration.

'I should like to see you on the subject either tomorrow or on Friday and would come to your office at any time convenient to you. The Works Committee of the Council are having a meeting at Bisley on Saturday and are going all over the ground and you might like to take the opportunity of being there and so making the acquaintance of the members of the Council who will have to take the subject most closely into consideration.

Arthur C. Pain Esq
Civil Engineer
17 Victoria Street
Westminster'

'18th November 1898

'Dear Sir Henry Fletcher

'I hear from Fremantle this morning that your function at Brighton will prevent him from being at the Works Committee tomorrow. I am writing this partly as you will probably like to know what I have done on the subjects of Water Supply and Tramcars but more especially to have a record of an interview I have had today with Mr Pain.

'Water Supply
-

'Supplementing what I said in my letter last night I now send for your perusal copy of a letter I sent to Mr Pain. Today I called on him and he is prepared to go thoroughly into the question of our supply and general arrangements and to give a report on what he considers necessary or desirable to meet our needs, for an inclusive fee of twenty guineas, it being understood that should any works be carried out as the result of his report and advice he shall act as our Engineer in regard to them and receive in remuneration the fees usual in his profession for work of that nature. Mr Pain does not ask for this to be reduced to writing. Mr Pain will be at Bisley tomorrow in accordance with the suggestions in the last paragraph of my letter to him.'

At the next Works Committee Meeting it was agreed that 'the arrangements with Mr. Pain as contained in the letter of the acting Secretary to Sir Henry Fletcher dated 18 November was approved. The Committee interviewed Mr. Pain and instructed him to report.'

During November, Matthews had a meeting with Quick, the Engineer of the Woking Water Co, who proposed that a large reservoir should be installed on the high ground at the north end of the Association's property. The best site was just outside the boundary of the Camp and so permission would have to be obtained from the War Office to install it on their land. Further discussions with Pain resulted in a suitable design in which the tank would be mounted on a structure which could be used as a store room. Pain had already located a suitable tank, the property of the Farnham Water Company, and this was the one finally obtained. Permission from the War Office was obtained after Matthews sent a letter explaining the requirements, to the CRE (Commanding Royal Engineer) Aldershot, in February 1899.

A Works Committee meeting held on 9 December had tried to deal with the water problem by involving the L&SWR.

'Water Supply – Mr Mortimer and the Acting Secretary to see the General Manager of the S.W. Rly. To ascertain if the Railway Co's pipes could be made use of to connect the Frimley Company's main with that of the Woking Company.'

However, at the Works Committee meeting held on 4 January, it was reported that the L&SWR was unable to assist with the pipes and that the War Office were not prepared to participate in any scheme. The Secretary therefore wrote Pain another letter to confirm that the new tank could definitely be filled before the meeting.

'I understand that you have arranged with Mr. Quick about filling the Tank with water before the Meeting, it would never do for the Woking Water Comp. to find out at the last moment, that owing to want of pressure they could not do so.'

Contracts for the 60,000 gallon Tank were signed in April.

'22nd April 1899

'Dear Mr. Pain

'I enclose your correspondence i.e. "Tanks" if convenient to you I will call at your office at 3.30p.m. on Tuesday 25th inst. as might then settle everything and have the Contracts signed. If this hour is not convenient anytime Wednesday will suit.'

The installation of the tank solved any further problems with the water supply and the tank itself still remains in situ on top of its 'store room', now converted for commercial use.

Train Services on the Main Line

Towards the turn of the century there were increasing complaints about the train service to Brookwood. At this time widening works on the main line were in full swing including substantial improvements at Waterloo Station and the problem may have been partially rooted in the disruption caused by those activities. In *The Times* of 11 July, their Special Correspondent recorded a journey to London and back which seemed to indicate a number of problems, especially on the return!

'THE BISLEY MEETING.
(FROM OUR SPECAL CORRESPONDENT.)
BISLEY, JULY 11.

'Now there is a matter of some little importance, albeit it has no direct connection with shooting, which must be mentioned. The main reason why men stay here as long as they can and go up to London as seldom as possible is, no doubt, that Bisley is a very delightful place under such conditions of weather as those which have prevailed to-day. Another reason, and a very unfortunate one, is that when once you have left Bisley it is sometimes very difficult to get back again. Now there are quite a large number of men, willing and anxious to shoot in the afternoon, who are none the less compelled to desert the camp occasionally and to

attend to their business. Few things are more wonderful than the manner in which doctors and lawyers, and all sorts of professional men, to say nothing of those of humbler rank, manage to combine the business of rifle-shooting with the business of life. For reasons of my own I put myself into the place of one of them this morning and travelled up to London. As to the up journey there was no ground for complaint; but the return journey, by the 1.5 p.m. from Waterloo, was far from creditable, and I mention some little facts about it at the suggestion of a member of council who happened to be my companion. We were ten minutes late in starting from Waterloo, and there was unconscionable delay at Woking. Of this I make but small account, being of opinion that at the worst of times it is better to be late than to occupy a railway carriage which gets into the way of another carriage in motion. But at Brookwood the delay was far greater and quite inexcusable. The member of council, knowing the ways of the tramway, got out and rode into camp on a bicycle. I remained. For unconscionably long time the through carriage stood idle in the sun. Every official in the little station deemed it his duty to examine tickets and to make sure that the passenger was going to Bisley Camp only. And when at last we crawled into the camp station fully an hour and a half had been occupied over the journey. This is surely a matter which might be mended.'

In the same year the *Volunteer Service Gazette* also had something to say about connections at Brookwood!

'With a little trouble the South Western Railway might succeed in improving the special service of trains between Brookwood and Bisley Camp. At present quite a number of trains seem to be so carefully timed that they continue to miss the main line connexion by a minute or two. The train leaving Camp at 9 a.m. misses the 8.57 from Brookwood to Waterloo; the 9.30 misses the 9.33, and necessitates waiting for nearly an hour; the 10.30 from Camp misses the 10.30 from Brookwood to Waterloo, and the 11.0 train from Camp misses the 11.5 from Brookwood. The same applies to trains later in the day, nor does there appear to be any attempt to steam out of the Camp Station up to time. We would strongly recommend the railway officials responsible to revise the time-table.'

Sam Fay, who went on to become the General Manager of the Great Central Railway, was the L&SWR Superintendent of the Line from 1899 until 1902. In a letter dated 21 March 1899 he asked Matthews to waive the latter's proportion of the Bisley Camp Tramway charge for a special train. This was in connection with the 'Home District Rifle Meeting' to be held on 17 May. He received an immediate reply agreeing to the request 'as a one off.'

By 1900, with the Boer War going against the British, the government had begun to absorb some important lessons about the importance of marksmanship in a modern campaign from the 'untrained' Boer Farmers who were putting up such an effective resistance to the Army in South Africa. They now fully supported such training through the medium of Regional Rifle Clubs and the NRA Secretary promptly wrote to the General Manager of the L&SWR to enquire whether the Company would be willing to extend the cheap rates of Volunteers to the members of such Clubs. This was immediately passed to Fay, who agreed to expedite a suitable arrangement.

'2nd March 1900
'The National Rifle Association in conjunction with the War Office are doing all in their power to encourage Rifle Clubs and to facilitate Rifle practice.

'Amongst many difficulties is the expense of Railway Travelling. Might I ask you to bring before your Clearing House this our application on behalf of our recognised Rifle Clubs that they may be allowed travelling to and fro from the Ranges the same privileges as allowed to Volunteers.'

'London and South Western Railway
Office of Superintendent of the Line
Waterloo Station
9th March 1900
'Referring to your letter of the 2nd instant, addressed to the General Manager, which has been passed to me, I beg to say that it has been decided to convey members of recognised Rifle Clubs bearing arms and travelling from Waterloo to Brookwood for shooting purposes upon the same terms as Volunteers and the Booking Clerks at Waterloo have been instructed accordingly.

'I may add that it will be necessary for each applicant to surrender to the Booking Clerk a form of certificate as a means of identification but this I will arrange direct upon receipt of applications from the various Secretaries of Rifle Clubs.

Yours faithfully
Sam Fay'

Fay's very positive response to this request enabled Crosse to use the precedent it set some ten years later by actually quoting the L&SWR letter.

In April 1899, Matthews had had to write a long and carefully worded letter to Charles Owens regarding alleged irregularities in issuing and collecting tickets on the Tramway.

'April 13th 1899
C. J. Owens Esq.
General Manager,
L. & S.W. Railway
Waterloo Station

'Bisley Tramway
'You may remember when I had the pleasure of seeing you some four or five weeks ago, I mentioned that there were one or two matters connected with the working of the Tramway from Brookwood to Bisley Camp Station which had been noticed by members of the Council of the National Rifle Association and which I had been directed to bring to your notice before this year's meeting

'The Council do not wish to make any definite complaint about the matters listed in this letter but from their personal observations and the evidence they have obtained from their Officials they think there is some slackness principally in the method of issuing and collecting tickets which offers undesirable facilities for irregularities on the part of the Staff employed in working the Trams.

'Passengers arriving at Brookwood or proceeding from Bisley Camp, who are not provided with through tickets, purchase single journey ticket @ 3p each at the special Booking Offices, either at Bisley Camp or Brookwood Station but it not infrequently happens that through want of attendants at the station offices, insufficient time and other causes a large number of passengers are able, and in many cases, obliged to get into the tram unprovided with tickets and their fares are collected by staff without any adequate measures of check.

Also the arrangements for collecting tickets are not uniformly satisfactory and the Council have had several substantial rumours brought to their notice of used but undefaced tickets being used a second time after having been obtained in a manner that points to probable irregularities.

'The Council do not wish to allege actual irregularities the subject was not brought prominently to their notice until after last years meeting; they have no evidence of a substantial character on which to base any such allegation but as they have an interest in the receipts from the tram line I am directed to ask that an interview may be arranged between our Secretary and our Superintendent of Turnstiles and the Officers of your Company responsible for matters of this nature with a view to considering whether any altered arrangements are desirable in the interests both of your Company and of this Association.

'The particular points I mention do not cover all the matters and I am directed to bring to your notice those that probably sufficiently indicate the general bearing of the matters to be discussed.

'If you see your way to arrange this interview I shall be glad if you would fix an appointment either here or at Waterloo (whichever would be most convenient to you) giving me at least three days clear notice.'

Owens passed this to Sam Fay and a meeting was arranged at Waterloo. A lack of further correspondence on the subject seems to indicate that a satisfactory resolution was reached.

The Saturday Train
By 1896, the number of Volunteers attending the ranges on Saturdays had grown to large proportions and Mackinnon wrote a letter to Charles Scotter proposing that the trains involved could run through to Bisley Camp Station

'21st April 1896
'I am desired by the Council to ask your favourable consideration of the following proposal.

'On Saturdays large numbers of Volunteers use the Bisley ranges, the majority going down by the 1.30 train returning by the 7.28. These men, many hundreds, crowd the platform and trains; many have been waiting some time and may be inclined to be disorderly; the trains become over full to the inconvenience of passengers and their own discomfort. I understand that on some occasions last year, and on Saturday last, a special had to be sent from Waterloo for them.

'The position is, might it not prove to the advantage of the Railway, it would be to our advantage, if, without increasing the fare, the train conveying them from London and Weybridge could run to our Camp station, wait, and take them back to London direct. The Council would gladly forego their share of the tramway fare.

'From our engagements so far we have reason to believe that this year the numbers will be greater than last year.

'Sir C. Scotter
General Manager
L.& S.W. Railway'

However nothing seems to have resulted from this request, although special through trains were provided as and when requested by Volunteer Division Commanders. It was not until August 1899, when a full shooting season concentrated on Saturdays from April to October, had become established, that the Association made a further attempt to introduce direct connections between Brookwood and the Camp on those days.

'Brookwood Tramway - The Secretary was instructed to approach the L.&S.W. Rly Authorities on the subject of running trains from Brookwood to Bisley Camp on Saturdays.'

The Assistant Secretary had once again raised with the L&SWR the possibility of establishing mixed gauge between Brookwood and Bisley so that *Wharncliffe* and its tramcars, from the Range tramway, could provide services outside the July Meeting; however, inspection of the track near Brookwood Station indicated this might not be possible. Fortunately an alternative scheme had already been discussed and Matthews put this to Fay.

'August 29th 99
'S. Fay Esq.
Supt. of the Line
Waterloo Station L&SWRy

'With reference to my call on you a few days ago about Railway communication between Brookwood and Bisley Camp on Saturday afternoons during the Musketry season other than during the Annual Prize Meeting. Mr. Andrews has not yet informed me whether or not he considered the proposed mixed gauge on this line to be within the range of practical policy, but from my interview with him and from subsequent examination of the points at Brookwood Station with the Station Master, I can see that this is likely to be more difficult to arrange than the Committee of the National Rifle Association thought would be the case, and I shall therefore be obliged if you will go into the alternative proposal more closely and let me know to what extent your Company could meet the wishes of the NRA in this matter should the mixed gauge scheme have to be abandoned.

'You will remember that the alternative scheme was that during the busy part of the Musketry season, that is to say, roughly from the middle of April to the middle or end of October, (except the three Saturdays in July covered by the Annual Meeting) your Company should run a short train on Saturday afternoons between Brookwood Station and Bisley Camp making such connections with your trains at Brookwood both up and down as experience would show the Volunteers are likely to be travelling by.

'The Council would like to know whether your Company will provide such trains. Assuming a satisfactory service is maintained, I think you may expect that at least 75 percent of those who now travel to Brookwood (for the Bisley ranges) would travel on to Bisley Station if the fare were not more than 3d return, or possibly 2d each journey; and although I have no definite authority for saying it, I have every reason to believe that the NRA would not require to receive any part of these fares if the service proposed was thereby facilitated.

'If you can arrange to let me have something definite in reply by the 18th of October I shall be glad, so as to be able to place before the next meeting of my Committee, and if there are any further points you would like to confirm with me about it, I shall be pleased to keep any appointment you may make.'

On 4 of September Fay delivered a favourable reply regarding the introduction of a Saturday service and this enabled the NRA Assistant Secretary to formulate

an acceptable proposal to put before the Council. The main points were reflected back to Fay in a letter dated 6 September 1899.

'I am obliged by yours of the 4th inst and note that it is considered impracticable to introduce a narrow gauge into Brookwood Station parallel with the existing line.

'I also note that your Company will be prepared, with a guarantee from this Association of not less than £5 on each day the train is required, to run a train on Saturdays during the Summer in the manner suggested in my letter of the 29th ult.

'I will bring this before the Council and communicated with you on the subject again in a short time.

'I presume the guarantee would extend over the whole Summer so that in calculating the amount which might have to be paid under this guarantee any excess of takings on one day would be set off against a deficit on another day.

'I shall be glad to have a line from you on this point at your convenience.'

This was duly passed on to the Association's Working Committee.

'Railway Tramway - The Secretary reported that he had approached the Railway Co on the subject of running trains between Brookwood and Bisley on Saturdays during the shooting season and that the L.&S.W. Rly Co had replied that they would do so on a minimum guarantee of £5 each Saturday. It was decided that it would be preferable for the NRA to pay a fixed sum each time to the Railway Co and to charge a little extra on the targets so as to partly cover the cost of running the tram free.'

At a meeting of the Finance Committee on 20 December 1899, confirmation of the arrangements by the Railway Company were read and minuted.

'Letter of 11th December from the L.& S.W.Rly Co:
'Agreeing to run a special train between Brookwood and Bisley Camp on Saturdays and Bank Holidays during the shooting season when ordered at a charge of £5 for each day; the service not to exceed three trips in each direction; Volunteers to be carried

without charge; the general public to pay the ordinary charge viz: 3d. in each direction, was read and approved. The Secretary was directed to make the necessary arrangements with the Railway Co: for the running of trains.'

The Council agreed to the proposals, which now also included Bank Holidays and other days.

'Report of the Finance Committee announcing that the South Western Rly: Co. would run a special train on Saturdays and Bank Holidays, and on other days when required during the Musketry season between Bisley Camp and Brookwood Station, making three journeys in each direction, at a charge of £5 for each day, conveying Volunteers and others using the Bisley ranges free, and the general public at a charge of 3d per each journey, and recommending that the charges for Practice Targets on Saturdays and Bank Holidays be increased by 1/- per target was submitted, and on the motion of Lord Waldegrave, seconded by Colonel Marsden, unanimously adopted.'

This was confirmed in a letter from Matthews to Fay, dated the 5th January 1900.

'Your letter of the 11th. December last with reference to a train between Bisley Camp and Brookwood Station on Saturday afternoons and Bank Holidays during the Musketry season was read at the Council Meeting on Wednesday, and I am directed to inform you that the Council accepts with thanks the arrangements you propose to make, and also agree to pay the charge you make for this service, £5 (on terms of your letter).

'I shall be glad to know how many days notice you require to make the necessary arrangements, and will inform you a little later on what our requirements are likely to be.'

The running of these services was put under the direct control of the Brookwood Stationmaster, as the local agent of the L&SWR Traffic Department, in liaison with the NRA Secretary, and were provided each year until the outbreak of war in 1914. For example, a very typical letter was written on 28 May 1910 by the Brookwood Stationmaster regarding additional Saturday trains.

'Traffic Department
Brookwood Station
'With reference to your enquiry per additional Service from here to Bisley Camp Station on Saturdays after the arrival of the 2.25 pm and 2.28 pm trains ex Waterloo. I am instructed to inform you that the Company would be pleased to provide such a service between the points named, but it could not be done without an extra payment of 30/- for the trip over and above the £5 paid for running two trains each way on each occasion, will you very kindly inform me, at your earliest convenience, if you are prepared to agree to these terms, and oblige.

Yours respectfully
L. Dennise'

FAMILIAR BISLEY SCENES.

No. 1. THE SATURDAY TRAIN AT THE PLATFORM.

THE L. & S.W.R. Co. have a special line to Bisley Camp Station and run special trains in the shooting season During the Bisley Meeting nearly 70 trains a day—over 30 journeys each way—are run between Brookwood and

Bisley Camp. From the ranges London is reached in an hour. Territorials and N.R.A. members and Rifle Club members are carried at cheap fares. On Saturdays in the season special trains run into and out of the camp.

A Saturday Train at the Platform headed by Adams Class O2 0-4-4 Tank Engine Number 235.

On 18 July 1910 A.P. Humphrey (who was temporarily acting for Crosse at the time) had complained to the Superintendent of Waterloo Station regarding the lack of porters to meet a special train from Brookwood at the end of the Annual Meeting at Bisley. He immediately received a reply from that official.

'Station Superintendents Office
Waterloo Station
20th July 1910

'In reply to your letter of the 18th ulto, with reference to the lack of Porters in attendance to meet the 6.0pm special train from Brookwood on Saturday last, I beg to inform you that owing to the congested state of the traffic this train was turned into the New South Station instead of the Main Line Arrival. The Inspector who met the train however, should have taken immediate steps to secure a number of Porters, and cabs should have been ordered round from the Main Line cab stand.

'I am taking the matter up sharply in order to prevent any similar trouble in future, and beg to express my regret that so much inconvenience and delay should have been experienced.

I am, Sir
Your obedient servant
(signed) J. P. King'

Lt. Col. Crosse and Henry Holmes

In 1901, following the negotiations regarding the 'Saturday' service, Lt. Col C. R. Crosse wrote to Fay on both the 11th and 18th September demanding to know why the NRA was being asked to pay for the services of the Attendant for the Bisley Camp level crossing.

'I am in receipt of your letter A/3/86222 of the 19th inst from which it is obvious that for the safe working of the line the provision of men experienced in the management of a level crossing is necessary and I am therefore at a loss to understand why the Association is asked to pay for the services of these men any more than for that of Guards, Engine Drivers, Stokers, &c. The only charge for the services of your staff which the Association has in previous years called upon to pay is the moiety of the Salaries of Booking Office Clerks.'

Sam Fay was appointed to the position of General Manager of the Great Central Railway in 1902 and was succeeded by Henry Holmes, making the latter almost the exact contemporary of Crosse in each of their respective positions. The two maintained an extensive business correspondence throughout this period with regular face-to-face meetings when necessary.

During and after the Boer War there was a great surge of patriotism and with it a massive expansion of Rifle Clubs, the country having begun to come to terms with how a comparative handful of Boer Farmers, in the early part of the war at least, had comprehensively out-shot the British Army in South Africa. This, in turn, lead to a vast increase in the number of Volunteers, private citizens and military personnel who now wished to hone their skills at Bisley during the expanded shooting season lasting from April to October. It was estimated that, by 1914, membership of rifle clubs in Great Britain alone was in the region of eighty eight thousand, most having an ambition to distinguish themselves on the Bisley Ranges, a destination they could only reach by train.

To accommodate this immense expansion in the use of the Ranges Crosse initiated regular negotiations with Holmes to improve train services at Brookwood Station, including through services to the Camp in parallel with arrangements for cheap fares. Special trains and saloons had also to be provided for important visitors and teams from overseas. There was also the occasional Royal Train for good measure! In those years King Edward VII and the Prince of Wales, the future George V, each made visits. The Saturday Camp tramway services were the responsibility of the Brookwood Station Master and Crosse took good care to build up a good working relationship with that Official.

He also took these responsibilities a step further. Being a regular passenger at Brookwood Station he became a keen observer of the railway scene on the main line and more than once wrote to Holmes suggesting the stopping of services at that station which would not have normally done so! Sometimes he had success and sometimes he did not, but it was not for want of trying.

Initially the omens were not promising. Main line trains that served Brookwood had become increasingly unpunctual throughout 1901 and this had led to a severe loss of business to the NRA causing Crosse to write a strong letter to Sam Fay, then still the L&SWR Superintendent of the Line, regarding the situation.

'November 7th 1901

'I beg to enclose a letter from the London Scottish Volunteers.

'This Corps began to use our Ranges for Class Firing for the first time in April last, and were so pleased with our arrangements that they practically decided to use the Bisley Ranges for all firing and applied to us to allot them a piece of ground for a Hut. As the season wore on, the traffic on your line became heavier and the train service most unpunctual and its continued unpunctuality has resulted in their deciding not to use our Ranges in future.

'I am directed by my Council to inform you that this is not only a serious monetary loss (some £350), but also that this very unpunctual train service does have, and will have the effect of preventing other Corps from coming to Bisley, and the Council would be glad if you could offer some kind of assurance and make some arrangements for next year that I could circulate amongst other Metropolitan Rifle Corps before they decide to abandon us, like the London Scottish.'

A major reason for this unpunctuality may have been due to the major widening works on the main line of the L&SWR between Woking and Basingstoke, the section to Brookwood not being completed until 1903, although this was never quoted as a reason during that period.

On 24 March 1902, in reply to a letter from Henry Holmes who had only recently been appointed as the new L&SWR Superintendent of the Line, Crosse made a pointed attack on the main line Saturday train service.

'I was unable to call on you this morning so now write in reply to your letter of the 20th inst.

'I regret to say that the arrangements you suggest are not at all what we require. I venture to point out to you that the Brookwood traffic receipts on Saturdays from now on through the Summer will compare favourably with any other station on your line. I therefore, writing on behalf of some thousands of Volunteers, do consider that some better arrangements should be made than one special train that loiters down from Waterloo to Brookwood in the appalling time of 1 hour 18 minutes at its best.

'What we require is as follows :-

'Punctuality in service of trains (last Saturdays 1.35pm train from Waterloo was more than ten minutes late at Brookwood).

'Train starting from the same platform always, stopping to pick up only, at Clapham Junction, Wimbledon, Surbiton, Weybridge and Woking, and running only to Brookwood, and doing the journey as advertised in 68 minutes.

'We most earnestly do not require a through train to the Camp it is quite useless as we have as you know a special every Saturday from Brookwood to Camp.

'May I venture to add that a good return service is of equal importance and I should be glad if you would arrange for this.'

By 1900 Crosse was in a position to request additional stops at Brookwood for certain main line trains and he did so in connection with the Annual Meeting of that year.

'10th July 1900

'The Traffic Manager
'London & South Western Railway
'It would be a great convenience to the Volunteers from Aldershot attending this Meeting and the Council would consider it a favour if arrangements could be made for stopping the 8.3 train from Aldershot at Brookwood.'

However in the same year he had to question the charging to the N.R.A's Account of certain through troop trains to the Camp.

'November 7th 1900

'With reference to your letter of the 9th inst. the troop trains to which referred are not the trains paid for by the NRA on Saturdays, but special trains that were run into Bisley Camp Station without any previous reference to the Association.

'With reference to Goods traffic – I should be much obliged if more detail could be given as we have to show the receipts under two headings. I should be grateful to see you personally on the matter.
'The Accountant
L. & S.W.R. Railway
Waterloo Station'

The 1908 Olympics

In 1908 the Olympic Games, originally awarded to Italy, were unexpectedly moved to London. This required the erection, at very short notice, of a new stadium located in White City where the main events were held with the shooting competitions being held at Bisley. It was not, however, until late June that the NRA Secretary wrote to the L&SWR to arrange a suitable train service for the events that were scheduled to start on July 9th! Nonetheless relations between the two organisations being what they were there was no problems in their provision.

'June 22nd 1908
'The Rifle Competitions in connection with the Olympic Games will be held at Bisley on July 9th, 10th and 11th and, as we expect a large number of Competitors and others I shall be glad if you will kindly make arrangements for the tramway between Bisley Camp and Brookwood to run on those days.'

The Superintendent of the Line replied by return and Crosse confirmed that he required a service over the Camp line similar to that provided for the annual Meeting and on 30 he put forward his ideas on the connections to be made at Brookwood.

'I would suggest that the tramway service on the 9th, 10th and 11th should be as follows:-
In connection with the 9.30 – 9.55 – 11.45- 12.8 – 1.10 – 2.28 – 3.5 and 4.12 trains from Waterloo, and

The L&SWR agree to run services over the Bisley Tramway to cover the 1908 Olympic Shooting. Written by George West, Henry Holmes' deputy.

in connection with the 1.45 – 2.28 – 3.5 – 3.15 – 4.4 – 4.26 – 4.51 and 5.58 up trains from Brookwood.'

Crosse noted from the reply that the Superintendent of the Line had not extended connections with the 9.30 and 12.8 trains from London and the 2.23, 3.15 and 4.4 from Brookwood, however he appeared to be satisfied.

The arrangements for the Olympic Shooting turned out to be very simple. No special trains from London were asked for or provided and the service of trains over the tramway was no more than an extension of that provided for the annual Meeting.

In a separate, but related, set of correspondence the captain of the Great British Britain Rifle Team wrote to three of the major railway companies, the London North Western, the North British and the Great Northern, desiring that the normal half fare arrangements be extended to members of the team using their services and this was readily agreed. The reply from the North British Railway coordinated the agreement of the main Scottish railways and was signed by Donald Deuchars, the Superintendent of the Line

Royal Visits and Special Saloons

The provision of special Saloons to transport colonial and overseas teams to Bisley became a regular negotiation by the NRA Secretary. In 1903, for example, a Saloon carriage was arranged to carry the American Team, who were taking part in the Palma International competition, from Liverpool to Bisley.

'June 8th 1903

'I beg to inform you that the American Rifle Team which is visiting Bisley to shoot for the Palma International Match will arrive at Liverpool on June 20th, and I am directed by the Council to ask if you could possibly arrange with the L. and N. W. Rly for a Saloon carriage to be placed at their disposal to convey them from Liverpool to Bisley Camp. In the event of this arrangement being impracticable, perhaps you could kindly arrange for a Saloon carriage from Waterloo to Bisley Camp.

'We expect that a number of Foreign and Colonial Teams will be in Camp here from June 22nd, and the Council hope that you will kindly give them the facilities which have in past years being granted to the members of the Canadian team to travel from Brookwood to the various Stations on your line at the single fare for the return journey. When Teams from England have gone abroad the Railway Companies have been so ready to grant every concession, the Council feel that the English Railways will not be backward in this respect.

'I am greatly obliged for your letter of yesterday informing me that you have arranged for the issue of cheap tickets to Lady members of the Association when production of their badge or card of membership whether they are proceeding to Bisley for rifle shooting or not.

'H. Holmes Esq.
Supt. of the Line, L.&.S.W.Rly
Waterloo Station'

Other Saloons to visit Bisley were those making up the Royal Train. On 29 1904, the Prince and Princess of Wales made the return trip between Waterloo and the Camp. In this case the L&SWR invoiced the NRA for the guaranteed sum of £5 which had been originally agreed with the Association to cover the special Saturday trains.

In 1905 Edward VII, the Patron of the NRA, inspected the Camp and presented the prizes on the last day of the Annual July Meeting. To publicise the visit the NRA produced a set of posters and requested Holmes to have them displayed at L&SWR Stations.

'July 18th 1905

'I have instructed our printers, Messrs. Reliker & Co., to forward to you tomorrow a parcel of posters announcing the visit of His Majesty the King to Bisley Camp on the 22nd instant and to request that you will be so kind as to have them prominently exhibited at the Stations on your line.

'As the time is short I shall be obliged if you would give the matter immediate attention.'

Following the 1905 Meeting Crosse wrote a letter of thanks to the L&SWR General Manager for the success of the arrangements including the decoration of Bisley Camp Station for the king's visit. He also took the opportunity to slip in a case for extra through trains during the Annual Meeting!

'July 31st 1905

'I am directed by the Council of the National Rifle Association to request that you will convey to the members of your Staff engaged at Bisley Camp during the late Meeting the recognition of the Council for the able manner in which they performed their duties.

I am further directed to thank you for the admirable arrangements which were made on the occasion of the visit of His Majesty the King on the last day of the Meeting both as regards the special train for the conveyance of His Majesty and the handsome way in which the Camp Station was decorated.

'With regard to the train service, I shall be extremely obliged if in future we could have at least 2 through trains each way on each day of the Meeting, especially on those days when competitors and others are arriving and departing in large numbers and have considerable quantities of luggage, as many complaints have reached me this year of the great inconvenience of having to change platforms at Brookwood Station.'

In early 1909, Crosse had received a letter from the officer responsible for the Colony of Natal's Rifle Team regarding railway travel concessions for the Bisley Meeting. –

'On previous years the Railway Company running the service from Waterloo to Brookwood have been good enough to grant members of Colonial Teams a reduction on the ordinary fares but each year we have had to ask for this reduction and do not get the advantage of it until we have been in England some time. Could this concession be arranged before the Teams arrive? It will affect all?'

This correspondence was of considerable historical interest as it occurred just prior to Natal becoming part of the

King Edward VII takes a salute at the end of his visit to the Camp on 22 of July 1905. The station had been especially decorated by the L&SWR for the occasion.

new Union of South Africa in 1910 as is explained in the same letter. Crosse had passed this on to the L&SWR and received a positive reply which he then passed on to the Natal Agent General in London.

In 1913 the Australian team made a visit to Bisley. This involved a six weeks voyage to the United Kingdom and Crosse made an extra-ordinary effort to ensure that they were provided with the best available transport to Bisley from their port of arrival at Plymouth. His first task was to write to Holmes.

'May 9th 1913
'The Australian Rifle Team which is expected to arrive at Plymouth by the P & O SS "Malwa" on June 13th have decided to disembark at Plymouth instead of proceeding to Tilbury, and I am directed to express the hope that you will be so kind as to make some arrangements for conveying the members of the Team and their baggage from Plymouth to Brookwood, and if possible place at their disposal a Saloon Carriage for the journey, and take any further steps you may be able to for the comfort and convenience of the Team.

My Council are anxious that a very cordial welcome should be given to the team, and that such facilities as can readily be arranged may be extended to its members.'

He received general agreement from Holmes but some perceived difficulties in running through to the docks were identified and Crosse passed this on to the shipping company.

'June 6th 1913
'With reference to our correspondence as to facilities for the conveyance of the Australian Rifle Team from Plymouth to Brookwood, the London and South Western Railway have promised to provide a Restaurant Car and possibly a luggage van from Millbay Station, but they say there is some difficulty as regards the special car running into the Docks. If this cannot be arranged it would necessitate some arrangement being made for the conveyance of the baggage from the Millbay Docks to Millbay Station, and I shall feel very much obliged if you would kindly inform me whether you make any special arrangements for this.

It would, however, be far more satisfactory and save no end of trouble and inconvenience if the special car could run through from the Docks, and if you can in any way assist with a view to such an arrangement being made I shall be greatly obliged as I am anxious to do all I can for the comfort of the Team.

'Might I ask you to be so kind as to let me have news of the "Malwa" for about 24 hours before arrival at Plymouth and also if the boat arrives at Marseilles within time.

'The P and O Steamship Co. Ltd.
122, Leadenhall Street
London EC'

In fact, the Great Western Railway operated the Docks in Plymouth and it was necessary to involve that Company in any arrangement to run the car through. Crosse was now able to take this up through the L&SWR.

'June 7th, 1913
'I thank you for your letter of 5th inst. informing me of the arrangements you propose Brookwood.

'The arrangements as far as they go will suit admirably, but I would remind you that your Representative promised to communicate with the Great Western Railway with a view to arrangements being made for the Saloon Carriage and luggage van to be run from the Docks.

'I very much hope that this can be done as it would save a great deal of inconvenience and delay.

'I agree to the charge of £1.0.0 for each day the Saloon and Staff are detained at Plymouth but as I now hear that the boat may not arrive until the 14th I shall be glad if you would let me know what is the latest date which I could advise you as to the date on which the Saloon is required. I am anxious to avoid the necessity of detaining the Saloon and Staff longer than actually necessary.'

Messrs Fox and Co, the P and O Agents at Plymouth successfully completed all the arrangements for the arrival of the *Malwa*, which finally occurred on 14 June and Crosse duly wrote letters of appreciation to P and O, the Great Western Railway and the L&SWR.

In 1914, less than three months before the Great War broke out, the Australian Rifle Team again came to Bisley and Crosse applied the experience gained in 1913.

'May 20th 1914

'The Supt. of the Line
L.& S.W.Rly. Co.

'Last year you were kind enough to arrange for a Saloon Carriage and Luggage Van to be provided at Plymouth to meet the Australian Rifle Team and bring them direct from the Docks to Brookwood Station. This arrangement was much appreciated and I would ask you to again provide this same accommodation for the team which will visit us this year and will arrive at Plymouth about June 11th by the P. & O. S.S. 'Mooltan'.

'You will remember that last year there was some difficulty as to running the Saloon from Millbay Docks, but this was eventually overcome and arrangements made with the P. & O. Agents at Plymouth for the Saloon Car and Luggage Van to be in waiting at the landing stage.

'I hope you will be able to make similar arrangements this year in every respect.'

He also sent a similar letter to P&O. This resulted in the GWR agreeing to accommodate a L&SWR dining car, attached to one of their luggage vans, at the Plymouth landing stage on the arrival of the SS *Mooltan*. On picking up the Australian team these would then be hauled to Exeter St David's station where they would be handed over to the L&SWR.

In 1914 very similar arrangements were again made for the Team. This time the L&SWR would supply a luggage van. Lunch or dinner would be offered at 5s per head for a guaranteed minimum of 20 passengers. If the restaurant car was delayed at Milbay Docks due to the late arrival of the ship there would be a charge of £1 per day for the saloon and staff.

At this time the possibility of the outbreak of a European conflict that, in turn, would involve Britain and its Empire was not even contemplated.

The Frimley Junction - Sturt Lane Junction connection

One of the slightly more exotic routes to Brookwood and Bisley involved the use of the complex triangular junction connecting the Ascot to North Camp (now Ash Vale) line to the main London and South Western line about a mile and a half east of Farnborough Station. In 1908 there existed a rather irregular service of trains which used the eastern curve of the triangle between Frimley Junction and Sturt Lane Junction; the majority of trains ran through the single line section to North Camp Station. During the annual Meeting at Bisley a considerable number of competitors used this route, giving them an early enough arrival at the Camp for squadding purposes with a corresponding return in the early evening. In 1908, a change in the timetable upset these arrangements and a prominent member of the NRA, Surgeon-Captain F. Blake-Campbell who lived at Ascot, wrote an urgent letter to Crosse to see if he could help. Blake-Campbell was Adjutant of the Irish XX Rifle Club.

'Ascot, Berks , 2nd June 1908
'Dear Colonel,
'The L&SWRy Co Summer timetable just out, and I find they have taken off the more popular of the forenoon to Brookwood that was as follows:
New Service, 1st June

Leave Ascot	8.22am	8.21
Bagshot	8.29	8.28
Camberley	9.39	8.37
Frimley	8.45	8.43
Brookwood	8.43	Non-Stop
Camp arrive about	9.10	Woking 8.55

Next train to Brookwood is as follows –

Leave Ascot	8.40am
arr North Camp	9.9
leave N. Camp	9.26
arr Brookwood	9.35
arr Camp	9.40

'Now this means that competitors coming from Reading – River area, Windsor, Ascot etc. Who all arrive at Ascot Junction about 8.18, and used to come in by the 8.22 arriving Brookwood 8.53 will in future have to cool their heels until 8.40 then hang about North Camp and not arrive at Brookwood until 9.35, fifty minutes – 50 later, practically one hour! – later into Camp

'Can you do anything to help us? Its a most serious matter fro the 11-27 July. The various Cadet Corps who stop at hotel here (Glenmond) and men on GWR line who come through Reading can't reach Camp until 9.35 – what about Squadding etc.

'Another matter is the return to Ascot in the evening – the trains are as follows:
Brookwood to Ascot

Leave Brookwood	4.42	5.10	6.07*	6.54#

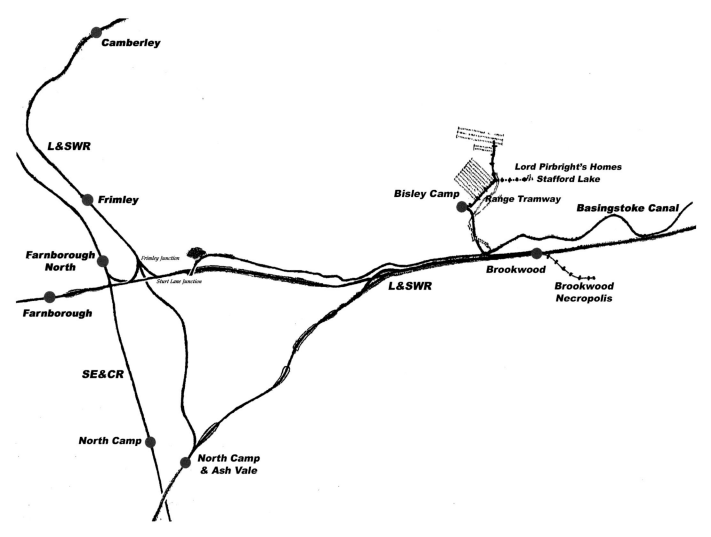

The railway network around Bisley c.1908. The line from Ascot passes through Camberley and Frimley to Frimley Junction and then round the east curve of the triangle to join the main line at Sturt Lane Junction while the now single line to North Camp and Ash Vale continues under the main line. The parallel South Eastern & Chatham line between Reading and Guildford passes through Farnborough North and North Camp on the left hand side of the map. The Bisley Range Tramway is also shown including the temporary extension (1900-1901) laid to bring in site materials for the new Princess Christian Homes at Stafford Lake.

Arr Frimley	3.52	5.20	6.37	7.05
' Camberley	3.58	5.26	6.42	7.11
' Bagshot	4.06	5.34	6.49	7.19
' Ascot	4.12	5.40	-?	7.25

*If the 6.07 ex-Broookwood would run on to Ascot, would be most convenient train in day meeting connections and home in good time for 7.30 dinner.

#This train is too late, always unpunctual, seldom reaching Ascot before 7.40 –

'It becomes a question of leaving Bisley either by the 5.10 or 6.54.

'At least if the L&SWR cannot make change altogether, can they have the 8.21 ex-Ascot from 11-27 July to stop at Brookwood, and the 6.07 ex-Brookwood run on to Ascot all Saturdays from Easter Monday until end of July and each day during meeting.

'I regret troubling you about this matter, but being so important, the sooner it is seen to the better before it becomes common property, and small entries thereby.

'With kind regards, Sincerely Yours, Frank Blake-Campbell.'

Blake-Campbell's letter landed on Crosse's desk the same day it was addressed. The latter, with his usual efficiency, passed this letter on to Holmes with his own comments added, again before the day was out!

London & South Western Railway.

Office of Superintendent of the Line.

Waterloo Station,

Henry Holmes,
Supt of Line. *London, S.E* **9th June, 190 8.**

Please copy this Nº in your reply

A4/ 3 0 6 1 3

16084

Dear Sir,

      In reply to your letter of the 3rd instant enclosing a communication from Dr. Blake-Campbell with reference to the train service between Ascot and Brookwood, I beg to say that I have had pleasure in giving instructions for the 8. 21a.m. train from Ascot to stop at Brookwood at 8. 51a.m. during the forthcoming Rifle Meetings July 9th - 25th.

      With regard to your correspondents suggestion that the 6.7p.m. train from Brookwood to Bagshot should run on to Ascot, I regret that this is impracticable as the train now returns from Bagshot at 7.0p.m. to form a connection at North Camp with the up train to London, and if it ran on to Ascot on the down journey it would not be able to take up its present timing from Bagshot, with the result that the connection at North Camp would be severed.

      Yours faithfully,

Henry Holmes

Lt. Col. C. R. Crosse,
    Bisley Camp,
      Brookwood,
        Surrey.

Henry Holmes responds to Blake-Campbell's letter.

'June 3rd 1908

'I enclose a letter from Dr. Blake-Campbell with reference to the train service between Ascot and Brookwood and shall be much obliged if you will kindly look into the matter with a view to granting better facilities between these places.'

Although the desired result was only partially achieved the correspondence emphasises the influence that Crosse was able to wield on train services in the area where the NRA was concerned.

Congestion at Brookwood Station

Crosse received a letter from a Mr F. Gould on 30 May 1910 regarding congestion at Brookwood Station experienced on the arrival of special Saturday trains carrying shooters to the Bisley Ranges. This lead to a short bout of correspondence involving the L&SWR Superintendent of the Line.

'Dear Col. Crosse,

'When I arrived at Brookwood by the 1.13 on Saturday, it took me about 7 minutes to get off the platform, in consequence of what I consider the very faulty and primitive arrangements which are made for taking the tickets.

'Every year that I go to Bisley in the Spring months I feel the same annoyance at the usual sight of two porters blocking up the exit and having a sort of scrimmage with the men who want to get across on to the other platform.

'I am not an expert in such a matter as this, but I feel sure that if the Railway Co. would send down an experienced official to watch the usual performance next Saturday, the latter would come to the conclusion that some more satisfactory method of collecting the tickets could easily be devised.

'At present there is lateral pressure on the exit from the converging crowd of men; and I would think that a much more rapid and less vexatious collection of the tickets could be devised by having them taken at the foot of the short staircase leading up to the Booking Office at the end of the tunnel.

'Unless the Ticket Collectors at Brookwood are old footballers, I can hardly imagine that they enjoy the weekly struggle, and I am only surprised that, in their own interests, that they have not tried long ago some other than the present plan.

'Perhaps if you would kindly make representations to the Railway Co. they would give my suggestion a trial. In the tunnel only so many can go abreast, and it would then work like the ordinary queue at a theatre. If there is any fear that some men would try to pop out of the door at foot of the stairs on the Arrival Platform, a porter could be stationed there for the few minutes to see that such did not occur.'

Crosse passed this on to the L&SWR Superintendent of the Line, who sent down his District Superintendent to observe the situation. The latter's report was reflected to Crosse.

'Office of Superintendent of the Line
June 15th 1910

'Dear Colonel Crosse,
'On the 31st ulto. you sent me a letter from Mr. F. A. Gould in reference to the arrangements at Brookwood Station, which I return herewith.

'I requested my District Superintendent to visit Brookwood and watch the train in question, and he reports that there is a certain amount of hustling and jostling on the part of the men of the Territorial Force arriving by that train, the majority of them trying to pass off the platform through the exit at the same moment, and that with the exercise of a little patience no difficulty would be experienced.

'I am afraid the suggestion made by Mr. Gould would not improve matters, but that the only effect would be that the pushing would take place in the subway instead of on the platform.

'As you are aware, Brookwood Station was reconstructed only a few years since. I really could not recommend my Directors to incur a considerable amount of expense in carrying out further

alterations there, in order to relieve a pressure which occurs only on the arrival of one or two trains on one day in the week, the remedy for which, as I have ventured to point out, rests with the men themselves

'Yours faithfully
Henry Holmes

Holmes' reply did not satisfy Crosse as he personally had also observed the situation first hand at the Station and he now sent a further letter fully supporting Gould's views.

'June 18th 1910
'Dear Mr Holmes,
'I thank you for your letter of 15th inst. with reference to Mr Gould's communication as to the arrangements at Brookwood Station for collecting tickets, and I cannot help thinking that your District Superintendent's view of the matter is much too favourable.

'I happened to be at the Station last Saturday when a train arrived and it was nearly a quarter of an hour before the platform was cleared and quite 5 minutes before there was any apparent decrease in the crowd at the gates.

'I am aware that there are difficulties in the matter, but I should have thought that the experience of your staff in such arrangements would have enabled them to suggest a means of avoiding the inconvenience and delay.

'To Henry Holmes Esq:
Supt. of the Line
L. & S.W. Rly.'

It would appear that the L&SWR took no further steps to alleviate the problem but Gould thanked Crosse for his efforts to obtain some kind of resolution. However, a year later on 26 June, Crosse came up with a possible solution. This was to re-open a footpath with direct access to the south side of the Station that lead to the Pirbright railway arch but nothing further is recorded on whether this was ever proceeded with.

Passes and Badges

Under Scotter, the L&SWR had maintained a close working relationship with the Association from the opening of

Bisley and had also donated a large sum of money. The NRA in response made him an Honorary Life Member and he was presented with the Association's Ivory Badge. This honour was extended to other senior officials of the Railway when the Court of Directors presented a valuable prize donation for a new rifle shooting competition (The London and South Western Competition) in 1895. A regular correspondence now commenced between the NRA Secretary and William Buckmaster, the long-serving Chief Clerk in the L&SWR General Manager's Office, regarding further recipients of these sought-after badges.

When Scotter died in 1910 his badge was returned to the NRA by the L&SWR Secretary and Crosse wrote a short letter of condolence.

> 'January 6th 1911
> 'I beg to acknowledge receipt of the ivory badge which belonged to the late Sir Charles Scotter who was a Life Member of the National Rifle Association, and of whose death my Council have heard with deep regret.
> 'Thank you for so kindly returning the badge.
> 'G. Knight Esq.
> Lon & S W Rwly
> Waterloo Station'

Crosse also wrote to A. W. Szlumper, the newly appointed L&SWR Chief Engineer, confirming that he should retain the NRA Passes, originally issued to his predecessor, Jacomb Hood, who had been found dead by the side of his horse earlier that year while out hunting on Dartmoor.

> 'I thank you for your letter of the 8th instant and shall be glad if you will kindly retain for your own use, the passes sent to your predecessor the late Mr. Jacombe Hood.
> A. W. Szlumper Esq.
> Engineers Office,
> Waterloo Station,
> S.E.'

It had been the practice since Wimbledon days, for the NRA to award Life Memberships to senior officers of organisations who had been of assistance to the Association. In the case of the L&SWR the assistance as well as prize money given by the latter had merited this award to a number of Directors as well as the General Manager and, as time went on, others further down the tree had become recipients.

Goods Traffic

The NRA's Account Books confirm a regular and fairly heavy flow of goods traffic into and, to a lesser extent, out of the Camp commencing with the opening of the Tramway in 1890 and continuing right through to the outbreak of the Second World War. These take the form of invoices sent to the NRA from both the L&SWR and the Southern Railway. This is especially true of the large quantities of ammunition, sometimes several tons, brought in for the Annual Meeting and which must have been carried in vans. Generally, this came from Woolwich Arsenal via the L&SWR Goods Station at Nine Elms. In addition, large quantities of military rifles moved between Weedon near Northampton on the LNWR, the location of a major Royal Ordnance depot, and the Camp.

There was an additional tariff for goods carried over the Tramway so parcels and certain goods were generally sent to Brookwood Station to be carted to the Camp by the L&SWR's carman, generally a contractor. Amongst the earliest deliveries recorded by this means was in June 1891 when a prefabricated hut arrived for the noted American pistol shot, Walter Winans, following shipment from the USA. This hut still exists today but is now known as the Elcho Lodge.

There were regular monthly deliveries of truckloads of coal for general Camp use. From 1890 until about 1922 these originated from the associated Digby and Gedling Collieries near Nottingham. After this date, up to the outbreak of Second World War the NRA dealt with the Griff Colliery near Nuneaton in North Warwickshire. Deliveries of coke came from the nearby Aldershot Gas Works at Tongham.

Rail deliveries into the Camp via the Tramway were by the local pick-up goods which shunted down any trucks and vans as necessary. Vans were used to carry ammunition and rifles and also domestic deliveries directly to the Pavilion which had its own gated siding. In addition, they were used to satisfy the requirements of the wealthier competitors before the Great War who liked to equip themselves with every home comfort to alleviate their otherwise spartan tented accommodation during the Annual Meeting. Temporary porters were employed to deliver these large amounts of luggage from the Camp station to its final destination. Such duties were normally allocated to boys from the Shoe Black Society, a leading charity of the time. Another fairly regular delivery were second hand railway sleepers which the NRA bought from the L&SWR mainly for reinforcing the Target Butts. There were also regular visits by battalions of Volunteers, and later Territorials, for shooting practice which were not recorded by the NRA. These required goods trains as appropriate to deal with stores, equipment and sometimes horses.

Nearly all building materials were brought in over the Camp Tramway and this particularly applied during the construction of the Princess Christian Homes in 1900 when a branch of the Range Tramway was specially built to access the site at Stafford Lake. The Camp terminus of this tramway was altered at the same time to be adjacent to Bisley Camp Station for the purpose of facilitating easy transhipment. The rails for these extensions were brought up by train from Devonport where they had been in use on the recently closed Tregantle Military Railway.

When major repairs to the Range Tramway locomotive *Wharncliffe* were required, it was sent initially to the Nine Elms Works of the L&SWR in both 1893 and 1898, in each case under an agreement between the NRA and the railway company. In 1901, it was sent to Merryweather's plant at Greenwich for a new boiler and, again, in 1909 for major repairs. The locomotive was transported each time on an L&SWR machinery wagon. In 1899 the new bogie tramcars for the Range Tramway were delivered by rail from Messrs J & F Howard's factory in Bedford, probably on similar vehicles.

During 1910, there were several incidents affecting deliveries to the Bisley Camp goods sidings. In July of that year the gateway on the siding to the back of the Pavilion was damaged after it swung back after an engine had passed through. The L&SWR accepted responsibility but requested that fastenings be fitted to the gate to prevent this happening again. Also that same year, considerable correspondence was generated over a 'missing coal' delivery, escalated on further charges that the load was below the recorded weight!

A very rare demurrage claim was made on the NRA by the L&SWR in 1911. 'Demurrage' was, in this case, a claim made on the excessive retention of goods trucks by the NRA. Crosse was able to make a strong rebuttal as the trucks in question were retained over the Easter Weekend when the staff responsible for their unloading were on holiday for the duration.

'13th May 1911
'With reference for the enclosed account for demurrage, I would point out that the two trucks in question loaded with gravel arrived at Bisley Camp at 6pm on Thursday the 13th of April, too late for unloading by our staff on that day. The day following was Good Friday. On the 15th (Saturday) run into the Camp, and the unloading the trucks would have inconvenienced this service. The 17th was a Bank Holiday (Easter Monday) on which day also no work could be done.

'The trucks were eventually unloaded on the 17th and 18th of April and returned on the latter date.

'Under these circumstances I consider that the charge for demurrage should not have been made, and I shall feel obliged if you will kindly cancel the account for 6/-

'The Goods Manager
L. & S. W. Rly
Waterloo Station
London SE'

Evidence suggests that the Railway Company withdrew the claim.

In the Great War, the tramway and the military extension to Blackdown Camp bore a very heavy goods traffic on behalf of the War Office who took over the complete line in 1917. This made life rather difficult for the NRA who were struggling to maintain their own regular deliveries of coal with the added problem of unloading the wagons in the time allocated with greatly diminished resources.

The London & South Western Competition
In 1895, the Railway Company, now on excellent terms with the NRA, offered to fund a new Bisley competition that was known, initially, as the 'Railway.' Mackinnon stated that the shooters preferred that competition names were made as short as possible but this, unsurprisingly, did not appear to go down well with the sponsor and it was changed the following year!

'2nd May 1895
'Dear Sir Charles Scotter,
'Your telegram arrived while our Council was sitting; they desire me to ask you to convey their thanks to

 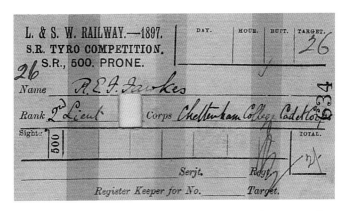

Competitor Register Cards for the L&SW "Railway" competition. In 1895 the L&SWR sponsored a new competition after a gap of nearly thirty years. This was for 'Tyros', those shooting at Bisley for the first time. It was called the 'Railway' initially to keep the title short. No doubt the sponsoring railway company had something to say about that and it was renamed the L.&S.W. Railway competition from 1896.

your directors for their handsome contribution to our prize list. This donation of 100 guineas entitles the London and South Western Railway to nominate five Life Members of the Association; when you send me the names I will be happy to register them. The competition will be called 'Railway', (we abbreviate all titles as they are more talked of than long titles), prizes by the London & South Western Railway, two distances, for tyros, it will be very popular - last year a similar competition had over 1000 entries.

I am, Dear Sir Charles,
Yours very truly
W. Mackinnon Col.
Sect. NRA

'Colonel Sir Charles Scotter
London & S.W. Railway
Waterloo Station"

The competition as originally conceived was for Tyros (newcomers) shooting with Martini-Henry Rifles shooting over two distances, 200 kneeling and 400 yards prone. The prize money offered was shared between the L&SWR and NRA who contributed £52 10s each.

The competition was renamed the 'L & SW Railway Competition' in 1896, most probably for the reasons stated, and remained in the NRA Competition List until 1923 when it was replaced, on a different basis, by the 'Southern Railway Competition.' At the 1896 general meeting Earl Waldegrave, alluding to a remark which had appeared in the press that the L&SWR Competition prize money had been reduced from one hundred guineas in 1895 to fifty guineas in 1896, explained that the

former was a special donation, whereas the latter was an annual contribution to the prize list.

On several occasions, just before the Annual Meeting, the NRA Secretary had to write a polite letter to the L&SWR reminding them to remit the prize money!

The L&SWR Rifle Club

The L&SWR had formed its own Rifle Club in 1901 and this quickly became affiliated to the NRA as No. 126 on the list. The Club's first Secretary was C.E. Worsdell and it was headquartered at Nine Elms. It was also a member of the London Railways Rifle League, made up of seven clubs representing the major railway companies, where it rapidly built up a reputation for the excellence of its shooting.

In 1903 Arthur Conan Doyle, whose views on rifle shooting had acted as an important catalyst in the formation of Rifle Clubs, held a rifle competition at his Undershaw Rifle Range at Hindhead. The prize, of a silver statuette depicting a Volunteer Rifleman, was won by the South Western RC who just beat Conan Doyle's own team.

In 1912 the Club was exceptionally successful and its annual muster that year was presided over by the Railway Company's new General Manager, Herbert Walker.

The extract following was published in the NRA winter *Journal* published in December 1912.

'The L&SWR Rifle Club
Railway League Champions

'The Club has had a very successful year. The main features of the work have been the winning of the championship of the London Railways Rifle League,

Mr. H. A. WALKER,
GENERAL MANAGER, L. & S.W.R.

"The London Scottish get there most times. The new General Manager of the L. & S.W. Ry., Mr. H. A. Walker, is an old member of 'I' now incorporated with 'F' Co. He joined in 1885, resigning 1890." So says the *London Scottish Regimental Gazette*. All our readers will be interested in the portrait of the new South Western's supreme

Chief of the Staff. He it is who will make the arrangements for trains to Bisley this year, including the heavy traffic of the Bisley fortnight. Marksmen, therefore, have an especial interest in Mr. Walker, as men from every part of the Empire come finally upon the South Western system ere being shot into camp. Territorials will also appreciate him as the General Manager who arranges their rapid transport in and out of camp in the south west countries. He came to Waterloo from the North Western Company, and has a brilliant administrative record. So far as the Territorial force is concerned, he is a "mobilisation keystone," for in time of war the S.W.R. will be a premier line, embracing as it does such centres and camps as Aldershot, Pirbright, Bisley and Salisbury Plain. All Territorials and shooting men will join in wishing him great success in his high and important post.

Herbert Walker becomes General Manager of the L&SWR - from the N.R.A. Spring Journal of 1912.

a league comprising of seven of the London Railway Clubs, viz., Great Eastern Railway, London and North Western Railway, Great Central Railway, London, Brighton and South Coast Railway, South Eastern & Chatham Railway, District Railway and London and South Western Railway. This necessitated twelve matches each, of which this club won all theirs, with an average per man per match of 96.5, and an average aggregate of 773 out of a possible 800 per match. Another feature was the strenuous fight made with Ham and Petersham RC for the Astor

Cup at Bisley, in which the club only succumbed to the ultimate winners of the County Championship by 5 points, and that only after its Captain had put a bull on the wrong target. The club also succeeded in winning the Surrey Advertiser Challenge Cup, open to tyros only, and given in connection with the National Service League Competition in the County of Surrey.

'The annual muster was held at Vauxhall last month. Mr. H.A. Walker, the General Manager of the Company, presided, and was supported by the Earl of Selborne and Colonel Williams, M.P., Director of the Company. There was also present Mr. J. H. Vickery, Assistant General Manager; Mr. A. H. Stanley, Manager of the Tube Railways of London; Mr. W. Bishop, Solicitor; Mr. Glyn Smith, Assistant Solicitor; Mr. Henry Holmes, Superintendent of the Line; Mr. G. F. West, Assistant Superintendent of the Line; Mr. F. Molyneux, London District Superintendent; Mr. A. W. Szlumper, District Engineer; Mr. J. Smeal, Goods Manager; Dr. T. Archer, Medical Officer; and Mr. S. E. March, Goods Superintendent, Nine Elms.

'Commenting on the shooting, Mr. Walker said that, although the South Western Team had come out so splendidly, it was a sad fact that the club was not being properly supported. It was essential that every man in this country should know how to handle a rifle. They all hoped that the time would never come when they would be called upon to use it. But he hoped that in future they would get many more members of the club. Mr. Stanley of the Underground Railways, had presented medals to the winning team.

'Lord Selborne thanked the company for their very kind reception. He emphasised the importance of the words which had fallen from Mr. Walker on the subject of Rifle Shooting. As has been said, they all hoped and prayed that the occasion would never arise when they would have to use their knowledge, but if there was one thing that recent events had impressed upon them more than another it was that in modern warfare an untrained man was useless. Even a man capable of using a rifle was not a perfectly trained man, but, nevertheless, a man who could be very valuable to his country in a crisis. Whatever their opinion on foreign politics, it seemed to him training in arms was as natural an obligation on them all as the paying of taxes. He respectfully suggested to the young men in particular that a few hours a year devoted to Rifle Shooting was a patriotic obligation. (Loud Cheers).'

Sleepers

The NRA had discovered at a fairly early stage that old railway sleepers made an extremely effective support to the earth bank at the back of the butts. In due course, they also found them useful for supplying to various temporary small-bore ranges to protect the wall behind the butts and were, naturally, of great benefit in repairs to the various tramway lines at Bisley.

Mackinnon was the instigator but it was Crosse who went on to build up a strong relationship with the L&SWR's Stores Department at Nine Elms under its successive Superintendents, G.R. Barrell and C. Alexander.

The earliest document on the subject that has been identified dates from 1893 and consists of an invoice for 200 sleepers presented by the L&SWR Accountant. There was then a considerable gap and the next communication on the subject was sent by Crosse to Barrell on 25 February 1904 referring to a requirement for 3-400 sleepers to accommodate a proposed extension to the Range Tramway. This request was modified in a further letter dated 4 March in order to accommodate a Miniature Rifle Meeting at Olympia in London.

'With reference to your letter "P" of the 25th inst. the sleepers will be required in the first place at Olympia, London at our Miniature Rifle Meeting and then at Bisley Camp when we extend our tramway. We shall require 400 and I shall be glad if you will let me know of a nearer place to Olympia where you have this number in stock.

'I appreciate your thoughtfulness in quoting for sleepers at Farnham as being close to Bisley but as we want them first in London it would be an unnecessary expense to convey them from Farnham to London and then back to Bisley.

'Mr. G.R. Barrell
Stores Department

London & S.W. Rwy
Wandsworth Rd
London
SW'

Further correspondence on the subject went into the rates to be charged and comments regarding the possibility of the sleepers being delivered to Addison Road Station which was immediately adjacent to Olympia. Shortly afterwards Crosse requested an additional 50 sleepers to be delivered directly from Farnham to Bisley Camp and, in the same letter, he mentioned that the L&SWR Goods Manager had stated that the original order would have to be sent to Nine Elms and carted from there to Olympia.

By mid-April Crosse had discovered that there were some deficiencies in the lighting arrangements at Olympia and he turned again to the railway company for assistance, this time to William Buckmaster, who was also a keen shooter at Bisley. Although much of the correspondence with him concerned the award of Honorary Life Memberships to senior officers of the Railway Company by the NRA there arose the odd occasion when Crosse felt able to call on Buckmaster's good offices for the benefit of the Association.

'April 18th 1904
'As you are doubtless aware the Association will hold a miniature rifle meeting at Olympia, Addison Road, from the 25th to 30th instant.

'The building will be lighted by gas, but the Authorities require in addition a separate system of lighting for the exits and I am wishful to obtain on loan 12 oil lamps for this purpose.

'Knowing that you take a personal interest in all matters connected with rifle shooting I thought you might be able to arrange for your Company to lend these lamps. If this does not come within the scope of your department perhaps you will kindly let me know to whom I should apply for the necessary sanction. An early reply will oblige.

'Mr Buckmaster
London & SW Rwy
Waterloo Station
London'

Somehow during the Meeting the original 400 sleepers had grown to a total of 500 and Crosse then duly requested their delivery to Bisley as soon as possible after the end of the Meeting!

Ever year thereafter, at least until 1912, Crosse put in orders for sleepers. In 1905, for example, there was a Miniature Rifle Meeting at the Exeter Drill Hall and Crosse again wrote to Barrell, this time requesting 110 sleepers, but seeing if he could keep the charge down by hiring them and returning those which were undamaged.

'These Sleepers are used to protect the wall behind the target and it is only about 10 per cent that are in any way damaged. I shall therefore be glad to know if you would be prepared to take back the undamaged Sleepers into store, making only a small charge for hire, or, if this could not be done, perhaps you would be able to arrange for undamaged Sleepers to be taken back into store at Exeter and the same quantity delivered at Bisley Camp from the nearest stores. This would save a considerable amount in carriage.'

Crosse followed this up with a letter to the Station Master of Exeter Queen Street, the South Western Station, asking him to make arrangements for delivering 120 sleepers to the Drill Hall.

'April 7 1905
'I have a letter from Mr. G. R. Barrell of the Stores Department dated March 31st in which he states that he has given instructions for a quantity of old Sleepers to be placed at my disposal at your Station

'Will you kindly give instructions for 120 Sleepers to be delivered at the Drill Hall 1st V.B. Devon Regm, commencing at 11a.m. on Monday morning next the 10th instant.

'I presume the Sleepers are the same size as supplied to us at Olympia London, last year, viz:

9ft   Long
5ins   Thick
10ins   Broad'

In February 1910 Crosse, who never seems to have missed a trick in this respect, observed repairs taking place on the line near Brookwood and promptly wrote to the Storekeeper to see if he could obtain some of the old sleepers. On a previous occasion he had been very successful with this approach.

'February 15th 1910
'The Storekeeper
L. & S.W.Rly.
Wandsworth Road
S.W.
'I notice that the old sleepers on the line near Brookwood are being replaced by new ones, and I shall be glad to know whether any of the second-hand ones which are being removed will be for disposal. Would you kindly let me have an early reply quoting price.'

But this time he was to draw a blank – Alexander, the L&SWR's Storekeeper, stating that he had again made enquiries and had been assured by his engineer that he had had the greatest difficulty fulfilling the Company's requirements and therefore, regretfully he could not comply with the request!

The Brookwood Cabmen's Shelter
At a meeting of the NRA General Committee held on 7 February 1900 the Secretary reported 'that he had been approached by several of the residents at Brookwood in view of the NRA giving one of the old tram-cars for the purpose of erecting a cabmen's shelter on it at Brookwood Station, and he further reported that the cost of converting one of these cars into a shelter would not exceed £10 and suggested that the N.R.A, should present a shelter.

The matter was discussed and favourably entertained and referred to the Finance Committee to consider and deal with.'

Cabmen's Shelter – The Secretary submitted a plan of the proposed Cabmen's' Shelter at Brookwood Station, the cost not to exceed £10. The plan was approved and the Secretary was directed to proceed with the erection of the Shelter.'

As far as can be ascertained bodies of the old tramcars had been already separated from their underframes and wheels and it would have been a comparatively straightforward job for the Association's workshop to equip one of them with some kind of a simple roof.

In March, the NRA Secretary wrote to the L&SWR Estate Agent, A.V. Haines, to see if the Company would waive any rental charges for the shelter.

> 'March 23rd 1900
>
> 'With reference to your letter of February 28th, I shall be glad to hear further from you respecting the proposed Cabmen's Shelter at Brookwood.
>
> 'Might I suggest that, as the Shelter is a gift on the part of the National Rifle Association for the benefit and convenience of the Cabmen at the Station, the charge for the site and the rent should either be quite nominal, or your Directors might see their way to forego any charge whatsoever, or allow it to be carried to expenses.
>
> 'A.V. Haines Esq
> L&SW Rwy Estate Office
> Addington Street
> Waterloo Station'

The L&SWR finally agreed to a nominal rental charge of 1/- per year. The cab drivers at Brookwood Station very much appreciated this gift and made good use of it. However, by 1912, the shelter was falling seriously into disrepair and was obviously becoming an eyesore. This had been noted by the Railway Company whose Estate Office was not amused and they wrote to the NRA to request it be repaired without delay!

The cab drivers, being fully aware that it had been a gift from the NRA in the first place and that the number of cab drivers now exceeded the capacity of the shelter, were keen to find their own solution although they did tentatively enquire whether the Association would be prepared to make a financial contribution towards a new shelter. In April 1913, the old shelter was carted to Bisley Camp for final disposal.

The Last Years of Peace - 1912 to 1914

In early 1912 Owens was elevated to the Board and replaced by Walker. Extremely keen on rifle shooting he proved to be a good friend of the NRA right through to his retirement as General Manager of the Southern Railway in 1937.

As had been customary in previous years, the Secretary circulated the major railway companies with details of the Annual Meeting in July, adding the hope that the usual concessions would apply to competitors.

London & South Western Railway.

SPECIAL TRAIN ACCOMMODATION

For Members of the Territorial Force and Rifle Clubs

Returning from the Bisley Ranges, Brookwood.

EVERY SATURDAY

UNTIL FURTHER NOTICE,

SPECIAL TRAINS

WILL RUN FROM

BROOKWOOD to WATERLOO

CALLING AT THE FOLLOWING STATIONS, VIZ. :—

WOKING	**WIMBLEDON**
WEYBRIDGE	**CLAPHAM JUNC.**
SURBITON	**VAUXHALL**

The departure time of these Trains will be altered as the Season advances, and it will be notified each Saturday at Brookwood and Bisley Camp Stations.

H. A. WALKER, General Manager.

14/ 5,000/344   Waterlow & Sons Limited, Printers, London Wall, London.

Saturday Specials from Brookwood to Waterloo. A notice issued during the 1913 Shooting Season.

He received an immediate acknowledgement from the office of the new General Manager, initialled by William Buckmaster.

Otherwise, however, things got off to a rather poor start. Problems in the coalfields had come to a head with the declaration of a strike in order to force the owners to concede a minimum wage. This naturally had severe repercussions on the delivery of coal which, in turn, had indirectly resulted in the L&SWR moving to cancel most of their cheap tickets for the duration. Crosse promptly advised Members that the

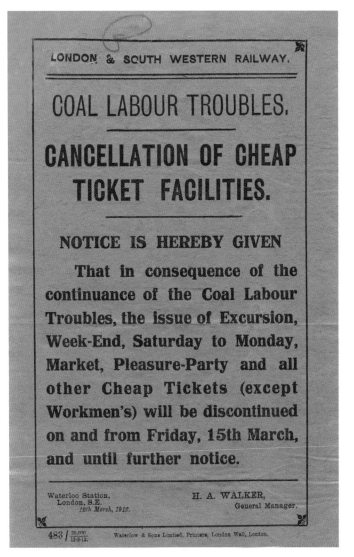

LONDON & SOUTH WESTERN RAILWAY.

COAL LABOUR TROUBLES.

CANCELLATION OF CHEAP TICKET FACILITIES.

NOTICE IS HEREBY GIVEN

That in consequence of the continuance of the Coal Labour Troubles, the issue of Excursion, Week-End, Saturday to Monday, Market, Pleasure-Party and all other Cheap Tickets (except Workmen's) will be discontinued on and from Friday, 15th March, and until further notice.

Waterloo Station,
London, S.E.
12th March, 1912.

H. A. WALKER,
General Manager.

483 / 20,000
13-3-12.   Waterlow & Sons Limited, Printers, London Wall, London.

The Coal Labour Troubles Notice issued by the L&SWR under the signature of their new General Manager, Herbert Walker, which was enclosed by Holmes with his letter.

L&SWR had suspended, without notice, the issue of special tickets.

'The Supt. of the Line
Lon. & South Western Rly.
Waterloo
March 29th 1912
'I beg to acknowledge the receipt of your letter of 27th instant confirming your decision to temporarily suspend the issue of the special tickets hitherto issued to members of the National Rifle Association.

'A decision so seriously affecting the convenience of our members is a matter which I must bring before my Council, and with a view to avoiding as far as possible any inconvenience arising at your Stations, I am sending the enclosed letter to those who have engaged targets at Bisley during the next fortnight.

'With regard to the special rate for the conveyance of passengers to Brookwood referred to in my letter of 25th instant, I have before me your letter of 8th November 1888 stating that your Company would be prepared to carry Volunteers from London to Brookwood and back for 1/6 each provided that the NRA select the site near Brookwood for their ranges, and also your letter of March 2nd 1900 agreeing to convey members of the Association at Volunteer rates.'

This brought a terse response from Henry Holmes (initialled on his behalf by his deputy, George West) dated 1 April, in which he made the point that the issue of cheap tickets to Territorials had not been disturbed. However it still affected NRA Members and Members of Rifle Clubs so Crosse was not satisfied with this explanation.

Crosse stuck to his guns and after several communications were exchanged, all in the space of about three days, the matter finally was brought to a satisfactory conclusion, at least for the time being.

'I am in receipt of your letter and telegram of 2nd instant and thank you for so promptly advising me of the withdrawal of your instructions to suspend the issue of special tickets to Members of the National Rifle Association and Members of Rifle Clubs travelling to Brookwood.

'I felt certain that when the facts of the case had been brought to your notice, you would realise that I was only asking you to carry out an arrangement which was specially agreed upon, and I would venture to ask you to kindly record the fact should your Company find it necessary at any future time to suspend the issue of Excursion and other cheap tickets, that such arrangements do not apply to the special tickets above referred to, which are granted under a specific promise, and are not therefore subject to the ordinary Regulations governing the issue of cheap tickets.

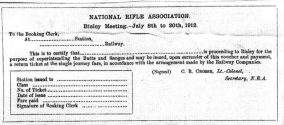

All letters to H. CUFF SMART. SECY

TELEGRAMS, "CLEARNESS. LONDON."

Railway Clearing House. 11667

Seymour Street, Euston Square.

London 13th May, 1912.
N.W.

Dear Sir,

Bisley Meeting.

I have the pleasure to inform you that the Railway Superintendents in conference have agreed that the following arrangements be adopted on the occasion of the National Rifle Association Meeting at Bisley, July 8th to 20th:-

(a) That 1st, 2nd, and 3rd Class single fare tickets to London and Reading, available for the double journey, be issued--

(1) To Officers and Men of the Territorial Force, either in uniform or upon production of tickets of admission to the competition,

(2) To Competitors from the Regular Troops, the Royal Navy, and the Royal Marines, upon production of Passes signed by their Commanding Officer, and certificates or shooting tickets showing they are intending competitors, and

(3) To members of Civilian Rifle Clubs affiliated to the National Rifle Association upon production of tickets of admission to the competition,

from the Thursday before the Meeting, except as to Stations in Scotland, from which Stations the tickets are to be issued from the Wednesday before the Meeting. These tickets to be available for return from London up to the night of the Thursday succeeding the close of the Meeting.

That.

11667

(b) That, on the occasion of the competition for the Loyd-Lindsay Prize, the Horses of Cavalry Corps and of the Territorial Force be conveyed at single rates per horse for the double journey.

(c) That the concession of "Single fare for the double journey" be understood to apply to Competitors only, except as stated in the following paragraph, and that the facility must not be extended to members of their families nor to members of the Association who are not competitors.

The concession granted to competitors may be extended to a number of Officers of the Territorial Force travelling to the Meeting in civilian dress for the purpose of superintending the Butts and Ranges provided a certificate in the following form be surrendered to the Booking Clerk:-

> **NATIONAL RIFLE ASSOCIATION.**
> Bisley Meeting.-July 8th to 20th, 1912.
>
> To the Booking Clerk,
> At.................Station,
> ....Railway.
>
> This is to certify that................................is proceeding to Bisley for the purpose of superintending the Butts and Ranges and may be issued, upon surrender of this voucher and payment, a return ticket at the single journey fare, in accordance with the arrangement made by the Railway Companies.
>
> (Signed) C. R. CROSSE, Lt.-Colonel,
> Secretary, N.R.A.
>
> Station issued to ....
> Class ....
> No. of Ticket ....
> Date of issue ....
> Fare paid ....
> Signature of Booking Clerk ....

Yours truly,

Lieut.-Col.C.R.Crosse,
National Rifle Association,
Bisley Camp,
Brookwood,
Surrey.

The Railway Clearing House agree to coordinate cheap fare arrangements with the major railway companies.

'It is possible that some of our Members who have paid the full fare under protest may apply to you for a refund of the excess fare paid, and I trust that their applications will be considered in the liberal spirit which your Company usually treats such matters.'

By July all seemed to be harmonious again with Henry Holmes, in a letter dated 16th July, agreeing to arrange a special saloon to convey the Lord Mayor of London and Sheriffs to the Annual Meeting stating that 'on Saturday next I shall be pleased to arrange for a saloon to be provided in the 11.45am train from Waterloo for the accommodation of the Lord Mayor of London and Sheriffs, and the vehicle will go through to Bisley Camp, where it will be due to arrive at 12.51pm, returning thence by the 6.0 p.m. special train, due Waterloo at 6.57pm.'

Fare concessions for competitors and officials requested by the NRA were co-ordinated through the Railway Clearing House. The letter from them for the 1912 Meeting is a typical example and shows details of these concessions. It also includes a sample of the certificate required by the officers from the Territorial Force who were appointed to superintend the butts and ranges.

Meanwhile the Station Master at Brookwood kept Crosse fully informed about changes to the train services affecting Bisley Camp, the former being specifically responsible for the special Saturday trains which operated as necessary throughout the shooting season.

Bisley Camp Station Developments

In late 1909 Crosse wrote to Owens regarding platform accommodation at the Camp Station. Certain trains were now arriving that were longer than the platform and some passengers had had to alight on the ballast at the Brookwood end of the station.

'November 15th 1909
'I am instructed to communicate with you with reference to the platform used by passengers at Bisley Camp Station. It has been doubtless been reported to you by your local officials that the length of this platform is quite inadequate for the length of trains which frequently come into the Camp station, and it is a common occurrence for passengers in the rear end

Adams O2 Class 0-4-4T No 2017, now with a Drummond chimney, prepares to run round its train probably towards the end of the Edwardian era but certainly before 1911 when the platform oil lamps were replaced with electric ones. The start of the 1 in 60 gradient behind the last coach is readily apparent. It was at this point that the 1898 accident, described elsewhere, occurred. (*Lens of Sutton*)

of the train on arriving in Camp to have to alight on the line at some risk of accident, the same inconvenience being experienced when leaving, as, when the carriage at the back part of the trains are crowded, it is only with considerable difficulty that passengers can enter the front coaches. Owing to the level crossing being close to one end of the platform it is impossible for the train to draw up so that passengers could alight with ease.

'My Council therefore hope that your Company will see their way before the next Shooting Season opens, to extend the platform end towards Brookwood to such a length as will accommodate any train which can be sent into the Camp.

'The General Manager
Ldn. & South Western Railway
Waterloo Station'

After further correspondence, the matter was placed in the hands of Henry Holmes, who then responded by offering to meet Crosse at Bisley on 25 May to discuss the matter. This was not in fact a convenient date for Crosse and further letters were exchanged on the subject. However, a measure of agreement was soon reached and at the same time Crosse sought tenders for lighting the Camp station by electricity. He received two replies from the railway company, one from J. Jacomb Hood, the Chief Engineer of the L&SWR, requesting details of the lighting scheme, and the other from Henry Holmes confirming authorisation of the expenditure. The overall expenditure was confirmed in a letter from Owens with the proviso that the NRA bore half the cost. The platform extension and the provision of electric light were completed in time for the 1911 Annual Meeting.

18850

London & South Western Railway.

Enclo:
Please copy this
N°. in your reply.

M. 4,310.

General Manager's Office,
Waterloo Station,

London S.E. July 18th 1910

Dear Sir,

Bisley Camp Station. Proposed extension of platform.

Referring to your previous letters with regard to the platform accommodation at Bisley Camp Station and suggesting that it should be extended, I now have pleasure in sending you herewith a plan prepared by our Engineer shewing how the platform could be lengthened by 110 feet at an estimated cost of £133.

It is also desirable that the electric light should be installed at the Station and this is estimated to cost a further £45.

My Directors have approved of these works being carried out upon the understanding that the National Rifle Association agree to bear one half of the total expenditure in each case.

Will you please let me hear from you thereon in due course.

Yours faithfully,

CHAS. J. OWENS.

Sir Charles Owens, the General Manager of the L.& S.W.R., confirms authorization of the platform extension and the electric lighting installation.

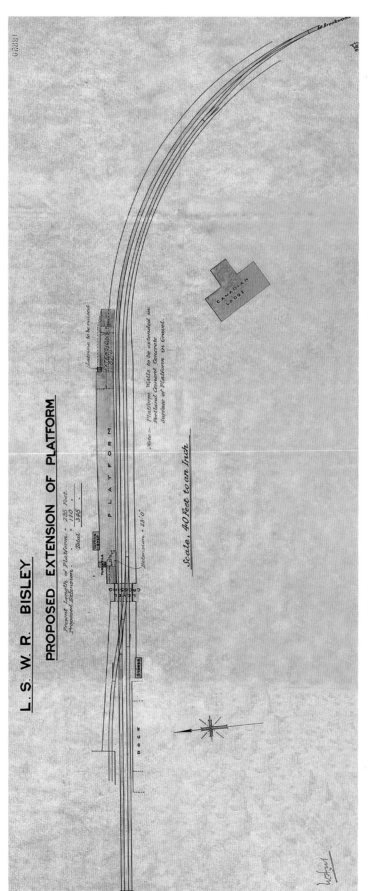

The L&SWR Plan of the Bisley Camp Station extension enclosed with Sir Charles Owen's letter regarding the authorisation of the extension and electric light provision.

July 1912, The *Bisley Bullet* departing from Bisley Camp Station. The *Bullet*, headed by an unidentified 02 class locomotive, accelerates away from the recently extended Camp Station towards Brookwood during the July 1912 Meeting. The Range Tramway diverges just behind the locomotive. The 'B and C Lines' Cabins (now the 'Crawford' Cabins) are prominent with the Bazaar Lines and some of the Club Houses visible in the middle distance. The Butts of the Century Range can be glimpsed in the background. The Siberia Ranges, the distant terminus of the Range Tramway, lie beyond.

The Fateful Year 1914

That year of world catastrophe, or at least the first half of it, also proved calamitous on the Tramway. Over this period there occurred three accidents and, although unspecified and apparently minor, the third one caused one of the important Saturday services to be cancelled, stranding and generally inconveniencing shooters at the Camp. This caused the Secretary to write a letter of complaint to the L&SWR Superintendent of the Line.

'June 29th 1914

'I am sorry to again have to report a third accident this season on the Railway from Bisley Camp to Brookwood two to our own Special Trains and one to a train engaged by the London Scottish, and would ask you to give your serious consideration in order that some steps should be taken to avoid such accidents in the future.

'On Saturday last the greatest inconvenience was caused and those who wished to catch the connection at Brookwood at 7.42 were compelled owing to the accident to take cabs and they are now naturally asking me the question as to whom they may look to refund the additional expense incurred on account of the accident.

'It is fortunate that no personal injuries have at present resulted from these accidents, but that is no reason why everything possible should not be done to prevent further accidents of this kind.'

Holmes, wrote back to say he would be dealing with the matter personally, but his following reply then stated that the Railway Company accepted no responsibility for any loss or inconvenience! This, of course, brought an immediate reaction from Crosse who demanded that the cost of the train involved in the accident, already paid for by the NRA, should be refunded.

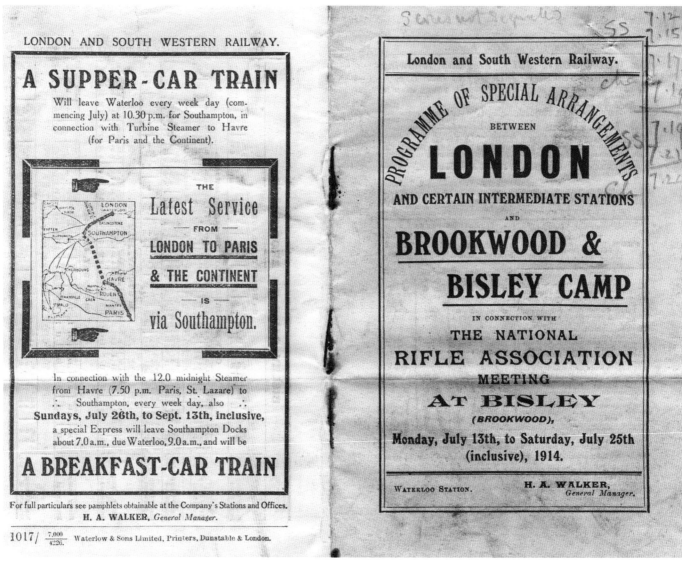

The first and last pages of the L&SWR Timetable booklet issued for the 1914 Meeting. Note the annotations regarding 'services not signalled' and the advertisement for luxury services to the Continent.

'July 10th 1914
'With reference to your letter of 7th inst. informing me that your Company do not accept responsibility for any loss or inconvenience caused by the accident which occurred at Bisley Camp on the 27th ult: and enclosing an extract for your Time Table with reference to the question of the liability of the Company in cases of delay, I would venture to draw your attention to the latter part of the paragraph referred to which reads 'or from any failure of a train to start at all (in which case the fare will be refunded)', and I think that under this clause we are justly entitled to a rebate on the enclosed account of £2.10.0 in respect of the trains charged and which to all intents and purposes, owing to the accidents, may not for all the use they were to intending passengers, have started at all.

'The claim for £2.10.0 is based on the charge of £5.0.0 for four special trains viz: 2 in and 2 out of the Camp i.e. 25/- each.'

On 7 July, just prior to the Annual Meeting, Crosse wrote to Holmes for advice respecting the temporary porters at the Camp Station. This was very necessary as many of the shooters brought vast amounts of luggage in order to equip their tents with every comfort for the fortnight.

'The Shoeblack Society which has for many years supplied boys who have acted as porters for the delivery of luggage at Bisley Station during the N.R.A Meeting is unable to let us have the boys this year and it is proposed in their place to have a few men, mostly pensioners, who are known to us as being reliable. These men would have access to the Station Platform at the Camp and would wear NRA Badges and if you wish it and would care to supply them on loan could also wear badges similar to those worn by your Outside Porters

'To enable us to make arrangements with the men I shall be glad if you would kindly inform me what are the usual charges authorised by you for the collection or delivery of luggage by Outside Porters.

'In our case the men would be expected to collect luggage on the platform and deliver it at the various Huts or Tents or vice versa.

'I shall much appreciate any information you may be able to give me in the matter, and as the time is short I would venture ask for a reply by return as soon as possible.'

At the end of the Meeting the luggage question had to be efficiently dealt with and the Secretary ensured this by writing to the Superintendent of Waterloo Station to ensure that there were enough Porters available in the right place to handle the load.

'July 23th 1914
'I shall be very much obliged if you will kindly make arrangements to have an adequate staff of Porters at Waterloo on the arrival of the Special Trains from Bisley Camp on Saturday next to deal with the luggage in an expeditious manner.

'The majority of those staying in the Camp leave by these trains and as you can well imagine take with them a large quantity of luggage and if they are unable to obtain the services of Porters would be in danger of missing their connections to other Railways.'

The Period of the Great War 1914-1918

With the declaration of war by Great Britain on Germany in August 1914 the National Rifle Association handed over the Camp to the War Office for the duration. At the same time, immediate steps were taken to form a School of Musketry at Bisley using instructors recruited from the ranks of the leading pre-war shooters. The normal peacetime traffic on the Bisley Tramway ceased, most competitions and the July Meeting having been suspended for the duration of the war.

Crosse had now been appointed Staff Officer for the School of Musketry; he wrote to the Railway Clearing House on 2 September regarding the introduction of half price return fare reductions in connection with this appointment.

'Under the Authority of the War Office the National Rifle Association is raising a Corps of Expert Rifle Shots to act as Musketry Instructors to the new Army which is now being raised.

'A number of these Instructors will be travelling to Bisley from all parts of the Country and I am directed to request that special facilities may be given to them to obtain return tickets at single fare.

'The matter being one of urgency, I shall be glad if you will give it your immediate attention.'

The normal peacetime traffic of Saturday trains during the shooting season and the services between Brookwood and Bisley during the annual Meeting were now suspended, being replaced by military trains carrying troop and goods traffic as and when required.

Motor traffic into the Camp was also now on the increase. A popular local taxi service run by Mrs E. Marshall, whose office was located at the Temperance Hotel adjacent to Brookwood Station, had started to use motor cabs just before the War but it seemed that by 1915 her drivers were tending to speed especially within the confines of the Camp. This had raised the ire of Crosse who now proceeded to send her a strong letter about their behaviour!

'September 20th 1915
'To Mrs Marshall
Brookwood
'I have to complain of the reckless pace your motor men drive your cabs into the Camp completely ignoring the notice 'Drive slowly' exhibited at the entrance.

'I have today had to personally warn one of your men who drove up to the Office at a furious pace regardless of the safety of pedestrians and other vehicles.

Unless you can take some steps to prevent a recurrence I shall reluctantly be compelled to prohibit your motor cabs from coming into the Camp.'

In 1916, the War Office decided to extend the Tramway for the purpose of serving the military camps at Pirbright, Deepcut and Blackdown. In its initial design this would have left Bisley Camp itself on a spur off the proposed new line. However the CRE at Deepcut, Colonel J. Fraser, suggested to the Association, on the advice of the L&SWR's Chief Engineer, that it might be preferable and more advantageous to all parties if the line was extended from Bisley Camp instead and this was agreed by the Council, the line being completed in early 1917.

The Military takeover and the Legal repercussions

In late February 1917 with the military railway virtually complete Lt. Col. Crosse received a bombshell. He had possibly anticipated that the military authorities would take control of the new line at some stage but not in the manner in which it came about. He was first informed of the intention to take over the Bisley Camp section, not by the military authorities or the General Manager of the L&SWR, as might have been expected, but by the Brookwood Station Master. This was followed, shortly after, by a visit from the Officer in charge of Construction and the Officer in charge of Military Camp Railways, Longmoor, who were under the impression that the War Office owned the whole line including the Brookwood to Bisley Camp section! As a result of this meeting the Officer in charge of Military Camp Railways, Major R. Godrey-Aston, sent a letter to Crosse which effectively threw the whole of the operating arrangements, and more specifically the agreement on payments that had been maintained between the NRA and the L&SWR since 1895, into disarray.

Crosse now had little choice but to hurriedly draft a letter to the Secretary of the L&SWR in an endeavour to clarify the position as seen by the Railway Company.

'March 3rd 1917

Dear Sir

'On the 22nd ult: I received a notification from the Station Master, Brookwood, that the Bisley Camp Railway would be taken over by the Military Authorities as from 1st March.

A few days later the Officer i/c Construction and the Officer i/c Military Camp Railways came to see me and expressed great surprise when I informed them that the line belongs, not to the War Office as they understood, but to the National Rifle Association and is worked by your Company under agreement, and further that we received from you an annual payment averaging £150 in respect of the Railway.

'I shall be very much obliged if you would kindly let me know what arrangements, if any, you have made with the War Office for taking over the line, so that I may have a record.

I am anxious to have a clear understanding in the matter, and as there are many points involved they could perhaps be better discussed at an interview, and I shall be pleased to come and see you if you think it necessary.'

A meeting was called at Waterloo on 12 March by Walker, at which the Railway Company's solicitor, W. Bishop was present. Crosse was accompanied by Col. Richardson, a Member of the Council.

Notes of the Meeting, which were drafted by Crosse, included a combative opening gambit by Bishop regarding the annual payments made to the NRA by the L&SWR.

A full report was presented at the next Council Meeting held on 23 March.

'The Secretary reported that he had received a notice from the London & South Western Railway Coy: that the Bisley Tramway line would be taken over on the 1st of March by the Military Authorities; that he had written to the General Manager enquiring who was responsible for the payment of the NRA proportion of fares etc. for running over the line and asked for an interview.

'Colonel Richardson and the Secretary saw the General Manager's representative (Mr. Bishop, Solicitor to the Company) on the 12th inst. and were then informed that in the absence of any special Agreement, the Solicitor was of opinion that the Agreement of August 1896 (sic - should read 1895) for conveyance to the London and South Western Railway of land and easements transferred all rights whatsoever to the Company in consideration of their keeping the line in repair and that all monies paid since that date were paid in error.

'It was pointed out that such an agreement would have been too one sided, so it was agreed that both sides should have a search for further correspondence etc.

'The Committee decided that Colonel Richardson and the Secretary should take any necessary steps before next meeting and report. The Solicitors to be consulted if required.'

Searches by Crosse in the registers of correspondence of the Association only turned up a record of receipt of such letters. He then turned to the NRA's solicitors, Messrs Raymond Barker and Co, whom he believed had been sent the original correspondence through their representative, Mr Wilde, who had drawn up the original agreement. However, although copies of the original agreements and other relevant letters proved elusive, on the 20th Crosse was able to inform the L&SWR's solicitor about some information that he had found regarding the original agreements.

'With reference to our interview on the 12th inst. when we discussed the question of the Agreement between the Association and the Railway Company, you asked me to help by referring to old correspondence on the subject of any agreement for payment of a moiety of receipts over the Tramway, and I find in our register of letters received that we had a letter from your Company dated June 25th 1891, stating that the Association would be credited with half receipts of the Tramway.

'There is also a note of a letter from the Railway Company's Solicitors dated 25th May, 1892, containing a proposal to give the Railway Company a small strip of land at the Canal Lock in return for which the Company would maintain and work the line into the Camp.

'You have doubtless copies of these letters in your letter books and could refer to them with much less trouble than it would take me to turn up the original correspondence. So if you are able to do so I shall be very much obliged if you would kindly let me have copies of these letters.

'Would you also be so kind as to let me know by whom the Agreement dated 14th August, 1897 (1896)

was signed on behalf of the Association when the Corporate Seal was affixed thereto.'

Unfortunately Bishop's reply did not provide much comfort although it did turn up the actual agreement, signed on 14 August, which transferred the parcel of land on the north side of the canal from the Association to the L&SWR. This was the land on which the northern pier of the canal bridge was situated, the bridge itself being owned by the Railway Company. This agreement turned out to be the only formal legal agreement between the two organisations regarding the Tramway.

Crosse, at the next meeting of the Council, was instructed to try and turn up further correspondence on the subject, with which he had some success, and also to contact Col. Marsden on the subject (Marsden had been the NRA Council Officer who had been in charge of the move from Wimbledon to Bisley). Crosse was also instructed to get in touch with the Association's Solicitors if necessary.

The L&SWR still had trouble in tracing the letters but Crosse made further efforts to assist.

'I thank you for your letter of 31st ult: and I am sorry that you have not been able to trace the letters referred to in my former letter.

'The enclosed, which is a copy of a communication received in 1911, seems to confirm the original agreement and will, I think, save me the trouble, which I am anxious to avoid, of turning up the original correspondence.

'I also find that, in May and June 1891, we had some correspondence with the General Manager bearing the reference To.6920. This may be of some assistance to you in tracing the letters.'

It was quickly realised that there were severe shortcomings in the original 'gentlemen's' agreements dating from 1890 and 1895 respectively which had never, of course, envisaged such a situation arising and this opened a lengthy period of legal argument. The negotiations regarding the ownership and legal aspects of the Bisley Tramway were now set to continue throughout the period of the military operation of the line.

Mr. James' Opinion

The debacle caused by the debate over the Tramway 'Agreements', the paucity of documents on the subject and the considerable difficulties in dealing with the military authorities over the issue had prompted the Council to call for an independent legal assessment of the situation. The solicitors to the NRA gave their view that an independent counsel's legal opinion should be sought and this was put into the hands of Ashworth James, a Barrister-at-Law of Lincoln's Inn Fields, who finally issued his 'Opinion' on 16 October 1917. The main requirement was naturally to ascertain 'whether the NRA could extract from the War Office the same tolls for use of the NRA part of the line, as had been extracted from the L.S.W.R.'

'National Rifle Association
Opinion

'The Tramways Order of 1890 confirmed by the Act of the 4th August 1890 empowered the promoters to construct and maintain the Tramway and also to charge certain Tolls and to acquire by purchase lease or otherwise the necessary land. Section 4 of the Order empowered the Promoters to assign the undertaking with its rights and liabilities to the NRA if and when incorporated but no other power or assignment was given.

'For the purpose of this Tramway Undertaking the Promoters obtained in November 1890 a Lease from the Secretary for War of the right to use certain land for the purpose of the Tramway Undertaking and to construct the Tramway thereover. But as I understand that the Tramway is not constructed on this land only but is continued beyond over other lands. Before the date of the Confirmatory Act, viz in June 1890, the N.R.A and the L.S.W.R. appear to have made an arrangement as to the terms on which the L.S.W.R. provided the necessary rolling stock viz half gross receipts. This Agreement seems to have been originally made for one year only but it seems to have been the fact that the L.S.W.R. accounted for half the gross receipts down to the beginning of the present war notwithstanding the transaction of 1895 below mentioned.

'In 1895 the NRA were apparently owners of a piece of land near the Railway which the L.S.W.R. wanted. At that time I gather that the L.S.W.R. was in fact carrying out the necessary maintenance of the Tramway from the junction of the Tramway with the Railway to the Terminus of the Tramway at the Camp. This included, as I understand, other parts of the Tramway besides those on the land held under the 1890 lease from the War Office. The NRA however were repaying them the cost of such maintenance.

'By a Conveyance of 1895 the NRA conveyed the piece of land to the L.S.W.R. in fee simple, and also assigned the L.S.W.R. the premises demised by the 1890 Lease, the L.S.W.R. assuming all the liability under that lease and also covenanting with the NRA to maintain and keep in sufficient repair for the purpose of the NRA Meeting in each year and for such other purposes as the Association may require to use the same the permanent way of the Tramway of the Association between Brookwood Station of the Company and the Camp Station of the Association and the signals, telegraphs and other accessories thereto. By a deed of the same date the Company agreed during the yearly Meeting of the Association at Bisley to provide sufficient train service between Waterloo and Bisley Camp.

'Nothing was said in these documents of 1895 about the Tolls or expenses. The Tolls were not 'premises demised by the lease of 1890' but depended on the Order of 1890, and it is at least doubtful whether the Association could assign the right to receive the Tolls to the L.S.W.R. or otherwise assign to it their Statutory Undertaking and the NRA did not purport to do so. However, if, as appears to be the case, the premises held under the lease of 1890 were an integral part of the statutory undertaking and were not surplus land, there is a difficulty in seeing how the Association could assign these rights and premises to the L.S.W.R. Moreover the Conveyance of 1895 appears to treat the Tramway between the Brookwood Station of the L.S.W.R. and the Camp Station of the NRA as still 'the Tramway of the Association notwithstanding the Assignment.

'I think that the transaction of 1895 really amounted to no more than this, namely: as the price of the freehold of certain land the Railway Coy took over the obligation of the Association to the War Office under the lease of 1890 and also undertook to bear the cost of maintaining the Association's Tramway between certain points (except the liability in respect of Bridges) but I think that subject to this, the Tramway Undertaking, including the Tolls, continued to belong to the Association, the Railway Coy., in fact, finding the necessary Rolling Stock and receiving half the gross receipts for so doing.

'It may be that these shares are open to revision, but, until the Association desires a revision presumably the equal sharing will continue. By the Agreement of 1895 the Railway Coy. has bound itself to provide certain train service without any definite provision as to the terms. It may be that this obligation was undertaken by the Railway Coy. as part of the consideration for the piece of land which the Association sold, and not for any additional remuneration. But I think it probable that in 1895 both parties knowing what was then the practice assumed that the equal sharing would go on, as it did, and forgot to deal with the point expressly at all.

'As to the Bridge, I think that the Association is bound to keep it in repair, but that the Road Authority should keep in repair the roadway over it.

C. Ashworth James
Linc. Inn
16th October 1917.'

After the Tramway was closed in 1952 the 'Opinion' was briefly summarised in the Secretary's report for 1953.

'This (the 'Opinion') declared inter alia:
1. It was doubtful if the relinquishing of the lease in 1895 was valid.
2. The responsibility for the brick railway bridge (the Cowshot bridge) rested on the NRA
3. The responsibility for the road over the bridge lay with the Local Authority.
4. As tolls had been paid by the L.S.W.R. for some 20 years, there seemed to be precedent for obtaining them.'

The last of these declarations pointed towards a resolution of the outstanding all-important revenue question but it now seemed to be more a matter of good will whether any money would be forthcoming from the War Office or the L&SWR.

On 25 October, Crosse wrote to the L&SWR to request their account for the year as the Association wished to close it. However, after a reminder, the Railway Company's accountant, A.E. Newhook, sent a letter announcing the suspension of the regular payments made by the Railway Company as no terms had

yet been agreed for the working of the Tramway by the War Office. The Council, however, being also anxious to close the accounts for the year requested the accountant to quote the amount the Association could expect to receive in due course. The accountant's reply caused Crosse further to enquire if any communication regarding such payment had been received from the War Office and mentioned that the amount anticipated had already been included in the 1917 accounts.

'April 10th 1918
'In reply to your letter A18/265 of 9th January with reference to payment of the moiety in respect of the Bisley Camp Railway, I beg to inform you that as we could not anticipate the suggestion that the amount which has been paid annually to the Association since 1914 would not be paid this year, it was included in our accounts for 1917.

'As the Railway is now being worked by the Military Authorities I shall be glad to know if you have received any communication from the War Office respecting any payment to the Association, which would justify my writing to them direct with reference to the matter or is the Company ready to pay what is due to the Association.'

This matter was finally resolved by the L&SWR's 1918 Agreement regarding the line when the railway company took over operational responsibility for it as agents of the War Office. At this time the L&SWR passed on a letter that they had received from the War Department agreeing to pay the NRA a sum of money for the use of the Tramway. This was acknowledged by Crosse in a letter dated 17 April to Newhook.

'I thank you for your letter of 16th inst. giving me particulars of the War Office letter dated 2.8.17 in which it is stated that an annual payment is to be made to the National Rifle Association so long as the Bisley Railway is worked by the War Department.'

However it was not until 1919 that the money became available.

Operations from 1918

Operation of the Military Railway had been handed over to the L&SWR as the agent of the War Office in

July 1918 and this restored an element of normality, as far as the NRA were concerned, to the running of the Camp Tramway. It also enabled Crosse to put forward some proposals regarding the provision of a shelter at Brookwood Station.

> 'September 21st 1918
>
> 'The Superintendent of the Line
> L. & S.W.Rly.
> Waterloo Station
>
> 'I receive frequent complaints as to the inadequacy of the arrangements at Brookwood Station for the convenience of passengers travelling on the Bisley Camp Railway.
>
> 'The chief complaint is that no provision is made for a shelter for those waiting for the trains and that the passengers have to wait in the open in all weathers.
>
> 'Various suggestions have been made; one is that the gate leading from the "Up" platform at Brookwood Station to the Camp Railway platform should be open for passengers travelling on the Bisley Camp Railway, who could, when waiting use the General Waiting Room until the train on the Camp Railway is in the Station.
>
> 'Another suggestion is that an empty coach should remain in the Camp line station at Brookwood which could be used by passengers as a shelter, the gates through which passengers now pass being left open. The tickets of those travelling could be examined on the train instead of at the gate as at present.
>
> 'It is quite evident that some arrangement for the comfort of passengers should be made in view of the approaching winter when the inconvenience of the present arrangements will become more pronounced.'

Although there seems to be no evidence of any action in this respect Crosse made a further attempt to revive the idea of a separate Waiting Room to be constructed at the Camp Station, the original having being taken over as a parcels office in 1917.

> 'October 10th 1918
>
> Bisley Camp Station
>
> 'When permission was given to the Military Camp Railway authorities to convert the covered in shelter used as a waiting room into a parcels office, it was on the understanding that a suitable shelter for the convenience of passengers should be erected, but this has not been done.
>
> 'Such a shelter has now become a necessity and I shall be glad if steps could be taken either to have a shelter erected, or to restore the building previously used for this purpose and provide another building for use as a parcels office.
>
> 'In view of the approach of winter some action should be taken without delay.'

However, events also overtook this proposal when the railway company closed the whole line in December 1918 as the military staff responsible for its operation had all been demobilised!

1919 The first post-war Meeting and re-opening of the Tramway

Although an Armistice had been in effect from 11am on 11 November 1918, and the war was effectively over, no peace treaty had been signed and the War Office continued to remain in control of the Camp and the Tramway together with the military extension to Blackdown, although operation of the latter had already been passed back to the L&SWR on a contractual basis. In 1919 the NRA wished to re-start the annual Meeting and with it a service over the Tramway to the Camp. At the same time they desired the reinstatement of the special cheap tickets. However the Government control of the railways under the Railway Executive forbade such an arrangement and the Association found themselves in yet another battle.

This letter had been sent to the NRA ironically signed on behalf of H.A. Walker, the acting Chairman of the Railway Executive but also the General Manager of the L&SWR; in normal circumstances, it would have attracted his total opposition.

Questions were immediately raised in the House of Commons about this decision with Hansard recording, under the heading of the National Rifle Association, that 'Major Barnett asked the President of the Board of Trade what arrangements are being made to give special railway facilities to competitors attending the meeting of the National Rifle Association next month. The reply received was that the matter is at present under consideration.' Shortly afterwards the Railway Executive ruling was reversed.

In March 1919, Crosse wrote to the railway company expressing the hope that the L&SWR Prize, originally

L.S.W.R.

National Rifle Association Meeting

AT
BISLEY (Brookwood)

JULY 9th to 19th inclusive.

Train Service from London (Waterloo Station) and intermediate stations to Brookwood.

On WEEK-DAYS, WEDNESDAY, 9th, to SATURDAY, 19th July, inclusive.

Down Trains.

			a.m.	a.m.	a.m.	a.m.	a.m.	a.m.	a.m. SO	a.m. SE	a.m.	a.m. SO	p.m.	p.m.	p.m.
Waterloo	...	dep.	5 50	7 0	...	7 38	8 50	9 20	10 25	10 35	11 20	11 35	...	12 35	1 20
Clapham Junction	...	dep.	...	..	6 25	7 35	8 35	9 5	10 35	10 35	...	11 35	...	12 35	...
Wimbledon	...	dep.	5 55	...	6 33	7 43	8 43	9 13	10 33	10 43	...	11 43	...	12 43	...
Surbiton	...	dep.	6 12	...	7 7	8 0	9 12	9 42	10 51	10 57	...	11 57	...	12 57	...
Esher	...	dep.	5 39	...	7 14	8 6	9 3	...	...	11 4	...	12 3	...	1 3	...
Walton	...	dep.	5 46	...	7 23	8 14	9 11	...	...	11 12	...	12 10	...	1 10	...
Weybridge	...	dep.	6 27	...	7 31	8 22	9 18	9 57	...	11 19	...	12 17	...	1 17	...
Woking	...	dep.	7 0	7 39	8 5	8 40	9 34	10 30	11 12	11 37	12 5	12 35	12 50	1 38	1 59
Brookwood	...	arr.	7 8	7 47	8 13	8 48	9 42	10 38	11 19	11 45	12 15	12 43	12 58	1 46	2 7
Brookwood	...	dep.	7 20	8 0	8 26	8 52	10 5	10 50	11 25	11 50	12 20	1 5	1 35	2 0	2 20
Bisley Camp	...	arr.	**7 26**	**8 6**	**8 32**	**8 58**	**10 11**	**10 56**	**11 31**	**11 56**	**12 26**	**1 11**	**1 41**	**2 6**	**2 26**

Down Trains.

			p.m.	p.m.	p.m. SO	p.m.	p.m.	p.m.	p.m.	p.m.	p.m.	p.m.	p.m.	p.m.	p.m.
Waterloo	...	dep.	1 35	...	3 20	...	4 0	5 0	...	5 20	6 0	6 20	7 0	7 35	8 35	9 35
Clapham Junction	...	dep.	1 35	...	3 5	...	3 55	4 55	...	6 5	6 5	6 35	7 35	8 35	9 35
Wimbledon	...	dep.	1 43	...	3 15	...	4 3	4 3	...	5 13	5 43	6 43	6 43	7 43	8 43	9 57
Surbiton	...	dep.	1 57	...	3 42	...	4 22	4 57	...	5 42	6 9	6 42	6 57	7 57	8 57	9 57
Esher	...	dep.	2 3	...	3 3	3 33	4 28	5 3	...	5 SO 33	6 15	...	7 3	8 3	9 3	10 3
Walton	...	dep.	2 10	...	3 10	3 40	4 35	5 10	...	5 SO 40	6 22	...	7 10	8 10	9 10	10 10
Weybridge	...	dep.	2 17	...	3 17	3 46	4 42	5 17	...	5 SO 46	6 29	...	7 17	8 17	9 17	10 17
Woking	...	dep.	2 40	2 50	4 5	4 5	4 59	5 44	5 50	6 10	6 45	7 10	7 44	8 40	9 40	10 40
Brookwood	...	arr.	2 48	2 58	4 13	4 13	5 7	5 52	5 58	6 18	6 53	7 18	7 52	8 48	9 48	10 48
Brookwood	...	dep.	2 55	3 25	4 25	4 25	5 20	5 56	6 16	6 36	6 57	7 24	8 20	9 8	10 15	11 10
Bisley Camp	...	arr.	**3 1**	**3 31**	**4 31**	**4 31**	**5 26**	**6 2**	**6 22**	**6 42**	**7 3**	**7 30**	**8 26**	**9 14**	**10 21**	**11 16**

Up Trains.

			a.m.	a.m.	a.m.	a.m.	a.m.	a.m.	noon	p.m. SO	p.m.	p.m. SE	p.m.	p.m. SO
Bisley Camp	...	dep.	7 35	8 14	8 36	9 2	10 25	11 0	12 0	12 30	12 30	1 25	1 25	1 50	...
Brookwood	...	arr.	7 41	8 20	8 42	9 8	10 31	11 6	12 6	12 36	12 36	1 31	1 31	1 56	...
Brookwood	...	dep.	7 57	8 28	8 45	9 15	10 46	11 16	12 14	12 54	12 54	1 43	1 50	2 15	...
Woking	...	arr.	8 4	8 35	8 52	9 22	...	11 23	12 21	1 1	1 1	1 50	1 50	2 22	...
Weybridge	...	arr.	8 32	...	9 32	10 12	...	11 40	12 39	1 15	1 40	...	2 14	2 33	...
Walton	...	arr.	8 38	8 57	9 41	10 18	...	11 47	12 46	1 22	1 47	...	2 21	...	...
Esher	...	arr.	...	9 10	9 49	...	...	11 55	12 54	...	1 55	...	2 30	...	...
Surbiton	...	arr.	8 49	...	9 56	...	...	12 2	1 1	1 33	2 2	...	2 37	2 47	...
Wimbledon	...	arr.	9 16	...	10 16	...	...	12 16	1 16	1 56	2 16	...	2 56	3 16	...
Clapham Junction	...	arr.	9 24	...	10 24	10 0	...	12 24	1 24	2 4	2 24	...	3 4	3 24	...
Waterloo	...	arr.	8 50	9 25	9 41	10 0	11 25	12 25	1 25	1 55	2 25	...	3 0	3 10	...

Up Trains.

			p.m.	p.m. S.O.	p.m.	p.m.	p.m.	p.m. S.E.	p.m.	p.m.	p.m.	p.m.	p.m.	p.m.	p.m.
Bisley Camp	...	dep.	2 33	3 5	3 50	4 36	5 0	5 36	6 26	7 7	7 34	8 10	8 50	9 30	10 35
Brookwood	...	arr.	2 39	3 11	3 56	4 41	5 6	5 42	6 32	7 13	7 40	8 16	8 56	9 36	10 41
Brookwood	...	dep.	2 50	3 22	4 6	4 53	5 15	5 48	6 42	7 18	7 46	8 31	9 6	9 52	11 3
Woking	...	arr.	2 57	3 29	4 15	5 0	5 20	5 55	6 49	7 25	7 53	8 38	9 13	9 59	11 10
															a.m.
Weybridge	...	arr.	...	...	4 30	...	5 37	6 41	...	7 46	8 30	...	9 30	11 7	3 10
Walton	...	arr	...	...	4 37	...	5 44	6 48	...	7 53	8 37	...	9 37	11 14	3 17
Esher	...	arr.	...	...	4 41	...	5 52	6 55	...	8 0	8 44	...	9 44	11 20	3 23
															p.m.
Surbiton	...	arr.	...	...	4 51	...	5 59	7 2	7 12	8 7	8 51	...	9 51	11 1	11 59
															a.m.
Wimbledon	...	arr.	...	...	5 16	...	6 16	7 16	7 26	8 26	...	9 16	10 26	11 26	12 10
Clapham Junction	...	arr.	...	...	5 24	...	6 24	7 24	7 34	8 34	...	9 24	10 34	11 34	12 19
Waterloo	...	arr.	3 35	3 40	5 15	...	6 23	7 25	7 35	8 30	9 15	9 25	10 15	11 24	12 30

S E—Saturdays excepted.   S O—Saturdays only.

Passengers change at Brookwood by all trains.
Passengers from and to intermediate stations between Waterloo and Woking are requested to ascertain at what points it will be necessary to change carriages.

[P.T.O.]

The 1919 Bisley Timetable page 1.

L.S.W.R.

NATIONAL RIFLE ASSOCIATION MEETING
at BISLEY (Brookwood).

Train Service from London (Waterloo Station) and intermediate stations to Brookwood—*continued.*

On SUNDAY, 13th July.

Down Trains.

		a.m.	a.m.	a.m.	a.m.	a.m.	p.m.	p.m.	p.m.	p.m.	p.m.	p.m.	p.m.	
Waterloo	dep.	...	8 20	9 0	10 0	11 30	2 20	3 0	5 0	6 0	...	9 30	10 35	...
Clapham Junction	dep.	...	8 31	...	9 43	11 42	1 43	...	4 43	5 43	...	9 23	...	...
Wimbledon	dep.	...	8 31	...	9 51	11 38	1 51	...	4 51	5 51	...	9 31	...	...
Surbiton	dep.	...	8 47	...	10 22	12 0	2 12	...	5 23	6 22	...	9 52	...	...
Esher	dep.	...	8 53	...	9 54	10 54	2 18	...	...	5 54	...	9 58	...	...
Walton	dep.	...	9 1	...	10 1	11 1	2 25	...	...	6 1	...	10 5	...	...
Weybridge	dep.	...	9 8	...	10 37	11 8	2 32	...	...	6 37	...	10 12	...	...
Woking	dep.	7 35	9 26	10 0	10 55	12 23	3 10	4 30	5 55	6 55	8 5	10 25	11 15	...
Brookwood	arr.	7 43	9 34	10 8	11 3	12 31	3 18	4 38	6 3	7 3	8 13	10 33	11 23	...
Brookwood	dep.	8 0	9 40	10 15	11 15	12 40	3 25	4 45	6 15	7 10	8 42	10 40	11 30	...
Bisley Camp	arr.	8 6	9 46	10 21	11 21	12 46	3 31	4 51	6 21	7 16	8 48	10 46	11 36	...

Up Trains.

		a.m.	a.m.	a.m.	a.m.	a.m.	a.m.	p.m.	p.m.	p.m.	p.m.			
Bisley Camp	dep.	8 10	9 5	9 50	10 30	11 25	11 50	12 15	5 42	8 0	9 15	...	...	...
Brookwood	arr.	8 16	9 11	9 56	10 36	11 31	11 56	12 21	5 48	8 6	9 21	...	...	...
Brookwood	dep.	8 23	9 17	9 59	10 44	11 37	12 9	12 34	6 0	8 19	9 36	...	...	...
Woking	arr.	8 30	9 24	10 6	10 51	11 44	12 16	12 41	6 7	8 26	9 43	...	...	...
Weybridge	arr.	8 47	...	10 22	11 19	...	12 33	1 57	6 55	9 12	10 34	...	...	...
Walton	arr.	9 4	...	10 29	11 30	...	1 5	2 4	7 2	9 19	10 40	...	...	...
Esher	arr.	9 11	...	10 36	...	...	1 12	2 11	7 9	9 26	10 46	...	...	...
Surbiton	arr.	9 3	...	10 43	11 46	...	12 48	1 4	6 38	8 55	10 23	...	...	...
Wimbledon	arr.	9 28	...	11 12	12 12	...	1 12	1 29	6 48	9 12	10 52	...	...	...
Clapham Junction	arr.	9 20	...	11 20	12 20	...	1 20	1 37	7 0	9 20	11 0	...	...	...
Waterloo	arr.	9 34	10 24	11 5	12 29	...	1 11	1 27	7 3	9 5	10 46	...	...	...

Passengers change at Brookwood by all trains.
Passengers from and to intermediate stations between Waterloo and Woking, are requested to ascertain at what points it will be necessary to change carriages.

Local Service between Brookwood and Bisley Camp.

SATURDAY 19th ~~On TUESDAY, 8th July.~~

		a.m.	a.m.	p.m.	p.m.	p.m.	p.m.	p.m.	p.m.				
Brookwood	dep.	10 5	11 25	1 5	2 20	2 55	4 25	5 20	7 0	...	...	...	...
Bisley Camp	arr.	10 11	11 31	1 11	2 26	3 1	4 31	5 26	7 6	...	...	...	...

		a.m.	noon	p.m.	p.m.	p.m.	p.m.	p.m.	p.m.				
Bisley Camp	dep.	10 25	12 0	1 25	2 33	3 10	4 38	5 36	7 30	...	...	...	...
Brookwood	arr.	10 31	12 6	1 31	2 39	3 16	4 44	5 42	7 36	...	...	...	...

On WEEK-DAYS, WEDNESDAY, 9th, to SATURDAY, 19th July, inclusive.

		a.m.	a.m.	a.m.	a.m.	a.m.	a.m.	a.m.	a.m.	a.m.	a.m.	a.m.	p.m.	p.m.	p.m.	p.m.
Brookwood	dep.	7 20	8 0	8 26	8 52	9 12	9 35	10 5	10 50	11 25	11 50	12 20	1 5	1 35	2 0	2 20	2 55
Bisley Camp	arr.	7 26	8 6	8 32	8 58	9 18	9 41	10 11	10 56	11 31	11 56	12 26	1 11	1 41	2 6	2 26	3 1

		p.m.	p.m.	p.m.	p.m.	p.m.	p.m.	p.m.	p.m.	p.m.	p.m.	p.m.	p.m.	p.m.	p.m.	p.m.
Brookwood	dep.	3 25	4 25	4 50	5 20	5 56	6 16	6 36	6 57	7 24	7 50	8 20	8 40	9 8	9 45	10 15	11 10
Bisley Camp	arr.	3 31	4 31	4 56	5 26	6 2	6 22	6 42	7 3	7 30	7 56	8 26	8 46	9 14	9 51	10 21	11 16

		p.m.	p.m.	p.m.	p.m.	p.m.	p.m.	p.m.	p.m.	noon	p.m.	p.m.	p.m.	p.m.	p.m.	p.m.
Bisley Camp	dep.	7 35	8 14	8 36	9 2	9 25	9 45	10 25	11 0	11 36	12 0	12 30	1 25	1 50	2 10	2 33	3 5
Brookwood	arr.	7 41	8 20	8 42	9 8	9 31	9 51	10 31	11 6	11 41	12 6	12 36	1 31	1 56	2 16	2 39	3 11

		p.m.	p.m.	p.m.	p.m.	p.m.	p.m.	p.m.	p.m.	p.m.	p.m.	p.m.	p.m.	p.m.	p.m.	
Bisley Camp	dep.	3 50	4 38	5 0	5 36	6 5	6 26	6 46	7 7	7 34	8 10	8 30	8 50	9 30	10 0	10 35	...
Brookwood	arr.	3 56	4 44	5 6	5 42	6 12	6 32	6 52	7 13	7 40	8 16	8 36	8 56	9 36	10 6	10 41	...

On SUNDAY, 13th July.

		a.m.	a.m.	a.m.	a.m.	a.m.	a.m.	p.m.	p.m.	p.m.	p.m.	p.m.	p.m.	p.m.	p.m.	p.m.	p.m.
Brookwood	dep.	8 0	8 30	9 40	10 15	11 15	11 35	12 2	12 40	2 40	3 25	4 45	6 15	7 10	8 42	9 45	10 40	11 30
Bisley Camp	arr.	8 6	8 36	9 46	10 21	11 21	11 41	12 8	12 46	2 46	3 31	4 51	6 21	7 16	8 48	9 51	10 46	11 36

		a.m.	a.m.	a.m.	a.m.	a.m.	a.m.	p.m.	p.m.	p.m.	p.m.	p.m.	p.m.	p.m.	p.m.	p.m.	p.m.
Bisley Camp	dep.	8 10	9 5	9 50	10 30	11 25	11 50	12 15	12 52	2 54	4 25	5 42	6 50	8 0	9 15	10 20	11 7	...
Brookwood	arr.	8 16	9 11	9 56	10 36	11 31	11 56	12 21	12 58	3 0	4 31	5 8	6 56	8 6	9 21	10 26	11 13	...

On SUNDAY, 20th July.

		a.m.	a.m.	a.m.	a.m.	a.m.	a.m.	p.m.	p.m.	p.m.	p.m.	p.m.			
Brookwood	dep.	8 0	8 30	9 40	10 15	11 15	11 35	12 2	12 40	2 40	3 25	...	...	...	...
Bisley Camp	arr.	8 6	8 36	9 46	10 21	11 21	11 41	12 8	12 46	2 46	3 31	...	...	...	...

		a.m.	a.m.	a.m.	a.m.	a.m.	a.m.	p.m.	p.m.	p.m.	p.m.			
Bisley Camp	dep.	8 10	9 5	9 50	10 30	11 25	11 50	12 15	12 52	2 54	4 25	...	...	...	...
Brookwood	arr.	8 16	9 11	9 56	10 36	11 31	11 56	12 21	12 58	3 0	4 31	...	...	...	...

On MONDAY, 21st July.

		p.m.	p.m.	p.m.						p.m.	p.m.	p.m.
Brookwood	dep.	2 0	3 30	5 20			Bisley Camp	dep.	2 30	3 50	5 36
Bisley Camp	arr.	2 6	3 36	5 26			Brookwood	arr.	2 36	3 56	5 42

WATERLOO STATION, S.E. 1.
1st July, 1919.

H. A. WALKER, *General Manager.*

Waterlow & Sons Limited, Printers, London Wall.

110

[P.T.O.]

The 1919 Bisley Timetable page 2 showing draft correction applying to the Tramway.

subscribed by the railway company in 1895 and discontinued during the War, be reinstated. The Company was amenable and the competition was included in the 1919 Meeting. The special L&SWR Timetable for the July Meeting was also reinstated.

The re-opening of the Tramway brought with it the introduction of the L&SWR's Pull-Push system in which the locomotive remained coupled to one end of its train. This dispensed with the necessity of 'running-round' at both termini, in the process increasing the efficiency of the service and lowering costs by a considerable degree. However the requirement for the run round loops still remained as through trains, including goods, from the main line still ran on occasion. In fact as early as 14 July, Crosse asked the Superintendent of the Line to provide a special Saturday through train from the Camp to Waterloo.

'The Superintendent of the Line
London & South Western Rly: Coy.
Waterloo Station. S.W.2
'I am directed by the Council to express the hope that you will be able to arrange as in pre-war years for a Special through train to run from Bisley Camp Station to Waterloo about 6p.m. on Friday next the 18th inst. on the occasion of the closing day of the Meeting when we expect a large attendance of visitors for the Distribution of Prizes, who will be returning to town about that hour.'

This was agreed by the Office of the Superintendent of the Line on 15 April. The train was scheduled to leave the Camp at 6pm, calling at Brookwood 6.15p.m., Woking 6.23, Surbiton 6.43, with arrival at Waterloo at 7.5 pm

However, Crosse had to amend his requirement as the Empire Match, between Britain, Australia, Canada and New Zealand, was scheduled to take place during the following week. He also requested that the reduced tickets available until the 20 April should be extended until the 24th to accommodate this match. Both of these were agreed by the railway company.

Fare increases during and after the War
In January 1917, an increase in fares had been announced by the railway company and Crosse raised the issue in respect of members of Rifle Clubs who were

still travelling to Bisley. At the same time the Secretary of one of the London Rifle Clubs had written to the L&SWR on the matter. The reply was that the Railway Executive, which had been set up by the Government to manage the railways for the duration of hostilities, had prohibited the issue of reduced fare tickets to members of these Clubs. Protestations by Crosse to the railway company were unavailing in the circumstances and in February the company proceeded to announce that the fares would rise to 3/5d return third class. This resulted in the Council apparently cancelling all remaining shooting fixtures for 1917 attracting further vehement protests from the Rifle Clubs.

By May, however, the Railway Executive either seems to have relented, or the railway company had been in error, and George West was able to announce the re-instatement of the original 1/6d fare for third class returns.

This situation remained undisturbed until 1920 when a combination of the unrelenting post war inflation and continued government control served to impose a massive increase in rail fares. In April of that year, in his reply to a query from Crosse about train services at the next annual Meeting, West released a thunderbolt involving a fundamental increase to the London-Bisley fare which equated to the amount of the short lived increase of 1917, the 3rd Class fare rising to 3/5d, more than double the 1/6d which had been in place since 1890.

This naturally created a crisis, not only for the Association which was still struggling to regain a significant proportion of the shooters who had attended Bisley before the war, but also rifle clubs who felt that such a fare rise was beyond the means of their members. Extensive correspondence and meetings between the parties followed with the railway company seemingly resolute although its hands were tied as the control of the railways was still effectively in the hands of the Government.

However, the government control of the railways ended in 1921 but it was not until May 1922 that the railway company found itself able to announce a small reduction in the fares.

The Extension of Electric Light from Bisley Camp Station to Brookwood Station
In January 1921, the L&SWR asked the Association if they would allow it to take electric current from the

Camp supply at Bisley Camp Station in order to light Brookwood Station. This was handed to the Association's Works Committee for consideration.

'An application by the L.S.W.R. Rly: Coy: to take electric current from Bisley Camp for the purpose of lighting Brookwood Station, referred to Captain Chick, Chairman of the Works Committee, was considered.

'Captain Chick reported that he had visited the Camp and was of opinion that the concession was a valuable one to the L. & S.W.Rly. Coy; that advantage should be taken of this opportunity to have definitely settled our outstanding claims such as Railway Ticket concessions, Share of tolls as agreed, possession of the new line running through our Camp.

The Council considered that the question should be settled amicably if possible, and suggested an interview between the Chairman and the Chairman of the Railway Coy. The Secretary was instructed to communicate with the Secretary of the L. & S.W.R.Rly.'

However, at this point tragedy struck when Crosse, who had then served twenty-two distinguished years as the Association's Secretary, died suddenly shortly after he had dispatched two letters on the subject to the railway company. When Walker became aware of this, he responded with a personal letter of condolence to the Association and at the same time arranged to set up a meeting with Lord Cheylesmore and the newly appointed Secretary, Major Etches. In the event this proved not to be possible and a meeting was eventually held between the Vice-Chairman and Secretary of the Association and other representatives of the L&SWR.

At a Council Meeting of the Association held on 24 April 1921 the meeting with the railway company was reported and the request from the railway company was agreed.

'The Vice Chairman reported that he and the Secretary had attended an interview with the Secretary, the Traffic Manager and the Sub-Manager of the L.S.W.R in the absence of the General Manager: that it had been agreed to allow the Railway Company to take ELECTRIC CURRENT necessary for the lighting of Brookwood Station over the NRA main: that he had pressed for an EARLY REDUCTION IN THE FARES from Waterloo to Bisley, and that the Company was most friendly disposed towards the Association, and would view its claims with every sympathy when it HAD THE POWER TO DO SO.'

The Secretary replied to the railway company in his letter of 7 April 1921.

'The General Manager
London & South Western Railway Company
'My Council now had the opportunity of considering the request contained in your letter L.A./11, 593 of 13th December 1920, and they are quite prepared to give every assistance to your Company as regards the supply of Electric current for the purpose of lighting Brookwood Station.

'I am, however, to explain that when the electric light was installed at Bisley Camp the National Rifle Association had to guarantee to the Woking Electric Supply Coy: a minimum annual payment which for many years fell far short of the cost of current consumed, and my Council feel that in order to recoup the Association for this outlay that your Company should pay to the Association a "way-leave" of £10 per year for the privilege.

'It is suggested that the extension is made from the existing 200V Cable at the Central Office at Bisley Camp and carried underground to the Booking Office at the Camp Station and connected up from the building to the overhead wires; the meter being fixed at Brookwood Station. I have not consulted the Woking Electric Supply Company at this point and would suggest that your Electrical Engineer should communicate directly with him as to whether the method I have suggested is a suitable one.'

This letter was passed to Szlumper, who strongly disagreed with the proposed wayleave charge and suggested that a nominal charge of £1 would meet the case! This was immediately accepted by the Association 'on the understanding that the Association was not to be put to any expense in the matter' and Szlumper agreed. Shortly afterwards a legal agreement covering the installation was drawn up by the L&SWR's solicitor.

London & South Western Railway.
I.J.

General Manager's Office,
Waterloo Station,
London S.E. 1 Feb. 23rd 1921

Please copy this
N°. in your reply.
B.

Dear Sir,

BISLEY RAILWAY.

It is with much regret that I have heard of the recent
death of Col. Crosse and beg to be allowed to express my
sympathy with the National Rifle Association in the great loss
they have sustained.

I am sorry that pressure of business has prevented
my replying to the two letters addressed by the late Col.
Crosse to the Company's Secretary dated the 11th and 27th
ulto. before this.

As you are doubtless aware the Bisley Railway is
still under Government control and continues to be worked
by this Company on behalf of the War Department under the
arrangements agreed with the Department in 1918, and while I
fear it will be very difficult to alter these arrangements
so long as the Government control lasts, I shall be pleased
to discuss with Lord Cheylesmore and yourself the points
mentioned in Col. Crosse's letter of the 11th ulto.

My engagements during the next few weeks are somewhat
numerous but if the morning either of the 2nd or the 3rd prox.
would be convenient to Lord Cheylesmore and yourself to call
at this Office, I shall be very pleased to see you.

Yours faithfully,

H. A. Walker

Major C. E. Etches,
National Rifle Association,
Bisley Camp,
Brookwood,
Surrey.

The letter of condolence personally signed by Sir Herbert Walker on the death of Lt. Col. Crosse, the N.R.A. Secretary. This also
reminded the Association that the Bisley Camp Tramway still remained under Government control.

London & South Western Railway
Engineer's Office.

Reference
M/L /82892

Your

Waterloo Station.

London, 3rd May 192 1

S.E. 1:

Telegraphic Address,
"TRACKROAD, LONDON."

Telephone No. 5100, Hop.

A. W. SZLUMPER,
Chief Engineer.

Dear Sir,

Brookwood Station - Lighting.

Your letter of the 7th ultimo addressed to the General Manager has been passed forward to me, and in reply thereto I have to say that the suggested wayleave of £10 per annum is in my opinion much too excessive.

With regard to the National Rifle Association's guarantee of a minimum annual payment, this I understand was under an agreement which expired in 1915 so that I cannot see how this can be brought into the present question.

I consider a nominal wayleave should meet the case, and unless the National Rifle Association are prepared to grant this, other arrangements must be made with the Woking Electric Supply Co.

It must not be overlooked that the electric lighting of Brookwood Station will be a direct asset to the Rifle Association and that being the case it is only natural to suppose they would wish to further the proposal.

I shall be glad to hear from you at your early convenience.

Yours faithfully,

Major C.E.Etches,
Secretary, N.R.A.,
Bisley Camp,
BROOKWOOD, SURREY.

The letter from Szlumper, the Chief Engineer of the L&SWR, disputing the £10 Wayleave, and the drawing, bearing Szlumper's initials, which showed the proposed connection at Bisley. The Association had suggested that the connection should be made at the Camp transformer to obviate unnecessary cutting of the current to Brookwood but Szlumper did not consider this to be a problem.

Electric Supply to Brookwood Station from Bisley.

Proposed Connection at Bisley.

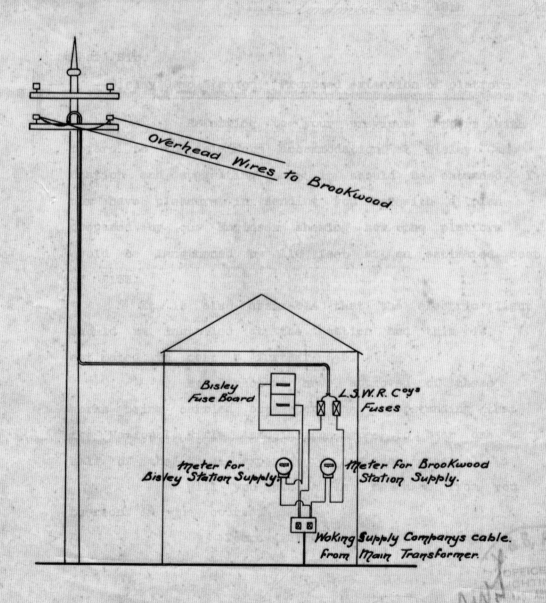

Overhead Wires to Brookwood.

Bisley Fuse Board

L.S.W.R. Coy.ⁱˢ Fuses

Meter for Bisley Station Supply.

Meter for Brookwood Station Supply.

Woking Supply Companys cable. from Main Transformer.

1208.
May 30 1921.

Repairs to the Camp Level Crossing

In August 1921, towards the end of the London & South Western Railway Company's existence as a separate company before becoming incorporated into the newly formed Southern Railway, the NRA Secretary wrote to the Superintendent of the Line regarding the uneven state of the Camp Level crossing. He received an immediate acknowledgement of receipt from the Office of the L&SWR Chief Engineer. A handwritten 'done' on this letter would appear to indicate a timely repair!

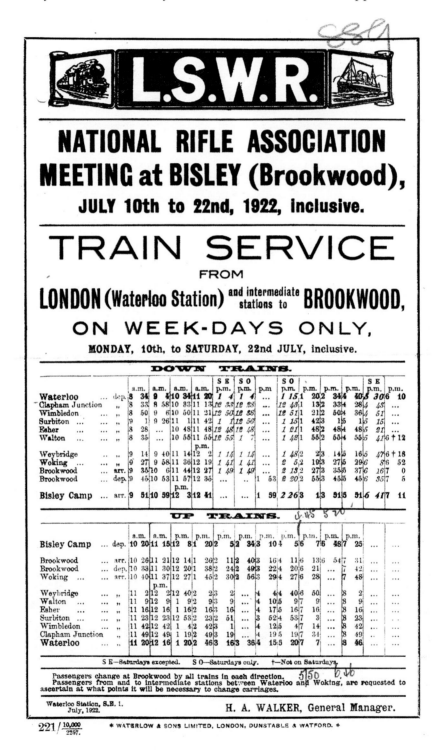

The railway timetable for the 1922 July Meeting - The final one to be issued by the London & South Western Railway before it became an integral part of the Southern Railway.

CHAPTER 8

THE BISLEY RANGE, BUTTS & TARGET TRAMWAYS

THE RANGE TRAMWAY

The Early Years at Bisley

It had been decided that the Range Tramway, laid annually for the July Meeting at Wimbledon and used to transport volunteers and visitors alike to the various firing points, should serve the same purpose at Bisley, although now it was to become a permanent feature. On 3 March 1890 the Bisley Common Committee minuted that it was agreed that the Light Tramway should be laid from the main tramway to a point near the Eastern Ranges. In June, with all the the Tramway equipment delivered to Bisley, the Secretary wrote to Aird requesting them to undertake the work.

'9th June 1890

To Messrs John Aird & Sons

Kindly undertake the laying of our tramway at Bisley Common on the same terms as heretofore at Wimbledon; repairing and replacing rails & sleepers etc. as you may find necessary.

As regards dimensions of sleepers, perhaps you will be good enough to discuss the matter with Mr. Hoey who may have something to say as regards portability, in case it should be desired to move any part or all of the line elsewhere or into store.'

Captain Hoey had been the NRA's Clerk of the Works at Wimbledon since 1882 and now assumed the same position at Bisley. Another strand of continuity was the role of Merryweather. Since 1878 the Company had held a contract with the NRA at Wimbledon to service *Wharncliffe*, move it to the tramway at the beginning of the annual Meeting and, at the conclusion, clean and grease it before moving it to storage. It therefore seems probable that they arranged the transportation of the engine from Wimbledon Common to its new location. A temporary wooden shed was erected at Bisley to house the engine but this had no physical rail connection to the tramway and, as at Wimbledon, the Tram Engine had to be manhandled on to a special horse-drawn trolley in order to move it between its shed and the tramway, normally at the beginning and end of the Meeting.

The route chosen started from the short-lived Cowshot Crossing station, located close to the Camp gate, and continued behind the firing points for the Mid Ranges (also known at this stage as 'The Queen's - and which were to be shortly renamed the '90-Butt' and finally 'Century Range'). It terminated south of the shorter and nearest of the two 'Permanent Ranges' which, because they were so remote, became known as the 'Short' and 'Long Siberia' Ranges respectively. The route was essentially level and the panels of ex-Wimbledon track were laid on sand ballast.

The *Volunteer Service Gazette*, which had reported on the Wimbledon Tramway from its inception in 1864, described its new location in some detail.

'... but we must now go back to the entrance of the enclosure. Leaving the branch railway here, we find the old Wimbledon tramway with its blue and white cars, and its little engine, the Wharncliffe. This tramway runs away first to the north east, where it brings us opposite to the great butt, nearly 500 yards long ...

'... after leaving the firing points for the 600 yd range, the tramway turns northwards, even a little to the west, till it approaches the firing points for the 'permanent' ranges, which are laid out at an entirely different angle from the other ranges.'

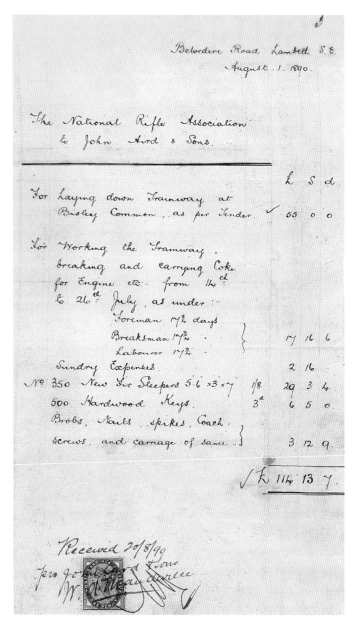

Invoices issued by Aird and Merryweather before the L&SWR took over all aspects of running the Range Tramway.

It also confirmed that the Range Tramway was ready for service well before the standard gauge Bisley Camp tramway that officially opened to the public on 14 July. The *Gazette* in its 'Notes of the Week' for Saturday 2 August commented on the necessity for the Range Tramway to be extended to the Long Range (later 'Stickledown') at the earliest opportunity. However, although this appeared in plans and maps well into Edwardian days it was never constructed although it was much commented upon.

'… The entire separation of the long range firing points from those for the Queen's ranges is undoubtedly an evil which, we think with Mr. Gratwicke,

will only be obviated, or rather mitigated, when it becomes possible to extend the narrow-gauge tramway, so that a competitor may travel from the Ninety Butt firing points to those for the long range.'

Mr Gratwicke, a Captain in the Devon Volunteers and a prominent member of the NRA (and one of the NRA's most voluble correspondents during the 1890s) wrote a letter at the end of the Meeting containing similar sentiments but with rather more ambitious proposals. He was also not enamoured with the riding of the ex-Wimbledon tramcars!

'For financial, if for no other reason, some steps need be taken to bring the firing points into closer connexion than at present. The only plan that occurs to me would be to extend the tramway from the present starting point to the entrance gateway to the range. Instead of one set of rails there should be two, so that two trams might be constantly running, instead of one. The tramway would have earned double the amount taken this year if the tram had only been

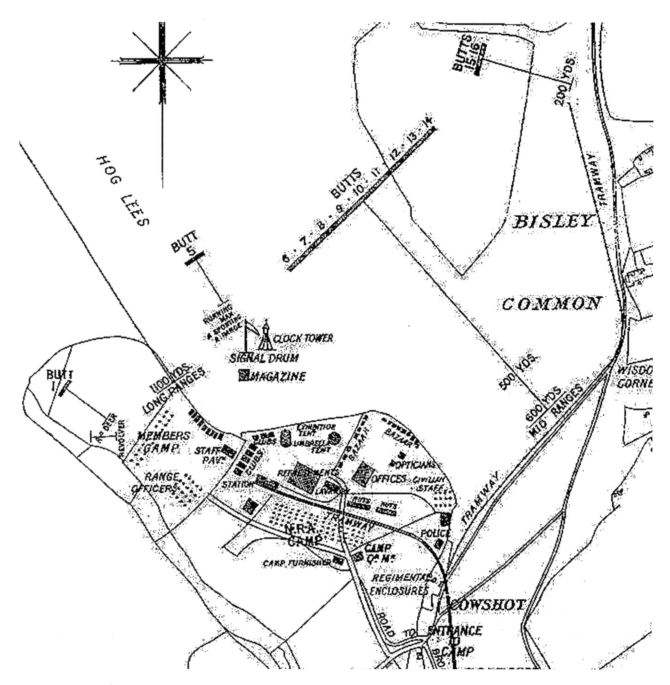

The original 1890 route of the Range Tramway between the short-lived Cowshot platform adjacent to the main gate of the Camp, and the 200yds firing point of the Short Siberia Range.

running more frequently. I venture to suggest, too, that any new cars should be placed on springs.'

The alterations of 1891 to the Camp Station and the abolition of the small station close to the Cowshot crossing entrance of the Camp made the adjacent Range Tramway terminus redundant. Instead the Tramway was cut back to the rear of the Butt 7 firing point of the 90 Butt Range. As described a small

shed had been constructed in 1890 to house *Wharncliffe* when not in use, but having no physical connection to the Range Tramway line. At Bisley the NRA Staff took over the task of manhandling the locomotive although Merryweather continued to include it in their annual bid! This arrangement lasted until the L&SWR took over responsibility for the tramway in 1893; a physical connection to the shed probably being made when the track was renewed between 1893 and 1894. The 1896

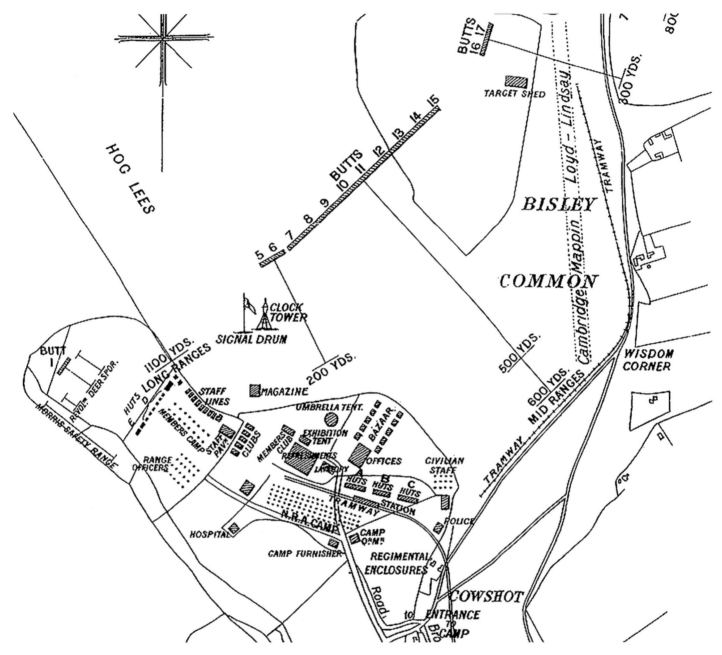

In 1891, with the abolition of the Cowshot platform, the Range Tramway was shortened to terminate near the 600yd firing point of Butt 7 (Mid Ranges). Note that the Short Siberia Range has now been extended to 300yds.

Ordnance Survey Map, based on the 1895 Survey, confirms that it was definitely in place by that time.

In November 1891, the Association's Finance Sub-Committee minuted that Aird's bill for maintenance of the Tramway was considered exceptionally high and they recommended to the Council that the task should be taken over by the Association's own labour establishment, this being agreed. However, in 1893 Scotter made a verbal offer to the NRA to take over the maintenance of the Range Tramway and its rolling stock,

as well as working *Wharncliffe*. The NRA accepted this with enthusiasm especially as Merryweather had already written to state that *Wharncliffe* now needed major repairs.

'15th May 1893

'Dear Colonel Scotter,
'Referring to our conversation which you may remember when you kindly said that the repairs of our small Tram line and working the Tram Engine

REGULATIONS
OF
RANGE TRAMWAY

(Running in rear of Firing Points).

1. The Charge for each Single Journey is··· .. **2D.**

2. A Ticket available for a Single Journey will be issued on payment of the fare, and must be given up on leaving the Car.

3. No person will be allowed to travel who has not paid the fare, unless such person be provided with a Tramway Pass or red or blue Ivory Pass signed by the Secretary, which must be produced on demand.

4. The Cars will start from the Camp every twenty minutes, beginning at 8.50 a.m., whether the Cars are full or not.

Season Tickets, 2s. 6d. each, and available for the duration of the Meeting, may be had on application to the Secretary's Office, No. 12.

By Order,

A. P. HUMPHRY,
Secretary.

The Range Tramway Regulations for 1892.

might be done by South Western Railway men; may we reckon upon this assistance?

'The work would be.

1: To repair the line.

2: To clean and put into working order the Tram Engine and to supply from 15th to 22nd July the necessary staff for driving the engine. After the Meeting to clean and tallow over the engine in proper order for storing.

'The Association to pay for labour and material.

Yours very truly

W Mackinnon Col.

Secr NRA'

Colonel Charles Scotter

General Superintendent

London & S.W. Railway.'

(Due to its 'Volunteer' origins the NRA tended to use military titles in its correspondence - Scotter was an officer of the 'Engineer and Railway Volunteer Staff Corps' as were many senior railway officials at the time. The NRA's use of military

titles, especially for competitors, was maintained up until about the 1970s).

On 5 June 1893 the NRA Secretary wrote to Merryweather, who had already put in their annual bid for moving *Wharncliffe* to and from store and operating it during the 1893 season, informing them that the L&SWR had now offered to take over this task.

'With reference to your tender for cleaning and working our small Tram Engine at Bisley this year, I am to inform you that the Council have arranged with the S.W. Railway to carry out this work.

'I notice in the form of tender, the wording of which remains the same as previous years, that part of the work to be done is supply of trolley and horses for moving the engine from the shed to the line and replacing it at the end of the Meeting. This work I am told was always done by your people at Wimbledon, but has not been done for the last three years at Bisley, the engine having been moved by our own men.

'You are doubtless not aware of that which must have considerably increased your expenditure; may I ask you to enquire into the matter.'

A summary of the repairs needed to *Wharncliffe*, already supplied by Merryweather, were forwarded to the L&SWR through Scotter's Office.

'We should recommend that before the engine is put to work again the boiler should be taken off and thoroughly examined, and the foundation ring, which has been leaking slightly for the past two years, repaired. It should then be tested by water pressure.

'Most of the working parts of the engine want some slight repairs, and the engine should be lifted to put the axle box bearers in order. There are also several other little matters that should be attended to. We mention this as we have been in the habit of sending our man some days beforehand in order to do anything that might be required. The Boiler and lifting the engine is however quite another matter, and should be attended to before the engine is again put to work.'

Scotter immediately passed this on to William Adams, the L&SWR Locomotive Superintendent, who then proposed that *Wharncliffe* be sent to Nine Elms for examination and

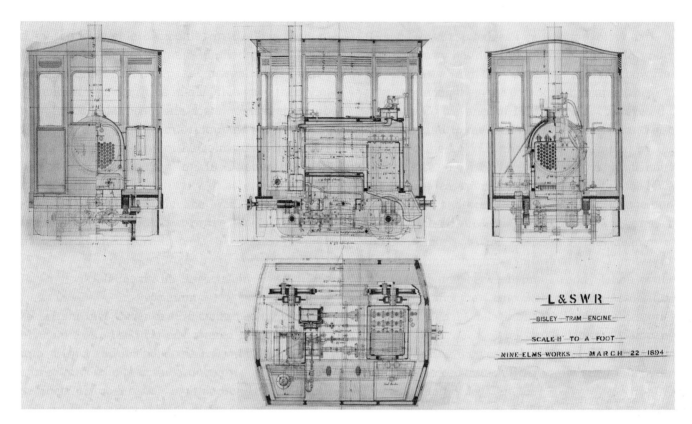

The 1894 LSWR General Arrangement Drawing of *Wharncliffe*. Produced by the L&SWR at Nine Elms Works probably to assist the repairs to the NRA's Tram Locomotive. The drawing shows the locomotive in its 'as built' condition (1878) as no modifications to it had been recorded since that date. Note - See Appendix 2 for large scale Drawings (*NRM – Science & Society Picture Library*)

thorough repair. The Council agreed to this and it was also decided to take out insurance on the boiler, Scotter being advised that the National Boiler & General Insurance Co. would be involved in boiler inspections during its repair.

On 20 September, the Secretary wrote to Scotter again, this time about both the Bisley-Brookwood 'Tramway' and the Range Tramway.

'I am much obliged to you for your letter 20582 of 19th being cover to your Engineers report on the insufficient waterway under our Tram embankment.

'I have a further favour to ask; would you allow one of your staff to inspect our little tramline. It is dreadfully rough, due I hope only to the truck wheel bearing worn hollow and there is a demand for extensions at both ends. I would meet your official there on any day he might appoint.'

This led directly to the appointment of the L&SWR's Resident Engineer to inspect the line and rolling stock.

By now the NRA Secretary was having a fairly regular correspondence with William Adams. On 21 September,

further instructions regarding the repairs to *Wharncliffe* were issued.

'Bisley Tramway Engine

'The Inspector National Boiler Co. reports that the engine should be retubed, and asks that all the tubes may be withdrawn to enable him to make special internal inspection of the barrel. Will your kindly have this done and let me know when the engine is ready for further inspection.

'I have told the Company that all the Inspector's suggestions shall be carried out.

'W. Adams Esq.
London & S.W. Railway
Locomotive Engineers Office
Nine Elms Works S.W.'

At end of the year Adams wrote to the NRA offering to have *Wharncliffe* repainted which, until then, seems to have carried its original two-tone Merryweather livery. He received the following rather engaging reply from the Secretary.

'3rd February 1894

Bisley Tram Engine

'By all means have the 'Wharncliffe' repainted.

'May I call at your works to see the engine?

Yours truly

W. Mackinnon   Col

Sect NRA

'W. Adams Esq.

Nine Elms Works

L & S.W.Railway

S.W.'

In the Council minutes for 7 February 1894 the Secretary reported that 'the *Wharncliffe* has been put into thorough repair at the L&SWR Co's works and that a Policy of Insurance has been granted by the Boiler Insurance Company.'

By March, the repair of *Wharncliffe* was nearing completion and Adams had written to confirm that the locomotive would shortly be returned to Bisley. The NRA Secretary, besides advising Adams on the necessary arrangements, raised the interesting possibility of extending the tram line to Brookwood over mixed gauge track.

'28th March 1894

Dear Mr Adams

'Wharncliffe Engine'

'Will you kindly give Mr Hoey our Foreman at Bisley at least three days notice of the despatch of the Engine, as he will have to make preparations for taking it off the truck, and please do not send it on a Saturday.

'Is the engine capable of drawing say two very light passenger trucks, over the tram line between Brookwood and Bisley Stations? If so we think a third rail might be laid on the existing sleepers and the line be utilised for conveyance of competitors at other times of the year than during the Meeting.

'The Chief Engineer

Nine Elms Works

London & S.W. Railway'

Three days later Mackinnon wrote to Scotter in which he listed the recommendations by Andrews, regarding the Range Tramway. It was now particularly evident that the sleepers of the old portable track from Wimbledon were worn out and needed urgent replacement. Three main alternatives were put forward.

Wharncliffe and its train of original Wimbledon cars at the Siberia Ranges pre-1894. The second car is one of the two supplied by the Metropolitan Carriage & Wagon Works of Birmingham in 1877. The cars are still in their blue and white livery. (*Tim Price Collection*)

Wharncliffe, mounted on L&SWR machinery wagon No 1131 ready to be returned to Bisley in April 1894 after its extensive repair at Nine Elms under the supervision of William Adams, the Locomotive Superintendent of the LSWR. He personally oversaw the application of the N.R.A. 'house colours' of blue and white to the locomotive. (*Peter Harding collection*)

'1. Replacing present worn out sleepers with new ones supplied by the L&SWR. Also the latter to find some 'good old flat bottom rail' to replace the existing.
2. Using the old rails with steel sleepers.
3. To lay down an entirely new line of 18 or 20 inch gauge.'

This was reflected in the winter 1894 NRA Report.

'… also that the Council had decided to extend the gravelled road to the Offices and the Army Service Corps Stables; to have the tramway re-laid and extended towards butts 16-17, and to have the "Wharncliffe" thoroughly repaired, as the latter works, though costly, could no longer, as measures of safety, be postponed.'

The Invoice from the L&SWR for the repairs to Wharncliffe totalled £66-18s-10d and appeared in the NRA's Revenue Account under 'exceptional amounts'.

The Council agreed to the first alternative, being the cheapest, and also requested that the line be extended 100yds into the Siberia Ranges. Meanwhile Mackinnon

had replied to an Adam's letter regarding the hauling power of *Wharncliffe*.

'8th April 1894
'Bisley Tramline
Wharncliffe Engine
'I am obliged to you for your letter of 30th March in reply to my question regarding the hauling power of the Wharncliffe, and asking one for the weight of the Passenger trucks and the number of passengers they will carry.

'I cannot get our trucks weighed, and they are nearly worn out. To carry out the idea of utilizing the engine between Brookwood station and Bisley Camp it would be necessary to have trucks especially made. If you could calculate approximately the hauling power of the engine, having regard to the gradients and curves of the line (information on which you can obtain from your Resident Engineer) one might perhaps get trucks made directed to the engine power.

'W. Adams Esq
Nine Elms Works
L.& S.W. Railway'

A Section from a Volunteer Cyclists Battalion at the start of the Starley Cyclists Competition held on the Century Range in 1896 with Martini Henry Rifles strapped to their bicycles. Ex-Wimbledon Range Tramway cars can be seen in the left background; the passengers are sitting in one of the MC&W cars of 1877. The original engine shed is in the right background and there is a glimpse of *Wharncliffe* at the front of the shed in the process of running round its train. John Starley is credited as the inventor of the modern bicycle in the late 1880s

This intriguing idea of putting in mixed gauge between Bisley Camp and Brookwood was never proceeded with although it was to be revived again at the turn of the century. The correspondence with Adams concluded with the anticipated return of Wharncliffe.

'20th April 1894
'Bisley Tram Engine 'Wharncliffe'
'I am much obliged to you for the information regarding the traction power of our Engine.
'Please forward the Engine to Bisley, but not on a Saturday, and giving a week's notice to
    Mr. Hoey
        Bisley Camp
           Pirbright
'To enable him to have labour ready.
'W. Adams Esq'

After *Wharncliffe* returned contract arrangements were made, based on an annual basis, for the locomotive to be maintained by an L&SWR fitter and operated by a driver and fireman from Guildford Shed, both during the Annual Meeting and at other periods as necessary. This arrangement required lodging turns at considerable extra expense to the NRA. Each year from 1894 until 1899 the Secretary sent a letter to the Railway Company requesting any minor repairs on *Wharncliffe* to be carried out and the loan of an engine crew for the duration of the Meeting. A typical letter was sent by Col Mackinnon on 14 June 1898.

'To General Manager
    Waterloo Station
'I am directed by the Council to ask you to kindly sanction the same assistance as afforded to us as last year.
'1st. Executing any necessary repairs to our small tramline and overhauling the Wharncliffe. Please inform me the date of the artificer going to Bisley for this duty that I may give notice to the National Boiler Insurance Co who have to examine and test the boiler.
'2nd Allowing us a driver and stoker for our tram engine *Wharncliffe* from Sunday 16th July to Saturday the 23rd July inclusive, the Association paying the expenses.'

In 1900 the NRA took on their own driver, at the same time taking the opportunity to dispense with the separate fireman, but arranged with the L&SWR that, in an emergency such as sickness, a driver from Guildford Shed could still be made available at short notice. At the same period, the NRA themselves took over the track maintenance of the Range Tramway.

During the Annual Meeting boys from nearby schools were employed for various tasks around the Camp including acting as ticket sellers on the Range Tramway. In 1895, for example, Mackinnon requested three boys from the nearby Gordon Boys Home (named after General Gordon, who had recently been killed at Khartoum; it was formed to look after destitute boys and was run on military lines) to attend the Tramway. In 1897, it was the turn of the local Shaftesbury School.

'July 6 1897
'I should be glad if the Association could have the services of Boys from the Shaftesbury School viz:
  '2 Boys, Tramway, 12th to 23rd @ 2/-
  '4 ' , Picking up paper, 12th to 24th @ 1/-
  '6 ' , Picking up paper, 19th to 24th @ 1/-
'The services of the boys would be required from 8am to 7pm, the lads providing their own meals
  'The Secretary
  Shaftesbury School'

By 1898, *Wharncliffe* needed repairs to the boiler, and Nine Elms was once again requested to carry these out. By this time, of course, Drummond was in charge of the L&SWR's motive power; his personal reaction to this request is not recorded!

'4th July 1898
'Wharncliffe'
'I enclose a communication from the National Boiler Insurance Co. and will feel obliged if you will issue instructions to have the required work carried out as far as may be practicable.
  'The Superintendent
  Loco Depmt
  L.&S.W.R.'

Details of the repair are not known but everything seems to have gone well. This repair also permitted the Association to seek an opinion from Drummond on the hauling power of *Wharncliffe* in respect of the new cars which the Council were intending to order.

The Range Tramway Alterations of 1898

At the Council Meeting held on 4 August 1897 A.P. Humphry moved – 'That it be referred to the "Works" Committee to consider whether by an extension of the small tramway or otherwise better communication between the "90" Butt Ranges, the Camp and the Long Ranges could be provided'. This was carried and referred to the Works Committee 'for report with power to obtain professional opinion'.

At the Works Committee Meeting of 20 August, Humphry proposed that the Range Tramway should be extended at both ends. This was taken up with some enthusiasm although it was not until April 1898 that a final decision was forthcoming.

'The Committee were of opinion that it would be advisable to extend the Tramway to the rear of the centre of the 600 yard firing point of butt 18, 19, and to end of Bazaar Road; Secretary to prepare an estimate. They do not see their way to further extensions at present in view of probable large expenditure in connection with Refreshment Contract.'

This was submitted to 'professional opinion' in the shape of the L&SWR who within a short time returned a set of estimates.

'Secretary submitted estimates for extension of the small tramway received from L.&S.W. Railway.
'Scheme A. to end of Bazaar Road £58 --
'   B. to butts 5.6.   £146 --
'   C. to centre of firing
       point 600 yards
       butts 18.19   £89 --
'It was decided to recommend Scheme A only.'

At a Works Committee meeting dated 5 March the proposed improvements to the Range Tramway were further considered.

'Considered the subject in all its bearings; condition of carriages and the possible necessity for a second engine - before deciding on any recommendation Secretary to prepare plan of proposed extensions on a larger scale, and get fresh estimates - Extension A, end of siding to be 10 yards South of Bazaar entrance - Extension C, to South end of 600 yard firing point butt 10 with siding behind 600 yard firing point - ascertain probable cost of another locomotive.'

The extension of the tramway was confirmed at the following Meeting held on 2 April.

'Recommend Extension A at an estimated cost of £54 - and C at an estimated cost of £69 - by L.&S.W. Railway Engineers Dept.'

The work was carried out under the control of A.W. Szlumper, then a District Engineer. However, the result was far from satisfactory resulting in the dispatch of a strong letter to Szlumper from a most disconcerted and probably terminally-ill Mackinnon.

'I was much disappointed on Saturday on seeing the way in which the western extension of our tram line is being carried out; I am sure it will not be approved by our Council, and it must be altered; it is a pity you did not let me see the plans before commencing the work. The curve is I fear too sharp for our long tramcars, and it passes so close to our 600 yard firing point that competitors firing at that end would have reason to complain.'

'At present the line is altered as largely shown AA; it should be as in BB so that it could be continued further if thought necessary another year. The engine

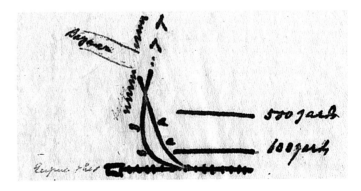

Mackinnon's sketch indicating the problem with the 1898 Range Tramway alteration.

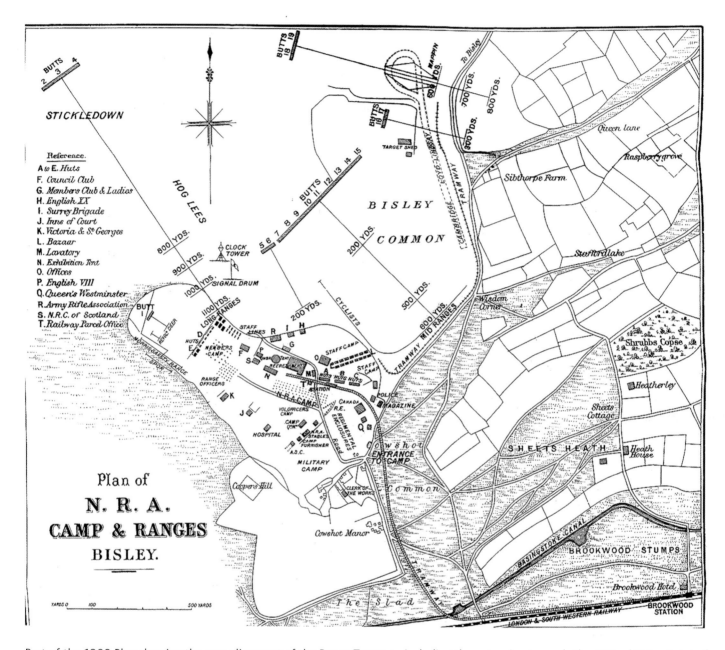

Part of the 1898 Plan showing the new alignment of the Range Tramway including the extension towards the 600 yd Firing Point of the long Siberia Range.

shed should remain where it is for use in winter and on bad nights and the short line bit should not have been taken up.'

This brought the Camp terminus round to the eastern end of the re-aligned Bazaar Lines, but the arrangement was only to last for two years. It was then again re-routed to terminate adjacent to the Camp Station as part of an agreement with Lord Pirbright's Homes for the carriage of building materials to the site of the new 'Princess Christian Home' from the Bisley Camp Station goods yard over the Range Tramway and via a temporary branch line to Stafford Lake from a junction at Wisdom Corner.

The New Tramcars

By November 1898, the Association had finally decided that the now thoroughly worn out ex-Wimbledon Tramcars should be replaced without further delay and the Works Committee, 'ordered that a letter be sent to the S.W.Rly Co enquiring if our engine was capable of hauling 2 bogie cars about 20ft, also if track was sufficiently strong, and if the Co would care to tender for their construction – Cars to be without roof, separate estimate to be asked for awning and fittings.' Matthews wrote to the General Manager of the Railway Company to ascertain whether they could supply suitable vehicles and was advised to write to J.W. Panter, the L&SWR Carriage and Wagon Superintendent, to find out if the Company had any surplus rolling stock that might be suitable for the Range Tramway.

'November 21st 1898

'The National Rifle Association are about to replace the cars which they use on their light tram-line running round the ranges at Bisley but before purchasing new Cars they instruct me to enquire whether you have any old carriages for sale which could be converted for use on our line and which you would be disposed to sell.

'Our line is 3ft 5¼ gauge and there are two sharp curves so that any of your old carriages would have to have new wheels and underframes and probably bogies.

'Your Engineer knows the capacity of our engine as you were good enough to have it repaired at your shops recently, and your Permanent Way Dept. knows all about the line as they have from time to time repaired and constructed portions of it.'

Panter provided drawings of carriages about to be withdrawn and Matthews replied in a letter dated 29 November.

'I am obliged by your letter of 25th inst. covering drawings of carriages which will shortly be withdrawn from traffic.

'The Council of the National Rifle Association are obtaining tenders from different Builders for new tram cars for use on the light railway on their ranges, but it occurred to them that you might have some old carriages which could be adapted for the purpose at a less cost than new cars could be constructed. Would you care to undertake the construction of the new underframes etc. necessary to enable

your old carriages to be used for our purpose. The gauge of our line is 3ft 5¼ ins and the curves on it would render it necessary for the carriages to be run on bogies.

'J.W. Panter Esq.
L.&S.W. Rly
Carriage Dept.
Eastleigh'

Panter then replied that it would be more economical to purchase new tramcars and, in fact, the NRA was already writing to obtain quotes from prospective suppliers. Thus the incongruous vision of superannuated L&SWR carriages, re-equipped with narrow gauge bogies, being hauled round the Bisley Ranges by the diminutive *Wharncliffe*, evaporated!

During the same period Matthews also wrote to Dugald Drummond, the Chief Mechanical Engineer of the L&SWR seeking his advice on the hauling power of *Wharncliffe* in respect of the new cars.

'Nov 14th 1898

'As you know all about the capacity of our *Wharncliffe* engine the Council of the National Rifle Association will be obliged if will give your opinion as to the capability of the engine to haul new tram cars which they are proposing to have built for them.

'It is proposed to have 2 bogie cars, each about 20ft long by about 7ft wide with iron underframes. To be open cars without roof. - I suppose the weight will be about a ton each unloaded.

'D. Drummond Esq.
Chief Engineer
L.&S.W. Rly
Nine Elms'

On 18 November, Matthews was able to write to Sir Henry Fletcher, the NRA Chairman, enclosing a copy of the letter he had sent 'to the three firms mentioned by the Works Committee – a representative of one the firms called on me today and I have arranged to go to Bisley with him one day next week so that he may see the line. The L&SWR Engineer has written to say that he considers our line sufficiently strong to carry cars such as we propose and our engine sufficiently strong to haul them.'

One of the firms contacted about the supply of new tramcars was the well-known Birmingham railway coach building company, Brown Marshall.

'22nd November 1898

'National Rifle Association

'Tram Car

'Replying to yours of yesterday - not date has yet been fixed when quotations will be required but it will probably be about a week before Xmas. The Council of the NRA meets on the 7th prox and will probably decide the date then.

'Delivery of the cars will be required not later than May 31st /99.

'Messrs Brown Marshall
Britannia Wagon Works
Birmingham'

Although they did produce drawings and specifications negotiations were handed over to the NRA's Agent, Messrs Kuhner Henderson and Co. of 115, Canon St, London E6, and a consulting Civil Engineer, Arthur C. Pain. They recommended that the contract be awarded to Messrs J and F Howard of the Britannia Ironworks in Bedford. Howard's were originally agricultural engineers who had diversified into light railways during the 1890s.

At the Works Committee meeting held in London on 20 January 1899 'it was resolved that the Council be recommended to purchase 2 cars of Messrs Kuhner Henderson & Co (Drawing No 1359) delivered at Bisley not to exceed £85 each.'

On 1 February, the Council agreed to order two tramcars with a carrying capacity of 42 passengers each, through Kuhner Henderson. Matthews confirmed the order in a letter of the 22nd February with a note of the same date to Arthur Pain.

'I beg to confirm the order given to you verbally for two tramcars (drawing No 1359) to be delivered free at Bisley Station by 1st June.

'The cars to be in accordance with the specification you have agreed with our engineer Mr. Pain and to cost £75 (Seventy five pounds) each.

'Dear Mr. Pain

'Thanks for your letter re Tramcars – I have now given the formal order.

'Arthur C. Pain Esq.
17 Victoria St
Westminster'

The Invoice from Kuhne Henderson, dated June 24th 1899, included a specification of the cars.

'2' 6" wide of 1 Open Passenger Cars, to drawing No.1359 – Platform 20' 0' long x $1\frac{3}{8}$" deal. 7 cross seats with pivot. Iron standards & hinged backs – wrought iron end Frames covered with steel plates. Frames of Channel Steel 4'x2' securely stayed & trussed & fitted with centre spring buffer & draw gear at each end. Foot board on each side running whole length of Car & carried by strong wrought iron brackets. Centre male & journal bearing casting with strong wrought iron pin. Carried upon 2 4 wheel bogies with wrought iron frames & Oak Beds – each fitted with 8 spiral springs – Cast Iron Axle boxes, for oil, with Gun metal bearings, steel axles, 23" diam Cast Steel wheels, 15" diam $1\frac{1}{8}$" flanges $2\frac{1}{8}$" on tread to 3' $5\frac{1}{4}$" gauge.'

It can be assumed that if the new tramcars had been as light as suggested Wha*rncliffe* would have handled both of them without any problem. Unfortunately, this proved a gross under-estimation; the final weight of the cars, which were mainly constructed of a mixture of iron and steel, turned out to be 3 tons unloaded and 5 tons loaded! Lt. Colonel C.R. Crosse had just been appointed as the new NRA Secretary, with A.C. Matthews as the Assistant Secretary, and one of his early tasks was to resolve this very awkward problem. But before that, he had to deal with some comparatively minor problems with the paint finish. The NRA had recently changed its house colours from blue and cream to vermilion and cream and the cars were initially intended to be in the new colours.

On 8 June, the Crosse had written to Kuhner Henderson :-

'In reply to your letter enclosing paint of colour for our tramcars [sic]. I am directed to say that we do not want to go to any extra expense in the matter and will be satisfied if you will (as suggested by your representative on Monday) pick the cars out in Vermilion or Lake so the scheme is complementary to the present one.

'Please advise we when this is done and I shall be prepared to accept delivery as arranged last Monday.'

On 13th June : -

'In reply to your letter re. cars, we are prepared to receive one as soon as you please. Kindly inform when we may expect it.'

On l4th June:

'… this morning received your letter … with reference to the extra charge for picking out in Black. Mr. Howard your representative told me that they intended picking out the tramcars in Black and I quite understood there was to be no extra charge of this so I do not wish it to be done.'

By late June the NRA was becoming concerned about the delivery of the new tramcars and Matthews wrote another letter to Kuhner Henderson.

'June 20 1899
'Replying to yours of the 19th inst. We have been daily expecting the delivery of the Cars, as Colonel Crosse is under the distinct impression that he gave definite instructions for their delivery - they should be sent (presumably by rail) addressed to The Secretary, Bisley Camp, at Brookwood Station L&SW Rly.
    'The contract price includes delivery at Brookwood Station.'

The tramcars in fact arrived shortly afterwards and, in early July 1899, the L&SWR arranged a trial run with *Wharncliffe*. This turned out to be unsuccessful causing Lt Colonel Crosse to write to Drummond blaming the type of coal that had been used.

'7th July 1899
'You were good enough to send a driver for our engine the other day, but as we had not got the proper coal the result was not quite satisfactory. I would be extremely obliged if you could again send him down on Saturday or Monday to see if the Wharncliffe is capable with steam coal of drawing the two new cars with ease.'

The problem was probably not so much the coal, as the weight of the pair of cars which proved to be beyond *Wharncliffe*'s capabilities with its existing 80lbs psi boiler and small cylinders. There was now little the L&SWR could do to assist, the Annual Meeting had arrived and *Wharncliffe* had to cope as best it could with a single tramcar. This was compounded by teething troubles with the tramcars themselves caused by bolts working loose. After narrowly avoiding a very severe accident with one of the cars at the height of the Meeting, primarily due to this cause, the NRA Secretary was compelled to take urgent action with a strongly worded demand for assistance from the car manufacturers.

'July 20th 1899
'Tramcars
'With reference to my telegram of yesterday, we find we are able keep the cars going with bolts we can provide locally.
    'Most of the bolts on the cars are working loose and require constant attention. This is especially the case with the bolts by which the wooden parts of the seats are fastened to the iron supports and appears to be owing to no washers or check nuts having been used.
    A very much more serious item, and one which might have caused a bad accident, arose with the brake apparatus. This worked loose and in consequence fell to such an extent that it caught a joint in the rails with the result that it was smashed to bits and the car thrown off the line. Fortunately no one was hurt but the design of the cars seems to show very little margin of safety in this respect.
    'Speaking generally the cars give great satisfaction, but with so many of these minor details working loose notwithstanding every care, passengers are beginning to talk about it and find fault with the construction and unless something is done to remedy it I fear that your name on the cars will not be an advertisement to your advantage, and I think on this account it would be worth your while to come and see if you cannot suggest anything to remedy these defects.
    'The cars will only be running tomorrow and Saturday for the present.
'Messrs J. and F. Howard
Britannia Works
Bedford'

Wharncliffe's New Boiler

This was a worrying time for Crosse as something equally urgent had also to be done about the power of the tram engine. Fortunately, towards the end of 1899, the NRA was approached by Merryweather with an offer either to construct a new engine or replace the existing boiler with one of 120lbs psi as it had now been established that *Wharncliffe*, with its existing boiler, in good repair, would only be capable of hauling a single bogie car. At this time, the change of route to terminate the tramway adjacent to the Camp Station meant that the tram engine now had to submit to a short length of steep gradient which the Works Committee estimated to be 1 in 30.

'He also reported that Messrs Merryweather had given an estimate to put a new boiler to the present engine so that it might give sufficient power to enable the engine to draw 27 tons on the level or 12 tons on an incline of 1 in 30 including the weight of the engine, at a cost of £168.

'...and it was unanimously resolved to recommend Council that Messrs Merryweather's estimate for the new boiler for the present engine be accepted.'

The NRA agreed to the supply of a new boiler, being the cheaper option, in a letter from Crosse, dated 8 February 1900, which contained however a few provisos. He also stated in his letter to Merryweather that the maximum gradient to be surmounted was 1 in 80 (instead of 1 in 30 stated in the Work's Committee's minutes) and one can only guess whether a significant error had been allowed to creep into the specification.

'Messrs Merryweather & Sons
Greenwich. S.E.
'Dear Sir,
'Bisley Camp Tramway Engine
'Your letter of the 19th ult. in which you tender to supply and fit a new boiler for this engine, and test the same complete for the sum of £168 net, was before the Council at their meeting yesterday when it was decided, that providing a satisfactory assurance can be obtained that the engine will be capable of performing the work required of it when re-boilered, your tender should be accepted.

'When I had the pleasure of seeing your Mr. Merryweather here sometime ago, he stated that if this engine were put into thorough repair it would only be able to draw one of our cars, (weight when loaded about 5 tons) as the cylinders are only 6 ins in diameter. From your telephone message of some days back, I understood you to state that when re-boilered as you propose the engine will be capable of drawing 27 tons (including its own weight) on the level, and 12 tons into an incline of 1 in 80. If the engine can do this it will be sufficient for our purpose, and before ordering the new boiler I am instructed to ask you whether after thoroughly examining the engine you will be prepared to guarantee the engine that, when re-boilered as you propose, it will be capable of doing the work mentioned in your telephone message as above.'

Crosse, having received the NRA Council's final approval for the fitting of a new boiler, then requested that Merryweather move *Wharncliffe* to their Greenwich Works for the work to be carried out.

'12 February 1900
Gentlemen
Bisley Camp Tramway Engine
'I am obliged by yours of the 9th inst in which you state that this engine with the new boiler you propose should be quite capable of doing the work we require of it.

'I think it would be best if you will take the engine to your works & thoroughly examine it and then if you will let me know that you are satisfied that it will come up to our requirements I will give the order for the new boiler and any minor repairs that may be necessary.

'As your men are much more capable than mine of handling the engine I shall be glad if you will make all arrangements to fetch it from Bisley. It should be done as soon as possible so that the work may be put in hand at once.

'The engine should be complete and ready for running by the beginning of June at the latest and earlier if possible as the line may be required earlier for running building materials over it.

'The only repairs that have been done since you left it have been done at the shops of the L&SWRy.'

On 2 March, after the locomotive had arrived at the Works, he was able to confirm that the necessary repairs and fitting of the new boiler could take place at a price not to exceed £200. Merryweather had not constructed a new steam tram engine since 1892 when the market collapsed due to the rapid development of electric traction. This order therefore throws an interesting light on their capabilities in this field a full eight years later.

The Alterations and Extensions of 1899 and 1900

During 1899 and 1900 further alterations and extensions to the Range Tramway, as well as new tramcars and a major rebuild to *Wharncliffe,* were discussed by the Works Committee. In the first instance, the Committee considered it would be advantageous to change the gauge of the Range Tramway to 'standard' (4ft 8½ins).

'Extension of Camp Tramway - A letter from Major Cowan stating that in all probability the necessary rails for extending the Camp tramway could be procured on loan from the War Office, was read; and it was decided that the Secretary was to find out the cost of converting the present line to a 3ft 6ins (should read 4ft 8½ins?) gauge and also the cost of buying or hiring an engine for same.'

'The Works Committee followed this with proposals for two possible schemes regarding the planned extension.

'Two schemes for the alteration and extension of Tramway were submitted.
  (a.) Starting from present engine house entering NRA enclosure 20 yards west and passing round by Fry's tent, across the level crossing round the NRA Camp and out to 1000 yards firing point.
  (b) Through NRA gate close to magazine, between railway and A.B.C. huts, alongside Pavilion siding, across the London Scottish camp, and out to 1000 yard Firing point.

'Letters from Messrs Stephenson & Co re engines were read, and it was decided that the Secretary should obtain an estimate for the conversion of present gauge to standard gauge, and for the continuation of the line (according to plan) as far as connecting with L & SW Rly at Bisley Camp Station.'

'November 15th 1899
'The Under Secretary of State for War
'War Office
'In the year 1890 you were good enough to issue to the National Rifle Association "on loan" a quantity of disused Railway material from the Suakin – Berber Railway for use on our Camp Tram Line.

'It is now intended to extend the Camp Tram Line & to replace these light rails with heavier metals to as to carry the heavier engine and larger cars required by the present traffic.

'I have the honor to request that issue may be made to us on loan of disused rails (if possible not lighter than 56 lbs per yard), sleepers, spikes etc. to enable us to renew the existing line so that the total length when extended will be 1½ miles requiring about: 5300 yds Rail, 2300 Sleepers, 9000 Dog Spikes, 1800 Fish Plates. I am informed that there is a quantity of disused Railway Material at Devonport possibly we might have some of that.'

At about this time, the Association were offered an electric tramway plant but this was turned down by the Council.

'November 20th 1899
'With reference to yours of the 9th inst. offering an electric tramway plant for sale – I will keep your letter before me but at present there is no intention on the part of the Council to go in for an electric tramline.
  'Messrs S.B. Saunders and Co
  Bush Lane House
  Cannon Street, London'

Following this Crosse wrote to the L&SWR regarding a recent survey of the Range Tramway that had been carried out by their Engineer.

'30th January 1900
'Chief Engineer
London & South Western Railway
Waterloo Station
'You were good enough to send us Mr Richards to survey our Camp Tramway line some few weeks ago, and the results of this inspection was that to carry a 25 tons Engine we should require about 2200 yds of new rails, 500 sleepers, 2500 dogs & 250 sleepers weights

of rails and also bolts. Could you kindly inform me if you have any second hand that would suit us and what would be cost delivered on ground.'

At the 31 January meeting of the Works Committee alterations and extensions to the Range Tramway were discussed in some detail. During the meeting, it was decided that there would be no change of gauge.

'The Secretary reported the result of his negotiations with the Railway Co. as to the purchase of sleepers etc. for the reconstruction of the Range Tramway.

'Considerable discussion then took place as to the route of the tramline, that the gauge of the line remain as at present, but that its route be altered from the rear of Firing Point 8 so as to enter the NRA ground on the east of the present work-shops and then follow the general line of the road leading from the work-shops to the Offices; the line to terminate near the Pool Payments Office; also that provision be made for the construction of a new engine shed near the terminus; the estimated cost being about £400.'

The Temporary Extension to the Princess Christian Homes

However, in early 1900 an enquiry was received from the Trustees of Lord Pirbright's Homes which entirely altered the perspective. This was regarding the construction nearby at Stafford Lake, about 700 yards east of the Century Range at Wisdom Corner, of what became known as the Princess Christian Homes of Rest for Soldiers. It was for a temporary line to be laid from a junction with the Range Tramway at Wisdom Corner to the site of the Homes for the purpose of carrying materials for the construction of the Homes. The correspondence was largely with Lord Pirbright's Architect, E.O. Sachs.

'Mr. Sachs
3 Waterloo Place
4th March 1900
'Your Engineer Mr Symons was here yesterday and went over the proposed Railway Line, generally approved of it. He however was most anxious for it to be extended about 100 yds close to our Goods Siding and this I am prepared to entertain and recommend to our Council on the following conditions.

1. That you will give us the free assistance of your Engineer to construct our line.
2. That you will contribute £100 towards its construction.
3. That you will return them to us free of charge, after you have finished with them, the second hand rails I propose to buy for you from the War Office.
'For this the NRA will give you the free running use of our Railway Range Line for one year (except from 9th to 23rd July) and provide you with 2 cars which you can adapt for goods use.'

The Meeting of the Council on 7 March 1900 noted the terms of the agreement.

'Correspondence between the Secretary and Lord Pirbright's Architect in connection with the construction of the Bisley Convalescent Homes was read from which it appeared that the Homes Committee were willing to pay £50 and all working expenses for the use of the Range Tramway line for the conveyance of building materials from Bisley Camp Station during their construction (not to include the Bisley Meeting), also that they asked the NRA to purchase for them from the Government sufficient rails to make the necessary extension of the line from Wisdom Corner to the Homes, and agreed when the buildings were finished to hand over these rails free of charge to the NRA; also that the Architect agreed to place his services and those of his technical staff at the disposal of the NRA without charge to advise on all matters of extension to the present tramway.'

Meanwhile the NRA had commenced negotiations with the War Office regarding the purchase of ex-Tregantle Military Railway track (originally constructed to serve forts on the west bank of the Tamar that protected the Naval Base at Devonport. These, in turn, had been repatriated from the military Suakin-Berber Railway in the Sudan). Confirming this with Sachs they also added a modified proviso – 'that you will undertake the post of Hon: Advisor and supply us gratis with such services as we may require of your Engineer for the laying out and construction of our line.'

Sachs immediately made a counter offer and this was accepted by the NRA

'March 8th 1900

'In reply to your letter of the 6th March re Range Tramway, I am directed by the Council to inform you that the National Rifle Association are prepared to accept your offer of a contribution of £50 and undertaking to leave us free of charge, the entire stock of rails, points, and sleepers laid down by you from our line to your Homes, a length of just over 700 yards, and for this the Association will so extend the present line as to run up close to the main siding and loan you two cars (such as they are) and loco on the understanding that you will run it at your own expense and be responsible that it is returned in good condition, and will grant you the running rights over the Range line (except from 6th to 23rd July) for one year.

'I also note that you will kindly undertake the honorary duties of Advisor as regards the construction of this extension, and assist us free of charge with the services of your Staff.'

It was now decided that the Engineer of the Homes and the Assistant Secretary of the NRA would travel down to Devonport for the purpose of inspecting the rails and any remaining details. Crosse confirmed the appointment with Sachs adding in his letter that he thought that 'the application for laying your line on War Office Land should be made by you direct to the War Office.'

On 30 March, Crosse sent the Assistant Secretary's report on the rails at Devonport to the War Office and quoted the price he was prepared to pay.

'With reference to your letter of the 9th February last, No.57/91/175, I have the honour to enclose the report of our Assistant Secretary who inspected the rails at Wacker, and now write to say I am prepared to take the 3 lots therein mentioned at an all-round price of 35/0 a ton, at Wacker, that being the price of old iron in the neighbourhood of Bisley Camp.'

Interestingly Crosse wrote to the L&SWR's Plymouth District Superintendent in April regarding the delivery of the rails from Wacker stating that he had been in touch with a Mr Wacker, Barge Owner, Queen Anne's Battery, and asked the Superintendent to act for him in respect of the transport of the rails as he was anxious to get them delivered to Bisley.

A Works Committee on 24 March confirmed the route of the Tramway to terminate near the Goods Siding and agreed a site for the Engine Shed. However the latter was not proceeded with as it was later decided to construct a new Engine Shed which would be large enough to house the tramcars as well.

'Engine Shed - The route of the extension of the Range Tramway was considered, and it was decided to adopt the one recommended by the Engineer. (as per plan).

The site of the engine shed was fixed in continuation of and south of the present railway station.

This, however, was quickly changed to a separate building that would be large enough to house *Wharncliffe* as well as the two tramcars.

In May Crosse had further thoughts about the original offer to hire out the tram engine and now offered to include the loan of the NRA's engine driver to assist the expenses of the Homes.

'23rd May 1900

'As I am sure you remember part of our agreement about the Tramway was that you should have the loan of our Tram Engine for a year (certain dates excepted) and use it at your own risk and expense you providing engine driver etc. It appears to me that this would be a great expense to you. I therefore propose that we should provide a qualified engine driver and fuel and that you should pay us at the rate of 10/- a half day when you employ him, you still bearing the same risks as you would have had you provided your own driver.

The proposal to lend the NRA's engine driver would seem to have been a little premature at this point as one had yet to be appointed although it was in hand and, as it turned out, was resolved in time for a decision made the following month when Sachs raised the possibility that supplying the engine with water on the spur out to the Homes might causes difficulties, but Crosse was able to reassure him on this point.

'14th June 1900

'I am sorry that there is any difficulty about watering the Engine, but I am of opinion that the present arrangements are good enough and have no

The invoice from John Westcott, a well-known Plymouth lighterage company proprietor, who had barged the ex-Tregantle rails (in turn from the Suakin – Berber Railway in the Sudan that had now been bought for use on the Bisley Range Tramway) across the Tamar from Wacker Quay to be loaded into LSWR Trucks.

intention of erecting another Stand pipe at the suggestion of Mr. Trollope. My engine driver confirms my opinion.

'By the way would you kindly ask Mr Symonds about the orders for the crossings as time is getting short and our line is useless without them.'

At the end of August, Crosse proposed that the account as it stood could be settled; the first cheque, for the cost of the rails, was received by 6 October,

although he had not received the initial account from Devonport, and had to send them a reminder letter as late as November.

'30th August 1900
'Many thanks for your letter of the 29th March. Now that the amount due for Rails is determined would it not be as well to have a general settlement of the account between us. I enumerate the items below.

Looking east from the Canadian Club in July 1901. The Range Tramway extension of 1900, laid under the control of the Engineer of Lord Pirbright's Homes, can be seen diverging to pass in front of the Workshop. It then rejoins the original route behind the Century Range 600 yard firing point. The frames of an old tramcar and some wheels can be glimpsed in front of the Workshop.

Bisley Camp Station platform in July 1901. The Range Tram shed of 1900 is immediately behind the platform on the right. To the left of the tree in the foreground can be glimpsed the Camp level crossing with the goods yard beyond. The latter was the site of the short-lived Pavilion station of 1890 and also the starting point of the Bisley - Blackdown Military Railway of 1917.

The 1902 'Ashburton' Competition in progress on the Century Range with the Range Tram behind (shown in the enlargement), heading towards the Camp. The boys are shooting with the .303 Long Lee rifle. The tram is approximately at the 1900 Wisdom Corner junction of the temporary line to the Princess Christian Homes, visible in the background.

Contribution as originally agreed		50.0.0
Rails		133.0.0
Repair of Trucks		5.0.0
Set of New Wheels		5.0.0
Working Engine June	16.17.0	
July	21. 9.0	
August	31. 2 0	69.8.0
Total		262.8.0'

'The Under Secretary of State for War
War Office
Pall Mall S.W.
7th November 1900
'I have the honour on behalf of the Council of the National Rifle Association to request that an account

may be furnished to this office of the cost of the 165 Tramway Rails supplied from Wacker, Devonport in May last.'

The extension to the homes remained in use, but on an increasingly intermittent basis until February 1901 with the final certificate for the contract being issued later that year.

The NRA appoints its own Engine Driver

By 1900, the growth in the use of the Ranges, assisted by the introduction of the Saturday trains between Brookwood and Bisley throughout the shooting season, required the Range Tramway to be pressed into regular use over the same period. The Association therefore decided that a permanent Driver for *Wharncliffe* should be appointed to replace the engine crews hired on a regular (and expensive) basis from the L&SWR. It was also decided at this time to dispense with the separate fireman on the Tram Engine.

A former Guildford engine driver, Charles Ginman, applied for the job and Crosse wrote to Drummond on 26 May 1900 seeking a recommendation.

'I shall be glad if you will kindly let me know the circumstances under which Charles Ginman, Engine Driver, left the employment of the London & SW Railway, and also if you think he is a man who may be trusted to take charge of the small locomotive which we use on our range tramway. A reply at your earliest convenience will oblige.'

The subsequent appointment of Ginman as the tram engine driver and his continued employment in this role

(he was also the NRA's blacksmith) is fully supported by the previous remarks regarding the water supply on the temporary extension to the new Princess Christian Homes and documents including a letter, dated 18 April 1912, to the Locomotive Superintendent at the L&SWR's Guildford Shed requesting a replacement driver. A doctor's sick note of a similar date stated that Ginman, of Bisley Green, had a poisoned foot with another note, dated a few days later, confirming his fitness to resume his employment.

'My Engine Driver has fallen ill and I am writing to ask if you could arrange for one of your engine drivers to do his work here tomorrow (Saturday April 20th).

'The work is that of driving our Small Range passenger Tramway Engine - the first trip with passengers is about 2.0pm and the last about 7.30pm. I can arrange to have steam got up if there is any

The Last Tram. One of the set of 1905 cartoons from 'the Humours of Bisley' by the artist Ernest Ibbetson. Possibly not too far from the truth from certain reports!

difficulty in your man arriving in time to do so. Though I would prefer it if he could be here in time to do so himself. In any event, as our line is only a very light tram line, he should be here in ample time to make a trial run over the line in company with our foreman; I would suggest that it be not later than 12.30pm

'If you can find me one of your men to do this I shall be greatly obliged, and shall be further obliged if you will let me know what pay I should give him & what payment (if any) your Company would require.'

The fact that Guildford Shed was able to provide an engine driver for the Range Tramway at such short notice is a tribute to the contingency arrangements that the NRA had arranged with the L&SWR. This probably took place around 1900 when the Association took over all the Range Tramway operations. Ginman was still listed as 'Engine Driver' into the 1920s, although the last time he seems to have 'driven' Wharncliffe was in 1919 when it underwent what turned out to be its final steam test for insurance purposes. Ginman continued in employment with the NRA until his death in 1931.

Range Tramway timetables of the period show the first and last trams of the day starting and finishing at the Long Siberia terminus respectively, rather than at the Camp, indicating that Ginman was permitted to 'stable' the tram overnight on that Range, only a short distance from his home.

The Range Tramway after 1900

Wharncliffe and the Tramcars continued to give good service until late in 1905 when the boiler was inspected and found to need repairs. These problems were serious enough to require its return to Merryweather at Greenwich.

'January 25th 1906
'With reference to your letter of Dec 11th I am now sending the Boiler per London & S.W. Railway.

'Will you kindly have it examined and, before proceeding with the repairs, let us have an estimate for putting it in thorough order.

'There is a leaky rivet in the fire hole doorway which is marked with chalk.

'Please supply new fixing studs and send separately when returning the boiler.
'Messrs Merryweather & Sons
Greenwich Road
London S.E.'

The NRA Secretary became a little concerned when the boiler was not returned until the end of March. However in July 1907, just at the time of the Annual Meeting, trouble was being experienced with the steam delivery pipe which kept fracturing.

'June 10 1907
'I am sending you today the Delivery Pipe of our engine to have a new Cone Flange fitted to it.

'Would you kindly put it in hand at once and return it so that it is delivered at Brookwood Station on Friday next so that we shall be able to mend the engine on Saturday.

'Please return by passenger train.
'Messrs Merryweather & Sons
Greenwich Road
S.E.'

A further problem occurred in the spring of 1908 when the Pressure Gauge became faulty. Merryweather pointed out that it would be cheaper to supply a new gauge and return the faulty one. This was agreed by the Secretary who wished as usual to avoid unnecessary expense.

In 1909, at the end of that year's Meeting, Wharncliffe again required extensive repairs which were serious enough to require return of the locomotive to Messrs Merryweather's Greenwich Works. At the same time, the Association enquired whether a larger and more powerful locomotive could be obtained. The locomotive was inspected at Bisley by Merryweather's Engineer whose report contained a comprehensive list of repairs needed, amply demonstrating just how hard the locomotive had been worked in the previous few years. At the same time, the Company advised against the purchase of a new locomotive. In November, they advised that it would be necessary to get the new firebox ready before sending the locomotive to their works, then revised this to announce that the engine would have to be sent before the firebox was constructed. When the locomotive was delivered to the Greenwich Works Merryweather immediately

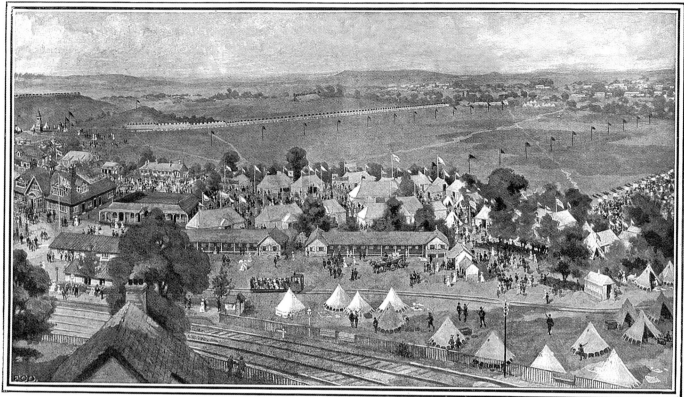

Stickledown Butts.

Siberia Butts.
The Century Butts.

The N.R.A. Offices.

The Bazaar Lines.

The Firing Line.

THE TENTED FIELD: GENERAL VIEW OF THE RANGES AND CAMP AT BISLEY
DRAWN BY F. C. DICKINSON

A 1909 panorama of Bisley in which *Wharncliffe* has just left the Camp terminus with its crowded single car bound for the firing points of the Century and distant Long Siberia Ranges, the butts of which can be seen behind those of the Century Range. The shed for the Range Tramway rolling stock can be seen just behind the platform of Bisley Camp Station. (*The Graphic*)

started to cut out the old firebox and discovered that it also had a crack in it. This was immediately notified to the NRA in case of an additional insurance claim.

At the beginning of February Crosse enquired how the repairs were progressing and Merryweather Reported that they expected to finish the job by the end of the month; but things then started to go wrong. By the beginning of March the Company was forced to disclose that they were having difficulty in obtaining the special plates for the firebox from the rolling mills due to the small order.

By now the locomotive was urgently required and this resulted in the exchange of increasingly heated telegrams and letters. The engine was finally returned towards the end of March.

In October 1910, the NRA asked Messrs J. & F. Howard of Bedford to quote for a complete set of eight wheels for the two tramcars, the old ones being worn out.

'October 18th 1910
'Would you kindly quote the price for a set of 8 wheels for the tram cars in use on the ranges at Bisley. The size of the wheels is 14½ inches in diameter – 3 inch sole. The wheels to be properly turned on sole and flange and fitted by you to our axles.

'Please note that the last set of wheels supplied by you were not truly round and we had to send them to Aldershot to be properly turned.

'Messrs J. & F. Howard
Britannia Works
Bedford'

The previous set had been supplied in 1907 and the complaint about the roundness of those wheels had been made at the time. However, when the new wheels, mounted on the old axles, were received it was now found that there were discrepancies in the gauge!

1655 & 4111.y.

PATENT FIRE ENGINE MANUFACTURERS,

The National Rifle Association.

OFFICES & WORKS :- *Greenwich Road, S.E.*

SHOW ROOMS :- *63, Long Acre, W.C.*

LONDON.

BY SPECIAL APPOINTMENT.

To Merryweather & Sons, Ltd.

GLYN, MILLS & Co.
a/c MERRYWEATHER & SONS, LTD.
Not Negotiable.

IF PAYMENT IS MADE BY CHEQUE PLEASE CROSS

P.

1909

Date	Description		£	s	d
Sep.21	Special attendance of Engineer inspecting tram engine and boiler including time out, rail fares and expenses.		1	11	6
1910 Apl.14	Repairing your locomotive engine as per our estimate and Engineers report of 23/9/1909 as under :- Boiler: Taking out firebox and supplying and fitting a new fire box together with a new set of boiler tubes. Supplying new ashpan and smoke box; grinding in all cocks and repacking glands; renewing injector and feedpump check valves and truing up seats. Engine: Turning up wheels and taking sharp edges off the flanges; renewing axle boxes; closing and adjusting all bearings; fitting new gunmetal slippers to the crosshead and guides and a new pin to the crosshead and forked end of connecting rods; supplying and fitting new sector blocks for link motion and regauging the sectors; rimering out all holes in the link gear and fitting new hardened pins; renewing neck rings in the stuffing boxes, rebushing glands, and truing up rods; refacing slide valves and refitting to cylinder face; throughly overhauling pistons and supplying and fitting new set rings; overhauling feedpump, grinding in valves of same and fitting new pin to pump rod; grinding in cocks and valves of injector and fitting a new water cock; grinding in all cocks and fittings on engine. Exclusive of carriage of engine either way. AS ESTIMATE NETT		145	17	"
	Cutting out boiler plate to instructions of Boiler Insurance Co's Inspector and supplying, fitting and rivetting on corner patch.		2	12	9
		£148.9.9 £	148	9	9

The major repairs to *Wharncliffe* which were carried out over the period 1909 to 1910 by Merryweather. But delays in the delivery of steel resulted in a late return to the NRA.

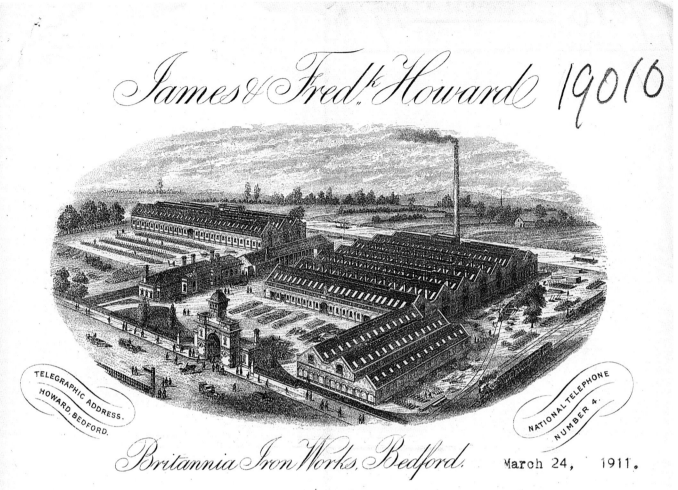

James & Fredᵏ Howard 19010

TELEGRAPHIC ADDRESS.
HOWARD, BEDFORD.

NATIONAL TELEPHONE
NUMBER 4.

Britannia Iron Works, Bedford.   March 24,   1911.

Dear Sirs,

We have today received back the Wheels and Axles.   On checking
them we find that the gauge is not the same as was originally supplied on the
Passenger Cars.   We understand from your letter that if we turn back
the front bosses of the wheels so that these are ½" from the journal of the
axle, as shown on the enclosed sketch that the wheels will be satisfactory.

We shall be glad however if you will confirm this by telegram
tomorrow morning.

Yours faithfully,

FOR JAMES & FREDˢ HOWARD
TG/SR.

Lt Col C.R.Crosse.
The National Rifle Association.

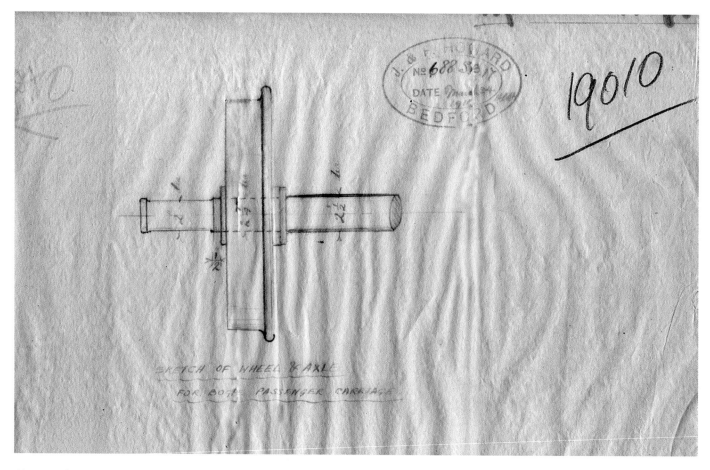

Above and Previous: Messrs J & F Howard's reply, with a journal and wheel drawing, to Crosse regarding the gauge problem on the tramcars.

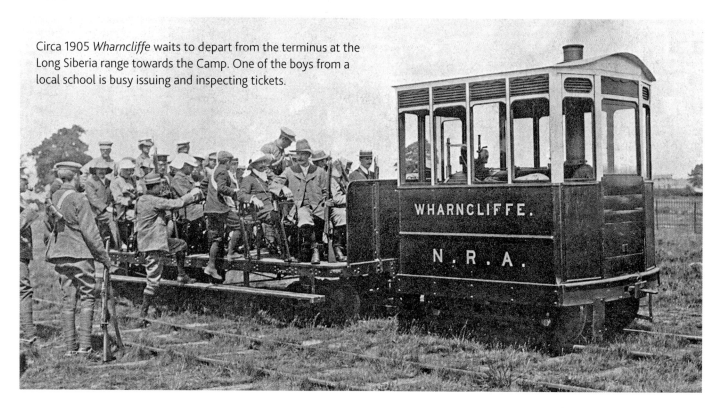

Circa 1905 *Wharncliffe* waits to depart from the terminus at the Long Siberia range towards the Camp. One of the boys from a local school is busy issuing and inspecting tickets.

'March 21st 1911

'In fixing the wheels and axles to our Tram Cars it is found that, with one exception, the boss of the wheels fixed to the axles by you are too long, and in the present state, are useless. The length of the boss in each case should be 4-1/8 in. but in those you have fixed 2 are 4-3/8, 2, 4-5/16, 3, 4-1/4. The matter is one of the greatest urgency and I shall therefore be glad if you will kindly let me know by wire what you would wish me to do to have the mistake rectified.

    'Messrs J. & F. Howard
    Britannia Works
    Bedford'

The wire from Messrs Howard's requested the return of the wheels to their works where, after further examination, they stated that the gauge was not the same as originally supplied, and included a drawing to confirm their findings. Crosse now requested them to proceed with the repair according to their drawing but asked them to clarify their statement on the change of gauge which he did not understand. Messrs Howard's reply pointed out the relative dimensions.

The Range Tramway Accident of 1911

In July 1911, *Wharncliffe* was involved in an accident with a four wheel cart belonging to the Guildford Brewery Firm of Lascelles, Tickner & Co. This was described in the daily edition of the *Military Mail* as well as a police Report on the incident, the police camp being conveniently adjacent to the scene of the accident! This seems to have been the only collision recorded on the Range Tramway during its time at Bisley.

The *Mail's* version was more graphic than that of the police.

'The Camp steam tram, in turning a curve at this place, crashed into a van belonging to Messrs Lascelles, Tickner & Co., brewers, which was crossing the line. The van was turned completely over, and the contents, consisting of barrels of beer, crates of minerals etc., were scattered in all directions. The driver of the van was hurled a considerable distance and was badly cut and bruised. While the horses were thrown over on their backs.

'Fortunately the tram, which was full of passengers, kept the rails, or the results might have been very serious.'

    'Police Camp
    Bisley
    10th July 1911

'At 7.25pm 7th inst, whilst a four wheel van owned by Lascelles Tickner & Co, Castle Brewery, Guildford laden with ginger beer etc. driven by Harry Avenall of 8 Keans Buildings, The Mount, Guildford, was crossing the tramway near the blacksmiths shop (by Police Camp) it was struck by the Camp light engine driven by Charles Ginman, NRA Employee, Bisley Camp whereby the van was overturned throwing Avenall and one of the two horses (a grey mare) to the ground. Damage: several bottles of cyder and lemonade broken, hind axle bent and springs strained of van and harness damaged. Avenall sustained contusions of face and left arm; he declined medical aid and after washing proceeded on his journey with van. The light engine had one buffer splintered and one pane of glass broken. The grey mare sustained a slight graze on off side, no further damage or injury. Avenall said 'I had not cleared the line when the tram struck me'. Ginman said 'I blew my whistle but before I could stop, I caught his hind wheel'. Witnessed by Pte John Rumble R.M.L.I. stationed at R.M.L.I. Camp who said 'The driver of tram blew his whistle but the van did not clear the line in time'. Rumble was a passenger on the tram.

    S Rolfe. Chf. Inspr.'

In August 1914, immediately after the annual Meeting, the pressure gauge of the locomotive was reported as reading incorrectly. Crosse immediately wrote to the Boiler Insurance Company to see if it required to be repaired.

    'August 18th 1914

'With reference to your report on the examination of the boiler of our locomotive Engine on July 31st in which attention is drawn to the pressure gauge which it is recommended should be overhauled, our Driver reports that the difference is on the side of safety and thinks there is no necessity to have it repaired.

Notices issued regarding the Range Tramway. The 1909 fare of 1d on the Range Tramway for any distance had halved since the 1890s. In real terms it was now much cheaper than the tram fares at Wimbledon had ever been.

'It appears that the gauge was overhauled a year or so ago and very soon after the engine was used the gauge registered the same pressure as it does now.

'Kindly let me know whether in these circumstances the suggested repairs are absolutely necessary.

The Insurance Company replied that it would be acceptable from the point of view of the boiler insurance and this was accepted by Crosse.

Each year the National Boiler and General Insurance Company wrote to the NRA in order to confirm the annual boiler inspection of Wharncliffe. However, with the outbreak of war and following the 1914 season, the locomotive and its cars were confined to their shed for what proved to be the duration and the inspections were continually deferred thereafter until 1919 when the Ranges were scheduled to re-open.

In 1915, in pursuit of the war effort the Government had issued an edict that all locomotive engines must be registered in order that they could be requisitioned if necessary. Wharncliffe was no exception. However no such demand was ever made although, in 1917, Colonel Fraser, the Commanding Royal Engineer at the nearby Blackdown Camp, made a request to hire

the locomotive presumably to help service those units who were based near both the Century and Siberia Ranges.

'April 2nd 1917
'With reference to your enquiry as to the terms on which you could hire our Locomotive Engine, my Committee are quite prepared to let you have it at a hired rental of £6.10.0. per month. The engine to be taken over by you in running order in the condition in which you saw it, without any expense to the Association, and to be maintained by you in repair whilst in your charge, and returned to us in good running order.'

By the next meeting of the Executive and Finance Committee on 20 April Crosse was able to report that Fraser had accepted the terms. However no further correspondence was recorded regarding this initiative and Wharncliffe was not steamed again until February 1919 and then only for boiler testing purposes, thus indicating that the Tramway had remained unused. With the possibility of the Ranges re-opening for the 1919 season it had been decided to get the National Boiler Insurance Co to carry out an internal and external inspection of Wharncliffe. For this purpose the locomotive was put into steam for the visit and this was carried out on the 14 February, with apparently satisfactory results. No attempt was made to otherwise run the locomotive and this was in fact the last time it was steamed.

An intention at least still remained to re-open the Range Tramway and at the Executive & Finance Committee held on 7 March 1920, the Secretary reported that the repairs to the Range Tramway would cost at least £150. It was suggested that steel sleepers might be purchased from Government Surplus Stores.

This was followed by a minute in the report of the Works Committee dated 21 September in which a radical suggestion to economise on the operation of the Range Tramway was approved.

'Approved of the suggestion that the present siding be done away with and in future the Range Tramway be used on the Push and Pull system as in present use on the L. & S.W. Ry. Brookwood to Bisley Camp.'

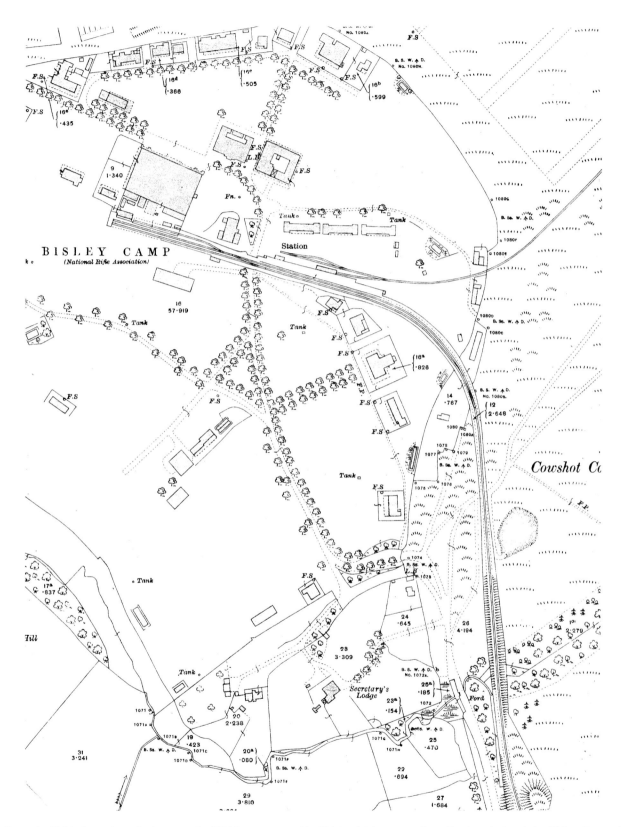

Bisley Camp in 1914. A section of a large scale OS Map, surveyed in 1914, which covers virtually the whole of the Bisley Camp site and the Ranges. The Camp termini of both 'Tramways' are prominent, showing three of the five turnouts on the Range Tramway (the other two being on the run-round loop at the Long Siberia Range) as well as the Tramway shed behind the branch platform. Other 'tramways' shown on the complete map served the Century and Siberia Butts for the movement of targets and also the combined Running Deer and Running Man Range. (*Ordnance Survey 1915 1-2500*)

Although the Committee had obviously been greatly impressed by the L&SWR's introduction of Pull-Push working for the 1919 Meeting this was destined to remain in abeyance. No doubt the likely abandonment of the run-round loops at either end of the Range Tramway appeared very attractive in cost terms, however, although the scheme received the Secretary's approval, it is probable that when the costs and feasibility of converting rolling stock with such basic couplings and no continuous brake system were looked into the whole scheme became unviable.

On 12 December 1925, Sir Lionel Fletcher, a member of the Council, wrote a letter to the Secretary which included comments on the re-opening of Siberia Range and putting the Range Tramway into working order. A quick reply from the Secretary enabled him to draw up a report for the information of the Council with estimates of the costs involved.

'Siberia
'It is within your knowledge the Railway Bn R.E. might well relay the railway to Siberia as a military exercise, though NRA might have to replace the sleepers.

'I will, therefore, be glad if you will place the whole question of the Siberia range on the agenda of the next Council meeting.

'I suggest you circulate the necessary data before the meeting.

1. Your estimate of the number of sleepers requiring renewal and dimensions of them.

2. Your idea as to route to be taken if the track be extended in the direction of Stickledown, and the length of such extension.

3. Cost of rejuvenating engine & trucks.

4. Extra personnel for using Siberia.

5. Cost of telephones, firing point & Butt overhauls.

'My reason for this request is that as a matter of policy the information should be made available.'

'22nd. December 1925
'Siberia Range and Repairs and Extension of Tramway

'It is impossible, unless we obtain professional advice, to give anything but an appropriate idea of the cost of repairs to the present tramway or for the extension towards Stickledown.

'To put the present tramway in order would require about 1,000 new sleepers, 6 ft. x 4 ins. x 6 ins., which would cost from 2s. 6d. each.

'The whole length would require re-laying, with possible replacement of some lengths of rail, dogs, spikes, etc.

Sleepers, say,	...	£150
Labour, say,	...	£150
Other replacements, say,		£100
		£400

'There appears to be no compensating set-off in the way of traffic if the line followed a route over the level crossing on the south side of the Pavilion via the Member's Field to the lower end of the Running Deer Field, about 650 yards; and the difficulties to be overcome in such a scheme are considerable.

'The Engine in any case would require complete overhauling, and I should not be surprised to find that the cost of putting it in thorough working order would amount to a considerable figure. It was last used before the war.

'The trucks are in running condition and would require only general overhauling which could be done by our own people.

'The extra personnel, viz: 8 Officers, 8 Sergeants, 60 Men, required for Siberia Ranges would cost about £10 per day.

'The cost of putting Siberia Ranges in working order would be slight as they are already fitted with telephones and are in fairly good condition.

'I would suggest that if it is decided to proceed with the scheme that I be authorised to engage an Engineer to go carefully into the question of cost and ascertain whether the Railway Bn. R.E. would help us.'

At the Council meeting in April 1926 'it was considered that the time had not yet arrived to take action in the matter' based on the fact that there was currently enough accommodation on other ranges.

The Roadrails System

In 1926, the Association was approached by the Managing Director of the Roadrails Company, Major-General Sir H.F.E. Freeland, regarding the possible trial of their hybrid road and rail system over the Range Tramway. This interesting and innovative system was designed to exploit the high tractive force exhibited by rail-adapted road vehicles running on tyres or tracks coupled with the low rolling resistance of railway vehicles; the whole being guided by a low-cost light-weight track.

The brochure of the Company contained a comprehensive description of the advantages of the system; the following is taken from the introduction.

'The Roadrails Company claim that their system of traction solves the problem that has confronted the railway engineer for the last forty years, namely, to obtain the maximum tractive effort of the engine while retaining the lowest tractive resistance to the load hauled.

'This result is obtained by running the driving wheels of the engine fitted with solid rubber or similar tyres, outside a rail track, on wheelways having a surface comparable with that of a road while the load is carried in trucks to form a train running on the rail track; or alternatively, the driving axle of the engine is fitted with a track-laying device, thereby obviating the preparation of special wheelways.

'This system of transport gives the combined advantages of Light Railway and motor lorry at a lower initial expenditure on construction and equipment, and a more economical cost of operation than either of these individual systems.'

Following this, however, in a letter to the Association Freeland explained that further examination had shown the scheme not to be viable and the grades and curves on the system would not be sufficiently severe to give a proper demonstration of the system so he was having to withdraw the offer.

Sir Lionel Fletcher's Report

On 17 October, later the same year, Sir Lionel Fletcher produced a much more comprehensive report on the viability of re-opening the Siberia Ranges again, coupling this with emphasis on the necessity to do something about the Range Tramway which had now been lying dormant since the end of the season in 1914.

'... To make the most efficient use of the ranges the railway must be put into running order.

'The first consideration in regard to this is the cost, and it follows that this will vary according to the route of the railway, and there are various schemes:-

1. Relay as at present.
2. - Ditto, - but extend the terminus further through the Camp either:-

    (a) behind the Pavilion,

    or (b) wheel to the 200 yards firing point outside the hedge at end of butt 10.

    or (c) as in (b) , but proceed up to the Clock Tower and run along Stickledown as far as, say, 1,100 yards.

'It is certain that *Wharncliffe* could not take any hill, and in any case may be beyond repair.

'The majority of sleepers have out-lived their usefulness and the whole line, it might well be said, would have to be re-laid.

The existing rails are serviceable and are the property of the War Office, but were loaned to the NRA for an indefinite period, as in the case of the telephone cables.

'If this work was let out to contract labour would absorb the vast proportion of the cost.

It is perhaps unfair to quote a personal conversation with a Minister, but I did mention this railway matter to the Secretary of State for War and asked him if this was not the sort of job which the Railway section of the R.E. would welcome, and I received a most encouraging reply.

'This question was discussed with Colonel Cowan during the Meeting and with the valuable points he mentioned well in mind, I think the time has now come to give this question serious consideration.

'I suggest that the whole matter be brought before Council at its first Meeting, but that in the meantime Secretary be authorised by Works Committee to obtain the assistance of the C.R.E., Aldershot, and to obtain from that or some other source a rough plan showing the extensions outlined in this memo. or any others, with additional length of rails, cubic yards material shifted, etc.

'With this information before it the council should then ask the War office to:-

1. Relay existing track with proposed extensions, but to another gauge, if needful.
2. Loan to NRA for an indefinite period, the additional rails and sleepers required.

3. Loan to NRA, as in 2., a suitable engine and trucks, ex stock at Woolwich, capable of taking Clock Tower gradient if necessary. It is asserted that suitable engines are in store against the next National Emergency.

4. Perform the entire work with the Railway Section R.E. and run the train for NRA during each Meeting as part of its annual training.

'Note. Whilst making allowance for the difference in the times when the rails and cables were loaned as compared with to-day, the only cost to the State would be that the sleepers which, unless of metal, would be a wasting asset. But these may be in stock to-day.

'It will thus be seen that the cost of rejuvenating the Railway on the foregoing basis would not be carried by the NRA

'Should this not be realised in its entirety we must decide how much NRA can afford to contribute to the cost, as against 'Roadrail Traction'.'

As with the Roadrails proposal little or nothing seems to have emerged from this, but at least one NRA member, who had been acquainted with the Range Tramway before the Great War, made his feelings generally known in a letter to the Journal.

'The Camp Train

'To the Editor of the NRA Journal
Sutton
Surrey
'August 14th, 1927
'Dear Sir –

'I want to add another suggestion to those already made for the next Bisley Meeting, viz. : that the old camp tramway should be revived. Looking through a scrap-book the other day I came upon a print of the camp tramway at Wimbledon. The truck has a knife-board, is well filled with riflemen and one lady, with a parasol, and is drawn by a cavalry-man, properly mounted, wearing the pill-box which we knew of old.

'If the cost of the locomotive is now prohibitive, perhaps there may still be one horse in the Bisley neighbourhood which could perform the necessary duties. The distance from Target 100 on the Century Range to the camp seems to have got much longer than it used to be, and if one penny per trip, any

distance, could be collected by the driver or postilion, the finances of the Association would benefit overwhelmingly. As an alternative to the horse, I suggest that Mr. Hinchcliffe, who doubtless comes to Bisley, should bring up a Navy petrol engine, and attach it to one of the old trucks.

'Seriously, as I get older, it seems to me that those useless rails might be made useful to the delectation of all concerned.

'Yours faithfully,
R. Langton Cole'

The End of the Range Tramway

Wharncliffe and its Tramcars slumbered on in their shed and, but for the intervention of the weather, may have survived indefinitely. By now they were unique relics of a byegone era, however, to a cash-strapped NRA at the start of the depressed 1930s, there was little room for sentiment when an autumn storm in 1929 destroyed the Range Tramway engine shed.

'The Secretary reported that the ENGINE SHED at Bisley was blown down during the recent gales. The Secretary asked for instructions as to whether a new one should be erected which would cost £150 - £200, or alternatively, as to the disposal of the Engine and Carriages.

'The Committee recommend that the engine and antiquated rolling stock together with such of the (heavy) rails as are NRA property be disposed of; the Secretary meanwhile to make enquiries as to possible purchasers.'

By January 1930, the Secretary was able to circulate a letter to those prospective purchasers of the tramway equipment who had already made enquiries, however some of the detailed measurements of the locomotive contained inaccuracies. Obviously, they had been mislaid or lost since it had been taken out of service sixteen years before!

Shortly after this, with replies coming in, the Council received a letter from Sir Lionel Fletcher regarding the problems of getting competitors to the Siberia Ranges in the absence of the tramway.

'A letter was received from Sir Lionel Fletcher with reference to the SIBERIA TRAMWAY and its sale as recommended in minute 9 of F.&G.P. 20.12.29.

The matter was again discussed at length and the Committee saw no reason to amend their previous recommendation. It was felt that if and when the number of competitors warranted the provision of easier communication with Siberia, a roadway would be generally more useful all the year round. So far as their information went the present rolling stock, to house which they were faced with an expenditure of £200, had only scrap value. They had received an offer of £2. 17s. 6d per ton for the rails of which there were 50 - 60 tons. Further tenders were being invited.'

The highest bid was submitted by the well-known scrap merchants, George Cohen and Son, and this was selected.

'Tenders for the purchase of the Siberia TRAM ENGINE and CARS and old RAILS were examined and the Secretary was instructed to accept that of Cohen, Sons & Co. for £95, all expenses in connection with taking up and removal to be born by the purchasers.

The sum received to be ear-marked for the proposed new road fund, if and when such a road to Wisdom Corner and Siberia were constructed.'

19300221 Finance & General Purposes Committee

The mystery surrounding the disappearance of *Wharncliffe* and its cars is explained by the total lack of public information in the NRA Annual Reports. There was neither a hint of the destruction of the Tram Shed in the 1929 storm, nor the subsequent disposal of the Tram Engine and rolling stock in 1930; on the contrary, everything was reported as remaining in good repair! Why there was such secrecy surrounding its demise and, perhaps, the failure to retain even a small 'souvenir' such as the Works Plate, remains the abiding mystery unexplained even in the Council Minutes. Coincidentally *Wharncliffes'* driver from 1900, Charles Ginman, fell ill the following year and died on 6 December 1931.

So sadly, an original Type 1 Merryweather Steam Tram Locomotive, which had long outlived the great majority of its sisters, was unceremoniously disposed of and was almost lost to history altogether.

The rails belonging to the NRA lay entirely within the Camp area and were thus disposed of, while those outside belonged to the War Department and probably remained in situ at least until the Second World War, finally to disappear in the insatiable scrap drive. Sleeper marks behind the firing points of the Century Range are reported as remaining visible into the 1960s.

THE BUTTS TRAMWAY

The date of the laying of the Butts Tramway – probably to the Century Range only - is subject to some confusion as very little reference documentation has been found. A drawing that appeared as one of a set in the *Illustrated London News* covering the opening of Bisley in July 1890 appears to show track being laid in the Butts of the new 90 Butt Range (the original name for the Century Range). Pictures from the 1891 *Bisley Album* indicate that it had certainly been laid in time for the Meeting of that year but there is no reference to it in the yearly Report. The 1893 Report states that 'Besides the ordinary annual work of maintaining buildings, butts and appliances, and of improving the capabilities of the ground, various new works were completed' – this included - 'extensive repairs to the long range butt and laying down tramways for conveyance of targets.' However, this is probably a reference to its extension out to the Butts of the Long Siberia Range as no tramway was ever laid to the

Stickledown range. This was re-stated in 1900 when the origin of the track was commented on (from the unfinished Suakin-Berber Railway in the Sudan, the track of which was repatriated after the death of General Gordon at Khartoum in 1886). Crosse sent a letter to the Secretary of War in October 1900 in which he requested that the ownership of the track should be transferred to the NRA although he stated that the track had been laid in 1892.

Tracks originated at the Target Sheds located on the north side of the 90 Butt Range and were laid to the Butts of both this and, later, the Siberia Ranges; the gauge was 18 inches. Unfortunately the records are otherwise silent on the tramway network other than the 1900 Report which stated that the track had been lent by the War Office. However, in 1891 Captain Maxwell of the Royal Engineers, who had been primarily responsible for the construction of the NRA's portion of the Bisley Camp Tramway between the north side of the canal bridge

The Target Sheds in 1891 with two of the original target trucks on view indicating that the Butts Tramway had been laid by that year.

and the Camp, had returned with his team to undertake various technical tasks. One of these was assisting with the construction of the new 200 yard range the butts of which were sited adjacent to the most westerly butt (now re-designated Butt 7) of the 90 Butt range. He is credited in later documents with obtaining and presumably laying the Butts tramway track. The track had been made available through the War Office who now had an enormous amount to dispose of. It is likely that the target trucks originated from Woolwich Arsenal which had operated an 18 inch gauge network for some years. In 1898 the Works Committee meeting of 9 December 'Ordered that Target Trolleys be thoroughly repaired' indicating that they had experienced a hard life even before they reached Bisley.

On 15 October 1900, the NRA Secretary wrote a letter to the War Office requesting that the rails supplied by the latter should continue on loan to the Association.

'With reference to the attached letter and Voucher, I am directed by the Council of the National Rifle Association to request that the plant shown on the Voucher may be struck off charge of the C.R.E. Aldershot and transferred to the NRA It consists of a about a mile of light Tramway 18inch gauge, originally a portion of the Suakin – Berber railway plant which was issued on loan to the NRA in 1892 (sic) and has been used on the Bisley Ranges since that date. This line though of great utility to us would be of little or no value if removed.'

On 6 February 1901, the Council discussed a letter from the War Office 'with reference to the target shed and Butts light tramway.' This seemed to have assented to the above proposal.

A rare piece of excitement hit the normally routine existence of the Butts Tramway in 1919 when boys from

Lt Col Crosse and his foreman discuss matters in the Century Butts during Edwardian times. One of the original target trucks (named 'Flag Ship!') is standing at the extreme end of the Butts Tramway.

the local Gordon Boys Home were caught joy riding on a Target Trolley. This caused Crosse to dispatch a letter to the Commandant of the Home, then a semi-military establishment.

'To the Commandant 20 Jan 1919
Gordon Boys Home
West End
Chobham
'Dear Sir
'I beg to inform you that for the last four week ends a Trolley has been taken from the Target Shed premises by the boys from your school for their amusement.

'Yesterday afternoon one of my employees was fortunate enough to catch them in the act. I shall be glad if you will kindly enquire into the matter as the Butts are out of Bounds.

'The boys gave their names as : -
Clifton, Walker and Walton.'

When the Camp was handed back to the Association in 1919 after the end of the war, the Long Siberia was not put back into use, efforts being concentrated on those ranges used for the main competitions. Nothing further seems to have been done until Sir Lionel Fletcher produced his report of 1927 which was mainly concerned with restoring the Long Siberia range.

In 1949 the Works Committee recommended that further consideration should be given to the repair or replacement of the rails for the target trolleys between the target sheds and butts, the Secretary being directed to produce possible schemes and costs. It noted that the rails were now showing signs of severe wear and in places would probably not last much longer.'

The Report for the year stated that the line behind the Century Range Butts had been re-laid and a start had been made on Long Siberia Range. The latter was re-laid in 1950 but there was no evidence that in either case was the track was actually renewed. However, in

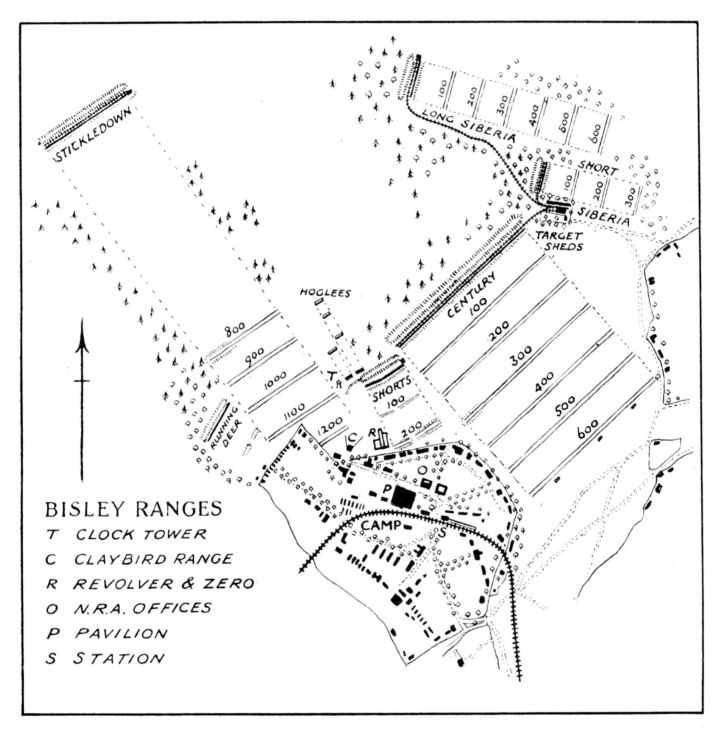

The Camp in 1943 showing the Butts Tramway system at its fullest extent. The 1940 military extension to Pirbright is apparent at the bottom of the map but there is no sign of the Range Tramway.

the following decade, the use of the Long Siberia Range became increasingly intermittent and by 1960, with most of the track of the Butts Tramway now requiring urgent renewal, a decision was made to remove the track to both Siberia Ranges leaving only that to the Century Range to be replaced. With the target trucks also having

come to the end of their lives the NRA searched for possible suppliers of suitable replacements. Initially this was pursued without much success but, fortunately, the Ministry of Defence found themselves able to supply 24in Gauge track complete with four target trucks of the correct gauge. The possibility of using a small locomotive

The Target Sheds and Butts Tramway as depicted in 1943. The junction of the Tramway for the Century and Siberia Ranges can be seen on the other side of the through shed.

in lieu of the former manual propulsion of the trolleys was also investigated and finally resulted in the procurement of a Lister diesel locomotive (Works Number 52579) in 1961 through ME Engineering. The track was laid as an exercise by a troop of Royal Engineers and the whole renewal was completed that year.

In the spring of 1975, the Century Range Stop Butts needed to be renewed and the Royal Engineers, equipped with heavy earth moving equipment, did the job. Unfortunately, during this activity scant regard was taken of the Butts Tramway track and the latter was damaged beyond repair. This caused the Secretary to express his feelings in the *Journal*.

'As soon as the Royal Engineers' work was completed the NRA had to re-lay their railway line, the engine having been thoroughly overhauled and refurbished due to various kind friends from a nearby establishment. Horror upon horror! Much of the railway line had been squashed by 'monster dragons'. Where to get a new line? British Railways, the Coal Board,

the Sports Council and other bodies were feverishly approached, all to no avail. Eventually, George Cohen and Company were contacted and delivered the goods. The final section of line was laid the day before the Services Meeting started!'

The tramway remained in use for a further thirteen years but a fire in October 1987, believed to have been started deliberately and which burnt down a large part of the Century Range target sheds and damaged the Lister and target trucks, caused the Council to review its use. A decision was made in early 1988 to close it completely and, as with the Range Tramway many years before, replace it with a road. This was announced in the Spring NRA *Journal* using a cartoon of a train that was totally unrelated to the appearance of the tramway rolling stock although this time members were asked to comment on how it could be disposed of. Luckily a private buyer came forward to purchase the Lister, rails and trucks, thus securing them for preservation.

The Butts Tramway train heads into the Century Range Butts to deliver refurbished targets.

The Lister and a Target Truck after the fire which destroyed the Target Sheds in September 1987. (*Tim Price collection*)

THE TARGET TRAMWAYS

In 1890 both the Running Deer and Running Man were transferred to the new site at Bisley where a separate range was built for the 'Man', near the Clock Tower. This was not well used and became regarded as something of an 'eyesore' in its exposed position up on the high ground. It was reunited the following year with the 'Deer' but on a separate parallel track. By 1896 the 'Man' had lost the barrel of his 'rifle', however both targets were replaced by penetrable versions in 1897, made necessary by the final passing of the lead bullet era.

In 1891 the Running Man and the Morris range were removed from the Clock Tower Hill with the former now co-located with the Running Deer but running on a separate track. They now operated on separate days to enable practice to be carried out at any time.

By 1896 the Running Deer and Man targets required replacement. The original targets, dating from 1863 and constructed of wrought iron, had become badly battered by the mid-1880s and the Running Deer target had been replaced with an identical steel version. They were both introduced when lead bullets reigned supreme but, by the mid-1890s, long discontinued on the main ranges. The Association wished to take the opportunity to standardise, as far as possible, on metal-jacketed ammunition and this demanded that the metal targets were replaced with penetrable versions. Therefore at a Council Meeting held on 13 January 1897 'on the proposal of Captain Fremantle and seconded by Col. Wilson it was decided that a penetrable Running Deer and Man be provided under the supervision of the Works Committee.'

The original trucks, although modified at some stage with additional support brackets for the target, were also badly worn having been in use since early Wimbledon days. One of the unfortunate results of this change was the inevitable loss of the Deer's stylish antlers. Both the

The later steel Running Deer, at Bisley during its final year of operation in 1896, ready for launch by its team of Markers. The truck is the original but apparently with some modifications to the frames. The following year it was replaced by a penetrative canvas deer (which did not possess antlers for obvious reasons), to accommodate contemporary bullets, and running on a new truck constructed by the L&SWR. The track in the foreground is that of the Running Man.

original Gooch wrought iron and later replacement steel Deer somehow escaped disposal and were eventually placed in position outside the Council Offices where they still remain.

Andrews was asked to report and he stated that the Railway Company could construct a new target truck and also supply and lay the rails for the reconstructed Range. This lead to the NRA Works Committee convening a meeting with a representative from the L&SWR Locomotive Department on 9 April 1897.

'Running Deer and Man - A representative from Loco. Dept. L&SWR attended. The system of penetrable target as devised was examined and approved. Decided that a new truck and new steel rails be provided by L&SWR. - pace for target should be about 12 miles the hour - the necessary measurements were taken and information as to price to be submitted.'

Adams, the L&SWR Locomotive Superintendent, had retired in May 1895 on health grounds at the age of 71 and was succeeded by Dugald Drummond, an outwardly fierce and abrasive Scot, and a completely different character from his friendly and obliging predecessor. However, Mackinnon seems to have established a productive working relationship with Drummond, for it was the latter who oversaw the construction of the new Deer target truck at Nine Elms while he was heavily engaged in the design of his classic T9 Class of 4-4-0 locomotives for the L&SWR's fastest expresses, after the Secretary had written to Scotter on 15 May requesting that the L&SWR construct a new target truck for the NRA at Nine Elms with rails supplied by the department concerned. The letter also acknowledged the help given by Drummond in allowing one of his assistants to give an opinion.

Scotter passed it on to Drummond mentioning, in his reply, that it would be presented at the next Locomotive Committee of the L&SWR. Drummond then put in his positive comments to the Committee enabling Macaulay to authorise the supply.

'26th May 1897
Running Deer Target
Bisley Camp
'Read letter from the Locomotive Superintendent of 21st May with application from the National Rifle

Association for the Company to make them, as shown on the plan submitted for the Running Deer Target at Bisley Camp, the cost of which is estimated at £10.
May be supplied
S. Macaulay'

The truck arrived in good time but the rails for the reconstructed range were not delivered and Mackinnon immediately wrote to Drummond as time was running out; it was less than a month before the Annual Meeting.

'14th June 1897
'Dear Sir,
'The truck for the running deer duly arrived; but the rails have not been sent; your assistant who met our Committee at Bisley went into the question of rails as well as truck and one understood that the rails would be supplied and laid by the Railway.
'I have applied to Sir Charles Scotter for the annual necessary overhaul of our small tram engine and tramway; if the requisite rails and stores for constructing the Running Deer line could be sent to Bisley, the party who will repair the tram line might be allowed to lay down the Running Deer line also.
Yours faithfully
W. Mackinnon   Col.
Sect NRA
'The Superintendent
Loco. Department
L&SW Railway
Nine Elms'

Drummond's reply has not been preserved however Mackinnon's following letter to Scotter, written on 16 June, probably reflects the temperature of its contents with some accuracy!

'We hope you will kindly assist us in the following matter as early as possible.
'Authority was given to your Locomotive Department to construct for us a truck for our new Running Deer and one of Mr. Drummond's Assistants came to Bisley and saw our Committee about it; we went into the whole matter with him, both of truck and of new rails to be laid; the pattern of rails being discussed and decided upon.

The Running Deer – from the 'Humours of Bisley' as depicted in 1907.

'But I ought, as advised by Mr. Drummond, to have written to you especially about the rails and about laying the line. Would you give authority to the Department concerned to supply and lay down the rails the particulars of which are known by Mr. Drummond's Assistant. The fault is mine and I am getting anxious about the matter the Meeting being so close on us. Perhaps, if the necessary rails and stores are sent, the party ordered to repair our tramline would be allowed to do the work.'

Fortunately for the Association the notable efficiency of the late-Victorian mail service and the excellent relationship with Scotter enabled the L&SWR to complete the job in time for the Meeting. Advantage was taken of the much lighter weight of the canvas Deer to dispense with the turntable used on the old system by substituting two Deers facing in opposite directions attached to an L-shaped frame with its apex mounted on a central hub. The frame was simply tilted over to substitute the correct target for the next run.

By the end of Edward VII's reign in 1910, the Running Deer had undergone further substantial modifications. A picture of it just after launch that year shows that the truck appears to have been made lighter than that constructed by the L&SWR.

Late the same year the Council raised the question of adopting a new apparatus for the Running Deer and Crosse circulated a letter to several authorities on this type of Range including the notable Running Deer expert Walter Winans and RSM J.A. Wallingford of the Hythe School of Musketry.

'November 22nd 1910
'The question of adapting a new Running Deer at Bisley is under consideration, and I shall be glad if you would kindly let me have your views on the proposal.

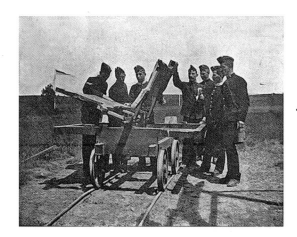

TURNING THE DEER

PATCHING THE DEER

STARTING THE DEER

SHOOTING THE DEER

Depictions of the new Running Deer Tramway, as reconstructed by the L&SWR in 1897. They show the new truck, constructed at Nine Elms, with the canvas target being 'turned', patched and then being prepared for launch by the same team of markers. The temporarily redundant Deer has been tilted over to rest on the deck of the truck. The 'shooters' complete the set.

The Running Deer being launched c1910 indicating the large number of markers necessary to operate the Range. The truck and the Deer support show signs of having been substantially modified or rebuilt at some stage during the previous decade, this work being carried out at Bisley.

'The proposed change will not necessitate any alteration in the figure of the Deer, but instead of being worked by gravity, and at a varying speed, it will be worked by hand on the level, the speed being an even one.'

The reply from Wallingford was less than enthusiastic regarding a hand worked apparatus, He especially pointing out the pitfalls from his own experience

'24th November 1910
'With ref to your letter this morning the following covers my observations :

Your Running Man and Deer targets are, from the competitors point of view, the fairest and best I have ever seen and I cannot think of anything to equal the principle.

From the markers point of view it certainly is expensive and dangerous. The latter can be obviated by building the banks out to the white posts. Orders to the markers would remain as now but in addition there ought to be an automatic catch to hold the trolley after arriving say ten feet inside the bank. You will, of course, say 'but the competitor ought not to shoot outside the posts', but we know that it is almost impossible to avoid it when one is young at the game. I myself have never been fined the 10/- but I won't say how often I ought to have been. One often sees, at the end of a hard day, the markers waiting to catch the trolley because they know that the opposite side are tired and are therefore are not taking the trolley to the top of the incline.

As regards working it by hand I have never seen such a one worked evenly, and the tricks that some of the markers get up to are unmentionable. If you watch your Pedestrian target you will often see him make a buck leap out of the mantlet and then stop dead for quite ½ to a whole second and then go on again at varying rates. I could tell you of many instances of unfairness in connection with hand worked targets but I'm sure you don't want to hear about them.

To sum up the whole matter in a few words – "I wouldn't have hand worked targets, in an individual competition at any price, and would keep the gravity-worked heavy trolley-on-rails until you have something better". I, to repeat myself, don't know of, and cannot think of anything to equal your present system, let alone beat it.

'I am Sir
Your obedient Servant
J A Wallingford Sgt Major
(for experiments)'

The reply from Winans avoided the hand worked aspect altogether but concentrated on the introduction of a 'galloping' deer (which when tried previously had not proved satisfactory). At the same period Crosse received a rather promising letter from the Rev. L.G. Hunt, the vicar of the small village of Canon-Ffrome in

Herefordshire, who had invented a Running Deer target system which could be operated by a single individual. This seemed to be just the thing that the Association had in mind.

'13th October 1910

'Colonel Hopton says I ought to write to tell you about an apparatus I have recently invented for working a full sized Running Deer, Running Man or Walking Man i.e. I can get any speed I like for the outward and homeward journey.

(1) My Deer does away with the necessity of more than one protecting butt for the person working the deer.

(2) It reduces the labour of working to a minimum i.e. it can be worked and is being successfully worked here by a boy aged 14.

(3) My invention also provides a contrivance for mechanically reversing the deer so that it faces the proper way on the return journey.

(4) If desired, the speed of the deer may be varied, thus affording a greater test of the sportsman's ability.

(5) I claim for my invention

(a) Its extreme cheapness.

(b) Its simpleness

(c) The ease with which it can be worked by even one boy

(6) Here, the marking is done by the boy after the return journey, the 1st signal being for the 1st shot, the 2nd for the 2nd, and the marking is done in the usual manner with disc on Dummy Deer. I use the Deer here myself with the members of my Rifle Club and I have found it always works well and satisfactorily.

'I have done the whole work of Construction myself with the exception of the iron work and roughly speaking, the whole thing has cost me £5!!

'I should feel very much indebted to you if you would take my apparatus into consideration in view of its being of use to the NRA in any way. I don't want to make money out of it but these Gentlemen seem to think you ought to know about it. Hence my excuse in troubling you in this way. With many apologies for doing so.'

After Crosse himself travelled down to see it in action there was further correspondence. Eventually Hunt offered to donate the apparatus to the Association and this was accepted by the Council. It was put into service by 1911 and is pictured in the 'Bisley Souvenir' of 1912 with a Running Man in place on a new range separate from the Running Deer.

The competitions held on both ranges re-started in 1919 but the Running Man was discontinued after the 1938 season with the advent of the new sporting range in 1939. This was constructed on the Hoglees site and included a 'Running Bear' mobile target. This target was automatic in action but was unidirectional from the shooter's point of view in that it made a visible pass in one direction only and then 'collapsed' at the end of the run to return, hidden from the firing point, to the start position. It had the disadvantage however that it was slower than the Running Deer for this very reason. In fact no competition on this Range was listed in 1939 when it opened and with the advent of war it was closed down for the duration. It was not until 1947 that it went into general use but eventually closed at the end of the 1953 season.

In 1962 the British Sporting Rifle Club (BSRC) was formed and took over the old Running Deer facilities at Bisley which had by then become very rundown.

The Running Man Butts in 1912 – using the newly installed Rev. Hunt's apparatus.

CHAPTER 9

THE MILITARY EXTENSIONS

The Bisley-Deepcut Military Railway 1916-1928

Planning and Construction

In late July 1916, the NRA received notification from Colonel J.F. Fraser, C.R.E. Blackdown Camp, that the War Office planned the construction of a railway to serve the three military camps at Pirbright, Deepcut and Blackdown.

'With further reference to our telephonic conversation this morning, I herewith forward, as promised, a rough sketch showing approximately the route the new Railway will take.

'You will observe on examining the plan that it was originally intended to take a junction off the Bisley branch railway at the point marked 162,80 on the right hand side of the plan and continue through Pirbright Camp as shown by the black and red dotted line.

'The plan has been approved by the Chief Engineer of the London and South Western Railway Co. but he suggests that instead of making a junction near that curve, as referred to above, it would be better to continue the line from Bisley Station along the alternate route shown on that plan.

'As in all probability a passenger service will be established between Blackdown, Deepcut and Brookwood Station it strikes me that it would be a distinct advantage to the NRA if the Railway did go as suggested, but as this is a question entirely for your Council I should be please if you would get an opinion from them, as from experience one knows that railway communication vastly improves the value of property, which is otherwise in an isolated situation.

'As I mentioned to you this morning we are at present moving rapidly, and I have to take advantage of the presence of a Pioneer Battalion which I want to put on to the work immediately, consequently you

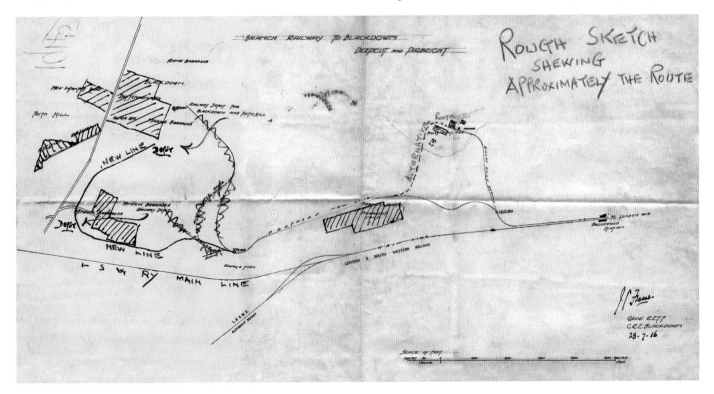

The draft plan for the military railway to Blackdown enclosed with Col. Fraser's letter.

will see the importance of getting a very early decision from your Council.

'Thanking you in anticipation
Signed J.P. Fraser
Colonel R.E.T.F.
C.R.E. Blackdown'

Major-General Lord Cheylesmore, the Chairman of the NRA, had expressed his preference for the second alternative route, and, rather than convene a Council Meeting with all the attendant delay (some members were on active service), instructed Crosse to write immediately to all the Council Members to ascertain their views. Replies by return were received from almost all the Members, the consensus being for the second alternative - an extension of the existing Tramway to form an end-on junction with the new line at the western end of the Camp Station goods yard. A representative reply came from T.F. Fremantle who was then instructing at the Northern Command School of Scouting and Sniping at Rugeley Camp in Staffordshire.

'It is no doubt too late for an expression of opinion about proposed extension of the Camp railway to

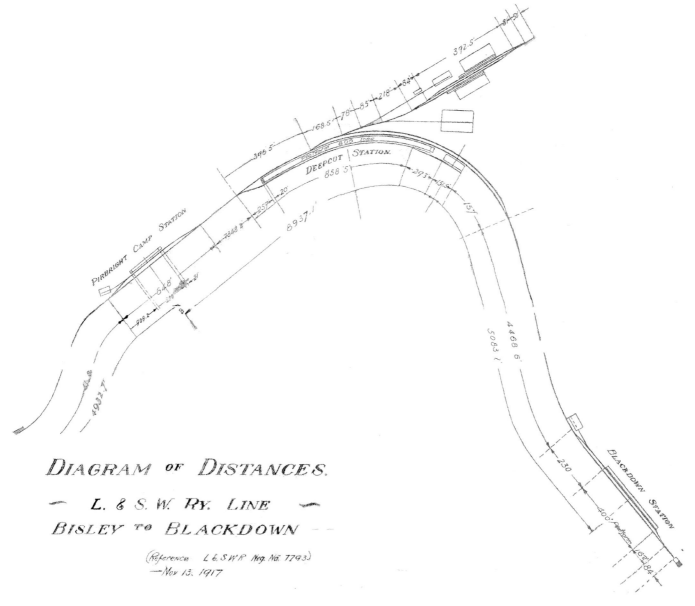

DIAGRAM OF DISTANCES.

L. & S. W. RY. LINE

BISLEY TO BLACKDOWN

(Reference L & S W R Neg. No. 7793.)
—Nov 13. 1917

The Diagram of Distances of the Bisley to Blackdown extension of the Military Railway as issued by the L&SWR on 13 November 1917 soon after the final extension to Blackdown was completed. This shows the line as built.

be useful, but I am confident that the consensus of opinion must be almost unanimous in favour of the alternative route; which would bring to the centre of the Camp a station on a through line with regular services instead of leaving us as the end of a little cul-de-sac of our own, almost stranded & with no train service except on special occasions.

'Armitage was here yesterday and we spoke of the scheme & he made the point that it is most important that there should be ample crossing places to facilitate the traffic through the Camp to the long ranges, running deer and other ranges in that corner. It is certainly important.'

The great majority of the Council having accepted the 'alternative' route, although there were some notable exceptions, a second plan was produced which gave three possible routes through Bisley Camp itself but, in view of the urgency of reaching a decision, Cheylesmore took it on himself to choose the shortest as the most logical and least affecting the Camp and this was ratified by the Council.

The extension was largely constructed by the Pioneer Battalion, assisted by German prisoners from the nearby Frith Hill PoW Camp. The chaired track components were supplied and most probably laid by the L&SWR however and were of that Company's standard design. The new station at Deepcut, seems to have been the only one on the extension to merit a platform building. This resulted in a distinctive structure designed and built by Canadian military engineers in the style of a North American railroad depot.

The L&SWR issued a notice on 21 July regarding the working of the line.

'The line between Brookwood and Bisley Camp, which is now being worked by the Military Authorities has been extended to Deepcut, with an intermediate station at Pirbright Camp, and will be open for goods traffic (authorised by the Military Authorities) as from Wednesday 25th July and for passengers and parcels traffic (authorised by the Military Authorities) as from Wednesday 1st August 1917. The following regulations for working the line will in future apply and must be observed by the L.&S.W. Company's staff.

a) The trains between Brookwood and Deepcut will be worked by the War Department's engines and manned by their staff.

b) The signal box at Brookwood (Bisley Camp Box) will be manned by the L.&S.W.Company's staff.

c) The line between Brookwood and Deepcut will be operated in three sections, viz: Brookwood to Bisley Camp, Bisley Camp to Pirbright Camp, and Pirbright Camp to Deepcut, and the passage of trains in those sections will be controlled by a system of train tickets and telephones.

d) The exchange of traffic between the L.& S.W.Company and the War Dept. will be made in the up sidings situated at the west end of Brookwood station and adjacent to the Bisley Camp Line, and under no circumstances whatever must the War Dept's engines working the Bisley Camp Line be permitted to enter upon or obstruct the L.&S.W. Main Line at Brookwood station.'

No doubt these regulations were subsequently modified as necessary when the railway was finally extended to Blackdown Camp later in the year.

The Military Takeover of the Line

On 22 February, the Secretary had received a notification from the Brookwood Stationmaster advising him that the new line, including the Bisley Camp Tramway, would be taken over by the War Office on 1 March. Having also noted that railway material was already being stacked on Bisley Camp Station – something which the Military Authorities had no authority to do at this time – he wrote to the Chief Engineer at Aldershot Command pointing out the existing arrangements with the L&SWR.

'February 24th 1917

'To/ The Chief Engineer
Aldershot Command
'I am informed by the London & South Western Railway Coy: that our line between Brookwood and Bisley Camp is to be taken over by the Military Authorities on March 1st.

'I would point out that we receive from the London & South Western Railway Coy: an annual payment of about £150 in respect of this line and I shall be glad to know to whom we are to look for this payment when the line is taken over, and also what arrangements will be made for the delivery at the Camp of coal and other Stores at present undertaken by the L.&S.W.Rly:

'I notice that the passenger platform at Bisley Camp Station is now being used as a Depot for heavy railway material. I assume you are responsible for damage and repair.'

No acknowledgement appears to have been received and it also became apparent that neither had the contents of the letter been transmitted to the two senior officers involved, the i/c Construction and i/c Military Railways respectively, when they visited him a few days later formally to take over the line, as they were still under the impression that the whole line was owned by the War Office! This had forced Crosse to dispatch a letter to the L&SWR General Manager asking for clarification of any agreement they had with the military authorities regarding the tramway.

At the same time, he also received a letter from Major Godfrey-Aston, Officer i/c Military Railways at Longmoor, one of the two officers who had visited him regarding the takeover of the line. This officer had finally received a copy of Crosse's letter to the Chief Engineer at Aldershot.

'I have received your letter dated March 1st addressed to Colonel Sinclair, together with copy of a letter addressed to the Chief Engineer Aldershot. I informed you when at Bisley last Monday that we were taking over the operation of the Bisley Railway on March 2nd. During construction the local control of this line will be under Lieut. Lewis, O.C., C.O.R.R.C. Res., Officer i/c Construction, and I do not anticipate any difficulty in delivering goods to the consignees which will have to be hauled from Brookwood to Bisley Camp. I think I told you last week that it was news to me to hear that the Railway belonged to the National Rifle Association, and I am now going into the question with the London and South Western Company as regards the annual payment of this £150.

'I do not anticipate any damage being done to the Bisley Camp Station platform, but should any damage arise I do not think there will be any trouble with making it good when the Line is handed back to the London & South Western Company. I will write you further in due course when I have more information to hand.

'Signed R. Godfrey-Aston, Major R.E.
Officer i/c Military Camp Railways

Longmoor Camp
2nd March, 1917'

Opening and Operation

Although goods trains had run earlier, the first part of the extension, to Deepcut only, was officially opened to traffic on 26 July 1917, however local newspapers gave the opening only brief coverage even though the King and Queen had performed the ceremony (probably as part of a general inspection of the encampments in the area). In fact, the *Woking News and Mail* gave more space to the crowds that turned out at Brookwood to cheer the royal party. The 1917 NRA Report, which carried the most comprehensive coverage, states that the royal party simply passed through Bisley Camp. It seems likely that any proceedings took place at Deepcut, the headquarters of Colonel Fraser, the senior military officer under whose overall control the extension came. The final section, to Blackdown Camp, was not opened until October that year. The completion and opening of the whole line was briefly reported in the NRA's Report for the year.

'Amongst other important changes at Bisley is the extension to Blackdown and Deepcut of the Brookwood and Bisley Camp Railway. This railway was taken over by the Military Authorities in March and a regular train service since August 1st has been maintained. Their Majesties, the King and Queen, performed the opening ceremony and passed through the Camp on that occasion.'

In a description of changes at the Camp taken from the same Report a little more information is forthcoming.

'Each year sees some change in the appearance of Bisley Camp, which during the three and a half years of war has passed through several phases of work and activity under Major General Cheylesmore. The chief change and the one most noticeable to a visitor who knew the Bisley of the Meeting days is the appearance of the new railway which links up Blackdown Barracks on the Chobham Ridges with the main London and South Western line at Brookwood. This new line, partly constructed by German prisoners of war, comes from the Ridges by way of Pirbright Camp and into Bisley where it

A selection of Military Camp Railway Tickets. Ticket Number 000 was probably presented to the NRA. Note the First Class Tickets, presumably for Officers. (*NRA Museum & Great Western Trust*)

joins the Camp line, whose dead end used to be at a point behind the Refreshment Pavilion.'

Goods traffic commenced before the official opening of the railway and the NRA was quickly billed by the 'new owners' for the delivery of a truck load of coal from the Gedling Coal Co. It was for this type of delivery that the Association soon enough suffered demurrage claims from the Military Authorities as they were unable to unload these trucks in the time allowed.

Deepcut Station just after construction. *Sir John French*, the 0-6-2T locomotive from Longmoor, heads a train of LSWR Carriages towards Blackdown.

At the Executive and Finance Committee Meeting of 22 June the Secretary reported that 'General Cowie, C.R.E. Aldershot Command, accompanied by Major Stewart his Staff Officer, and Colonel Sinclair and Colonel Godfrey-Aston of the Military Controlled Railways, had been to see him on Wednesday the 6th June with reference to the charges for traffic on the Brookwood, Bisley, Pirbright Camp Railway. It was decided that the charge for goods conveyed from Brookwood to Bisley Camp should be at the rate of 7d per ton. As regards Passenger traffic the Secretary explained that the N.R.A Council was not in any way desirous of making a profit out of their railway in war time, but would like a clear understanding that any arrangement made now were not to be considered as a precedent in subsequent arrangements with the Government or with the L.&S.W.Rly. To continue the system of payment as at present existing between the NRA and the L.&S.W.Rly would necessitate a considerable amount of book-keeping etc. and he suggested that instead the M.C. Railways should as a royalty make a payment of £25 per quarter to the NRA for

running over their land and using their station, from the date they commenced to run their passenger service, and that the whole of the upkeep should be born by the M.C.R. who also undertook not to block the public roads through the Bisley Camp.'

At the end of June Crosse received a private communication from Brigadier General A.L. Cowie, the Chief Engineer at Aldershot, in which he passed on the contents of a document drawn up by the War Department regarding the working of the Camp Tramway which alluded to the meeting on 6 June.

'Chief Engineer's Office
Headquarters
Aldershot
28th June, 1917

'Dear Crosse,
'I am writing privately to you in regard to the arrangements re working of the Brookwood – Bisley Branch Railway. Extract from W.O.Letter just received.
'Now that the working of the branch and of the new extension has been taken over, for the period

of the war at any rate by the War Department, it is considered that the fairest arrangement would be to continue so far as possible the existing terms as agreed between the NRA and the Company namely:-

'(a) The War Department to allow the NRA the same special rates on their goods, etc., as have hitherto been given by the L&SWR Co.

'(b) The War Department to pay the NRA an annual sum in full settlement of their pre-war right, under the agreement with the L&SWR Co., to 50% of the gross receipts on all traffic. This annual sum should not exceed the £155 hitherto paid by the L&SWR Co. under the special agreement for the period of Government control; on the other hand it appears from a report from the Commandant, Railway Troops, Longmoor, of a meeting held at Bisley on June 6th, at which Brig. General Cowie was present, that the NRA would be prepared to accept a lesser sum, £100 being suggested.

'(c) The NRA to continue to meet any liabilities such as the maintenance of Bisley Station and of the over-bridge referred to by Sir Herbert Walker, imposed on them by their existing agreement with the London & South Western Railway.

'Will you discuss this in the train on Saturday.

'(sgd) A.L, Cowie'

Towards the end of July Crosse received a copy of the draft timetable from Godfrey-Aston and found he had a number of questions regarding the running of services through the Camp Station.

'25 July 1917

'Lieut; Colonel R. Godfrey-Aston
Officer i/c MCR
Longmoor Camp
'With further reference to your letter M.C.R 66 of 21st inst, enclosing copy of the timetable. Would you kindly let me know what arrangements you propose making for the use of the platform at Bisley Camp, and, as you

BISLEY - DEEPCUT MILITARY CAMP RAILWAY.

PASSENGER SERVICE TIME-TABLE.

(Subject to alteration at short notice.)

UP TRAINS.

		WEEK DAYS.									SUNDAYS.			
Train Number.	1	3	5	7	9	11	13	15	17	1	3		5	7
	am	am	am	pm	pm	pm	pm	pm	pm	am	am		pm	pm
DEEPCUT. Dep.	6.20	8.55	10.15	12.15	1.45	3.0	4.50	8.15	10.45	8.59	10.20		5.16	8.20
PIRBRIGHT. "	6.28	9.3	10.23	12.23	1.53	3.8	4.58	8.23	10.53	9.7	10.23		5.24	8.28
BISLEY "	6.33	9.8	10.28	12.28	1.58	3.13	5.3	8.28	10.58	9.12	10.33		5.29	8.33
BROOKWOOD. Arr.	6.40	9.15	10.35	12.35	2.5 (SO)	3.20	5.10	8.35	11.5	9.19	10.40		5.36	8.40
BROOKWOOD. Dep.	6.53	9.28	10.46	12.46	2.15 2.25	3.32	5.25	8.43	11.12	9.29	10.50	11.54	5.46	8.45
WATERLOO. Arr.	7.47	10.12	11.28	1.28	3.7 3.8	4.33	6.34	9.28	12.27	10.42	12.9	1.2	6.58	9.42
	M				M				M					M

DOWN TRAINS.

		WEEK DAYS.									SUNDAYS.			
Train Number.	2	4	6	8	10	12	14	16	18	2	4		6	8
	am	am	am	am	pm SE pm SO	pm	pm	pm	pm	am	am	am	pm	pm
WATERLOO. Dep.	4.42	8.0	9.15	11.45	1.5 1.10	2.25	5.0	7.25	10.35	8.25	9.5	10.5	5.0	9.35
BROOKWOOD. Arr	6.29	9.18	10.36	12.39	2.13 2.10	3.33	5.47	8.38	11.28	9.37	10.22	11.8	6.19	10.35
BROOKWOOD. Dep.	6.55	9.25	10.45	12.50	2.20	3.45	5.55	8.50	11.35	9.45		11.15	6.29	10.45
BISLEY Dep	7.2	9.32	10.52	12.57	2.27	3.52	6.2	8.57	11.42	9.52		11.22	6.36	10.52
PIRBRIGHT. "	7.7	9.37	10.57	1.2	2.32	3.57	6.7	9.2	11.47	9.57		11.27	6.41	10.57
DEEPCUT. Arr.	7.15	9.45	11.5	1.10	2.40	4.5	6.15	9.10	11.55	10.5		11.35	6.49	11.5
	M		M		M					M				

SE Saturdays excepted.
SO Saturdays only.
M Mails.

AUGUST 1st 1917.

Draft Military Railway Timetable issued before the extension to Blackdown was opened.

propose running a night service of trains, what steps you are taking for lighting the platform, etc.

'Would you also let me (know) what precautions you are taking against accidents on the level crossing.'

Which attracted the following reply from Longmoor.

'I have received your letter dated July 25th but hardly understand what you mean by asking 'what arrangements you propose making for the use of the Station at Bisley Camp'. This, as you should be aware, is one of the stations on the Military Railway and all trains will stop there. You are not right in stating that we propose to run a night service of trains. The last train on week-days will leave Brookwood for Deepcut at 11.35 p.m. and on Sundays at 10.45 p.m. and it was at your request mainly that a train was arranged to connect with a late train from London.

'Lighting arrangements for the platform should be dealt with by Col. Fraser, C.R.E., Blackdown, who has provided lights at Deepcut Station, and I am to-day writing him about it.

'Accidents at level crossings will be guarded against by having Flagmen stationed there.

'Signed by R Godfrey-Aston
Lieut. Colonel R.E.
Officer i/c Military Camp Railways
LONGMOOR CAMP
26th July1917.'

However, Crosse remained adamant and also pointed out that the Camp Station was NRA property and had not yet been formally handed over to the military authorities.

'July 31st 1917
'I am in receipt of your M.C.R./66 of 26th inst.

'My enquiry re Bisley Camp Station is owing to the fact that it is the property of the National Rifle Association and should be formally taken over by

Sir John French, a Hawthorn Leslie 0-6-2T Locomotive built in 1914 was an outside cylinder version, equipped with Walschaerts valve gear, of two locomotives previously supplied to the Plymouth, Devonport and South Western Jct. Railway and was used on the Military Extensions in both World Wars.

the M.C. Railway Authorities and the same remark applies to the lighting arrangements.

'I am not incorrect in stating that you propose running trains at night as your Time Table shows one at 10.45pm and 11.35pm. I have no recollection of asking for these, on the contrary I think they are quite useless and a disturbance to this Camp and should be withdrawn.

'As regards the other trains, the 5.25 p.m. train from Brookwood to Waterloo has been cancelled.'

The Military Extension, now known as the Bisley-Deepcut Railway, was run in conjunction with the Camp Tramway as a single entity. Locomotives were provided by the War Office from the Longmoor Military Railway and the coaches for the passenger trains came from the L&SWR. In fact, only two locomotives appear to have been used. These were *Sir John French*, a powerful Hawthorn-Leslie 0-6-2 Tank Engine for 'main line' use, built in 1914 and a small tank engine for shunting purposes, thus ignoring the 'one engine in steam' order originally applied to the Bisley Camp Tramway. Facilities for maintenance were located at Deepcut where a small engine shed had been erected.

Shortly after the start of operations the Commanding Officer of No 1 Machine Gun Corps wrote to Crosse to complain about dangers due to lack of fencing and the loose nature of the banks in the cutting beyond Bisley Camp Station. This of course came under the responsibility of the Officer i/c Military Railways and Crosse passed the letter on with his added comments.

'The Secretary
NRA
'I wish to bring to your notice the necessity for fencing in the railway cutting through the Camp.

'The soil above the cutting is loose, the banks are high; many Cadets and others pass to and from between the parts of the Camp divided by the cutting; it is probable that want of fencing will conduce to a serious accident.

'Fence posts were put in last winter but the work was not proceeded with, and the posts have since been removed.

'G.N. Powell Lt. Col.
Bisley Camp
7/8/17'

'August 9th 1917

'The Office i/c
Military Camp Railways
Longmoor Camp
'Dear Sir,
'I beg to forward a letter which I have received from the O.C. No.1 Cadet Battalion Machine Gun Corps pointing out how necessary it is that the railway running through the property of the National Rifle Association at Bisley Camp should be properly fenced in. I am quite in accord with the views expressed in his letter.

'With reference to this matter, my Council though they do not accept any responsibility for accidents, have directed me to draw your attention to what appears to them to be the general insecurity of the railway owing to the lack of fencing and other safeguards.'

By September 1917, after military personnel had taken over the running of Bisley Camp Station booking office but before it had been formally handed over, Crosse continued to take a close interest in the operations of the railway, especially the timekeeping. In that month he encountered difficulties with the clerk at Bisley Camp Station, a corporal, when he found reason to make comments to the latter on the time keeping of a late afternoon train. This caused him to draft a strong letter of complaint to the Officer i/c Military Camp Railways at Longmoor!

'September 10th. 1917

'The Officer i/c
Military Camp Railways
Longmoor Camp.
'With reference to the official time table of the Bisley - Deepcut M.C. Railway you were good enough to send me. I have to report that the train advertised to leave Bisley Camp at 5.28 p.m. yesterday (Sunday) left at 5.15 p.m. I went on to the platform to enquire the reason and was told by Corp. Appleman in a very off-hand manner, that 'it left 10 minutes earlier today'. As he was at the telephone talking to Deepcut, I asked him to enquire there if any arrangement was being made for possible passengers by the 5.28 p.m. train; this he distinctly refused to do. I then asked him for his name. He at first replied 'I have nothing to do

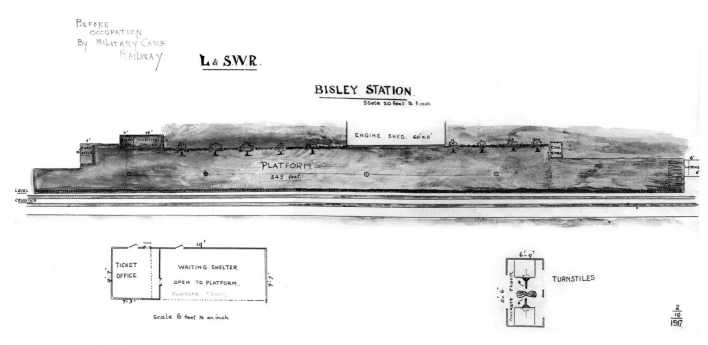

The L&SWR plan of the Camp Station made just before the takeover by the War Office. The chief focus became the Ticket Office, now scheduled to be transformed into a Parcels Office, whose inventory included 'a Telephone (Property of L&SWR), Electric light Fittings inclusive of Fuse Box & Switch, set of three Switches controlling platform lights. 1 lamp on ceiling & 1 switch and a joint box.' The inventory also stated that 'the Platform is faced with a brick wall (in good condition) height 3' 1" above surface'. The 'Engine Shed' behind the platform housed the Range Tramway locomotive *Wharncliffe* and its two cars.

BISLEY—DEEPCUT MILITARY CAMP RAILWAY.

TIME-TABLE.
(Subject to alteration without previous notice.)

UP TRAINS.		WEEK DAYS.								SUNDAYS.			
	A.M.	A.M.	P.M.	P.M.	*P.M.	P.M.	P.M.	P.M.	P.M.	A.M.	P.M.	P.M.	...
BLACKDOWN .... dep.	...	10-12	12-15	1-55	3-30	5-40	8-5	9-52	...	...	...	...	...
DEEPCUT .... ,,	8-50	10-17	12-20	2-0	3-35	5-45	8-10	9-57	...	9-18	5-3	8-8	..
PIRBRIGHT .... ,,	8-57	10-24	12-27	2-7	3-42	5-52	8-17	10-4	...	9-25	5-10	8-15	
BISLEY .... ,,	9-2	10-29	12-32	2-12	3-47	5-57	8-22	10-9	...	9-30	5-15	8-20	
BROOKWOOD .... arr.	9-7	10-34	12-37	2-17	3-52	6-2	8-27	10-16	...	9-35	5-20	8-25	
BROOKWOOD .... dep.	9-24	10-43	12-53	2-36	4-7	6-26	8-47	10-21	...	9-49	5-34	8-42	
WOKING .... ,,	9-35	...	1-4	2-47	4-19	6-38	8-59	*10-55	...	10-0	5-47	8-54	
CLAPHAM JUNCTION ...... ,,	...	...	...	...	...	...	...	11-50	...	10-48	6-39	9-44	
VAUXHALL .... ,,	...	11-19	...	...	...	7-18	9-33	...	...	10-57	...	9-52	
WATERLOO .... arr.	10-9	11-24	1-38	3-21	5-12	7-23	9-38	12-0	...	11-2	6-48	9-57	

DOWN TRAINS.		WEEK DAYS.								SUNDAYS.			
	A.M.	A.M.	P.M.	P.M.	P.M.	P.M.	P.M.	P.M.	P.M.	A.M.	P.M.	P.M.	
WATERLOO .... dep.	8-50	9-15	12-5	1-15	2-55	5-5	7-55	9-30	11-40	10-0	5-30	10-35	...
VAUXHALL .... ,,	...	...	...	...	...	...	...	...	...	...	5-35	...	
CLAPHAM JUNCTION ...... ,,	...	9-25	12-16	...	...	...	8-6	9-41	11-50	10-10	...	...	
WOKING .... ,,	9-32	10-26	12-50	2-8	*3-40	5-47	9-0	10-33	12-40	11-1	6-18	11-15	
BROOKWOOD .... arr.	9-39	10-34	12-57	2-16	3-47	5-55	9-8	10-41	12-48	11-8	6-26	11-23	
BROOKWOOD .... dep.	9-45	10-50	1-10	2-30	4-0	6-10	9-20	10-55	1-0	11-25	6-40	11-40	
BISLEY .... ,,	9-50	10-55	1-15	2-35	4-5	6-15	9-25	11-0	1-5	11-30	6-45	11-45	
PIRBRIGHT .... ,,	9-55	11-0	1-20	2-40	4-10	6-20	9-30	11-5	1-10	11-35	6-50	11-50	
DEEPCUT .... ,,	10-2	11-7	1-27	2-47	4-17	6-27	9-37	11-12	1-17	11-42	6-57	11-57	
BLACKDOWN .... arr.	10-7	11-12	1-32	2-52	4-22	6-32	9-42	...	...	...	...	...	

(Down trains, P.M. column with 1-0, 1-5, 1-10, 1-17: "Wed. & Sat. mornings only.")

1st May, 1918.   * Change at Woking.

The timetable as marked by Crosse for the 6-10 p.m. from Brookwood and the 8-5 p.m. from Blackdown.

with it', but when I said 'I order you to give me your name', he did so, but in such an insolent manner that I had to tell him that was not the way to speak to an Officer.

I afterwards ascertained that the alteration in time was known to the Booking Clerk on Saturday morning. I would therefore suggest for the credit of the Railway and the convenience of the passengers that any alteration be posted in a conspicuous place on the Station.

'I should like to add that the erratic time kept by the train is the subject of a good deal of comment and I think your attention should be drawn to it'

However this caused the Officer i/c Military Railways Longmoor Camp to hurry to the defence of his staff and suggested that Crosse had not been correct in interrupting an operations telephone call!

'With reference to your letter dated September 10th. I have made careful enquiries into the matter, and have to inform you that the train service on the Bisley and Deepcut Railway, the same as on all the other Camp lines, is subject to Military requirements, and for that reason the 5.29 pm train on Sunday last, the 9th instant, left at 5.15 p.m. In accordance with arrangements made with the London and South Western Railway a special order giving full particulars of the alterations to take place in the train service was issued by the Officer i/c of the Deepcut Railway to all concerned about 3.30 p.m.

'As regards Corporal Appleman's conduct, I find that your conversation with him took place while he was in telephonic communication with Brookwood Station. This may account for his seeming to be offhand and rude. The man has been cautioned as regards his future conduct, and I regret that you should have anything to complain of regarding our staff, but I would draw your attention to the fact that it is contrary to Railway regulations for any person to speak to, or endeavour to detract the attention of any Railway employee whilst he is giving orders or signals with regard to the movement of trains.

'The orders concerning the alterations in this train service was only issued about 3.30 p.m. on Sunday. With regard to any orders placed on the station platforms I shall be glad if you will kindly bear in mind that at present we are working this Railway under the very greatest difficulties, and we are making all endeavours to supply Notice Boards, etc., but as overseas requirements have to be considered first it has not always been possible to keep Carpenters employed on such work.

'The Officer i/c of this Railway informs me that the Garrison Adjutant of the district is always given particulars in regard to the alteration in the train service and he issues notices in Orders to the effect whenever possible.

'I trust you will have no more inconvenience.
'Signed R. Godfrey-Aston
Lieut. Colonel R.E.
Longmoor Camp
14th September 1917'

This bout of jousting seems to have terminated with a crushing letter from Crosse.

'September 13th 1917
'The Officer i/c
Military Camp Railways
Longmoor Camp
'I am in receipt of your letter of the 14th inst.
'With reference to para. 3, Sapper Godfrey R.E. the Booking Clerk, informed me that the notice of the alteration in the service was received on the Saturday morning previous.

With regard to the provision of Notice Boards on which alterations should be posted, there is a permanent Board at Bisley Camp Station for giving information as to the time at which the next train will start, and the use of this board for notifying any change might save much inconvenience to passengers.'

A decision to devolve the running of the line seems to have already been taken by the military authorities and by the end of September 1917 the responsibility for the Military Railway had been transferred from Longmoor to Deepcut where the local position of Officer i/c Military Railways, Deepcut, had been created. On 1 October, Crosse met Captain M. Greenfield R.E., the officer appointed to the position, for the purpose of discussing alterations to Bisley Camp Station including conversion of the Booking Office into a Parcels Office and the provision of a waiting shelter in lieu.

'1st October 1917

'Captain M. Greenfield
Officer-in-Charge
Military Camp Railway
Deepcut Station
'With reference to your visit here this morning, I am quite willing to agree to the proposed alterations and improvements to the Railway Station at Bisley Camp being carried out provided they become the property of the National Rifle Association without any charge.'

On the same day he also wrote about securing the free passes on the railway, originally issued by the L&SWR, as these now came under the responsibility of the same Officer.

'The London & South Western Railway Co. issue annually to the National Rifle Association 4 free passes between Waterloo and Bisley Camp Station, and I am informed that these passes are not now available over the Brookwood & Bisley Camp Railway.

If this is so, I shall be glad if you will arrange for the issue to the Association of passes available over the Camp line, in lieu of those issued by the London & South Western Railway Company.'

On 3 December, Crosse reminded the C.R.E Blackdown about the possibility of erecting a waiting shelter at Bisley Camp Station as the existing accommodation at the station had already been taken over as a parcels office as agreed. Nothing, however, had been done about the shelter, a necessity now that the line was being operated during the winter months for the first time.

'When I saw Captain Greenfield here some time ago with reference to the Booking Office at Bisley Camp Station being used as a Parcels Office, I understood from him that some provision should be made for a waiting shelter for the convenience of passengers by screening off the end of the building. Some sort of shelter is certainly required and should be provided as soon as possible.'

Again, nothing seems to have happened and it was almost a year before Crosse tried again but in very different circumstances. However, in the meantime the military authorities had finally made the decision to take over the Camp Station in a memo to the CRE. Blackdown from General Cowie of the Aldershot Command. This resulted in the Deepcut Lieutenant and Quartermaster RE requesting an interview with the NRA Secretary to arrange the handover in a memo dated 13 December on which Crosse noted '10.30 Monday'.

Within days of the Station takeover the Military Authorities decided to install a stove in the Station Booking Office to cope with the winter weather – the single gesture made by them regarding the use of the Station at that time of year. The Station, of course, had never been used in winter in the past and the War Department declined to insure it against fire thus forcing Crosse to contact the NRA's insurance company. However, this 'problem' seems to have been quickly solved from the NRA's point of view when the insurance company modified the policy to give an open cover on all buildings 'that pipe stoves can be used in all or any of the buildings covered in the Policy.'

On 6 February 1918 Greenfield wrote to Crosse regarding withdrawing the attendants at the Cowshot Crossing due to the paucity of vehicular traffic and substituting an alternate method of controlling it safely.

It had been suggested that trains should come to a full stop but this was ruled out owing to the steepness of the prevailing gradient and Greenfield suggested that they should slow to 5mph and sound a prolonged blast on the steam whistle (a method he had already experienced on the Bentley – Bordon branch which had proved quite successful). To this Crosse willingly agreed.

'Officer i/c Military Camp Railway
'In reply to your letter DC.218 of 6th inst., I quite appreciate the necessity of economising man power and am quite willing to acquiesce in your suggestion that the method adopted on the Bentley-Bordon branch should be introduced here.'

An exchange of letters in 1918 gives an insight into the operating procedures used on the Military Railway. Crosse, having had considerable success in dealing with the L&SWR in improving the train services through Brookwood for the benefit of Bisley Camp passengers, now turned his attention to the Bisley-Deepcut Railway. It was unclear, except to him, whether he had any business doing so but it seemed to be effective none-theless. In a letter to the Officer i/c Military Railway Deepcut, for instance, he pointed out some alterations to assist connections at Brookwood.

'July 20th 1918
'With reference to the Time Table of the Bisley-Deepcut Railway. I would suggest the following alteration as one which would add greatly to the convenience of passengers from London and intermediate Stations in the evening.

'The 6.10 p.m. train. Brookwood to Deepcut, at present only takes passengers from the 5.5 p.m. train ex Waterloo. If the time of departure of this train could be delayed until about 6.25 it would enable the passengers from both the 5.5 and 5.32 fast trains ex Waterloo which arrive at Brookwood at 5.56 and 6.15 respectively and also the 5.15 slow train from Surbiton to Woking due at Brookwood at 6.19, to travel by it. The Brookwood-Deepcut train would then be about 15 minutes later and would arrive at Deepcut about 6.47 instead of 6.32, but as it does not depart on the return journey until 8.5 there would be plenty of time, over an hour and a quarter, to prepare for the next journey.

'I think you will agree with me that the suggestion is worth considering.'

The hard-pressed Officer i/c Military Railways at Deepcut, in his reply, gave an explanation of some of the difficulties under which he was trying to operate the service leaving us with a vision of *Sir John French*, in trying to meet the timetable, scuttling between various points on its own little branch line rather like an engine in a model train set!

'I have to thank you for your letter of 20th instant, and much appreciate your remarks, but while I quite agree that your suggestion would improve the time-table it is much regretted that same is not practical.

'In the first case, the 6.10pm train ex Brookwood invariably arrives late at Blackdown, say at 6.35pm, the engine has then to be uncoupled, return to Deepcut, take water and coal, and back on to a Goods train, which departs for Brookwood at approxi-mately 6.55pm. The journey, including shunting, takes some thirty minutes, and the same engine has

to work another Goods train from Brookwood to Deepcut, where it arrives at about 8pm and immedi-ately has to run to Blackdown for the purpose of tak-ing up the working of the 8.5pm Up passenger train.

'From this you will see that the margin is very small, and it would not be wise to delay the departure of the 6.10pm train from Brookwood as you suggest.
'Signed - M. Greenfield
Capt.
Officer i/c Military Camp Rly.
Deepcut Station
22nd July 1918'

Demurrage and a Form of Indemnity
Demurrage was a charge applied when equipment such as rolling stock was detained for longer than the time allotted and amounted to a siding rental. Apart from an isolated incident in 1911 the National Rifle Association had never received a demurrage demand from the L&SWR; however, in early 1918 with the line being operated by the military, invoices were received that included such charges. In the one case, that of a truck which had carried coke from Tongham on 13 December 1917, things seem to have been dealt with in a letter sent to the Officer i/c Bisley-Deepcut Military Railway who had originally forwarded the invoice.

'January 26th 1918
With reference to the charge for demurrage in the accompanying account for the truck of coke, I would state that it was unloaded as soon as possible after arrival, but an unavoidable delay was caused by the state of the roads through frost, the horse had to be roughed and there is difficulty in getting this done. I therefore trust under the circumstances that you will have the charge withdrawn.'

However, when the military authorities declined to waive the payment Crosse refused to meet the demand and the matter was now escalated further up the mili-tary chain, this time to Aldershot. New demands for the amount owing for demurrage were delivered in both January and February 1918 and included other instances involving private owner wagons, carrying coal from collieries to the Camp, during December 1917.

Crosse was adamant that these charges were unjusti-fied and continued to withhold payment. He had good

The demand note from Capt. Greenfield, the Officer i/c Bisley-Deepcut Military Camp Railway, for payment of the demurrage charge which Crosse had refused.

reason for so doing; other than the case of the coke wagon the military themselves had placed barriers in the way of expeditious unloading of the trucks, he was also short of labour caused by the call up of his men and, not least, the Association was now being effectively billed by the military authorities in connection with goods delivered solely for the benefit of the army who had entirely taken over the Camp since 1914 (when it was handed to them by the Association for the duration)!

'March 9th 1918

'I enclose a cheque 19/1 for carriage of goods during February. With reference to the charge for demurrage I cannot hold myself responsible for this as the trucks were unloaded after arrival without due delay.

'In the case of the truck arriving late on Friday 22nd Feb., there was no time to complete the unloading on Saturday and it had to be finished on the Monday

following. Considerable delay is caused by the Gates being closed for shunting operations and for the passing of trains which prevents our cart crossing the line.

'I should like to hear from you as to the actual time allowed for unloading the trucks after arrival.

'The O i/c
Bisley Deepcut Military Camp Railway'

Concurrently with the demurrage issue the military authorities also thought it necessary to protect themselves by attempting to inflict on the NRA a Form of Indemnity. This was essentially a legal agreement by which the Association, in providing a railway facility to the War Office, would become liable if anything went wrong with that facility. This document, which had been channelled through the Officer i/c Military Railway at Deepcut, duly arrived on Crosse's desk with a demand for an instant signature. Crosse, naturally enough, was not in a position to do this without consultation and forthwith replied to that Officer, explaining his position.

'February 16th 1918

'The Officer i/c Military Camp Railway
Deepcut

'With reference to the Form of Indemnity which has been left here for my signature. As the railway between Brookwood and Bisley belongs to the National Rifle Association and we have certain rights which we are not prepared to surrender, I cannot sign the Form of Indemnity until I have referred the matter to my Council and possibly to our Solicitors for instruction.'

The Secretary was directed to refer the Form of Indemnity to the Association's solicitors and their reply was tabled at the Meeting of the Executive and Finance Committee held on 11 March.

'9 New Square W.C.2
11th March 1918

'Referring to your letter of 25th ult: and also to my interview with you on Friday last. I cannot advise the National Rifle Association to sign the document which has been sent to them, which I return, without further explanation from the Military Authorities.

'It seems to me that the document entirely ignores the arrangements with the London & S.Western

Railway Coy: as to which you will remember that my partner Mr Coulson had an interview with Mr Bishop on the 13th July last as set out in my letter to you of that date.

'I think the best course would be for you to apply for an interview with General Ellison with the view of going into the whole matter.

'I also think that either you should communicate again with the Railway Company, or if you prefer it I will communicate from here with Mr Bishop.

'The document the Association is now asked to sign provides for the Association supplying trucks and so forth, which is quite foreign to the arrangements between the Association and the Company.

'Should the Association come to the conclusion to sign any such document as for the period until the end of the War, it must be distinctly agreed, not only by the Military Authorities but by the Railway Company that such an arrangement is entirely without prejudice to the position between the Association and the Company.'

The Meeting heard that the NRA Chairman, Cheylesmore, had seen General Ellison, the Deputy Quartermaster-General based at Aldershot, who had referred the matter to the Director of Movements at the War Office. An interim letter had been received and the Secretary was instructed to pass this on to the Association's solicitors with a view to their seeing the L&SWR solicitor as soon as possible. Crosse also ensured that the Officer i/c Military Camp Railway was kept informed of progress.

Meanwhile the 'demurrage' issue was still present and Crosse drafted a letter to the Chief Engineer at Aldershot laying out the difficulties he had with unloading the wagons within the specified time.

'March 21st 1918
The Chief Engineer,
Aldershot
'Bisley-Deepcut M.C Railway
'With the reference to the question of demurrage on trucks used for delivering coal etc. at Bisley Camp, I am afraid that in view of the many difficulties with which we have to contend that I must ask for an extension of the usual time limit for unloading.

'On several occasions much delay has been caused as our carts are prevented from crossing the line at the level crossing owing to the usual traffic and shunting operations. This, and our depleted staff, makes it impossible for us to unload trucks in the specified time.

'Before the Railway was extended we were at liberty to draw the wagons on to the level crossing and could unload them without any interruption or delay.'

This letter was now passed to the War Office who, having apparently completely ignored Crosse's remarks, proceeded further to demand that the demurrage charge be paid. However Crosse remained adamant in his refusal to settle.

'The Secretary
War Office Annexe
London S.W.1.
May 21st 1918
'In reply to your letter S.R.4. Accounts 118-307 of 15th inst. enclosing an account in respect of Siding Rent and carriage of goods on the Bisley-Deepcut Railway, I am afraid I must decline to pay this siding rent, as I maintain that owing to the lack of proper accommodation for unloading trucks at the Camp Station it is impossible for us with our depleted staff to clear the goods in the time allowed.

'This view is shared by the Officer i/c of the Railway who suggested that a siding giving proper facilities for goods etc. to be unloaded without delay being occasioned by the traffic and shunting and I understood that the Railway Authorities were prepared to make such a siding.'

The reply to this letter from the War Office suggested a breath-taking lack of understanding and general refusal to compromise in any respect.

'War Office
25th May 1918
'I am directed to acknowledge receipt of your letter of the 25th. instant in which you state that you decline to pay the Military Camp Railway charges for siding rent incurred by your Association as per the accounts rendered to you by the Officer i/c Bisley – Deepcut Military Railway, owing to the alleged lack of proper accommodation for unloading trucks at the Camp Station, and of staff at your disposal to clear

the wagons in the time allowed, and to state that the reasons advanced for non-payment are not considered adequate to warrant the withdrawal of accounts referred to. Twenty four hours is thought to be ample time for unloading purposes, and the fact that your Association have insufficient staff to deal with wagons which they had arranged to be consigned to them, is purely a matter for them to deal with, and not a reason why the War Department's charges should be waived.

'In these circumstances I am directed to again request that a remittance for £1: 8s: 10d., be made to the Command Paymaster, Aldershot Command, without delay.

'Signed W. Clow
Lieut-Colonel
For Director of Movements'

Crosse now hit back with an uncompromising letter of his own but included an olive branch by again suggesting that an authorised officer be sent to see the situation on the ground. After further skirmishes the latter solution was eventually agreed.

'May 27th 1918

'I am in receipt of your letter of the 25th inst. S.R.4/Accounts/118 and am not prepared to pay the demurrage in question.

'I do not appreciate your remarks as to my not supplying sufficient staff and should be glad to know on what authority this statement is made.

'For various reasons totally outside our control principally the alteration of the place for unloading we require 1/3 (one third) more time.

'Might I again suggest that an authorised Officer be detailed to see me and inspect the arrangements. I am quite sure he will see the disabilities under which we are suffering and the reasonableness of my request.'

The uncompromising and bureaucratic reply from the War Office seem to have totally ignored the underlying problems being experienced and in true military fashion demanded that the account be settled forthwith. Crosse, of course, was adept at this type of trench warfare and was quite prepared to fight his corner against this insurgent attack on 'his' Camp and finances.

In late May, the War Office again requested the return of the Form of Indemnity, however things had moved on and Crosse was now in a position to state that the matter was now entirely in the hands of the Association's and the Railway Company's Solicitors. He also, as usual, made sure that the Officer i/c Military Camp Railway was kept in the picture.

'June 3rd 1918

'The Officer i/c Military Camp Railway
Deepcut
'In reply to your letter D.C. 284 of 30th ult: requesting me to return the Form of Indemnity, I beg to inform you that all matters as to terms connected with the working of the Railway are now being dealt with by our Solicitors and the Solicitors of the L.&S.W.Rly: Company who are acting on behalf of the War Department, and to whom I would refer you.'

In early June Crosse had received more letters from the War Office that included re-defining 'demurrage' as 'siding rental' and also proceeded to remind the Association, for the purposes of the Form of Indemnity, that they were classified as a 'Private Trader' as opposed to 'Government Traffic' being the only two designations permissible. In the circumstances he sent back two very restrained letters the first of which took the War Office to task for their unfortunate remarks on the demurrage issue regarding the supply of staff!

'June 7th 1918

'The Director of Movements
War Office Annexe
London S.W.1
'In reply to your letter of S.R.4/Accounts/118-307 of 4th inst. I cannot see that the question as to whether the charge is for 'siding rent' or 'demurrage' has any particular bearing on the matter but I should like to point out that in a letter from the Chief Engineer, Aldershot, and in a requisition from the Paymaster, Aldershot the term 'Demurrage' is used.

'With regard to the second paragraph of your letter I requested in my letter of 27th ult: to be informed on what authority the statement was made as to our not supplying sufficient staff to deal with the wagons.

'I think I made it quite clear in my letter of 21st ult: that owing to the lack of facilities for unloading trucks it was impossible with our depleted staff to clear the goods in the time allowed.

'I note that you will arrange for an Officer to see me with reference to the arrangements. Might I request that a few days notice may be given as to the day on which he is coming in order to ensure my being here.'

The second letter made the points, yet again, that the NRA was not a 'Private Trader' and that now all the issues were now being dealt with by the Solicitors of both the NRA and the L&SWR.

'June 11th 1918

'With reference to the second paragraph of your letter, we do not consider ourselves "Private Traders". As I pointed out in my letter to the Officer i/c Military Railways, Deepcut, all the matters as to the terms connected with the working of the Railway are now being dealt with by our Solicitors, to whom I have sent a copy of your letter, and the Solicitors of the London and South Western Railway who are acting on behalf of the War Office.'

However, by this time everything had been thrown into the melting pot when the War Office agreed that the L&SWR should take over the running of the military railway. Crosse now took the opportunity to write to the Association's Solicitors for the purpose of ensuring that any such agreement with the L&SWR included relevant clauses to prevent the 'demurrage' problems arising again. This however brought a response from Bishop, stating that as no such problem had previously arisen between them (ignoring the isolated incident in 1911) there was no necessity to include it. Crosse did not press the issue.

Shortly thereafter a welcome respite appeared when the War Office decided to cancel the 'demurrage' demand. But even then, there remained some small disagreement about the accounts. Crosse was now able to reply including a reference to the fact that an agreement between the Association and the L&SWR, acting on behalf of the War Office, was being drawn up.

'July 2nd 1918

I am in receipt of your letter S.R.Accounts of 27th ult: and note that arrangements have been made for the outstanding accounts referred to the National Rifle Association for siding rental have been cancelled. I would point out in your letters of 13th and 25th May that the amount is stated to be £1.8.10. not 9/- as mentioned in your letter under reply.

'With regard to the Form of Indemnity I will, if you wish me to do so, communicate with our Solicitors in the matter, but in view of the fact that they are engaged with the Solicitors of the London and South Western Railway Coy: acting on behalf of the War Office in drawing up an Agreement with the Association for the working of the Railway, part of which is our property. I do not wish to press them unnecessarily in the matter especially as the Form of Indemnity has already been submitted to them and their reply was to the effect that they would not advise us to sign the document.

'I pointed out to you in my letter of 11th June that the National Rifle Association are not 'Private Traders' and as owners of a section of the line now worked by the Military Authorities and under a special agreement which is now being drawn up, I agree with our Solicitors that we should not sign the Form of Indemnity.'

Meanwhile the 'Form of Indemnity' issue rumbled on and, in spite of Crosse's remarks the War Office still attempted to re-affirm that the NRA was a 'Private Trader' in their eyes. Their reply amply demonstrated that the military authorities seemed resolute in their determination that their classification of the Association must fall within their own limited definition to the very end!

'War Office Annexe
London SW1
5th. July 1918

'With reference to your letter of 2nd instant. It should be pointed out that the sum of £1:8:10d., include £1:2:10d., for freight charges which amount has already been paid by your Association, leaving a balance of 6/- plus 3/- on another account.

'With regard to the form of Indemnity, we are agreeable to this matter remaining over for the present but your attention is drawn to the contents of this Office letter under above reference dated 7th. ultimo with the explanation that traffic handled over the Military Camp Railways is covered under two heads viz. Government Traffic and Private Trader's Traffic and as the merchandise carried for your Association does not come under the former head, the term 'Private Trader's Traffic' applies for the purposes of the Form of Identity.'

Shortly after this exchange Crosse received a letter from Bishop confirming the latter's view that the paragraph in the agreement referring to 'demurrage' was unnecessary and he had therefore deleted it.

> 'Solicitors Office
> Waterloo Station
> 24th July 1918
> 'Bisley Railway and Extension to Blackdown
> L&SW Rly and National Rifle Association
> 'With reference to your letter of the 15th ult: enclosing draft of the proposed terms in connection with the working of this Railway and the extension by the Company on behalf of the War Department with your amendments on behalf of the National Rifle Association shown in red ink. With regard to your suggested Clause 3, I am instructed that when the line terminated at Bisley Camp Station, the National Association staff were accustomed to unload wagons at the road level crossing at the farther end of the Camp Station but in view of the extension of the Line this cannot now be done and the traffic has to be dealt with in one of the sidings immediately adjacent.
>
> 'The road access to the sidings is not quite so convenient from the point of view of the National Rifle Association but this cannot be obviated.
>
> 'Further, I am informed that the Company are unable to discover that any demurrage charges have been made against the National Rifle Association or that any wagons have been detained by them beyond the free period allowed since the Bisley Railway was taken over by the Government.
>
> 'In these circumstances the proposed new Clause would appear to be unnecessary and I have therefore deleted it.
>
> 'With regard to your amendments to Clause 11 I can accept these as further amended in green ink.
>
> 'As I understand the arrangements with the War Office, it is proposed that this Memorandum of terms shall be signed by someone on behalf of that department and by someone on behalf of the Railway Company merely as a record of the terms accepted and agreed to by both sides.'

In any case time was running out and, with the takeover of the line by the L&SWR on 8 August, the Demurrage claims and the Form of Indemnity just faded away.

The L&SWR takes over the Line

In the spring of 1918 the War Office decided to place the working of the line in the L&SWR's hands and the conditions for this were included in a draft agreement. drawn up by Bishop. It was entitled 'Bisley Railway and Extension to Blackdown – Proposed Terms of Working by the London and South Western Railway Company on behalf of the War Department.' The draft of this was discussed at a meeting, attended by all three of the interested parties at the War Office on 9 May.

The draft agreement was discussed at the Executive & Finance Committee Meeting of 24 May.

> 'Minute 5 - The Chairman informed the Committee that, accompanied by General Sir Henry Mackinnon, Mr. Coulson (our Solicitor) and the Secretary, he had interviewed Major Micklem (as representing the Director of Movements) and a representative from the London & South Western Railway Company, at the War Office, on the subject of an agreement for the use of the Bisley Camp Railway, and then read to the meeting the draft of the new agreement which briefly was as follows :-
>
> 'Proposed terms of working the Bisley Camp Railway and extension to Blackdown by the L. & S.W.Rly. on behalf of the War Department.
>
> --------------------------
>
> 'The Company to work the railway and provide all necessary rolling stock and to maintain the railway between Brookwood Station and Bisley Station and pay all expenses incurred in working. Expenses incurred in maintaining Bisley Camp Station and the bridges to be charged to the Company's working expenses in account with the Government.
>
> 'The Company to provide such a service of trains as may be required, the scale of charges between Brookwood and Bisley Camp as arranged with the National Rifle Association and in operation at the outbreak of the War is to continue in force.

'The Company to pay to the National Rifle Association the sum of £100 per annum in respect of receipts from traffic as from 1st January, 1917.'

The L&SWR finally took over operational responsibility for the whole line as the War Office's Agent in August 1918. However, although the Agreement secured the Association's annual moiety, it was still felt that they needed to try to restore the direct pre-war arrangements with the L&SWR, rather than through some sort of tripartite operating committee in which they were, very obviously the junior partner! An extract of a letter from the NRA Secretary to their solicitors, Messrs Johnson Raymond Barker and Co laid out these views.

'August 17th 1918
'I enclose a letter from the Director of Railway Transport Aldershot Command stating that the Railway has now been taken over by the London & South Western Railway Coy. Under these circumstances would it not be as well for the Association, instead of being one of the parties included in connection with the working of the Railway, at present under consideration, to have an agreement direct with the London & South Western Railway Coy. If you think this would place the Association in a better position and the proposal is entertained, I presume we should look to the War Office for the annual payment of £100 for the period the Railway was worked by the Military Authorities.'

Further communications followed, culminating in a letter to their solicitors which made the NRA's position very clear.

'With reference to our conversation yesterday on the subject of the proposed agreement in connection with the working of the Bisley Camp Railway, the matter was considered by my Committee at their meeting on Friday last and, as I explained to you, there was a very strong opinion that as the Railway has been taken over by the London & South Western Railway Company, the circumstances had so completely changed that any agreement which the Association should be party to should be one with the L&SWR and not a third party agreement as is present suggested.
'As long as the Railway was run by the Military Authorities we were quite prepared to meet the War

Office in every way possible and to accept the proposed nominal annual rent of £100 in satisfaction of all claims, but as the Railway Company is now working the line, and it is presumed that we shall have to look to them and not the War Office for all payments, it seems only reasonable that any agreement entered into by the Association should be direct with the Company.
'Such an agreement should clearly define the position of the Association not only as owners of part of the Railway, but owners of the land over which a considerable part portion of the line runs and their right to receive dues as heretofore.
'The agreement should provide for the payment to the Association of the usual portion of the receipts from traffic, the Company undertaking to maintain the line, provide all necessary rolling stock, and also make provision for an efficient service of trains both for passengers and goods.'

With the approach of winter in 1918 and the line still in the hands of the War Office, although being worked by the L&SWR, Crosse tried once again to get a shelter built at the Camp Station in place of the existing shelter which was still used as a parcels office. This time, however, with the operation of the line back in the hands of the railway company, he wrote to the L&SWR's Superintendent of the Line, George West.

'October 10th 1918
'Bisley Camp Station
'When permission was given to the Military Camp Railway Authorities to convert the covered-in shelter used as a waiting room into a parcels office, it was on the understanding that a suitable shelter for the convenience of passengers should be erected, but this has not been done.
'Such a shelter has become a necessity and I shall be glad if steps could be taken either to have a shelter erected or to restore the building previously used for this purpose and provide another building for use as a parcels office.
'In view of the approach of winter some action should be taken without delay.'

There is no indication of a reply; however to build such a shelter it must be assumed that the authority of the

War Department would have to be obtained in that the L&SWR were only responsible for operating the line on the former's behalf. In any case the war was rapidly reaching a conclusion and the Armistice of 11 November completely altered the situation. By December the necessity for it had all but evaporated as the railway company had effectively closed the line. The NRA wrote to their solicitors in March 1919 expressing their views.

'C.S. Raymond-Barker Esq:
9. New Square
London WC
'Dear Mr. Raymond-Barker,
'With reference to our conference yesterday on the subject of the proposed agreement with the Railway Company, as the position, since our previous correspondence with you, and our conference with Mr. Ashworth James, has undergone a great change, it might be well to re-consider our action.

'It appears that the L. & S.W. Railway so far as the Bisley Camp Railway with extension to Blackdown is concerned, are only Contractors on behalf of the War Office and that, towards the end of December last the working Staff transferred to them from the Military Authorities was demobilised and the Company being unable to staff the line closed it.

'It is likely to remain closed, as under the present conditions it would appear an un-remunerative undertaking which, I think, the Company would not be prepared to work on their own account.

'They might confine themselves to running a service between Brookwood and Bisley Camp Stations during the Annual Meeting in accordance with the obligations under former agreements.

'Under these altered conditions it might perhaps be as well for us, if we can do so without prejudice to cash the two cheques for £100 each, and await developments.'

The Military Railway, having ceased regular operations in December 1918, now seems to have entered a phase in which trains operated on an irregular basis but no details have been discovered. The Brookwood-Bisley section, however, although it remained under War Office control until 1921, reverted to the normal pre-war pattern starting with the 1919 Meeting, the first to be held after the War. It is not clear at this time whether the Longmoor locomotive *Sir John French* was still on the line (under the terms of the agreement the L&SWR had a right to use it if they desired) but with the demobilisation of the military staff it is likely that the engine shed would have been closed with the L&SWR providing

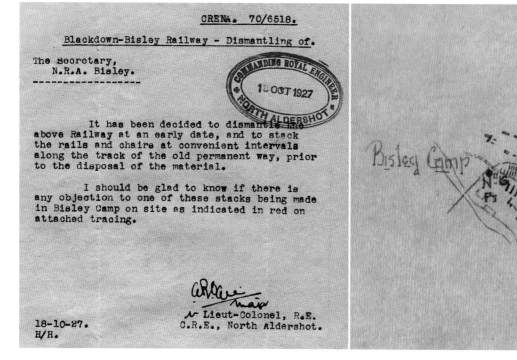

The decision to dismantle the Military Extension.

their own locomotive as and when required under the one-engine-in-steam order.

The line beyond the Camp Station therefore seems to have become all but abandoned by 1921 when the War Office finally relinquished control of the Bisley-Brookwood section. However, in 1924, with the Southern Railway now operating the Camp Tramway, there was a brief revival with the requirement to construct new barracks at Blackdown when the War Office approached the NRA and Railway Company for permission to run goods trains through the Camp to the site in case the contractors should require them.

In June 1926 a Military Train staff ticket was issued for a driver to proceed to Pirbright from Bisley when he had seen the train staff. This ticket had the words 'Bisley-Deepcut MCR' and 'Bisley to Pirbright' printed, rather than stamped, indicating continued occasional use of the line, but to Pirbright only. In 1927, however, the War Office decided that the line should be closed and dismantled and the NRA's permission was sought to store material within Bisley Camp in anticipation of final removal. This was readily granted by the Association who, no doubt, were glad to see this obstructive relic of the Great War disappear from the heart of the Camp. The extension was removed in early 1928 but within twelve years, of course, it would return with the advent of the next world crisis!

'19th October 1927

'The C.R.E.
North Aldershot,
H.Q. Aldershot,
Hants
'In reply to your letter 70/6518 of 18th October, there will be no objection to one of the stacks of old railway material being made in Bisley Camp on the site marked in your tracing.

'I presume the material will be disposed of and removed before our Meeting in 1928, for which preparations commence about the beginning of June.'

THE MILITARY EXTENSION IN THE SECOND WORLD WAR

Although the Military Extension of 1917 had been completely dismantled in 1928 the military camps at Pirbright, Deepcut and Blackdown still remained in use so it was not surprising that, with the national emergency and outbreak of a new war in 1939, consideration was given to relaying all or part of the track through these Camps. By 1940 a decision to extend the line to Pirbright Camp only had been reached. This ended just short of the original Pirbright Camp Station in the form of a new island platform, avoiding a level crossing.

The type of track used was military pattern flat-bottom as used at Longmoor Camp. The head shunt of the goods sidings was re-laid on the stub end of the old run round loop at Bisley Camp Station, which had been taken out of service in 1939, and this used the same type of spiked track in place of the former chaired track using bull-head rail.

Although, on paper at least, such things such as requisition orders and the resultant compensation entitlements were supposedly better organised than in the Great War, it did not quite turn out this way for the unfortunate NRA At the end of June 1940 the Acting Secretary of the Association observed that certain work had already commenced at Bisley Camp Station and wrote a letter to the Military C.R.E. Aldershot as no official notification for such activity had been received.

'1 July 1940
'The C.R.E. Aldershot Command
Headquarters
Aldershot
Hampshire
'Dear Sir
'I understand that the Bisley Camp Railway line is about to be extended and that certain work in connection with same has already been commenced in Bisley Camp.

'I shall be glad to receive, for the information of my Committee, an official confirmation of this in view of the fact that the land in question is private property.'
19400701 Railway Box File Extension of Railway

The dispatch of a further letter on 15 July finally elicited a reply from the Land Agent's Office of the Aldershot Command and, belatedly, this was followed by the official notification dated 22 August which included a plan.

A form of apology, however, was eventually received from the Office of the Chief Engineer, Aldershot Command dated 16 August. Just before this was received, however, the NRA also had cause to complain about the state of the level crossings in Bisley Camp.

'29th July 1940

'The C.R.E.

Headquarters

Aldershot Command

'With reference to the recent extension of the Bisley Camp Railway, I am instructed by my Committee to draw your attention to the unsatisfactory state of the level crossings in Bisley Camp consequent on the laying of the line, and to request that they be restored to the same good condition as they were prior to July 1st.

'The present state of the crossings is such as to be dangerous to motor cars and their passengers.

'I am also to ask that notice boards – "Beware of Trains" – be erected at the level crossings.'

19400729 DB4 State of Level Crossing

In mid-June representatives of the Association had visited Aldershot Command to lay out their case for claims on the use of the land under the terms of the notification of the requisition issued in 1940. The reply from the Lands Branch suggested that the claims issue could be dealt with at the end of the emergency although they had already stated that the Association's claims were 'excessive'. A copy of the relevant Acts was included with the letter.

Captain J.H. Whiteing, the Camp Quartermaster representing the NRA, compiled a short report on the new railway, which was intended to clarify how it had affected Bisley Camp itself. The main points of this were incorporated into a longer report from the NRA's solicitor, dated 28 September, which covered the subject in greater detail and concluded with comments on how much compensation should be claimed by the NRA from the War Department for the use of the Tramway.

'Bisley Camp Railway

Extension by War Department

'About the end of June the C.R.E. Aldershot Command commenced work on the railway, putting in a shunting siding with cross-over by the Camp Station. The track of the siding crossed the main Camp roadway at the station level crossing, and this was for a time left in an unsatisfactory state. A railway track was laid from near the station on the line of the former Bisley, Deepcut and Blackdown Railway, leaving the NRA land at a point S.W. of the Inns of Court Compound. The Report made by the Association's Camp Quartermaster, Captain Whiteing, on the 21st ultimo, shows that the excavations made were surface only and unlikely to cause subsidence to any N.R.A buildings. The Military, however, removed thirty-four young trees of about 20 years' growth, including six oaks. The line was taken across the lower Camp road without gates or other protection.

'It was not until 22nd August that formal notice was given to the Association by the Quartering Officer, Blackdown and Deepcut area. The notice states that in pursuance of Regulation 50 of the Defence Regulations 1939 "it is necessary to do the specified work below on the land occupied by you at Bisley Camp" and "It is proposed to begin the work specified on July 1st 1940".

'The Association were content with the proposal to settle the claims at the end of the emergency and it was not until 1944 that the question was re-opened. In May 1944 an enquiry was received by the NRA Secretary from the Lands Branch which re-kindled the subject. However it was decided that the matter could be left over until the War Department surrendered the emergency occupations at Bisley and this was reflected back to the Lands Branch.

'The details of Works are described as:

"Excavations, levelling, Track-laying in connection with extension of railway".

'The right of the Association to Compensation on account of the doing of the work is regulated by Section 3 of the Compensation (Defence) Act 1939. Compensation is payable only if the annual value of the land is diminished by reason of the doing of the work and it is to be 'a sum calculated by reference to the diminution of the annual value of the land ascribable to the doing of the work'. This compensation ceases if possession of the land is taken on behalf of the Crown. There is eventually a right to further Compensation if the land is not restored to its original condition.

'It is difficult to assess the diminution of annual value of Bisley Camp ascribable to the doing of the work described above, but I suggest a claim of One hundred pounds per annum and that Claim Forms be completed and lodged in accordance with the draft enclosed.'

It was not until May 1944 that the Acting Secretary of the NRA wrote again concerning the extension to the Bisley Camp Railway. He had received a letter from the Lands Branch at Aldershot with a query which he now referred to the Solicitors to the NRA.

'19th May 1944
'Bisley Camp Railway – Extension of.

'In June 1941 my Committee considered a letter from the Aldershot Area Land Agent suggesting that this case was one which called for settlement under Section 3 (4) of the Compensation (Defence) Act 1939, at the termination of the emergency, rather than have diminution of rental value under Section 3 (2), and it was decided that Mr. Milne should negotiate with the Aldershot Area Land Agent and might, if necessary, agree to a settlement under Section 3 (4) of the Compensation (Defence) Act, 1939. Could you please inform me whether Mr. Milne was able to make a settlement in this case and if so the terms of same.'

It would appear that he received a positive reply from the solicitors and that it had been agreed that the compensation issue would be left until the end of the Emergency. He passed this on to the Land Branch and received their agreement.

Construction and Operations

In August 1940, questions had been asked in the House of Lords regarding the transport of Territorials to and from Bisley Camp for shooting practice as there were now large and increasing numbers of them who required it. It was requested that the railway company should be asked to make trains available as and when required, however at this time the Tramway section was in the progress of being taken over by the army and it seems most likely that the military authorities would have organised troop trains over the branch for the duration.

An official requisition notice had been belatedly issued to the NRA by the War Office stamped 'Headquarters Blackdown and Deepcut', dated 28 August. This included a handwritten list of 'Details of Work' which included 'Excavations, levelling, Track laying in connection with extension of railway' with a start date of 1 July.

Records of day to day operation over the military extension have not been located but some invaluable observations were made by the late D.L. Bradley towards the end of 1941 when he was on a course at Pirbright Camp. He noted the following.

'W.D. Military Camp extension line October – December 1941
'0-6-2T Hawthorne Leslie No 3088 *Sir John French* built 1914 Longmoor Military Railway No 203. The livery was dull khaki.

The forlorn remains of Pirbright Station in 1964; the terminus of the Second World War extension from Bisley. (*Peter Harding collection*)

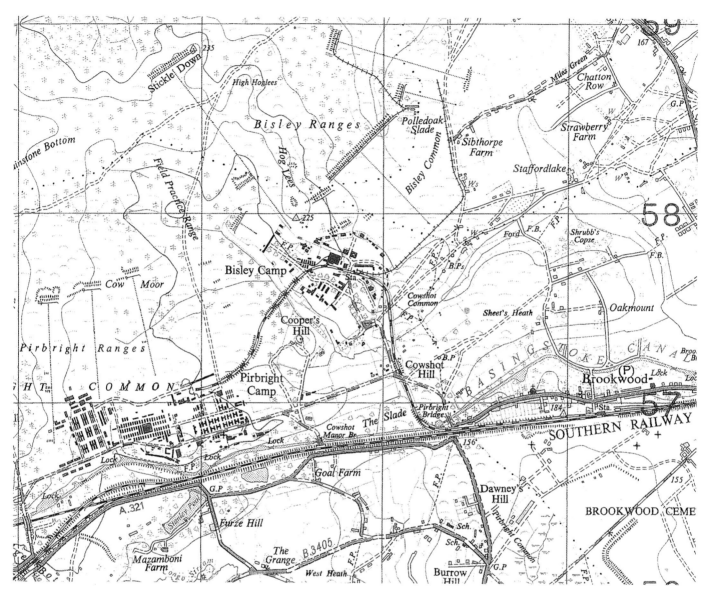

The large scale OS map issued in 1949, which included parts of earlier maps, showing the WW2 Military Railway extension to Pirbright which followed the identical route of the WW1 military railway. It also shows the Butts Tramway at its fullest extent and the whole of the Range Tramway whose track had been at least partially removed in 1930. (*Ordance Survey*)

'0-4-0T Andrew Barclay No 2027 built 1937. The original livery was dark green with red lining and lettered *Royal Navy Whale Island No. 7*. This locomotive also supplied steam for the laundry and bath unit when available! Later the locomotive was re-painted a dull khaki/green colour but with the same lettering.'

Sir John French was the same locomotive that was used on the line during the First World War. After its sojourn during the earlier conflict it was given an overhaul on its return to Longmoor and further one at Eastleigh in 1936. After the Second World War it was sold for scrap.

At the end of the war the extension was abandoned and the crossing gates at Bisley Camp station were padlocked but the track remained in-situ until 1950 when final dismantling took place. An internal British Railways Southern Region memo stated, in a pencil note, that the War Department Extension west of Bisley Camp Station was completely removed in 1950 and the NRA Report for the year stated that 'the rails of the level crossing had been removed and the road made up.'

CHAPTER 10

THE BISLEY CAMP TRAMWAY FROM 1923

At midnight on the 31 December 1922 the L&SWR ended its illustrious existence as an independent company and became the South Western division of the newly formed Southern Railway. Fortunately for the NRA the new General Manager of the amalgamated railway company was their old friend Sir Herbert Walker, who was able to give them a welcome sense of continuity in very difficult times. However, certain things had changed and not for the better; although the Association was still able to negotiate fare reductions for the shooting fraternity arriving at Brookwood and Bisley by train. These were proportional to the inflationary pressures of the Great War which had long overtaken Scotter's 1/6d offer of 1889 covering Volunteers travelling from London. The number of competitors was down by two thirds compared with the pre-war figure, already severely stretching the Association's finances. In addition, motor vehicles, an increasingly competitive method of transport to the Camp, were beginning to make severe inroads into the Tramway revenue, to the extent that its operating costs could no longer be covered.

The Southern Railway produced accounts for the years 1923 and 1924. These showed expenditure in 1923 of £326 8d with receipts of £95 6s 5d and in 1924, expenditure of £386 1s 10d and receipts of £94 8s 11d. A very heavy and increasing loss.

In 1924, the Southern Railway, in its efforts to reduce costs, suggested to the NRA that the annual Tramway payment, maintained until the end of the L&SWR's existence, should be suspended for the next two years in the pious hope that things might have improved. Until then, of course, the Association's share of the Tramway revenue, which had already been reduced to £100 pa at the end of the War, formed an important consideration in the Association's income; but there was little choice now but to agree to this measure. The Association did not accept the proposal to hand over the lines in the Camp, no doubt viewing this as an infringement on their property rights – probably the problems with the military authorities in

the war still loomed large. The 'temporary' suspension of the half share of the revenues became permanent as the NRA never pressed for a resumption of revenue sharing. However, the Southern Railway did agree to pay £100 for each of the previous two years.

At this period the parcels and goods invoices from the railway company demonstrated a dramatic drop. This appears to have confirmed the huge impact that the general introduction of motor vehicles had had on this type of delivery. Before the war it was not unusual for the Association to receive two or more such invoices almost on a daily basis. This had reduced to one or two a month by 1925.

The Southern Railway Prizes

After the 1923 Annual Meeting the L&SWR Prize was withdrawn to be replaced, in 1924, by a Southern Railway Prize shot for under revised conditions. Early in 1925 Walker expressed a wish to present prizes to be competed for by employees of the Railway Company and, following this, Major Etches, who had already met the General Manager's Chief Clerk, W.G. Pape, was requested to call in at Waterloo at his convenience to see the latter in order to further discuss these proposals.

The Secretary met Pape at Waterloo on 30 March and as a result of this drew up a comprehensive explanatory letter regarding the inducements for the Railwaymen to take up full range shooting.

'March 31st 1925

'Reference our conversation yesterday re: inducements to Southern Railmen to take up full range shooting.

'I find you have two miniature clubs affiliated to us:-

No. 126. Southern Railway (Western Section). Surrey. Secretary - F.T. Gray, Goods Superintendent's Office, Waterloo. This club seems to have about 40 members.

No. 1305. (Brighton Section). London. Secretary - S.C. Edwards, Engineering A/c's Section, Waterloo. About 110 members.

'Full Range Shooting is of course more expensive than miniature: our object is to make it as cheap as possible.

'The first step therefore I would suggest (if members agree) is affiliation (full Range Clubs £1 per annum) to the NRA: this brings rifles, ammunition and range accommodation within economical reach.

'Excellent .303 rifles can be hired at £1 per year, ammunition @ £2.10.0. per 1,000, and targets and markers as required on three days notice (see enclosures).

'Your mentioned the possibility of making a range of your own: it is an expensive proposition in construction and upkeep and requires a great deal of ground: Bisley with all its amenities and atmosphere is in the centre of your sections, and always at your disposal.

'Special Prizes for S. Railmen at the Bisley meeting:

'As many of your employees are 'All Comers', (i.e. not Past or Present Members of H.M.Forces), I confirm the suggestion that you should form a small prize list in connection with the Stock Exchange Competition, viz:- open to S. Railway competitors only:-

1st Prize	...	N.R.A Life Membership
2nd	...	£4
3rd	...	£2
4 prizes of	...	£1

'The Stock Exchange (see enclosure) is a species of aggregate of the Graphic and Wimbledon Cup; 300, 500 and 600 yards. Competitors can enter either for the Stock Exchange prize list only (and yours) at 10s., 5s. or 3s., according to their class or qualification (see definitions), or for the class or classes above them,

or

'They can enter in addition for the Graphic and Wimbledon Cup or either, by class or classes, and so participate in further prize lists.

'It is a good sporting contest and occupies all Saturday 11th July, and the prizes are liberal, a 50 guinea cup, a £20 cup, 15 Graphic originals and £8-0-0.

'A class C man can enter for the lot for 8s 6d.

'Please let me know if there is any further information or help I can give you.

'Publicity could be given to your special prizes by handbills, my programme etc. is already published. I enclose copy.

'W.G. Pape, Esq.
General-Manager's Office,
Southern Railway,
Waterloo Station,
London S.E.1.'

Pape passed this to E.A. Richards, the Welfare Assistant, who then queried with Etches the fact that Life Membership offered to a prize-winner, to be given by Walker, appeared to be one of those to which the Southern Railway was already entitled by reason of its donations regarding the existing Southern Railway Prize. To this Etches agreed.

Richards now also wrote back to state that he had been able to secure the names of 20 good shots from the ranks of the Southern Railway but queried whether each required Associate Membership of the NRA in order to compete. Etches immediately clarified these points in his letter of the 20th – 'to get over this difficulty I am arranging to issue Associate Members' tickets at 1s. each to such Railway Competitors who are not members of the NRA provided their entries are made on the enclosed forms, which have been specially marked.'

The Report of 1926 carried the list of prize-winners for the Southern Railway prizes and mentioned that Walker had presented prizes to be shot for by employees of the Southern Railway and also that the Company had again extended the half fare facility for competitors.

The 1926 Visit of the Canadian Rifle Team

In the middle of June 1926, the Secretary wrote to the Indoor Commercial Manager of the Southern Railway seeking the same reduced fares for the visit of the Canadian Rifle Team as had been obtained in previous years. He also enquired whether any special boat train put on could be specially stopped at Brookwood for the convenience of the team. However, the circumstances were not propitious as the railway company was still recovering from the effects of the 1926 General Strike, which had been called on behalf of the coal miners, and could only offer certain limited services.

'15th June 1926

'F.H. Willis Esq.
Indoor Commercial Manager
Southern Railway

London Bridge Station
London S.E.1
'I am directed to request that the same concessions as in former years may be accorded to the members of the Canadian Team on their arrival in England by the issue on production of the enclosed vouchers, of return tickets at the single fare from Plymouth to Brookwood. The Commandant will, I am sure, greatly appreciate the concession to the Team.

'They will arrive at Plymouth by the SS *Alaunia* on Sunday, June 20th, and hope to reach Brookwood in the evening.

'If you are running a special Boat Train for the convenience of passengers by the 'Alaunia' would it be possible, should the Commandant wish for it, to stop at Brookwood in order to expedite their journey as far as possible. They would be glad, I am sure, if any such special arrangements could be made for them.

'As the time is short would you be so kind as to let me have a reply by a return of post or by telephone (13 Brookwood).

The office of the Indoor Commercial Manager of the Southern Railway, F.W. Willis, located at London Bridge Station, replied on 18 June with details of the service to be offered.

The railway company was unable to offer a saloon or a convenient direct train between Plymouth and Brookwood and confirmed that the best service which could be provided in the circumstances was one that took slightly less than nine hours for the journey involving two changes and a long wait at Exeter! Such a journey, under normal circumstances would not have exceeded three and a half hours.

'I am in receipt of your letter of the 17th instant, and provided the party reaches Plymouth Friary in time for the 10.55 a.m. the service will be as follows : -

Plymouth Friary	leave	10.55 a.m.
Exeter Queen Street	arrive	1.40 p.m.
'	leave	3.30 p.m.
Salisbury	arrive	6.57 p.m.
'	leave	7.15 p.m.
Brookwood	arrive	8.25p.m.

'17th June 1926
Dear Major Crowe
'This is to wish you and the members of the Team a most hearty welcome and to let you know that I have made arrangements with the Railway Company:-

1. For the issue of Return Tickets from Plymouth to Brookwood at the single fare on production of the enclosed vouchers.

and

2. If you find it possible to catch the 10.55 a.m. train from Plymouth on Sunday, the Southern Railway Company will stop the express train from Salisbury to Brookwood Station.

'I enclose a copy of the letter from the Railway Company.

'I hope you have had a pleasant voyage and that you and all the members of the Team are quite well.

'I sent the Import License for the rifles to Colonel Birdwhistle in April last. I presume you have it with you and that you will have no difficulty in passing through the Customs.'

At the same time Etches wrote to Cunard to ascertain the time of arrival of the ship bringing the team.

'Pressing
17th June 1926

'The Secretary
Cunard Steamship Company, Ltd.
51 Bishopsgate
London E.C.2.
'I shall be very much obliged if you would be so kind as to telephone to me – 13 Brookwood – before 11 a.m. to-morrow (Friday) the probable day and hour of the arrival of the SS *Alaunia* at Plymouth.

'The Canadian Rifle Team will arrive by this boat and I am anxious to get in touch with the Commandant as regards the railway arrangements and issue of reduced fare tickets.'

The Secretary also sent letters of thanks to the railway company for making arrangements for the team's arrival at Plymouth as well as allowing fare concessions and arranging to stop the Salisbury express at Brookwood.

Following the Meeting and in view of the travel problems directly arising from the Strike the Canadians

SOUTHERN RAILWAY

NATIONAL RIFLE ASSOCIATION MEETING at BISLEY (BROOKWOOD), JULY 2nd to 16th, 1927, inclusive.

TRAIN SERVICE

FROM

LONDON (Waterloo Station) and intermediate stations to BROOKWOOD.

On SATURDAY, 2nd to SATURDAY, 9th JULY, inclusive.

DOWN TRAINS (Weekdays only).

	a.m.	a.m.	a.m.	a.m.	a.m.	a.m.	a.m.	p.m. (E)	p.m. (S)	p.m.	p.m.	p.m.	p.m.	p.m.	p.m.	p.m.	p.m.
Waterloo ... dep.	6 30	6 55	8 37	9 10	10 10	10 43	11 24	1 0	1 42	2 03	3 53	4 44	4 20		5 C10	5 47	6 F20
Clapham Jct. ... ,,	6 23	6 53	8 23	8 43	10 3	10 43	11 23	12 23	12 43	2 23	2 23	3 43	...		4 23	5 23	
Wimbledon ... ,,	6 30	7 9	8 30	8 50	10 10	10 50	11 30	12 50	1 30	2 30	3 50		...		4 30	5 30	
Surbiton ... ,,	6 49	7 19	8 57	9 4	10 25	11 6	11 45	12 45	1 51	4 52	4 54	5	...		4 58	5 46	
Esher ... ,,	6 41	7 25	8 35	...	10 31	10 51	11 51	1 10	1 51	5 12	5 51		...		5 35	5 26	E 4
Walton ... ,,	6 48	7 33	8 42	...	10 38	10 58	11 58	12 58	1 17	1 58	2 58	4 16	...		5 10	5 59	E 11
Weybridge ... ,,	7 4	7 40	8 49	...	10 45	11 5	12 5	1 5	1 24	2 5	3	5 4	4 23	...	5 17	6 6	E 18
Woking ... ,,	7 22	7 57	9 10	10 0	11 6	11 32	12 26	1 39	1 39	2 35	3 39	4 34	4 52		5 45	6 22	E 58
Brookwood ... arr.	7 30	8 7	9 27	10 8	11 16	11 40	12 36	1 48	1 48	2 44	3 48	4 44	4 45	5 1	5 54	6 32	E 7
Brookwood ... dep.	7 40	8 25	9 34	10 20	11 28	12 0	12 40	1 55	1 55	2 50	4 5	4 49	5 16		6 10	6 46	7 12
Bisley Camp ... arr.	7 46	8 31	9 40	10 26	11 24	12 6	12 46	2 1	2 12	2 56	4 11	4 55	5 22		6 16	6 52	7 18

UP TRAINS (Weekdays only).

	a.m.	a.m.	a.m.	a.m.	a.m.	p.m.	p.m.	p.m.	p.m.	p.m.	p.m.	p.m.	p.m. (A)	p.m.	p.m.	p.m.
Bisley Camp ... dep.	7 55	8 40	9 50	10 35	11 40	12 15	12 56	2 10	3 10	4 20	5 0	5 30	6 29	6 29	6 58	7 26
Brookwood ... arr.	8 1	8 46	9 56	10 41	11 46	12 21	1 2	2 16	3 16	4 26	5 6	5 36	6 35		7 4	7 32
Brookwood ... dep.	8 6	8 50	10 15	11 20	11 54	12 31	1 11	2 17	3 19	4 39	5 12	5 40	6 50	6 36	7E33	7 39
Woking ... arr.	8 13	8 57	10 22	11 31	12 2	12 39	1 19	2 25	3 26	4 47	5 19	5 48	6 59	6 44	7E40	7 46
Weybridge ... ,,	8 30	9 29	11 13	12 12	...	1 9	2 15	3 12	3 40	5 12	5 38	6 13		7 7		8 6
Walton ... ,,	8 36	9 35	11 19	12 20	...	1 16	2 22	3 18	4 25	5 18	5 45	6 21		7 14		8 12
Esher ... ,,	8 50	9 42	11 26	12 27	...	1 24	2 30	3 25	4 32	5 25	6 29	6 29		7 21		8 19
Surbiton ... ,,	8 57	9 49	11 33	12 34	...	1 33	1 42	2 57	3 54	5 32	5 56	6 37		7 28		8 19
Wimbledon ... ,,	9 21	10 2	12 3	1 1	...		2 3	3 21	4 21	6 1	6 21	7 1		8 1		8 41
Clapham Jct. ... ,,	9 28	10 8	12 10	1 8	...		2 9	3 29	4 28	6 8	6 29	7 8		8 8		8 48
Waterloo ... ,,	9 7	9 35	11 4	11 D59	12 39	1 21	2 5	3 19	4 16	5 54	6 19	7 07	7 36	7 51		8 40

A—Thursday, 7th July only. B—Depart 1.4 p.m. on Saturdays. C—Depart 5.0 p.m. on Saturdays.
D—Arrive 12.9 p.m. on Saturdays. E—Not Saturdays. F—Depart 6.8 p.m. on Saturdays. S—Saturdays only.

Passengers change at Brookwood by all trains in each direction.
Passengers from and to intermediate stations between Waterloo and Woking are requested to ascertain at what points it will be necessary to change carriages.

✴ Waterlow & Sons Limited, London, Dunstable & Watford.

FOR PARTICULARS OF TRAIN SERVICE FROM JULY 11th TO JULY 16th, SEE OTHER SIDE.

The Southern Railway Timetable for the first half of the 1927 Meeting.

Class O2 No 232 at Bisley Camp Station on the 16th July 1927 waiting to propel the 6.24pm train back to Brookwood. Hidden behind the trees lay the engine shed for the Range Tramway which still housed the Merryweather tram engine "Wharncliffe" and its two cars. They were last used in 1914. (*H.C. Casserley – collection R.M. Casserley*)

decided to radically alter their return arrangements. This required them to return their railway tickets to Etches so that they could be altered Etches immediately forwarded this request to the Brookwood Stationmaster.

'Very Urgent (by hand)

17th July 1926

'The Stationmaster
Brookwood
'I enclose a letter from the Adjutant, Canadian Rifle Team with reference to the availability of the return portion of the tickets issued to them from Plymouth to Brookwood they request that same may be made available to Liverpool, some to Southampton, and others to the Surrey Docks.

'I shall be very much obliged if you could get into communication with Head Office as soon as possible and let me have a reply by Monday morning as many members of the team will be leaving Bisley on that day.'

However, the weekend got in the way and the Stationmaster at Brookwood, being unable to get in contact with his head office at Waterloo Station, put forward suggestions as to how the situation could be handled on an individual basis.

'July 18th 1926
'Canadian Rifle Team
'I am in receipt of your letter of the 17th inst. enclosing twenty return halves 1st class Brookwood to Plymouth with the request that they may be made available to other destinations.

'I regret that due to Sunday intervening I cannot get in touch with our Head Office, and the only alternative is for the Members of the Team to take fresh tickets to their respective destinations and apply for refund for any difference in fare.

'I might mention that passengers for Southampton could use their tickets as far as Basingstoke & pay the excess fares at Southampton if desired.

'Further, as the original tickets were issued as Single fare for the return journey, I do not think that any allowance would be made on the unused portion to passengers travelling to Surrey Docks and Liverpool.

'I return herewith the 20 tickets together with the Canadian Adjutant's letter.'

In 1928, with the railway network long since restored to normal, the Secretary was requested to arrange a special saloon to carry the Australian Rifle Team from Southampton to Brookwood. Arrangements were immediately put in hand with the Southern Railway. The Indoor Commercial Manager's Department replied agreeing to reduced rate tickets for the members of the team and the Brookwood Station Master wrote to confirm the arrangements made including the provision of a 24-seat saloon carriage with the luggage following in a later train.

Suggestions to improve the Layout at Brookwood Station

In 1927 a Southern Railway driver, familiar with the crossovers at Brookwood that had been put in to enable easy access to the Bisley Camp Tramway for through trains in the early 1900s, drafted a staff suggestion aimed at simplifying the arrangements.

'There is a slip road at Brookwood No 9 which was put in to deal with the Volunteer trains on Saturdays from Waterloo to make one shunt from Down Local or Down Through to the Bisley Camp Platform.

As I have backed these trains into same you had to be careful as you were backing same into a dead end and

would not take much longer to back them to the up Local Line and pull in on the Bisley Camp Line through No 14 with safety.

Since then the Volunteer trains have ceased and the Territorials never come to Brookwood so much as in the old Volunteer days.

The slip line is still there and is never used and will never be required again and can be done away with at once to save expense as it will have to be renewed in time if left there and useless.'

'29/7/29 Discussed with OM and agreed that long crossover stand over until time arrives for its renewal when it can be dealt with.'

However it was not until 27 November 1930 that the connection was abolished.

Miscellaneous Items

By 1932 several motor accidents had occurred close to the narrow Cowshot Bridge which was situated at the junction of the roads to Bisley and Pirbright Camps from Brookwood. This bridge, which was owned by the Association, had been erected at the behest of the Board of Trade in 1890 for the opening of the Bisley Tramway as they had refused to countenance the provision of a level crossing at this point. The Secretary wrote to the Guildford Rural District Council seeking permission to erect road signs marked 'Slow – Road Narrows' as advised by the AA. He also had to secure permission from the War Department for an additional sign to be erected on their land. All these signs had to be erected at the Association's expense!

In June that year and shortly before the annual Meeting the War Office unilaterally issued an edict that

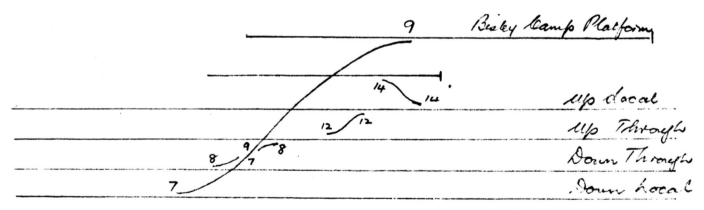

The sketch of the existing Crossover at Brookwood with a Driver's suggestion that it had now become redundant. (*Dennis Cullum – Peter Harding Collection*)

Southern Railway Travel Voucher. The transport of large numbers of Service Personnel by rail from their bases to Bisley Camp for Range duties during the Annual Meeting were commonplace in the 1930s with the NRA paying the fare. This Voucher was issued on 5 July 1936 for 181 men of the RASC to travel from Bulford Camp Station, on Salisbury Plain, to Brookwood for these duties. Passenger Services over the Amesbury and Military Camp Light Railway, linking the South Western mainline to Bulford, were withdrawn in 1952 with the line closing in 1963.

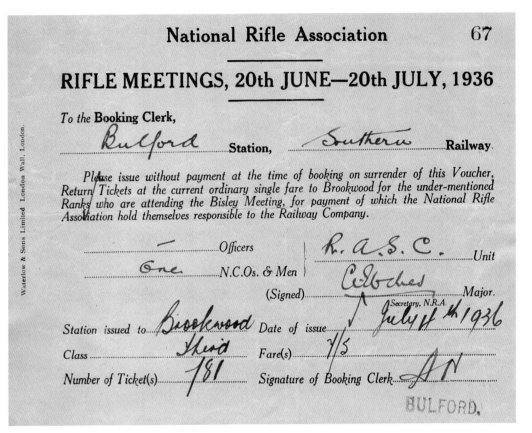

army railway warrants for military personnel detailed for duty during the Bisley Meeting were no longer to be issued. A very worried Etches was able to negotiate an alternate arrangement with the Southern Railway in which a special travel voucher would be issued instead. Fortunately, however, the War Office quickly rescinded this notice after Etches got in touch with them to express his concern.

'25th June 1932

'G. H. Wheeler Esq.,
Commercial Assistant,
Traffic Manager's Office – Southern Railway,
London Bridge Station
London, S.E.1

'With reference to my letter of 22nd June and your letter B/5 of same date. I have been in communication with the War Office as to the order issued by Aldershot Command intimating that Army Rail Warrants will not be issued for journeys by rail of Military Personnel proceeding to and from Bisley Camp, and I am pleased to inform you that the order which emanated from the War Office has been cancelled and that the same arrangements as in former years for the issue of travelling warrants will be in force for this year.

'I feel I owe you many thanks for the expeditious manner in which the matter was dealt with by your office in obtaining the approval of the special travel voucher it was proposed to issue, but which I am glad to say is not now necessary. I am afraid the matter caused you and your staff a great deal of trouble which I very much regret.'

During the same month Etches wrote to the Bill Department of the Railway Company forwarding 400 posters to advertise the special attractions that would be available at the annual Meeting that year.

In 1928 a load of coal from the Griff Colliery Company was delayed by a 'hot-box' in Woking Yard and, in 1936, a covered goods wagon, No. 276030 belonging to the LMS, sustained damage to its axle-box and axle guard tie rod in the Bisley Camp goods yard caused by a derailment. In this instance, the NRA received a claim from the Department of the Chief Mechanical Engineer of the Southern Railway, R.E.L. Maunsell, and, being the owners of the yard, agreed to pay for the damage.

COME TO BISLEY

SATURDAY, JULY 22nd, 1933

The 100 Best Shots in the Empire in

H. M.
THE KING'S PRIZE

Final Range (1000 yards) at 3.0 p.m.

Massed Bands of
4 Regiments

Presentation of Prizes by
THE VISCOUNT HAILSHAM
(SECRETARY OF STATE FOR WAR)
AT 5.15 P.M.

Teas and Refreshments at the N.R.A. Pavilion.

ADMISSION TO THE GROUND 1/3
(INCLUDING TAX)

THE SOUTHERN RAILWAY
WILL ISSUE
CHEAP TICKETS
BY ALL TRAINS

The Southern Railway Poster announcing the 1933 King's Prize Final.

Consideration of Closure and the Aldershot and District Traction Co

The end of the War had brought with it exceptional monetary inflation and the Bisley Tramway was not immune. The L&SWR had maintained the status quo as far as they could but the formation of the Southern Railway brought a different attitude. Despite significant fare increases, but below those otherwise pertaining, the Tramway was now losing money quite heavily and economies in running costs now had to be sought.

In 1932 the Southern Railway mooted a proposal to close the Tramway and substitute a bus service. The local bus company, the Aldershot and District Traction Company, agreed this in principal, however further consideration in respect of the freight service to the Camp and a direct intervention by Walker effectively ruled it out.

The Bus Company addressed their reply to the Railway Company's proposal on the 3rd March 1932.

'NRA Meeting at Bisley July 2nd – 16th, 1932
'With reference to your letter of 23rd ultimo, we have now had the opportunity of considering your suggestion, that we should this year operate a road service between Brookwood and Bisley Camp in place of your train service previously operated.

'We are pleased to inform you that we are agreeable in principle to operate this service, provided that it is dealt with under Clause 8 of the Working Agreement, and provided you are prepared to Guarantee us a revenue amounting to 1s 2d per mile on all mileage run in connection with the proposed service.

'We have examined your loading return for last year and we find that if we had operated the necessary mileage to carry the traffic the cost at the above rate would work out at £70-12s-5.

'If you decide to proceed with this suggestion, you will no doubt give us ample notice in order that we may make the necessary application for Road Service Licenses. There will also be certain matters to consider such as: -

1. Whether you intend to issue through tickets to all passengers, and whether passengers will be able to board our vehicles at Brookwood and pay their bus fare independently. If this latter is the case we should require to know from you what fares you desire us to charge.
2. Permission would have to be obtained from the Military Authorities to operate a service over the road between Brookwood and Bisley and suitable arrangements would have to be made for parking at Bisley.'

However an internal Southern Railway memo, while in favour of this proposal, pointed out that a freight service still had to be maintained and interestingly enough referred to a profit still being made!

'In the event of it being decided to ask the Aldershot Company to operate the road service in question we should of course still require to open the line for the morning freight service, as it is probably not an economical proposition to convey this traffic by road.

'In these circumstances it would not be possible to eliminate the whole of the costs shown in the enclosure and it would appear, seeing that we already make a profit, that prima facie there is no material financial benefit to be obtained by the proposal now under review. If, however, you consider the matter is one which warrants further investigation I will approach the Locomotive and Engineers Departments with a view to ascertain what will be the saving in expenditure if the passenger services which have hitherto been provided are eliminated.

'I think there is a very important point to bear in mind here, viz, that we do not take on additional staff to deal with this traffic, and further our wages expenses are not actually saved if we do not run this service.'

The line's immediate future, however, was secured when Walker made it clear that it should be maintained for the Annual Meeting. This was confirmed in an internal memo from the Traffic Manager to the Chief Engineer.

'Tfc Mgr to CE 3/10/34
'With reference to your letter of the 2nd inst. I shall be pleased to accompany you over this line on a date in the near future.

'In order that there may be no misunderstanding, however, I should like to say that the General Manager has expressed a very definite opinion that the Bisley Camp line shall be maintained for future meetings.

'It therefore becomes a question of what is the least expenditure it is necessary to incur in order to maintain it in a fit and useful condition.'

In this way, the tramway was permitted to survive right through to the end of the Southern regime at midnight on 31 December 1947 and, miraculously, lasted a further four and a half years under the Southern Region of the nationalised British Railways.

Topping and Tailing
Although the run-round loop at Bisley Camp Station had been made virtually redundant by the introduction of Pull-Push trains following the Great War, the continued

appearance of goods trains and the occasional through passenger train from the main line meant that it had had to be maintained to accommodate such services as regulations laid down that the locomotive must always be at the head of a conventional train where a 'one engine in steam' arrangement existed, such as on the Branch. Southern Railway officials had continued their search for cost reductions on such lines and in June 1933 they identified an ultimately far reaching solution.

An internal Southern Railway memo originating from the Traffic Manager's Department, dated 28 June 1933, seems to have acted as the catalyst for introducing the concept of 'topping and tailing.'

'Bisley Camp Line
So far as I am aware, the 'one engine in steam' arrangement, or 'two or more engines coupled together', referred to in the Ministry of Transport Requirement No. 3, shewn under the heading of 'Modes of Working Single Lines' of that Department's Requirements, has never covered the case of a passenger train with an engine coupled to it at each end, but it seems to me that the spirit of this requirement would be maintained by such an arrangement, if decided upon, and I may say that I have ascertained this morning from Colonel Trench, of the Ministry of Transport, that he is in agreement with this view.

'A revised instruction would, of course have to be issued to the staff that the rear engine must remain completely coupled (including brake) to the train from Brookwood to Bisley Camp and vice-versa.'

This was immediately followed on the 29 June by a memo from E.C. Cox to G Ellson confirming that he saw no difficulty if the loop at Bisley Camp were to be taken out of use during the forthcoming Meeting in July.

'Bisley Camp Line
'I duly received your letter of the 13th instant, and note that a considerable saving would accrue to your Department in repairs if the connection (the eastern end of the run-round loop) at Bisley Camp Station were put out of use during the forthcoming meeting of the National Rifle Association.

'There would be no difficulty, so far as this Department is concerned, in making the necessary working arrangements to comply with the 'one engine

S O U T H E R N   R A I L W A Y

LONDON (WEST) DIVISIONAL SUPERINTENDENT'S OFFICE,
WATERLOO STATION. S.E.1.

SPECIAL NOTICE NO.S.1391.L.W.D.   7TH JULY, 1933.

(1). WORKING OF EMPTY WAGONS.   All empties to Bolsover Colliery
(MID) MAY NOW BE SENT FORWARD.   (TF.8)
-----

(2). BISLEY CAMP LINE.   Passenger trains may work between Brookwood
and Bisley Camp with an engine at both front and rear. The rear engine
must be coupled to the train, and the continuous brake pipe must be
coupled up.
    The Driver & Fireman of the train engine are responsible for the
observance of signals and the working of the continuous brake; the
Driver of the engine at the rear must watch for and act upon signals
given by the Driver of the train engine, but the Driver of the engine
at the rear is not relieved from the due observance of all signals
affecting the working of the train, and in case of need he must apply
the continuous brake.
    The staff must be shewn to the Driver of the train engine and
handed to and carried by the Driver of the engine at the rear.
    The provisions of Rule 133 (c) must be observed.
    The rear engine must remain coupled (including brake) to the
train after its attachment at Brookwood until the return journey from
Bisley Camp to Brookwood has been completed.
    A goods train may, when necessary, be propelled from Brookwood
to Bisley Camp. The load of such train must not exceed 4 vehicles,
including the van, and the leading vehicle must be a brake van in which
the Guard must ride. It will be the duty of the Guard to keep in touch
with the Enginemen by means of hand signals during the time the train
is being propelled.   (R.51524B. A.69878)

Left: The Special Notice issued by the Southern Railway that appeared to have pioneered 'Topping and Tailing'.

Below: The Camp 'Tram' at Bisley Station during the Annual Meeting in the early 1930s. The locomotive is an ex- Ex London, Brighton & South Coast Railway Class D1 0-4-2 Tank Engine originally Numbered 260 and named *Lavington*. It was re-numbered by the Southern Railway as 2260. Note that the track on the right is part of the original run-round loop taken out of service in 1933. The stop block, represented by a sleeper placed across the track, can just be discerned at the head of the 1 in 60 incline in the distance. (*R. Mundy collection*)

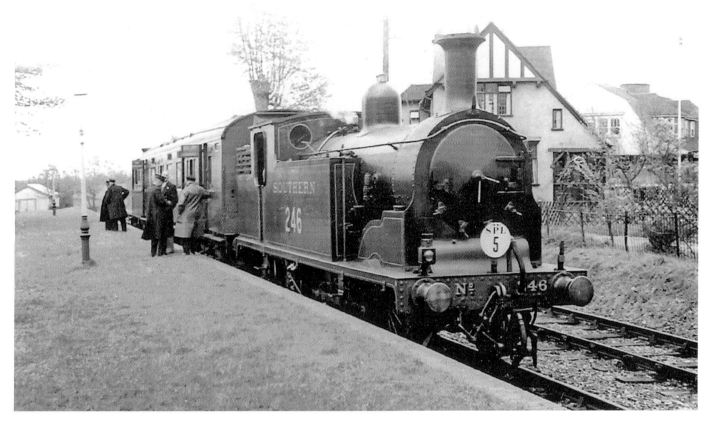

23 April 1939 – A Special Train 'topped and tailed' between Brookwood and Bisley Camp by Class M7 0-4-4 Tank Engines Nos 246 and 672 (at the far end). The occasion was a special 'footplate excursion' for visitors which included a footplate ride over the branch. At the same time a Lord Nelson Class 4-6-0 No 864 *Sir Martin Frobisher* was parked in the branch bay at Brookwood on general exhibition for the visitors.

in steam' arrangement, i.e. by providing an engine at each end of the through trains worked to and from Waterloo when working over the Camp line, and, from an informal conversation with Col. Trench of the Ministry of Transport, it is gathered that the Ministry would not take exception to such working provided the necessary safeguards were taken to see that the rear engine remained completely coupled to the train.

'I shall be glad if you will be good enough to let me know immediately whether you propose to put the connection in question out of use, in order that the necessary working arrangements may be completed, and if it is proposed subsequently to remove the connection you will, no doubt, furnish a financial statement prepared in the usual form; also let me know what immediate saving would be effected.

'May I take it, please, that the National Rifle Association are not affected in the matter?'

Immediate steps were now taken to achieve this by locking the point at the east end of the run-round loop and securing a stop block across the loop at the top of the incline into the station area. The remains of the now out-of-use loop opposite the station platform, after being left in-situ as a head shunt, were finally dismantled before the 1939 Meeting.

The Resumption of Services after the War
The outbreak of war in September 1939 had seen the NRA hand over the Camp, as in the First World War, for military use and the Tramway was taken over by the War Office in 1940 as in 1917 with the Camp becoming a major training facility for the new Home Guard movement. The end of the war in 1945 permitted the resumption of peacetime shooting and the Annual July Meeting was held for the first time since 1939, albeit on a very limited basis lasting one day only. However the 'Bisley

The *Bisley Bullet* (Southern Railway 'decorated' M7 Class locomotive No 128) at the Camp Station on 12 July 1947. The out-of-use head shunt of the Second World War with its characteristic flat bottom rail is on the left with the locked crossing gates in the background. (*Nash - Peter Harding collection*)

Bullet' service to the Camp did not re-appear until the following year, 1946.

'Railway Concessions

The Southern Railway Company resumed the running of the 'Bisley Special' between Brookwood and Bisley Camp during the Meeting and was a great help to many Competitors.

Despite several requests on our part the Railway Company has not found it possible to restore the special concessions of reduced fares for riflemen between London and Brookwood.'

Sir Herbert Walker died in 1949 and this was recognised in the Association's Report for that year. A highly supportive Life Member of the Association since 1912 when he was appointed General Manager of the L&SWR, he had retired as General Manager of the Southern Railway in 1937 where he had been instrumental in keeping the Camp Tramway open when it became threatened with closure in 1932.

The special fare concessions were not in fact renewed until 1949 with the line now under the control of British Railways since nationalisation on January 1st 1948.

The Cowshot Crossing Accident

A potentially serious accident on the Bisley Tramway occurred at the Cowshot Crossing on Friday 4 July 1947 when a van proceeding from the Brookwood direction was in collision with the 3.37pm push and pull train to Brookwood, which had just left Bisley Camp Station. Although the van was completely wrecked the occupants were lucky to escape with only minor injuries and shock. A full investigation was carried out by officials of the Southern Railway from which they were able to conclude that the cause of the accident was the van driver misunderstanding or neglecting to obey the flagman's signals.

LPS(¹⁄₁₀)

SOUTHERN RAILWAY.

Stock
(750 N)
10/45

RETURN OF ACCIDENT, under the Regulation of Railways Act, 1871, the Railway Employment (Prevention of Accidents) Act, 1900, Section 13 (2) and Board of Trade Order of 21st December, 1906.

Date and Time of Accident.	**Friday 4th July. 3.39pm.**
Place at which Accident occurred. Name of Crossing, and whether public or private road, or footpath.	**Cowshott Level Crossing situated at 0m. 75 ch. between Brookwood and Bisley Camp — Public Road.**

Nature and Cause of Accident, including particulars of damage to Trains or Works.

The 3.37pm Push and Pull train, engine leading, Bisley to Brookwood struck a motor van, Registration No. EPH.680 belonging to the Woking Gas Coy. proceeding from the direction of Brookwood towards Cowshott, completely wrecking it and carrying it a distance of 50 yards.
Two men were riding in the van, names and injuries as below, and they were dealt with at the Military First Aid Post and later taken home by ambulance.
A flagman was stationed at the Crossing at the time of the incident in connection with the National Rifle Association Meeting.
~~**Rough Sketch enclosed.**~~

A further report will be sent you in due course

Particulars of Persons killed or injured.	Name	**H.Grace (Driver)** **109 Boundary Rd.,Woking.**	**Mr. R. Baker,** **4, Grove Villas, Sandy Lane, Maybury, Woking.**	
	Nature of Injury	**Cuts on head and neck. and shock**	**Shock**	
	Whether person killed or injured was— Passenger, Servant of Company, Servant of Contractor, Trespasser, Other Person.	**Other Persons.**		
	Copy of Verdict at Coroner's Inquest, or Finding at Procurator Fiscal's or Sheriff's Inquiry, with rider or recommendation.	—		
Level-Crossing.	Whether gates and wickets provided. Whether gates close alternately across Railway and road. Whether gates are equipped with targets or discs and lamps.	**Gates and Wickets not provided.**		

The summary of the accident as entered on the official 'Return of Accident' form. (*Dennis Cullum - Peter Harding collection*)

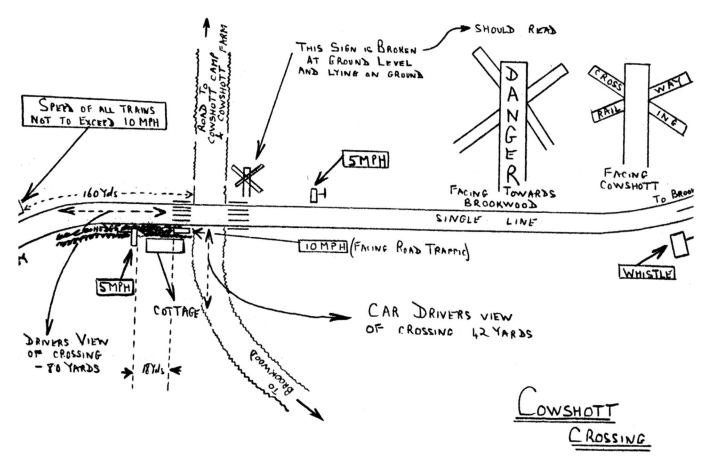

Below: The Plan of the Accident scene. (*Dennis Cullum - Peter Harding collection*)

Following an investigation by the Southern Railway authorities a comprehensive report complete with diagram was issued.

Repatriation of the Bodies of American Casualties of the Second World War

During the Second World War American Servicemen, who had died of wounds or for other reasons in mainland Britain, were buried in the War Cemetery at the Brookwood Necropolis. After the war, the American authorities proceeded to make arrangements for the repatriation of their bodies.

In early 1948, very shortly after the Southern Railway had become absorbed into the nationalised British Railways as its Southern Region, the authorities requested the use of the Bisley Camp line in order to load the coffins. A Southern Region internal memo requested that the number of vehicles authorised to be propelled along the line from Brookwood should be temporarily increased for the duration of the operation.

'28/2/48

'The American Authorities are exhuming the bodies of the American Servicemen buried at Brookwood Cemetery and have erected two platforms on the Bisley Camp Line for this purpose each capable of accommodating two vans and they will require two vans to be loaded at each platform at the same time, by two squads of men. This will operate in the near future and Mr. Scutt has asked me to get in touch with you and ask if you will consider revising the instruction in the Appendix, page 7, which says only 4 vehicles including a van may be propelled from Brookwood to Bisley Camp, to read 5 vehicles including a van for the period of this work.

'Told Mr. Julian to get more details, actual date and actual location of these platforms as it may only need issuing a special shunt movement instruction.'

Under the rules, established since the abolition of the run round loop at Bisley Camp Station, a goods train had to be propelled towards Bisley Camp with the engine at the rear. The reply clarified the situation and agreed the temporary arrangement.

'The site at which this platform has been constructed is just under a mile from Brookwood Station on the Bisley side of Cowshot Crossing. At the moment three wagons and brake van are being propelled as per Appendix instructions, the three wagons being loaded with empty coffins, but when the coffins are dispatched at a later date they will be worked away in ambulance vans.

'A man is posted at Cowshot Crossing during the movement for protection of the crossing.

'Mr. Piper seen by Mr. Bennett and agreed to the vehicle limit being increased to 4 wagons and a van.

'Working Rules so advised.'

Two months after this decision, in order further to expedite the clearance of coffins, permission to use an additional vehicle, to make up a total of 5 wagons and a van, was authorised.

The temporary platform seems to have been erected roughly on the site of that constructed for the Bisley opening in 1890, close to the main entrance to the Camp, and closed and removed before the 1891 Meeting. It was therefore on the NRA's property.

The 1948 Olympic Games

In 1948 the first Olympic Games after the war were held in London and, although chiefly based at Wembley, the shooting took place at Bisley. Transport of teams to and from this venue resulted in additional workings over the Bisley Tramway with the two car push-pull train normally employed being given a minor 'facelift' by the application of a rim of white paint round the driver's cab with the well-known symbol of the Olympics pasted in the non-driving window. The buffers were also painted white.

An Olympic Small Bore Shooting Special at Brookwood on 7 August 1948, made up of a suitably embellished ex-LBSCR Arc-Roof Push-Pull Set No 727, about to leave for Bisley Camp. The Coaches and the locomotive, probably Class M7 0-4-4T No. 110, are all still in Southern Railway livery eight months after Nationalisation. (*R.F.Roberts – Peter Harding collection*)

Above: The *Bullet* crosses the Canal Bridge on its way to Brookwood Station on 12 July 1952, a few days before closure of the Tramway. (*Denis Cullum – Peter Harding collection*)

Below: Push-Pull Unit no 734 at Bisley Station during the 1952 Annual Meeting and the final year of operation of the Camp Tramway.

Berthing of Trains on Bisley Camp Line

In October 1949, an internal Southern Region memo raised the possibility of the Bisley Camp Tramway being used as a temporary berthing siding, except during the Annual Meeting. It was also mooted that the one engine in steam regulation on the branch should be withdrawn during its use as a siding. By the following January it had been agreed, under the original terms of the lease of the land to the NRA by the War Office and the subsequent assignment to the railway company, that this was permitted. The original restriction of 64 wheels over the Tramway only applied to the passenger trains from the main line which had not run for many years. The only restriction on freight trains was that they needed to be propelled due to the lack of run round facilities.

In November, the London West Divisional Superintendent at Woking answered a memo from the Superintendent of Operation, Waterloo, regarding the used made of this facility. He mentioned engineering trains unloading material and occasions when Feltham Marshalling Yard was unable to accept goods trains due to fog or other adverse conditions, and also to short notice restricted acceptances by other Regions via Kew.

The Closure of the Camp Tramway

On 28 May 1952, the British Transport Commission issued a Notice of Termination of the Lease on the Tramway.

It remained open for the duration of the 1952 Annual Meeting, finally closing on Saturday 19 July with great and unconstrained ceremony. The winner of the Queen's Prize, the first of the new reign, was a Cambridge Graduate, Major A.B. Kinnear-Wilson late RAMC, resulting in the 'celebrations' being led by members of the Cambridge University RC, who not only kidnapped the winner but 'forced' him to 'drive' the final train.

The *Bullet*, pulled by M7 0-4-4T No. 30022 on its way to Bisley Camp, is flagged across the Cowshot Crossing on 12 of July 1952 during the final Meeting, at the end of which the Tramway closed. (*Peter Harding collection*)

1890   **1952**

[*Photo: Gale & Polden Ltd., Aldershot*

The Last Journey of "The Bisley Bullet" 19th July, 1952

The Bisley Tramway, to give it its official title, between Brookwood Station and Bisley Camp was opened by the Prince of Wales on 12th July, 1890, the L.& S.W.R. engine used being No. 185, with the name Alexandra and the Prince of Wales's feathers painted on its sides for the ceremony. These decorations it bore until 1896. (In recent years, but notably not this year, the engine has had the name "Bisley Bullet" chalked on its sides.)

The length of the line between Brookwood and the Camp was one mile 55 chains. The gradients were severe—the steepest 1 in 50. A 10 m.p.h. speed limit was imposed, restricted to 1 m.p.h. at the unprotected and rather "blind" Cowshott crossing. The line was extended to Deepcut during the First World War, but afterwards this extension was disused and subsequently dismantled.

The fares in 1890 were, for Volunteers in uniform, 1s. 6d. third class return from Waterloo, and for competitors with N.R.A. vouchers, 3s. first class return. At one time in its early days one or two through trains ran to and from Waterloo and the Camp on Saturdays and special occasions.

WHEN it was known that "The Bisley Bullet" would make its last journey on Saturday, 19th July, the N.R.A. Public Relations Committee took the matter in hand, and deputed Major T. Anstey, T.D., one of its members, to organize a suitable farewell ceremony.

In his able hands, and with the willing and efficient co-operation of the Traffic Superintendent at Woking, the Publicity Department at Waterloo, the 1st Bn. The Gloucestershire Regiment and the Cambridge University R.A., a remarkable finale was arranged. The C.U.R.A.s' particular task was to kidnap the Queen's Prize winner and take him to Brookwood to drive the last train.

The Gloucesters, determined to speed "The Bisley Bullet" on its last flight in a right and proper manner, formed a procession, headed by the Regiment's Band and Drums, in which to solemn music marched a "Banner Carrier," "Undertaker," "Prime Movers," "Pall Bearers," "Medal Carrier," "Markers" and a large and increasing number of "mourners" in its progress from the A.R.A. Officers' Mess to the Camp Station. There a large crowd assembled and spread over the permanent way beyond the platform to wait more or less patiently, soothed by the plaintive music of the band, the arrival of the last down train.

Here there was some delay, caused by an excited passenger pulling the communication cord, and an exuberant assistant driver or fireman blowing the whistle so often that the head of steam was insufficient to drag the overloaded train. However it eventually arrived, full inside and out—engine cab, carriages, all crammed and overflowing.

After some speechmaking, N.R.A. spoons were presented on behalf of the N.R.A. by the Queen's Prize winner to the crew of the train, the Brookwood Stationmaster and the Bisley Camp Station Superintendent.

As the still loaded train drew slowly out of the station on its last journey, under the volleys of a firing party and over a series of fog-signals, thoughtfully placed in its path so that it would "go off with a bang," there were, in the midst of the hilarious merry-making, some "old stagers" who felt a little sad at the breaking of one more link with the "good old days" of happy memory.

The Last Journey of the *Bullet*. It is not clear when the endearing term 'The Bisley Bullet' was first applied. It was in common use after the Second World War however. (*NRA Journal*)

The extraordinary scene on the embankment up to Brookwood Station just before the 'Bullet' reached its final destination.

The Railway Correspondence and Travel Society (RCTS) arranged a final trip over the Tramway. This used pull-push unit number 363 in tandem with Drummond 0-4-4T M7 Class No 30027, the same locomotive used on the last official train from Bisley.

Removal and Sale of Tramway

It was not until late in 1953 that the Tramway was dismantled. In the October/November Secretary's report it was stated that a letter had been received from Thomas Ward & Co., saying that they had bought the Bisley Railway and were proposing to dismantle it at once. They had also made an offer for that part of the line owned by the NRA. It was agreed that they should be asked the same price as they pay the Southern Railway, pro rata for the length of the line within the property.

That part of the line bought by Thomas Ward consisted of the section between the northern end of the Canal Bridge and the southern boundary of the Camp. The land here belonged to the War Department while the section between and including the Canal Bridge and Brookwood remained in the ownership of British Railways. The NRA owned all that part of the railway within the Camp boundaries.

In the Association's November/December Report reference was made to the disposal of railway equipment in the Camp: -

'Railway Line

'The track has been taken up. The Secretary has sold the lines, chairs and buffer stop for £200. (The sleepers have been retained as being useful for building up butts etc.).

Railway Bridge

'The W.D. Land Agent has received a letter from the Southern Railway, pointing out that under the Bisley Tramway Act of 1890, the Railway Company were not responsible for any bridges except that over the Basingstoke Canal.'

19531200 Report

Although all the line north of the Canal Bridge had been removed by November there was now a legal problem regarding ownership of the Cowshot Bridge which had to be resolved. British Railways had also decided to retain the Brookwood – Canal Bridge section as a long siding sufficient for the storage of up to seventy wagons.

However, on 7 May 1954, a report was sent to the Chief Regional Manager containing an inventory of material recovered from the closed section of the tramway. This also included a further appraisal of the 'long siding' and in its introduction, references to the future of the Cowshot and Canal Bridges.

'It has been the practice in the past to treat the portion of the Bisley Camp line between Brookwood and the bridge over the Basingstoke Canal as a lay-by for berthing freight trains comprising up to 70 wagons, and as it is essential that this facility should be retained as far as possible, the additional work necessary to provide for this in the most economical manner has been incorporated in the estimates now submitted. (The letter attached) depicts a minimal scheme, after a careful consideration of all factors, namely, as the gradient falling towards the Basingstoke Canal is 1 in 90, the provision of a heavy mass concrete buffer stop within a portion of the siding covered by a 100ft pebble drag, turned and canted towards the main line embankment. A cushion of Meldon dust will be tipped down the slope of the embankment to meet the pebble drag and buffer stop with a view to reducing damage to run-a-way vehicles should this occur. The existing connection to the branch line at the west end of No.3 siding to be moved to the east (Brookwood end), as shown by red colour, to afford the berthing space required and to give direct access to the up local line.

'In respect of Item 5, it is noted that the proposal contained in the report of the Branch Lines Committee was to withdraw the passenger service and recover the Commission's assets on the branch line, leaving a length of track sufficient to berth a 70 wagon freight train at Brookwood. Over a representative period the berthing of freight trains occurred on an average eleven times per month, and the facility, having existed and been used for this purpose for very many years, it was recognised during the investigation that it should remain available. In order that Pirbright Bridge No. 1 might be removed, however, accommodation for a 53 wagon train be proposed and, incidentally the least costly scheme, was agreed as suitable to meet requirements.

'It is recommended, therefore, that the Civil Engineer be authorised to take in hand the requisite works per item 3, 4 and 5 on the basis of the estimates furnished, thus bringing this matter to a conclusion so far as possible at the moment.

'In view of what is stated in the second paragraph of this report, however, the expenditure now detailed cannot necessarily be regarded as complete, but on the contrary, must be subject to what may arise as to liability for future maintenance of Cowshott Road Bridge No. 3 and any further requirement of the War Department as to restoration of Crown Land.

'Enclosed is a schedule of requirements furnished by the War Department Land Agent on the 5th October, 1953, and the Civil Engineer has confirmed that these have been complied with apart from the removal of the Commission's Bridge over the Basingstoke Canal. Immediately authority is forthcoming to proceed, arrangements will at one be made for the removal of this bridge to be taken in hand as requisite.'

The protracted winding up of the Tramway

Although the last train had run in 1952 and the British Railways' owned track between the Canal and the Cowshot Crossing, as well as that belonging to the Association within the Camp perimeter, had all been removed in 1953 the final elimination of the various loose ends was destined to drag on for many more years.

A bus service had been provided as a substitute for the Tramway during the annual Meeting but this seems to have attracted little custom and in 1958 the Southern Region of British Railways who had arranged the service through the Aldershot and District Traction Company, wrote to the Association notifying them that the bus company wished to withdraw this service.

The Secretary wrote to the Bus Company and their reply implied that if the Association required the maintenance of the service they would have to provide a subsidy. The Association now reluctantly accepted that the service was no longer necessary as by now the vast majority of competitors arrived at the Camp by private transport.

The Cowshot Bridge

After the demise of the Tramway the Association still retained ownership of the Cowshot Bridge, which it had been forced to construct in 1890 at the behest of the Board of Trade. Also, under the terms of the determination of the original lease, British Railways, as the current lessees, were required to fill in the cutting on the north side of the bridge but for some reason this was never carried out.

In January 1958 the War Department demanded that the Association demolish the, by now, inadequate bridge and fill in the cutting so that the road could be brought up to a standard capable of handling the traffic. This invoked a rapid response from the Association who had taken legal advice. Although they retained ownership of the bridge, they were not responsible for the maintenance of the road over it. Capt. E.K. Le Mesurier, the Secretary of the Association, wrote a strongly worded letter to the Ministry of Defence making the position perfectly clear.

'The Council of the National Rifle Association have taken legal advice on the question of the responsibility for the maintenance of the brick bridge at Cowshott Hill, carrying the Pirbright Camp to Brookwood road over the cutting in which the Bisley Camp Railway used to run.

> 2. (sic) We are advised that the position is as follows :-
> (a) The NRA is under an obligation, until the bridge is demolished to maintain the bridge so that it will carry the volume of traffic that it carried in 1890.
> (b) The demolition and reinstatement contemplated by the War Department are far in excess of any liability which could rest on the NRA either at common law or by contract.

The Cowshot Bridge looking north in 1952 just before the Tramway closed. Compare this with the drawing of the Bridge in 1890 (Chapter 6) although the latter showed the Bridge facing south. (*A K.G. Carr collection*)

3. My Council wish me to inform you that if the Surrey County Council wish to demolish the bridge and relay the road, the NRA will have no objection: but they (the NRA) will make no contribution to the cost.

4. It must be realised that, up to 1916 or so when Pirbright Camp was much enlarged, the access to that Camp and Blackdown by any metalled road ran South of the Southern Railway main line embankment. The road up to the bridge from Brookwood was only a by-road and little heavy traffic used it. When Pirbright Camp was enlarged by the War Department they built a proper road, from the bridge at Cowshott Hill to the east end of Pirbright Camp. It is the creation of this new (and shorter road) to Pirbright and Blackdown Camps etc., plus the great increase of motor traffic of all kinds, that has made the brick bridge in question so inadequate. Since by far the greater proportion of the vehicles that use the bridge nowadays are military or civilian vehicles on business in connection with the military Camps, it would seem quite inequitable and contrary to common sense, to hold the NRA responsible for removing the present bridge and filling in the cutting under it, in order to build a newer and more adequate bridge for the modern volume of traffic.'

However it was not until 1965 that real action was taken when, in April that year, terms were finally agreed with Surrey County Council in which the latter would take over responsibility for the bridge. They undertook to demolish it and reconstruct the road on the payment of £250 by the NRA. Another relic of the Tramway disappeared in 1979 when the landmark girder bridge over the canal was finally demolished by British Railways. The abutments were left however and still remain.

The 'Southern Railway' competition, latterly sponsored by British Railways, was withdrawn at the end of the 1962 Meeting. In 1963, however, Major T. Anstey, who had also arranged the 1952 festivities surrounding the last 'Bullet' over the line, sponsored a new competition, aptly named the 'Bisley Bullet', in the form of a Challenge Cup and a sum of money to commemorate the old tramway. As it states in the 'Bisley Bible' each year the competition is 'Named after the train that ran between Brookwood and the Camp 1890 – 1952.'

In 1984, extending a further gesture to the memory of the old tramway, a Standard Mark 1 British Railways Sleeping Car was installed on a length of track adjacent to the station platform roughly on the alignment of the old run round loop. This provided sleeping accommodation to the Club House located in the station building. Originally resplendent in British Railways 'blood and custard' (carmine and cream) it was later re-painted in Southern Green.

The 1998 Survey

The abandoned line lay dormant until the 1990s when the Military Authorities requested the Royal Logistic Corps to carry out a feasibility study regarding the possibility of re-opening the line through to Blackdown Camp. The survey, carried out on 18 February 1998, considered each section of the old track bed starting from Brookwood.

'Brookwood Station. The bay platform that served trains operating on the branch still exists. It is at the south end of the station, it is likely that the land that it stands on belongs to Railtrack. The former line out towards the railbridge over the A324 is still visible, though it is heavily overgrown.

Railbridge A324. The abutments of the former branch line bridge are still intact and the approach from Brookwood is visible as an embankment.

Canal Bridge. The abutments for the bridge over the Basingstoke Canal are still intact. The approach to the bridge can clearly be seen as an embankment and across the canal the former line can also be seen as embankment into a heavily wooded area.

Cowshot. The line from the canal bridge can be followed through the woods but comes to an abrupt end by a road in front of a row of married quarters. Behind the quarters the trackbed can be found again as a cutting leading through a wooded area to the former Cowshot level crossing. The line can be picked up again over the road leading off as a pathway into a caravan site on Bisley Camp.

Bisley Camp. By the caravan site the trackbed is lost under a new range shed, but can be picked up again after the shed where the platform and station building of Bisley Camp can still be seen. Here stands a BR former Mk1 sleeper coach on a rail plinth which stands on the former trackbed. The line can be followed as a path/track to the edge of Bisley Camp into a wooded area towards Pirbright Camp.

Pirbright Camp. There are no signs of the railway at all within the confines of Pirbright Camp.

Lodgehill. Just beyond the Curzon bridges it is possible to make out parts of the line as embankments through the woods towards Deepcut. The line touches the road between Deepcut – Pirbright before descending to an embankment just west of Lodgehill. The line can be followed at this point as a track past the lock gates on the Basingstoke Canal. A small portion of the line can be seen just beyond the Canal preservation building but then stops by a track on the outside of the security fence of Deepcut Camp.

Deepcut. The line can be followed as a track along the fence behind the Det of 41 Sqn RLC towards the Deepcut bridges over the canal and main railway line. Just before the B3015 the former loco shed foundations can be found complete with partially filled in inspection pit. The line that curved round into Blackdown Camp can be seen in the woods adjacent to the path/track. The line can just be made out as a small embankment but stops by the access road into Blackdown Camp.

Blackdown Camp. Across the access road there are no signs of the railway from then on.

Summary. Although the track bed is still in situ from Brookwood station towards Bisley Camp there are a number of obstacles that may preclude the reinstatement of the railway. The missing bridge over the A324 is one, the abutments are still there but they will require a detailed examination to determine their current state and may even require rebuilding. The same goes for the missing bridge over the Basingstoke Canal which also has its abutments, but requires further examination.'

Since the Survey the only major change observable between Bisley and Brookwood is the total obliteration of the remaining traces of the old bay platform at Brookwood Station by housing development. Another break with the past was the conversion of the Brookwood Hotel (originally the Temperance Hotel) into offices. It was here that discussions with the L&SWR had taken place during the early planning stages that finally resulted in the Tramway.

NOTES ON OFFICERS OF THE NRA, THE LSWR AND OTHER PERSONALITIES REFERRED TO IN THE TEXT

NRA

Officers, Members and Associates of the NRA

Cambridge, George Duke of, 1819-1904. Commander in Chief of the British Army 1856-95 and President of the NRA 1861-1905. Although he encouraged the use of breech loading rifles he was generally regarded as resistant to change in the Army. He was a cousin of Queen Victoria.

Cheylesmore, Lord, (Herbert Francis Eaton, 3rd Baron) 1848-1925. Chairman of the NRA from 1903 to 1925. He had been the Wimbledon Camp Commandant during the final Meetings there. As a Major-General he was the Commandant of the School of Musketry established at Bisley during the First World War.

Crosse, Lt. Col. Charles Robert. NRA Secretary 1899-1921. He had been the Chief Range Officer for the previous eight years and had been an Official at Wimbledon before that. He was appointed a Member of the Royal Victorian Order in 1909.

Elcho, Lord, 1818-1914 (Francis Richard Charteris), from 1853 to 1883 and then 10th Earl of Wemyss. British Whig Politician; co-founder and Chairman of the NRA from 1860 until 1867 and again in 1871.

Etches, C.R., Major. NRA Secretary 1921-37. A fine shooter before the First World War, he was largely responsible for re-building the fortunes of the NRA afterwards.

Fremantle, T.F., Lord Cottesloe, 1862-1956. Proficient Marksman. Member of the NRA Council. Assistant Secretary during the move to Bisley. Chairman 1931-9.

Halford, Sir Henry, 1828-1897. Rifleman and highly distinguished shot. He had a strong influence on the development of the breech loading rifle and was a member of the War Office Small Arms Committee responsible for the Lee-Metford Rifle. He was a great friend of William Metford and acted as his assistant in the latter's experiments.

Hoey, Capt. John, Appointed NRA Clerk of the Works 1882 in succession to Stockman at Wimbledon and then at Bisley. He had been the Regimental Sergeant Major of the 1st Royal Scots and later the Sergeant Major of the 3rd Surrey Rifles. He oversaw the move to Bisley where he had been responsible for the layout of the ranges. He had constructed the Staff Pavilion (which became the Council Club at Bisley) on Wimbledon Common in 1885. His excellent relationship with the London and South Western Railway was such that he was the subject of a special article in their staff journal, the South Western Gazette, when he retired in 1900. He died in 1902.

Humphry, A.P. He won the Queen's Prize in 1871. He became a member of Council and acted as Secretary during the move to Bisley and the first Meeting there in 1890.

Mackinnon, Colonel William, Formerly Chief Instructor at the Hythe School of Musketry. Secretary of the NRA from 1890-8 when he resigned through ill-health. He presented the Mackinnon Prize in 1891 followed by his Challenge Trophy in 1892. He died in 1899.

Matthews, Capt. M. C. A prominent member of the NRA Council who became Executive Officer then Assistant Secretary on the appointment of Crosse as Secretary in 1899.

Metford. William Ellis, 1824-99. A leading engineer and inventor who was fundamental in the development of ammunition and the breech-loading British military rifle. He designed the barrel for the .303 calibre Lee-Metford Rifle, the first magazine rifle used by the British Army (which evolved into the classic Short Magazine Lee Enfield rifle of the First World War).

Mildmay, Capt. Edmond H. St John. NRA Secretary from 1860-89. He remained in office throughout the entire Wimbledon period. He resigned in 1889 but was then appointed a Vice-President.

Spencer, Earl, (John Poyntz Spencer), 1835-1910. Co-founder and Chairman of the NRA from 1867-8. He was a Liberal Politician and a close friend of William Ewart Gladstone, under whom he also served. He was twice Lord Lieutenant of Ireland. He had extensive landholdings in the Wimbledon area and was Lord of the Manor of Wimbledon Common.

Stockman, Charles R., Former Royal Engineer. NRA Clerk of the Works at Wimbledon from 1868 until his death in 1882. He set up and managed the NRA's workshops on Wimbledon Common where he constructed two large prefabricated buildings for the Association. These were the Pavilion (1871) and the Council Offices (1876). The latter building still survives at Bisley.

Wantage, Lord, (Robert Loyd-Lindsay). 1st Baron Wantage, VC, KCB, VD, 1832-1901, was a British soldier, politician, philanthropist, and one of the founders of the British Red Cross. Chairman of the NRA from 1887 until 1891. He was a major sponsor and Chairman of the Didcot, Newbury and Southampton Railway and also Chairman of the Wantage Tramway.

Winans, Walter, 1852-1920. An NRA Life Member, he was an American citizen born in Russia but lived in Britain. He was a great sportsman, a champion pistol shot in the 1890s and later shot for the USA in both the 1908 (winning a gold medal) and 1912 Olympics. He was a great enthusiast for the Running Deer and Man targets at both Wimbledon and Bisley and wrote a number of books on shooting. He was a grandson of the distinguished American Railroad Engineer, Ross Winans, who had attended the Rainhill Trials on behalf of the Baltimore and Ohio Railroad.

London and South Western Railway

Senior Officers of the LSWR who dealt directly with the NRA.

Adams, William, 1823-1904. Locomotive Superintendent 1877-1895. Well-known for the efficiency and elegance of his locomotives. He was especially helpful to the NRA during 1893-94 when he oversaw the repairs to their tram engine *Wharncliffe* at Nine Elms Works.

Alexander, C. Storekeeper 1909-1920. Successor to Barrell, and continued the assistance with the supply of sleepers.

Andrews, Edmund, Resident Engineer 1887-1901. Greatly assisted the NRA on their move to Bisley. Responsible for the new central station at Bisley Camp in 1891.

Barrell, G. R. Storekeeper. Was of great assistance in supplying sleepers used by the NRA, chiefly for the protection of butts.

Bircham, Sam – L&SWR Solicitor 1900-10. He was involved in the legal aspects of the planning for the Bisley Camp Tramway before he joined the railway company.

Bishop, William - Solicitor 1910-22 (Solicitor for the Southern Railway from 1923). He liaised closely with the NRA during the legal problems with the War Office over the operation of the Tramway (and its extension) during the First World War.

Drummond, Dugald, 1840-1912 - Locomotive Superintendent (Chief Mechanical Engineer from 1904) 1895-1912. He had previously been Locomotive Superintendent of the North British Railway followed by the Caledonian Railway.

Dutton, The Hon. Ralph H. 1821-92. – Chairman of the Board 1875-1892. Strongly backed his company's relationship with the NRA especially in respect of the move to Bisley.

Fay, Sam, 1856-1953 Superintendent of the Line 1899-1902. He was seconded as the General Manager of the Midland and South Western Junction Railway from 1893 until 1899 and was appointed as General Manager of the Great Central Railway in 1902. After Grouping in 1923 he became Chairman of the locomotive builders, Beyer-Peacock until 1933.

Galbraith, W.R. Consulting Engineer 1862-1907.

Hartnell, F. Accountant 1890-1913.

Holmes, Henry, 1863-1933. Superintendent of the Line 1902-16. Maintained a close and effective working relationship with the contemporary NRA Secretary, C.R. Crosse, during his period in office. He resigned from his post in 1916.

Jacomb Hood, William, 1859-1914. Resident Engineer, 1901-14.

Macaulay, Frederick Julius. Company Secretary 1880-98.

Newhook, A. E. Accountant 1913-22.

Owens, Sir Charles J, 1855-1933. Formerly Goods Manager then General Manager 1898–1912. A strong supporter of Target Rifle Shooting. Assisted the NRA with the platform extension to Bisley Camp Station in 1910. He became a director of the company on his retirement and then of the Southern Railway until 1930.

Panter. W. Carriage and Wagon Superintendent 1890-1906.

Scott, Archibald – General Manager 1852-1885 (Titled Traffic Manager 1852-70).

Scotter, Sir Charles – General Manager 1885-98 & Chairman 1904-10. Instructed by his Board to try and ensure that the NRA remained on 'LSWR Territory' he gave every assistance to the Association in their search for a new site and the construction and operation of the Bisley Common Tramway as well as the management of the Range Tramway between 1894 and 1899. He was instrumental in agreeing cheap fares for Volunteers and others in travelling to Bisley which continued until after the First World War. He was knighted in 1895 for his services to the railway.

Szlumper, A. W. – Chief Engineer 1914-22. Appointed to the same position on the Southern Railway from 1923 to 1927.

Verrinder, E.W. Traffic Superintendent 1873-93.

Walker, Sir Herbert. General Manager 1912-22 (and General Manager of the Southern Railway 1923-37). A very strong supporter of Target Rifle Shooting including his own staff. He awarded shooting prizes at Bisley. He refused to countenance the closure of the Bisley Tramway in the early 1930s.

West, George F.P. Deputy to Henry Holmes then Superintendent of the Line 1916-22.

White, G.T. Traffic Superintendent 1895-9.

Other Associated Personalities

Adams, George Gammon, 1821-98. Distinguished Sculptor. Executed the NRA's Gold Medal from Watt's design.

Aird, Sir John (1833-1911) & the firm of John Aird. Became one of the greatest of all the late Victorian contractors. Assisted the NRA with the operation of the Range Tramway at Wimbledon and the first three years at Bisley. Coincidentally, it was his firm who were appointed as the main contractor for the widening of the Woking to Basingstoke section of the L&SWR Main Line that ran adjacent to the N.R.A's Bisley Camp, between 1899 and 1905.

Conan Doyle, Sir Arthur, 1859-1930. The famous Author. During the second Boer War (1899-1901) in which he served as a doctor, he observed the skills of Boers shooting from cover and recommended the setting up of Civilian Rifle Clubs in Britain in which he was supported by the N.R.A. He became a member of the NRA Civilian Rifle Clubs Committee.

Fenton, Roger 1819-69. Famous for his photographs of the Crimean Campaign in 1854-5. He was one of the early Volunteers and attended the first Volunteer Course at the Hythe School of Musketry in 1860 He was commissioned by the NRA to photograph their first Meeting on Wimbledon Common in 1860.

Gooch, William Frederick 1825-1915. A Captain in the 11th Wiltshire Volunteers, he was the Superintendent of Swindon Works from 1857 to 1864. He was responsible for the design and construction of the original Running Deer Target in 1863. In 1864, he probably supplied the wheels and axle boxes for the new Range Tramway cars. He left the GWR in 1864 to become the Managing Director of the Vulcan Foundry at Newton-le-Willows, near Warrington. He was the younger brother of Daniel Gooch who designed the first successful Great Western Railway locomotives under Isambard Kingdom Brunel. Daniel was the 'father' of Swindon Works, and eventually became the Chairman of the GWR.

Landseer, Edwin Henry, 1802-73. Great Victorian animal painter. He designed the Running Deer target at the behest of Lord Elcho.

Pain, Arthur Cadlick, 1844-1937. Notable civil engineer who became well-known for his design of the now listed Cannington Viaduct on the Axminster Light Railway, of which he was also the Engineer. He owned and managed the Frimley and Farnborough District Water Works, near to Bisley, and assisted in the design of the new Range Tramcars of 1898.

Paxton, Joseph, 1803-65. Designer of the Crystal Palace for the Great Exhibition of 1851. He was a Volunteer and a member of the NRA Council at the end of his life.

Salmond, Sir William, 1840-1932. Engineer Officer in charge of the Wimbledon Camp in succession to Capt. Drake RE whom he had previously assisted. He designed the original prefabricated Council Offices at Wimbledon which were then transferred to Bisley where they still exist. He rose to the rank of Major-General and his two sons both came to hold the highest ranks in the RAF.

Watts, George Frederick, 1817-1904. Great Victorian painter who designed the NRA's Gold Medal as well as the Elcho Shield and original Running Man target.

Whitworth, Sir Joseph W, 1803-87. He supplied and oversaw the setting up of the Whitworth Rifle on its stand for Queen Victoria to fire the 'First Shot' at the opening of the Wimbledon Meeting. The pioneer of precision engineering techniques and the inventor of the standard screw thread system that carries his name. He had been requested by the Government to improve the manufacturing of the Enfield Military Rifle whose shortcomings had become evident in the Crimean War. This lead to the development of the Whitworth Rifle, in collaboration with the gun maker Westley Richards, which employed hexagonal rifling with a bore diameter of .451 inches.

LONDON AND SOUTH WESTERN RAILWAY DRAWINGS OF "WHARNCLIFFE"

The following drawings are taken from the General Arrangement Drawing produced by the London & South Western Railway at Nine Works in 1894 under the supervision of William Adams, the Chief Mechanical Engineer of the L&SWR, where "Wharncliffe" had been sent for repair in late 1893.

The locomotive as shown is in its original condition as built by Merryweather in 1878.

(All Drawings - National Railway Museum/Science & Society Picture Library)

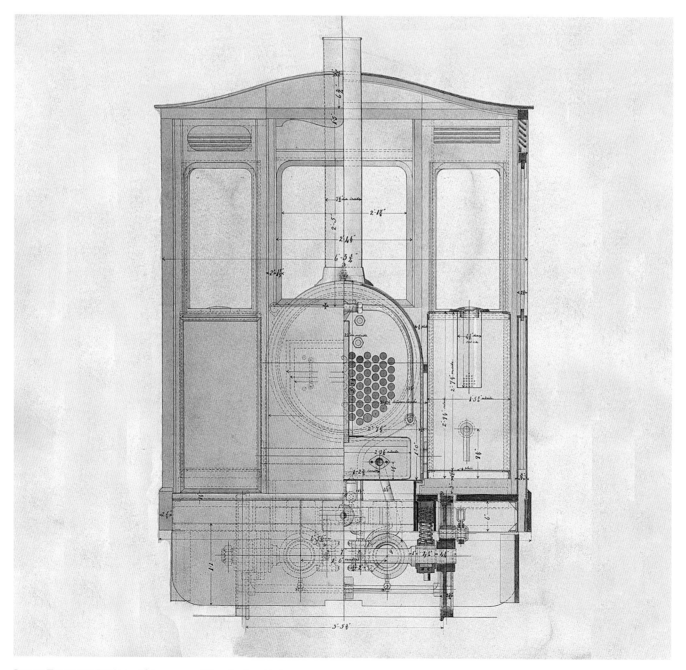

Range Tramway Engine - Chimney and Smoke Box End

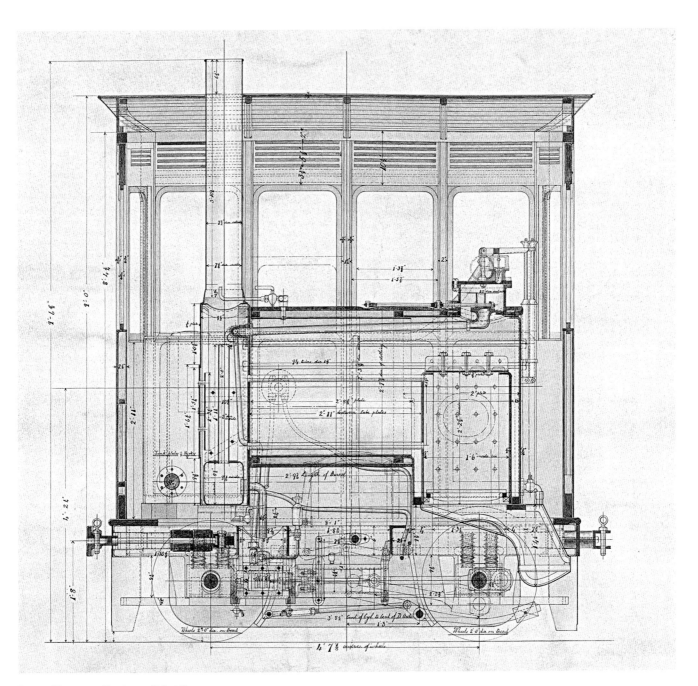

Range Tramway Engine – Side View

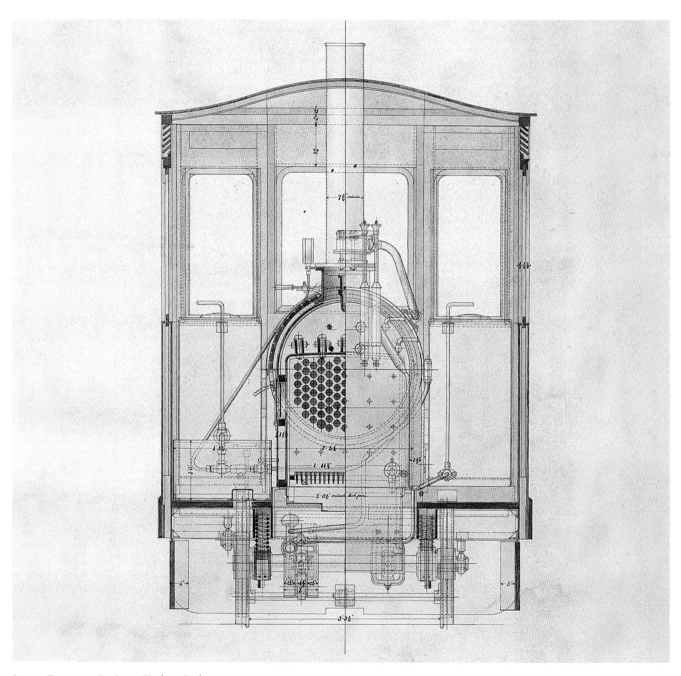

Range Tramway Engine – Firebox End

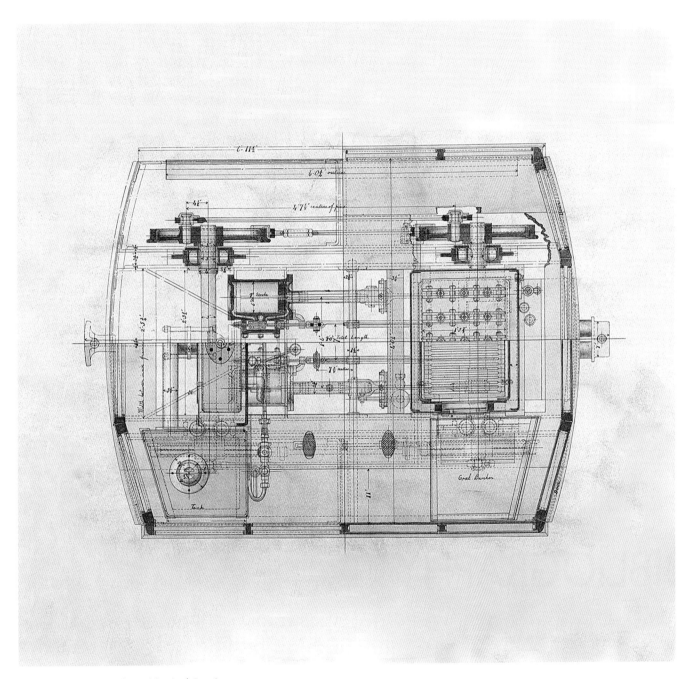

Range Tramway Engine – Vertical Section

MOTIVE POWER USED OVER THE BISLEY TRAMWAY

The normal passenger services over the line were handled by just three classes of locomotive throughout its history.

L&SWR Adams Class O2 0-4-4T 1890 – 1914 and 1919 – 1931. These were based at Nine Elms Shed. The more logical Guildford Shed took over in the summer of 1932.

LBSCR D1 Stroudley Class 0-4-2T 1932 – 1939 and normally used over the Guildford-Horsham branch.

L&SWR Drummond Class M7 0-4-4T 1946 – 1952 (these first appeared just before the Second World War on special workings).

During the First and Second World Wars, War Department locomotives were used, the main hauler in both conflicts being the Hawthorne Leslie No 3088 0-6-2T *Sir John French* from the Longmoor Military Railway. Incidentally this locomotive was to the same design as two on the Plymouth, Devonport and South Western Junction Railway but was especially equipped with Walschaerts Valve Gear for training purposes. It was sold for scrap after the end of the Second World War. In each case a small tank engine for shunting duties was also used. In the Second World War, this was Andrew Barclay No 2027 0-4-0T *Royal Navy Whale Island No 7*.

From the early days, the axle load was restricted to 14 tons with all the Adams Classes permitted, however, in the 1909 Working Timetable, the Adams T1 Class 0-4-4T and all the Drummond Classes were barred with the exception of K10 Class 4-4-0s and 700 Class 0-6-0s. An Adams Class 0395 0-6-0 tender locomotive was recorded as being involved in the Bisley Camp accident of 1898. The 1911 Appendix to the Rule Book limited the 'number of wheels' on the branch to sixty-four.

Goods services were generally handled by the normal 'pick-up' goods trains on the main line using the available locomotive. The most numerous service of this type was for the handling of wagon loads of coal and coke as there had been a substantial reduction of general goods traffic from the end of the First World War due to the increasing use of motor transport.

On 23 April 1939, in conjunction with a special train over the Bisley Branch, a Lord Nelson Class 4-6-0 Express Locomotive, Number 864 *Sir Martin Frobisher*, was parked in the Brookwood bay of the Tramway with visitors being allowed into the cab and operate the controls. Over the branch passengers were permitted to 'drive' the M7 Class locomotives that topped and tailed the one coach train.

BIBLIOGRAPHY

The National Rifle Association 1859 – 1909 Humphry and Fremantle, Bowes & Bowes 1914

The Queen's Prize – The Story of the National Rifle Association – Susie Cornfield, Pelham Books 1987

A Hundred Years Behind the Times – The History of Bisley in Surrey, Tim Price - Melrose Books 2012

The London & South Western Railway Volume 2: Growth and Consolidation – R. A. Williams, David & Charles 1973

The LSWR in the Twentieth Century – J.N. Faulkner & R. A. Williams, David & Charles 1988

NRA Reports

NRA Journals

The Volunteer and Territorial Service Gazettes

The Volunteer Service Review

Council Books of the National Rifle Association

NRA Letter Books, Invoice Ledgers and many other documents held in the NRA Museum Archive

INDEX